Memorial Books of
Eastern European Jewry

Memorial Books of Eastern European Jewry

Essays on the History and Meanings of Yizker Volumes

EDITED BY
ROSEMARY HOROWITZ

McFarland & Company, Inc., Publishers
Jefferson, North Carolina, and London

LIBRARY OF CONGRESS CATALOGUING-IN-PUBLICATION DATA

Memorial books of Eastern European Jewry : essays on the history
and meanings of Yizker volumes / Edited by Rosemary Horowitz.
        p.   cm.
    Includes bibliographical references and index.

    ISBN 978-0-7864-4199-0
    softcover : 50# alkaline paper

    1. Memorial books (Holocaust) — History.   2. Holocaust,
Jewish (1939–1945)   3. Jews — Europe, Eastern — History —
20th century.   4. Holocaust survivors — Intellectual life.
I. Horowitz, Rosemary.
D804.195.M46   2011
940.53'18 — dc22   2011002748

BRITISH LIBRARY CATALOGUING DATA ARE AVAILABLE

Front cover image © 2011 Shutterstock

Manufactured in the United States of America

*McFarland & Company, Inc., Publishers
  Box 611, Jefferson, North Carolina 28640
  www.mcfarlandpub.com*

Contents

Part V: Bibliography

Introduction

From the Russian civil wars through the Nazi years, the Jews of Eastern Europe were targets of ongoing violence throughout the first half of the twentieth century. One response by some people to their extreme personal and communal losses was to compile a memorial book. The earliest such books from that time are the 1921 volume to Zhitomir; the 1924 volume to Proskurov; and the 1937 volume to Felshtin.[1] To an extent, those books, written during the interwar period, established the pattern for the Holocaust-era volumes. Influenced by religious, historical, and cultural practices, the Holocaust-era works, known variously as *yizker bikher*, *sifre zikaron*, or *pinkeysim*, are monuments in print commemorating the life and death of a place and its people. While these volumes started appearing in the 1940s, their numbers peaked in the 1960s and 1970s. Distilling information from one bibliography shows that 25 books were issued in the 1940s, 117 in the 1950s, 188 in the 1960s, 180 in the 1970s, 65 in the 1980s, 37 in the 1990s, and a few later on.[2] About language, one analysis finds that 216 of 348 volumes were written predominately in Hebrew, 82 in Yiddish, 35 in English, 8 in Hungarian, and 7 in other languages.[3] Some books have the same article in two languages making it possible for those who did not know one language to read about their ancestral hometowns in the other; others have summaries or introductions in English. Ultimately, about 75 percent of all books were published in Israel. Publication trends changed in the 1980s when English translations of earlier books started to be issued, and then again in the 1990s, when new media versions appeared.

No conclusive total number of Holocaust-era books is available due to various ways of defining the genre. Some people restrict the definition to those volumes prepared by *landsmanshaftn*, the mutual aid organizations comprised of immigrants from the same region or town; others count volumes written by individuals. Thus, the more narrow definition would not classify Melody Amsel's *Between Galicia and Hungary: The Jews of Stropkov* as a yizker book.

1

Similarly, neither Liliana Picciotto Fargion's *Il libro della memoria, gli Ebrei deportti dall'Italia 1943–45,* a reckoning of Jewish Italian losses, nor the books commemorating Western European communities would be included. The significant work *Lerer yizker bukh*, a volume dedicated to the teachers of Poland, would not count either.

The total number of books published during any particular period depends on how and when the books were counted. In 1973, Abraham Wein estimated that about 400 books had been published in the previous thirty years; that same year, David Bass counted 342 books. David Kranzler identified about 600 in 1979, and Paul Hamburg identified 800 in 1998.[4] Currently, *Yad Vashem* lists over 1,000 books in its yizker book collection. Counting translations would further increase the total.

For the Holocaust survivors and their compatriots, yizker books were oriented toward the past, as well as the future. Among other reasons, the books were written to memorialize the hometown and to inspire its descendants. Genealogists, academics, librarians, and curators have also expressed interest in the books. For instance, to genealogists, the books are very useful for the pictures that may show a relative in a class or a youth group meeting; the maps that may show the name of the street where the family lived and the proximity of the home to the school, synagogue, or market; the descriptions of common local professions that may apply to family members; and the necrologies and lists that may contain family names. For librarians, in addition to an interest in contents, there are professional issues related to collection development, collection management, and other concerns. For curators, the books are artifacts, the actual products of the survivor community, which may be displayed as material culture.

Critical attention to the volumes has varied. The first group of scholars to evaluate the books, which included Jacob Shatzky, Beryl Mark, Philip Friedman, Elias Schulman, and Abraham Wein, primarily viewed the books as flawed historical sources. While aware of the quantity of material in the books and its usefulness for certain types of studies, the reviewers in the 1950s and 1960s tended to point out the deficiencies in the books for historians. As Philip Friedman articulates in one assessment:

> It is true that it is not easy to write historical monographs when it is known that all archival sources, national as well as communal, have been destroyed or are now behind the Iron Curtain. Even the local periodicals and newspapers, so important to the history of previous decades, are mostly no longer in existence. We must therefore reconstruct the historical past from available fragments and rely on recollections and memoirs. Jewish historians and editors of yizker books have more than once pointed to these difficulties. Compare for example Dr. Jacob Shatzky's foreword in *Pinkes Mlave* to Dr. Refoel

Mahler's foreword in *Tshenstokhover yidn*. As a result, the place of honor in many yizker books is not relegated to historical material but rather to descriptions of ways of life; institutions, folklore, idioms, contemporary memoirs, biographies, various episodes and experiences of the Nazi era, and the like.[5]

His point is that while the books may be problematic sources for the study of history, they contain much material for the study of culture. In the 1970s, researchers started re-evaluating the books. During that period, a couple of monographs using the books as sources were published, specifically William Glicksman's volume on Jewish social welfare institutions in Poland and Isaiah Trunk's on the *Judenrat*. During the 1980s, Jack Kugelmass and Jonathan Boyarin's *From a Ruined Garden: The Memorial Books of Polish Jewry* and Annette Wieviorka and Itzhok Noborski's *Les Livres du Souvenir: Memoriaux Juifs de Pologne*, two groundbreaking publications, introduced the genre to a new audience.

Memorial books continue to receive attention. The work of Robert Moses Shapiro and Andrew Koss shows that yizker books may be useful for the study of previously overlooked topics, such as Soviet Jewry. Besides that, new approaches of study with new units of analysis are also emerging. The work of Natalia Aleksiun, Daniel Magilow, Katharina Hall, and Jeffrey Veidlinger represents these new directions in research. Aleksiun uses the concept of gender to examine the representation of women in yizker books; Magilow studies photographs to examine the visual aspects of yizker books; Hall uses the concept of memory to examine literature and yizker book traditions; and Veidlinger uses the books to study Jewish cultural life. International interest in the books is growing as scholars in Germany, France, Israel, Australia, Poland, and elsewhere turn to the books. The work of Monika Adamczyk-Garbowska, Adam Kopciowski, and Andrzej Trzciński, who are introducing the books in translation to a new generation of Polish readers, is especially exciting.

Taken together, these studies underscore the value of yizker books as objects from the survivor culture and as sources for genealogical and scholarly research. They also suggest different theoretical and methodological approaches from which the books may be analyzed. Much may still be gleaned from the books, including information about education, religion, politics, commerce, recreation, language, culture, youth, social welfare, literature, and other topics. Additionally, along with their memory maps and photographs, the books contain other illustrative material, for instance, line drawings, paintings, reproductions, and religious images. All that and more needs to be studied. Thus, the overarching goal of this collection is to deepen the appreciation of the books and encourage their use.

Notes

1. See *Yizkor dem ondeynken Zshitomirer kdoyshim* (New York: United Zhitomir Relief Committee, 1921); *Hurbn Proskurov: tsum ondenken fun di heylige neshomes* (New York: Levant Press, 1924); *Felshtin: zamlbukh tsum ondenk fun di Felshtiner kedoyshim* (New York: First Felshteener Benevolent Association, 1937).

2. See Zachary Baker's appendix in *From a Ruined Garden: The Memorial Books of Polish Jewry,* eds. and trans. Jack Kugelmass and Jonathan Boyarin. Second, expanded edition (Bloomington and Indianapolis: Indiana University Press in association with the United States Holocaust Memorial Museum, Washington D.C., 1998), 273–339.

3. See Michlean Amir, "From Memorials to Invaluable Historical Documentation: Using *Yizker Books* as Resources for Studying a Vanished World." Proceedings of the 36th Annual Convention of the Association of Jewish Librarians. La Jolla, CA, June 24–27, 2001. Amir's data are based on a sample of about half of the books in the New York Public Library collection and validate a similar study she did of the 500 books at the U.S. Holocaust Memorial Museum's library.

4. See Abraham Wein, "'Memorial Books' as a Source for Research into the History of Jewish Communities in Europe," *Yad Vashem Studies on the Eastern European Catastrophe and Resistance* 9 (1973): 255–272; David Kranzler, *My Jewish Roots: A Practical Guide to Tracing and Recording Your Genealogy and Family History* (New York: Sepher-Hermon, 1979); and Paul Hamburg, "Closing Circles, Opening Pathways," *The Reference Librarian* http://www.informa world.com/smpp/title~db=all~content=t792306953~tab=issueslist~branches=29-v2929, Issues 61 & 62 (April 1998): 235–243.

5. Philip Friedman, "*Di landsmanshaftn literatur in di fareyniktn shtatn far di letstn ten yor,*" *Jewish Book Annual* Volume 10 (5712/1951–1952): 82.

PART I

HISTORY

1

A History of Yizker Books

ROSEMARY HOROWITZ

This chapter focuses mainly on the memorial books compiled by *lands-manshaftn*. The preparation of those books was a grassroots enterprise involving thousands of people. More than a hundred could take part in the preparation of a single volume. The editor of the Szydlowiec volume, for example, notes that about 200 articles were received from about 150 people.[1] In general, a book committee was formed by the leadership of the association to coordinate the project. The committee members solicited photographs, letters, essays, testimony, maps, lists, and other materials from the membership of the organization. These materials were then edited and compiled into a volume. Production costs were covered through donations, as well as through the sale of advertisements or tributes in the book to family and friends. Copies were printed in quantities sufficient to meet orders. While some well-known editors, such as David Shtokfish and Berl Kagan, were hired to help with a book, and some well-known historians, such as Joseph Kermish and Philip Friedman, were hired to write articles, generally the material for a book was supplied by ordinary people from the particular town who responded to the solicitation from their organization.

Not surprisingly, the people in the organization had differing beliefs about commemoration, differing ideas for financing a book, conflicting personalities, varying levels of interest in a book, and differing visions of a book. These matters could delay a project for years. In the case of the volume to Białystok, for example, calls for a memorial book were made at the Białystok convention in 1970. After the convention, the Israeli and United States chapters of the organization spent several years collaborating on a book. This joint effort ended in 1979 due to disagreements over style, content, and finances. Shortly thereafter, members of the Białystok Center in New York City took over the project and published *Der Bialystoker yisker bukh* in 1982.

A project could also take years to get underway. The idea for a book to the Jewish communities of Manyevitz, Horodok, Lishnivka, Troyanuka, Povursk, and Kolki seems to have germinated for decades. Gathering the material for what eventually became *The Memorial Book to the Jewish Communities of Manyevitz, Horodok, Lishnivka, Troyanuka, Povursk* started at the end of World War II and continued for more than fifty-four years. The volume was issued in 2002.

Some Influences on Yizker Books

When people decided to compile a memorial book, they drew on a variety of religious, cultural, literacy, and literary practices. Religious practices are foundational to the books since yizker refers to the memorial service for remembering the dead. After the First Crusade, the practice of memorializing ordinary people, not only the renowned, took hold among the Jews, and by the fifteenth century, the *kaddish* prayer and the *yortzeyt* remembrance, as well as the yizker service were incorporated into Jewish practices.[2] Along with related images, such as eternal lights, memorial candles, and gravestones, yizker books refer those practices. From *Sefer Dereczyn*:

> With respect for the Almighty, we will take this Book in our hands and we will read it, as if it were a silent Kaddish, in memory of our nearest and dearest.[3]

Also, during the fifteenth century, the idea of *kiddush hashem* [dying for the sanctification of God] and *kodesh* [martyr] were applied to Jews who were killed in their defense of Judaism or who killed themselves to avoid converting from Judaism. This concept of martyrdom was extended to the Holocaust victims, and references to it abound in yizker books. From *Hurbn Glubok*:

> We request of all former landsleit that on the day of the yahrzeit the eldest in the family read to his relatives some chapters from this book. In this way we will identify with our beloved and dearest who died in God's name.[4]

From *Zabludove, yizker bukh:*

> Every word from this book shall be like a light burning for the souls of our martyrs.[5]

In addition, most books contain a necrology. The practice of listing names and reading those lists at memorial services in the synagogue has been traced to the thirteenth-century genre of *memorbucher*.[6] In yizker books, necrologies are presented in a variety of ways. Some necrologies are simply lists of names; others are memorial pages with photographs or drawings. An interesting necrology appears in the 1949 *Volkovisker yizker bukh*. The author of that necrology provides the lists of people by house and street. Some yizker books contain the names of Jews killed in prewar pogroms. Still others contain the names of Israelis killed in that country's wars. Along with its liturgical purpose, the necrology also connects the descendants of a place to their ancestral hometown.

Another major influence on the memorial book genre is the Bible. Some writers mention biblical events, especially the battle between the Amalek and Israelites from the books of Exodus and Deuteronomy. Other writers cite or paraphrase biblical passages. *Sefer yizkor Goniadz* references Job 19:23 for example. Still others seem to be acting on biblical injunctions. From *Sefer zikaron Czyzewo*:

> Those of us who have had the honor to be saved from that immense conflagration, always see before our eyes our ancestors' commandment that remains engraved with letters of fire and blood: "remember what Amalek did to you" — the Amalek of the twentieth century.[7]

From *Sefer zikaron le-kehilat Kolno*:

> This, of course, is the book's purpose — to erect a monument to a life wiped out and to Jews cut-down. "That the generation to come might know, even the children, which should be born, who should arise and declare them to their children" (Psalms, Chapter 78).[8]

In addition, passages in Exodus 17:14 and Deuteronomy 25: 17–19 may have influenced book projects insofar as writers often note that a memorial book is a sacred text and that writing the book is a sacred act. From *Pinkes Kovel*:

> We, the Kovel compatriots in Argentina do this sacred work so that the memory of the holy congregation of Kovel, Volynia, will live on forever, generation after generation.[9]

The belief in the writer as witness could be related to *sifrut ha'edut*, the Jewish literature of testimony.[10] This is expressed in *Pinkes Varshe*, where the editors call the front matter: "a monument and a witness."[11] Likewise, in *Pinkes Zshirardov*, Mordechai Bauman calls his chapter "a witness to the destruction."[12] From *A Tale of One City*:

> There are few of us left and we are disappearing day by day, one by one. Soon history will speak with the impersonal voice of scholars, at worst with the poisonous voice of the anti–Semites and falsifiers. It is therefore important to those of us who are still here to bear witness put everything on record and make it available to our children and the generations to come — an undistorted record, in all its tragedy and all its glory....[13]

Although found primarily in the early memorial books, the term *she'erit hapletah* [surviving remnant] is another biblical reference. This is an allusion to Isaiah 37:31: "The surviving remnant of the house of Judah will again take root downward and bear fruit upward." In fact, during the 1940s, the term was used within the displaced persons camps by those who lived through the war to refer to themselves, as well as all surviving Jews in Europe.[14] From *Pinkes Byten*:

> The majority of the surviving remnant from Byten, the eyewitnesses to our great disaster....[15]

From *Belkhatov: yizker-bukh*:

> As soon as the Second World War ended, the Belchatover assistance organization was created to help the surviving remnant from our hometown.[16]

To the extent that readers and writers view the books as the last entry in their town's *pinkes*, a yizker book may be viewed in terms of a communal recordkeeping tradition. Historically, the *pinkes* was the register of records or minutes book kept by Eastern European Jewish governing bodies or communal organizations. The practice of chronicling begins in the sixteenth century, when sets of historical records were kept by provincial governing bodies, such as town councils and courts, and by local communal organizations, such as houses of prayer, synagogues, professional guilds, burial societies, and philanthropic societies.[17] The *pinkes* contained vital administrative or communal records and served as a guide for decisions. For example, *Pinkes seyfer hazikronot* from Posen contained entries on town rules, housing policy, population policy, economic regulations, finances, taxes, budgets, imprisonments, bonds, expulsions, sumptuary regulations, tolls, welfare, and other administrative issues. This information was available for many purposes, including settling disputes or keeping track of taxes.[18]

Yizker book writers make associations to this chronicling function by using the term *pinkes* or by alluding to the recording function. From *Gombin: dos lebn un umkum fun a yiddish shtetl in Poylin*:

> With deep respect and piety we present to our Landsleit and the Yiddish reader this "Pincus."[19]

From *Pinkas Kolomey*:

> The idea of a "pinkas Kolomey," which would tell about the once splendid past of our now, in the Jewish sense, destroyed native city, and which would, through the accounts of eye-witnesses, victims who miraculously survived, mourn the annihilation of the Jewish Community of Kolomey — arose simultaneously among the "olei Kolomey" in Israel and among the "sharit haplita," the survivors in New York.[20]

In rare instances, a yizker book may actually include pages from the town's *pinkes*. This is the case with *Pinkes Bendin*.

In terms of their structure, yizker books are generally divided into four sections: the town and its people before the war, the town and its people during the war, the fate of the town and its survivors after the war, and the necrology. This organization suggests that historiography also had an impact on the books. About that Annette Wieviorka notes:

> Curiously enough, the two corpuses — the mass testimonies about the destruction and the memory books — are rooted in a tradition that began with the First World War.... With the First World War, humanity entered the era of mass murder. The Jewish reaction to the destruction of a number of its communities prefigures the response to the genocide: Jews wrote works that were anchored in the Jewish tradition while simultaneously borrowing from the non–Jews the genre of historical narration.[21]

Compared to Wieviorka who claims that the Eastern European Jewish practice of writing started around World War I, Elias Tcherikower considers the nineteenth century to be the start of Jewish historical narration, and Lucjan Dobroszycki considers the establishment of the first academic institution of Jewish historiography in Vilna, Poland by YIVO, the Jewish Scientific Institute, in 1925 to be its beginning.[22] About the specific writing of yizker books as a historical enterprise, Abraham Wein notes that the writing of history

> which had been performed in earlier periods by various chroniclers and scholars, was now an enterprise in which thousands from all classes and strata of the nation participated: from political leaders and intellectuals to ordinary people having some sort of knowledge of their community and its past. They felt very deeply that professional historians in their analytical and synthetic research would not be able to encompass the problem in its enormity; meanwhile, their contemporaries whose own memory was an invaluable source of rich information would gradually pass away.[23]

Although it is not clear why yizker book writers felt that professionals were not able to fulfill the task of writing about the town, the basic responsibility for writing the history of the destroyed town seems to have shifted from scholars to descendants from the place. Writers and editors state this view in their works. From the publishers of the Korczyner memorial book:

> We know that we don't have the necessary literary skills to create a fitting memorial but the remnants of the Jewish community of Korczyn demand that we undertake the task in spite of the fact that we are not priests (cohens) or writers. Of course we can ask whether any professional or literary writer can do justice to the Jewish destruction in our times. The object of the memorial book is not to create a literary or historical masterpiece but to create a memorial, a tombstone in the memory of our fathers, our mothers, our brothers, our sisters and our children from Korczyn that were innocently killed by the Germans. The object of the memorial is that the children and their children should read and especially see the book in order to remember what the Ger-

mans did to our community. The future generations must remember that there once existed a Jewish community in Korczyn that consisted of 786 people who lead a simple and pious life. In 1942, the Germans cleared the Jews from the entire area about 800 into the ghetto of Korczyn and then destroyed the entire Jewish community of about 1600 people. This deed can't be forgotten. It must be memorialized for eternity. Perhaps the future generations will be able to see in the German defeat some consolation as the German philosopher Nietzsche stated: "A token revenge is better than none." May their memory be erased forever.[24]

Even though the writers acknowledge that they are not professionals, they wonder whether even the skills of the professional are sufficient to describe the scope of the Holocaust. Another possibility is that ordinary people may have written by default because there were too few scholars for the job and too many towns to commemorate. Whatever the reasons, writers clearly consider their volumes as historical, as well as personal accounts. From *Sefer hazikaron le-kehilat Kamien Koszyrski ve-ha-seviva:*

> This book is a modest addition by the survivors of the town to the history of the Holocaust, written testimony of Jewish suffering and supreme courage and heroism. It is a testimony that cries out to the world not to forget and not to forgive the German murderers.[25]

From *Plotsk: bletlekh geshikhte fun idishn lebn in der alter heym:*

> We, people of Plotsk, in Argentina, have accordingly taken on the duty of recording at least a few of the pages of the history of the Jews of Plotsk.[26]

This reliance on communal writing may reflect another sensibility, which is suggested in the foreword to *Sefer zikaron kehilat Vileike*, where the editor writes about the book:

> It was a hard and difficult task, and we asked ourselves: Will we be able to accomplish it? Can we find within our ranks people who are gifted enough to put into writing the feelings and emotions of the hearts, the material and spiritual life, the joys and sorrows of our town, from its beginning to its bitter end — there are neither writers nor poets amongst us. But, on an afterthought, we realized that the mission imposed on us by the very fate as it were, does not call for a literary masterpiece, and neither is expected to be composed of superb poetry. All we want to bequeath ... [are] simple, honest stories....[27]

While recognizing the importance of scholarly accounts, writers definitely believed that their personal accounts were more suited to describe the catastrophe. This suggests that the genre of autobiography, a relatively new one among Eastern European Jewry, also exerted an influence on yizker books. People believed in the value of writing about their own experiences. For some, writing was a cathartic experience. From *Sefer Dereczyn:*

> Scores of Deretchiners wrote this Memorial Book, simple people and not writers by vocation, but their souls could not rest until they had recounted the memories, thoughts, struggles of those dearest to them, who were lost in the streets, fields, and forests of their town, the town which had been a peaceful home of a carefree childhood and adolescence, and which the war and Holocaust turned into a place of death. It is these unpretentious people who built this Memorial Monument.[28]

Hagiography may have also have exerted an influence on the projects since many books profile spiritual leaders from the town. Including luminaries from the town serves to elevate the stature of the town. Interestingly, although descriptions of the town's religious life are common, the religious inhabitants from the town did not usually contribute entries because the books are products of secular organizations.

Although it is not possible to know with certainty the level of their familiarity with all these practices or the depth of their religious beliefs, readers and writers clearly seem to have drawn from a shared repertoire of knowledge. The commonalities across the books suggest that people relied on shared practices, genres, and images to commemorate their losses, contextualizing those losses within a continuity of Jewish experience.

The Original Books in Print

Although most memorial books were issued in the 1960s and 1970s, a few were issued even before the final defeat of the Nazis. Examples are *Toyznt yor Pinsk: geshikhte fun der shtot, der yidisher yishuv, institutsies* published in New York by the Pinsker Branch of the Arbeter-Ring in 1941 and the *Lodzsher yizker-bukh* published in New York by the United Emergency Relief Committee for the City of Lodz in 1943. Several books were actually written in the displaced persons camps. These include volumes to Rovne, Skalat, Krasnystaw, Chrzanow, Otwock, Czenstochow, Radom, and Siepec.[29] An interest volume is the Czenstochower one, which is set in roman letters because editors did not have access to Yiddish type.

Some of the early books issued outside of Europe were those published in Argentina. That is perhaps due to the centralized nature of that country's Jewish community, the vibrancy of its publishing industry, and the offer of subsidies. Mark Turkow, one of Argentina's major publishers of the 1930s, was very interested in works about Polish Jewry.[30] His series, *Dos poylishe yidntum*, includes a number of memorial volumes. For example, the 1945 Sokolow book was the 4th title in that series; the 1949 Tshenstokhov book was the 46th; and the 1951 Belchatow book was the 80th. By comparison,

Elie Weisel's 1956 *Un di velt hot geshivgn*, the precursor to *Night*, was the 117th book in the series. Volumes printed in Argentina by other presses include the 1945 book dedicated to Plotsk, the 1949 book to Ostrovtse, the 1951 book to Kobryn, and the 1951 book to Kowel.

In the United States, the war in Europe prompted some *landsmanshaftn* to hold fund drives and undertake other relief efforts on behalf of their compatriots. After the war, when the refugees arrived in the United States, they invigorated those organizations. Although their exact number is difficult to ascertain, about 140,000 Jewish refugees eventually settled in the United States after the end of the war.[31] Despite the myth of silence attributed to them, refugees were expressing their losses in ceremonies, monuments, print, and in other ways from the start.[32] The yizker ceremony held in 1947 at the Academy Hall in New York by the United Sherpser Relief Committee is one example. Another is the memorial plaque to the Warsaw ghetto heroes and the six million killed placed on the banks of the Hudson River in New York City in 1947.[33] Early yizker books issued in the United States include the 1947 volume to Tshenstokhov, the 1947 volume to Nowy Dwor, and the 1948 volume to Braynsk.

Ultimately, the majority of Eastern European refugees settled in Israel, where the role of the survivor was part of the public discussions among politicians, educators, rabbis, jurists, journalists, poets, novelists, and others. The establishment of *Yad Vashem* in 1953 is one type of commemoration. For example, when Rachel Auerbach, a chronicler of the Holocaust who survived the Warsaw ghetto, joined the staff of *Yad Vashem* in 1955, she introduced an initiative to the directorate of *Yad Vashem* to collect testimonies from survivors. After the initiative was approved, she was appointed Director of the Collection of Testimonies Department. Applying the principles of documentation learned in the Warsaw ghetto from Emanuel Ringelblum, she issued a call to survivors to submit their testimonies to *Yad Vashem*. Thousands of pages of written materials, along with photographs and other materials were submitted. At same time on a private level, hundreds of Israeli *landsmanshaftn* were encouraging their members to submit materials for a memorial book. Examples of early yizker books published in Israel include the 1948 volume to Lachowicze and the 1952 volume to Luniniec. In 1961, an exhibit of yizker books held in Tel Aviv displayed about 150 volumes.

Despite historical, political, economic, demographic, and other differences in the countries where they lived, survivors and their compatriots wrote to commemorate the hometown, record its history, testify about its destruction, tell the story of their own lives and those ancestors, friends, relatives, and others who lost their lives in the Holocaust, and guard against future acts of anti–Semitism. Survivors wanted the books to include description of the town's pre–Holocaust history in order to emphasize its active life and tragic loss. As a result, most yizker books contain a survey of the town from its Jewish beginning to the modern period. In some cases, a historian was hired to write the introductory chapter; in other cases, an editor summarized a number of texts, took excerpts from texts, or used encyclopedia entries for that chapter. The introduction was not intended to be a comprehensive history, but rather to present an image of the town. Writers selected what they believed would best honor the life and death of the town. Along with these descriptions of historical events, editors used illustrative material, such as maps, photographs, drawings, and other images to convey the richness of the Jewish life of the town. Many books also contain biographical sketches of prominent citizens as way to emphasize the intellectual, cultural, economic, and religious life of the town and provide a level of prestige to the hometown.

Although the books share a common structure and purpose, each one was the result of a specific group of writers and editors working under a specific set of conditions. Writers made decisions about what to include and exclude in their own accounts. Their experiences during the war, as well as the distance from it, affected their image of the past. For instance, since most survivors were young adults at the war's end, the affective voice that many use in their writing suggests an eviction from paradise and serves to idealize the town. In retrospect, writers changed the small town into a major place and made the ordinary extraordinary, because they had to reconcile their traumatic wartime experience, their realism and romanticism about the hometown, and their longing for the past. Also, people often avoided maligning each other in print.[34] The consequences of printing negative material, such as naming Nazi collaborators, were very serious. Reputations were at stake. Legal action was occasionally threatened. Sometimes negative material was omitted to idealize the town or to defend someone's actions.

Editors used criteria to select personal accounts for the book that were not always related to the writer's Holocaust experience. For example, one factor for including the testimony of a particular writer might be the amount of money that the writer's family contributed to the publishing of the book. Regardless, the original readers viewed the books as accurate portrayals of the life and destruction of their hometown. They tended not to question the knowledge contained in the books or to make distinctions between memory and history. Along with the historical essays and chronologies contained in each book, the experience of the original readers counted as important sources of knowledge about the former life of the hometown.

Although the editorial committee made the final decisions about content and style, and everyone was encouraged to submit articles, editors were not bound to include all the material they received. In the end, each publication was the product of a group of individuals who created the memory for the community, operating under varying constraints of time and money and using selected historical material and personal testimonies. As one editor of the Brzeziny book writes:

> And it may sound a little strange but building the houses of stone and cement went easier than creating the monument on paper, the yizker book. Yes, there were all kinds of difficulties on the way — material, technical. Let us forget all the difficulties today, when before us open the pages of our modest history, when we get down to reading and remembering everything and everyone that are for us loved and dear — the individuals who are with us and those who are no longer with us, above all the *kedoyshim-otehoyrim* (sainted martyrs) who have vanished with the annihilated portion of the Jewish people.[35]

This editor is eager for the readers to overlook the problems that occurred during the compilation of the book and accept the book in honor of their town and its people and descendants.

Miriam Hoffman's in-depth study of the Zwolen yizker book details the ways in which one specific book was shaped by the conflicts among the people who supported the project and those who did not, the formation of the book committee, the differences in opinion between the *landsmanshaft* members and the professional editor, the mixed reception of the book by its readers, the manner of funding the book, the concern over the children and grand-children, the rationale for including an English synopsis in the book, and the disagreements between New Yorkers and Israelis.[36]

In fact, conflict and consensus regarding politics, religiosity, gender, age, language, personality, money, time, and nationality shaped all the books. Yet, despite these problems, once a book was published, the memorial to the place was fixed in print. However, a translation could change all that.

The Translations in Print

Over time, as the readers of the books changed so did their facility with language. For instance, if a yizker book was originally written in Hebrew and Yiddish, the Israeli descendants from the ancestral hometown could at least read the Hebrew sections of the volume. By contrast, generally American descendants could not read either section. A book originally written only in Yiddish would have no new readers. Over the years, Jews living in the United States grew interested in their heritage and looked for information about East-ern Europe Jewry written in English. The emerging ethnicity movements in the United States during the 1970s helped to stimulate that interest in genealogy. Motivated by similar interests, young Israelis wanted Yiddish volumes translated into Hebrew. Simultaneously, the sources continued to be useful for research purposes.

These matters of nationality, language, genealogy, and scholarship prompted some organizations, as well as some individuals to seek a translation of an original yizker book. As it happened, a translation could assume a number of forms. A translation could be a complete version of the original text, an abridged version of the original text, an updated version of the original text, an expanded version of the original text, a supplement to the original text, or a combination. Also, the time span between the publication of the original and its translation could vary. In addition, between an original and its translation, there could be variations in size, binding, color, paper, artwork, photographs, and other aspects of production. And even more interestingly, a change in contents often accompanied the change in language since there was a willingness among the survivors to favor continuity of culture over continuity of language.

For example, *A Tale of One City*, the 1991 English-language book to Piotrokow Trybunalski, contains articles from the original 1965 *Piotrkow Trybunalski ve ha seviva*, as well as material from other sources, such as *landsmanshaft* newsletters. At the end of each essay in the volume the source of the material is noted. For instance, at the end of an article describing Piotrkower rabbis are the words "*Izkor* Book," a reference to *Piotrkow Trybunalski ve ha seviva*. Similarly, the 1997 English-language book *Luboml: The Memorial Book of a Vanished Shtetl* contains numerous articles not included in the 1974 *Seyfer yisker le kehilat Luboml*.

The Chrzanower memorial book is another illustration of how an original volume could change over time. In 1948, the Chrzanower Young Men's Association issued *Sefer Chrzanow*, a Yiddish-language book. Forty years later, since many descendants could not read that volume, the *landsmanshaft* prepared a Yiddish-English version. In a letter to the membership about the 1948 volume, Solomon Gross writes:

> Time has taken its toll. The pages of his book are disintegrating and the binding is falling apart. Saddest of all, very few people are able to read it in Yiddish. The time has come to correct this situation. I hope that with the cooperation of the membership and friends of the Chrzanower Association, I will be able to have it properly translated and rebound into a new Yiddish-English edition.[37]

In the same letter, Gross also calls for additional photographs. Eventually, this letter is printed in the bi-lingual volume, which was issued in 1989. Then in 1992, the English portion of the 1989 volume was translated into Hebrew. That English portion is also available online.

Still another example of a variation in the translation is illustrated by the volume to Manyevitz, which was completed in two stages. From the start, the *landsmanshaft* intended to have a Hebrew version, as well as an English one. The Hebrew-language book was planned first and published in 2002; the English version followed in 2004. The initial materials were generally written in Yiddish and then translated into Hebrew. The material for the English version was translated from Hebrew or Yiddish.

A few books went through several translations. For instance, a Hebrew-language book to Kamenetz-Podolsk was published in Israel in 1965. Since Kamenetzers in New York could not read Hebrew, they decided in 1966 to issue an abridged English language edition of the Hebrew version, which included additional material. In 1990, a descendant from the Kamenetz-Podolsk region translated a portion of the original Hebrew book into English and published those excerpts as a typewritten version. Then, in 1999, a typeset edition of that 1990 version, with an added index, a glossary, and other material, but without the photographs from the 1965 book, was published in the United States.

The English version of the yizker book dedicated to the city of Volkovysk highlights another type of change. The city has three original yizker books: *Hurban Volkovysk*, a Hebrew-language book published in 1947; *Wolkovisker yizker book*, a Yiddish-language book published in 1949; and *Volkovysk*, a Hebrew-language book published in 1988. The 2002 English translation, *The Volkovysk Memorial Book—The Trilogy*, contains the three earlier volumes. This English volume, which is photocopied and has a velo binding, contains no photographs from the original books.

Whatever the final outcome, the decision to translate a volume could be financially, organizationally, and personally difficult. The completion of a translation depended on numerous factors. Sometimes an editor wanted to include two descriptions of the same event by two different authors for the sake of harmony between the writers; whereas the translator was more concerned with repetition and less with harmony. Matters of autonomy were another source of tension between editors and translators. Editors exercised varying levels of control, causing friction between some editors and translators. The degree of control in part reflected the personality of the editors, as well as the degree of affiliation between the translator and *landsmanshaft*. Conflicts between insider and outsider perspectives on the books were another source of tension. Since the translated texts were primarily intended for the survivors and their families, a translator sometimes misunderstand the urgency of the aging survivors. The dependence of the editors on the translators added more stress. Knowing that the translators were necessary for the completion of the project created a situation in which the editors were dependent on others for the work. Tensions between editors and the members also existed because of personal agendas.

In some cases, a translation was prompted by an individual, not a *landsmanshaft*. For example, in 1998, a descendant from Felshtin initiated the English translation of the 1937 Felshtin book. As one journalist writes about that project:

> Shaievitz produced a few copies of a second translation — on paper and CD, this time including copies of the drawings from the original. And he continued reworking the 650 pages of Yiddish himself, inserting footnotes and explanations for the benefit of readers who may not have a Jewish background.[38]

Shaievitz decided to re-do some of the translator's work and add the explanatory material to the text. Jacob Solomon Berger, the translator of *Sefer zikaron Zelwa*, *Sefer Dereczyn*, and other books explains his work in this way:

> The preparation of this English *Dereczin Memorial Book* represents another step in my continuing effort to make histories of Eastern European Jewish *shtetl* life more accessible to the English-speaking world.[39]

His motivation is two-fold: to preserve his own family history and to make the works available to English readers. Eventually, as interest in the books increased, the limited supply of original copies became a problem. To address that shortage, people looked to new technologies for solutions.

The New Media Versions

The creation of a digital library of yizker books by the National Yiddish Book Center and the New York Public Library offered one solution to the shortage of books. During the 1990s, the recognition that the books were scarce and deteriorating prompted staff at the National Yiddish Book Center and New York Public Library to digitize approximately 650 of 700 titles in the New York Public Library's collection.[40] Processed as .gif files, these digitized versions are scanned images of every page in a volume. As a result, patrons may read an entire volume online at the New York Public Library's website or buy a print on-demand volume from the National Yiddish Book Center's website. While the original books continue to be valued and carefully guarded historical documents, this digital library makes the books more accessible than before. The reprints limit the handling of original copies and fill in gaps in collections. They are also useful for developing collections, such as the recent one established at the Institute for Strategic Studies in Poland.

The establishment in 1987 of JewishGen, the online site for genealogical research, also addresses the problems of limited availability and accessibility of yizker books.[41] Along with its other initiatives, JewishGen started a yizker book translation project in the 1990s. In some cases, when a town does not have an actual yizker book, JewishGen includes an entry from the *Encyclopedia of Jewish Communities* as a substitute. Hundreds of partial translations are available online as .html files. Using the JewishGen listserv, volunteers issue announcements about new projects. From a recent email about *Grayeve yisker-bukh*:

> It is with great pleasure that we announce the official start of the Grajewo Yizker book translation project. As a brief summary, the Yizker book is written in Yiddish, Hebrew, Polish, German and English. We are about to hire a professional translator to translate the Yiddish sections into English, with an anticipated cost of approximately $8000. She is a delightful woman who not only has experience translating Yizker books, she also once managed the Institute of Yiddish Studies in Vilnius. She will begin translating the first chapter once a minimum of $500 USD is raised, and will continue to completion as we raise additional funds. Additionally, we have two very generous landsmen who graciously offered to translate the Hebrew and German sections. We hope to find a Polish translator in the very near future. I want to stress this Yizker book was written approximately 60 years ago with the goal of keeping the memory of Grajewo alive. As many of you may know, Yiddish is a dying language and we consider ourselves very fortunate to have found someone very passionate about the language. So my dear friends and family, it may be only a matter of time before Yiddish becomes a language of the past. Therefore, we feel it is our duty to translate the Grajewo Yizker into English as soon as possible. This is one way of ensuring the memory of Grajewo and all of her souls who were brutally murdered during the Holocaust is kept alive for generations to come. What can you do to help? Please consider donating money. We also encourage you to talk to your friends and relatives who you think would be willing to help us raise the $8000 USD necessary to complete this very worthwhile project.[42]

The coordinators of the Grayever project mention duty, language, and memory as the reasons to translate the book. In many ways, this solicitation is similar to the ones issued by the *landsmanshaftn* for the original book projects. The channel for the request is different.

Also regarding new media features, hyperlinks on the JewishGen site augment the information in the original books. For instance, the Horodenka and Rohatyn entries on the JewishGen site include portions from the original book, along with links to other sources of information about the places. The JewishGen site also hosts a number of regional special interest groups; the sites of some of these groups contain information from yizker books, For example, the website BIALYGen provides details from more than a dozen yizker books dedicated to towns in the Białystoker region. BIALYGen also contains an excerpt from a yizker book not listed on the main JewishGen site.

BIALYGen are also provide links to other websites dedicated to the Białystok region, such as the Jewish Records Indexing site, the Belarus special interest group site, Ada Holtzman's Zchor.org, Tilford Bartman's Zabludow.com, Andrew Blumberg's Bielsk Podlaski site, ShtetLinks, and Gary Mokotoff and David Gordon's Jalowka site. Ada Holtzman and Tilford Bartman are among a number of individuals who maintain personal websites dedicated to their ancestral hometowns.

Many of these sites contain portions of yizker books or provide links to the books. For example, Holtzman's homepage has a link to the pages of the Plock Remembrance Initiative, which contains the English portion of the yizker book issued by the Plotzker Association in Israel in 1967. Likewise, Jose Gutstein's homepage provides a link to an English translation of the original 1954 Szczuczyn yizker book published in Tel Aviv by former residents of Szczuczyn in Israel. Chapters from an English translation of the book are included on the site with photographs from the original book. Gutstein's homepage for the town of Radzilow uses hyperlinks creatively. Since Radzilow does not have its own yizker book and is near the towns of Goniadz, Jedwabne, Kolna, Szczuczyn, and Stawiski, Gutstein provides links to those JewishGen books. Other examples are the web-based only books for Czortkov and Sudilkov, created by descendants from those towns. One limitation to the online material is that there is no guarantee that the site will be maintained on the web for posterity.

In addition to an organization's or individual's website, a *landsmanshaft* may maintain a website. The Felshtin Society is an example of an active online association. According to its website, the original organization became inactive in the late 1970s, but in the 1990s, was revitalized by a group of descendants interested in Jewish history and genealogy.[43] The goals of the group include translating and publishing an English version of the Felshtin yizker book, restoring the Felshtiner section of the Baron Hirsch cemetery in Staten Island, and providing forums for social and educational interchange. Regarding the Felshtin yizker book in particular, the website site provides links to the National Yiddish Book Center and New York Public Library websites, excerpts and pictures from the volume, and articles about it.

Besides providing greater access to the contents of yizker books, the web makes information about collections of yizker books more readily available. A number of libraries, archives, and museums have placed information about their collections online. Some libraries, for example, YIVO and the St. Louis County Library, have placed their list of yizker books online. Sometimes these lists are linked to sites where the contents of a yizker book may be found. For instance, the St. Louis County Library provides links to JewishGen; whereas the Holocaust Center of North California links its online list to the New York

Public Library website. This online information about holdings and catalogues increases the use of the books as well.

And finally, there is even a YouTube video describing how to use the New York Public Library and the JewishGen sites to find out about yizker books, as well as a JewishGen listserv.

Change and Continuity of Yizker Books

At the same time that the translations and new technologies are making the books more available, they are changing the function, form, structure, contents, language, and value of the books. For example, the documentation function of the books is shifting. About that, Annette Wieviorka finds that

> the purpose of testimony is no longer to obtain knowledge.... The mission that has devolved to testimony is no longer to bear witness to inadequately known events, but rather to keep them before our eyes. Testimony is to be a means of transmission to future generations.[44]

The point is that survivor accounts no longer fulfill their initial purpose of providing first-hand evidence of events rather they act as a means of intergenerational transmission of information.

Another shift concerns the audience of yizker books. The original readers and writers were reading and writing for each other since many were born in the town, were acquainted with or related to writers, were friends with other readers, recognized names and faces printed in the book, were members of the *landsmanshaftn,* or lived through the actual events. In addition to sharing a range of experiences, they knew the scope of the book's audience, because the original books were usually printed in small quantities in response to the number of subscriptions. At first, the books were even disparaged by outside readers. As a rule, the familiarity between readers and writers does not extend to the readers of the translations or new media versions. An exception would be an English-language reader with an affiliation to the *landsmanshaft.* For example, an adult child of a Holocaust survivor would bring a measure of first-hand experiences to the book. This reader might know another reader, a writer, the name of person or place, or the story of an event included in the book. A reader without such an affiliation might not have any first-hand experience. As outsiders, these readers did not know the audience at all. These new readers may not know about the role of the *landsmanshaftn* in compiling the books either because dust jackets on the print-on-demand versions credit the National Yiddish Book Center as the publisher. The readers of the original works used the volumes for communal purposes; whereas the readers of the translations and new media versions use the books for research purposes. For instance, in *Ritevas seyfer zikharon,* the editors address their compatriots directly:

> To all the townspeople who did not spare of their time and labored days and nights collecting the materials that would reflect the history and life of our town, our heartfelt thanks. We wrote this book the best we could. We told as best as we could remember.... While we are aware that there are errors, we do know that we did all that we could, always recognizing the sacred duty we undertook.[45]

The editors are appealing to their readers within the organization. By contrast, the editors of the English version, *A Yizker Book to Riteve*, include a historical overview, footnotes, summaries of articles, and an index to help the contemporary reader. The rationale for adding this new material is given by the editor in the book's foreword:

> It is perhaps the combination of personal memoirs, written by the townsfolk, added to the efforts of the historian to supply context and details, glossary and archival material, which offers a meaningful contribution to an understanding of one's roots.[46]

The books are also becoming more secular to the extent that the liturgical use of the necrology is diminishing. For example, many of the JewishGen versions contain the necrologies from the originals. However, these lists originally served memorial purposes, but now the lists are often used for genealogical reasons. For instance, the lists of names in the JewishGen translations are not used to commemorate the losses from the place, but rather by descendants to find their relatives. Moreover, in those cases when a JewishGen translation does not include the necrology, such as the online translation of *Pinkes Zshirardov,* the version does not act as a gravestone at all. This is a major shift in function since the book as gravestone was among the earliest motifs. And in the case when a book is not translated at all, the early hopes for collective memory are not realized whatsoever for current readers.

Language is also affected. In the English translations, the trend is toward secular language. Translators often use popular discourse, which tends to universalize the Jewish experience. For instance, the terms *kodesh* and *she'erit hapletah* are being replaced by the terms *victim* and *survivor*. Victim and survivor are the language of popular culture, and thus hide the Jewish dimension of the catastrophe. Another traditional Jewish term found in the early yizker books is *churbn*, which refers to the destruction of the first and second temples in Jerusalem is also disappearing. That word appears in the title of the 1948 yizker book to *Czenstochow*, which was published by the cultural committee of the Czenstochower *landsmanshaft* in the American Zone in West Germany. By using the word *churbn*, the writers place the events within a Jewish history of destruction. Some even call the Nazi period, the *dritn churbn*, the third catastrophe. Over time, though, the words *shoah* and Holocaust have replaced *churbn*. That glosses over the fact that Yiddish speakers were annihilated.

Another change is that the new media formats tend to fragment the representation of the town for the current reader. Additionally, many of the JewishGen versions are incomplete translations. The level of completeness depends on many factors, including the donations to the project, the number of volunteers working on the project, and the duration of the project. In some cases, only the table of contents of the original is available online; and in other cases, numerous chapters from the original are available. To the original writers, readers, and editors, the books commemorated death and affirmed life, To emphasize that dual orientation, books contain separate sections to the period before the war, during the war, and afterwards. This reflects a belief in the continuity of Jewish life. To provide the descriptions of the pre–Holocaust life in the town, books contained a history of the town, as well as reprints from historical records. Whereas, an array of historical documents provided the basis for the overview of the town, the personal narratives form the core of the books. The articles about the townspeople after the war celebrate their survival. While web features augment the information in the original books, those features impact how the books are read and what the books mean. Hyperlinks permit readers to seek specific information rather than an understanding of the entire text. For example, by following a series of links connecting victim names, the reader bypasses the material about the institutions and organizations of the town, an extensive section in the original book. That shifts the image of the town away from its rich descriptions and reduces the book to a list. This overlooks the commemorative or celebratory nature of the book.

While the informal definition of yizker books used by JewishGen, coupled with the overall informality of the site, changes the intentions of the original writers, this is not the case with the National Yiddish Book Center and the New York Public Library project, which maintains the content of the original books in the reprints. Possible confusion may result from differences in copyright dates between the original and the reprint. For example, the 1943 Lodz volume held by YIVO library is a reprint. The cover lists the National Yiddish Book Center and The New York Public Library as copyright holders and the copyright date as 2003.

From print to online and from language to language, the form and structure of a book may also change. The transition of the Zabludow books provides a case example. *Zabludove yizker bukh* was printed in 1961 in Yiddish. Then in 1987, a Hebrew volume *Zabludov: dapim mi-tokh yizker bukh* was issued. A portion of the Hebrew version was translated into English. Never published in print, that English version is currently on the Zabludow homepage maintained by Tilford Bartman, a descendant from the town. The original Yiddish and Hebrew texts are available from the New York Public Library and National Yiddish Book Center's digitized collection. However, there are two JewishGen entries. One is a translation of the table of contents, a single article, and the necrology from *Zabludove yizker bukh*; whereas the other is a translation of the Holocaust chapters from *Zabludov: dapim mi-tokh yizker bukh.*

The value of a yizker book is also shifting. The original readers thought of the volumes as monuments in print. For instance, in the preface to their town's book, the members of the Yizker Book Committee of the People of Belchatow write:

> With this Yizker Book we wanted to erect a memorial on the unknown graves of our martyrs and to create an eternal monument to commemorate our town Belchatow.[47]

From this vantage point, the book is the gravestone for the people from the town who died without one. Some readers and writers of the original versions also viewed their book as the last entry in the town's chronicle. In addition to its value as a monument and chronicle, for those people who had few possessions from their hometown, the book also serves as an heirloom. The book was a tangible item that could be handed from parent to child. With the publication of the original book, people felt that they had partially fulfilled their obligation to the past by honoring their town and their obligation to the future by passing on the legacy about the town.

In sum, this diachronic examination of memorial books shows the ways in which the works are moving from the private setting of the *landsmanshaft* to the public space of the library or database. One result of that shift is that the value of the books as monument, chronicle, and heirloom is diminishing while their value as artifact and source document is increasing. In this way, new readers are transforming the books to meet new goals.

Notes

1. The Yizker Book Committee, "Brief History of the Szydlowiec (Shidlovtse) Yizker Book," in *Szydlowiec Memorial Book,* ed. Berl Kagan and trans. Max Rosenfeld (New York: Shidlowtzer Benevolent Association in New York, 1989), 12.

2. See Alan Mintz, *Hurban: Responses to Catastrophe in Hebrew Literature* (Syracuse, N.Y.: Syracuse University Press, 1996).

3. Y. Raban, ed., *Sefer Dereczyn* (Tel Aviv: Deretchiners Societies in Israel and the USA, 1966), 10.

4. M. and T. Rayak, eds., *Khurbn Glubok, Sharkoystsene, Dunilovitsh, Postav, Droye, Kazan: dos lebn un umkum fun yidishn shtetlekh in Vaysrusland-Lite (Vilne gegent)* (Buenos Aires: Former Residents' Association in Argentina, 1956), iii.

5. Itsak Tesler, "*Yizker*," in *Zabludow yizker-bukh,* eds. Itsak Tesler, Joseph Reznik, and Isaac Chesler (Buenos Aires: Zabludowo Book Committee, 1961), 13.

6. Y.H. Yerushalmi, *Zakhor: Jewish Memory and Jewish History* (Seattle: University of Washington Press, 1996), 46.

7. S. Kanc, ed., *Sefer zikaron Czyzewo* (Tel Aviv: Czyzewer Landsmanshaft in Israel and America, 1961), 43.

8. A. Rembah and B. Halevi, eds., *Sefer zikaron le-kehilat Kolno* (Tel Aviv: Kolner Organization and Sifirat Poalim, 1971), 10.

9. B. Baler, ed., *Pinkes Kowel* (Buenos Aires: Former Residents of Kowel and Surroundings in Argentina, 1951), 5.

10. James Young, *Writing and Rewriting the Holocaust: Narrative and the Consequences of Interpretation* (Bloomington: Indiana University Press, 1988), 19–21.

11. P. Katz, ed., *Pinkes Varshe* (Buenos Aires: Former Residents of Warsaw and Surroundings in Argentina, 1955), 9.

12. M.V. Bernshtayn, ed., *Pinkes Zshirardov, Amshinov un Viskit: Yizker-bukh tsu der geshikhte fun di kehiles ... fun zeyer oyfkum biz zeyer hurbn durkh di natsis yimah shemam* (Buenos Aires: Association of Former Residents in the USA, Israel, France, and Argentina, 1961), 474.

13. B. Giladi, ed., *A Tale of One City* (New York: Shengold Publishers and the Piotrkow Trybunalski Relief Association in New York, 1991), 11–12.

14. See Zeev Mankowitz, *Life Between Memory and Hope: The Survivors of the Holocaust in Occupied Germany* (New York: Cambridge University Press, 2002).

15. D. Abramovitsh and M.V. Bernshtayn, eds., *Pinkes Biten: Der oyfkum un untergang fun a yidisher kehile* (Buenos Aires: Bitaner landslayt in Argentina, 1954), v.

16. A. Laib, Z. Przedborksi, and H. Goldminc, eds., *Belkhatov: yizker-bukh* (Buenos Aires: Association of Polish Jews in Argentina, 1951), 11.

17. See Salo Baron, *The Jewish Community: Its History and Structure to the American Revolution* (Philadelphia: The Jewish Publication Society of America, 1942). See also Lucjan Dobroszycki, "YIVO in Interwar Poland: Work in the Historical Sciences," in *The Jews of Poland Between the Two World Wars,* eds. Yisrael Gutman, E. Mendelsohn, J. Reinhatz, and C. Shmeruk (Hanover, New Hampshire: University Press of New England, 1989), 494–519.

18. See Salo Baron, *The Jewish Community.*

19. J. Zicklin, "A Few Words," in *Gombin: Dos lebn un umkum fun a yidish shtetl in Poyln,* ed. Jack Zicklin et al. (New York: Gombin Society in Amerikca, 1969), 5.

20. Shlomo Bickel, "Introduction," in *Pinkas Kolomey,* ed. Shlomo Bickel (New York: Kolomeyer Memorial Book, 1957), vii.

21. Annette Wieviorka, "On Testimony," in *Holocaust Remembrance: The Shapes of Memory,* ed. Geoffrey Hartman (Oxford: Basil Blackwell, Ltd., 1994), 31–32.

22. See Elias Tcherikower, "Jewish Martyrology and Jewish Historiography," *YIVO Annual of Jewish Social Science* Volume 1 (1946): 9–23; and Lucjan Dobroszycki, "YIVO in Interwar Poland: Work in the Historical Sciences," in *The Jews of Poland Between the Two World Wars,* eds. Yisrael Gutman, E. Mendelsohn, J. Reinhatz, and C. Shmeruk (Hanover, New Hampshire: University Press of New England, 1989), 494–519.

23. Wein, "Memorial Books as a Source," 255–256.

24. Korczyna Book Editorial Committee, "Some Words from the Publishers of the Korczyner Memorial Book," in *Korczyna; sefer zikaron,* ed. Korczyna Relief Committee (New York: Committee of the Korczyna Memorial Book, 1967), 11.

25. Chaim Lazar-Litai, "Introduction," in *Sefer ha-zikaron le-kehilat Kamien Koszyrski ve-ha-seviva,* ed. A. A. Stein, et al. (Former Residents of Kamin Koshirsky and Surroundings in Israel, 1965), 20.

26. Y. Horn, ed., *Plotsk: bletlekh geshikhte fun idishn lebn in der alter heym* (Buenos Aires: Association of Plock Residents in Argentina, 1945), 5.

27. The editors, "Foreword," in *Sefer zikaron kehilat Vileike,* eds. K. Farber and J. Se'evri (Tel Aviv: Society of Vileykah and Surroundings, 1972), 326.

28. Y. Raban, ed. *Sefer Dereczyn* (Tel Aviv: Deretchiners Societies in Israel and the USA, 1966), 5.

29. See Gabriel Finder, "Yizker! Commemoration of the Dead by Jewish Displaced Persons in Postwar Germany," in *Between Mass Death and Individual Loss: The Place of the Dead in Twentieth-Century Germany*, eds. P. Betts, A. Confino, and D. Schumann (New York: Berghahn Books, 2008), 232–257.

30. Robert Weisbrot, *The Jews of Argentina: From the Inquisition to Perón*, with the research assistance of Robert Murciano (Philadelphia: Jewish Publication Society of America, 1979), 108–109.

31. Beth Cohen, *Case Closed* (New Brunswick: Rutgers University Press in association with the United States Holocaust Memorial Museum, 2007), 9.

32. *Ibid.*, 168. Also see Hasia Diner, *We Remember with Reverence and Love: American Jews and the Myth of Silence After the Holocaust, 1945–1962* (New York: New York University Press, 2009).

33. Annette Wieviorka, *The Era of the Witness* (Ithaca: Cornell University Press, 2006), 47.

34. See Rosemary Horowitz, *Literacy and Cultural Transmission in the Reading, Writing, and Rewriting of Jewish Memorial Books* (Published dissertation) (San Francisco: Austin & Winfield, Publishers, 1998).

35. Jacob-David Berg, "Our Book," in *Brzeziny Memorial Book*, http://www.jewishgen.org/yizker/brzeziny/Brzeziny.brz001.html #TOC (Accessed March 30, 2010).

36. See Miriam Hoffman, *Memory and Memorial: An Investigation into the Making of the Zwolen Memorial Book* (Unpublished M.A. thesis) (Columbia University, NY, 1983).

37. Solomon Gross, "Foreword," in *Sefer Chrzanow*, ed. M. Bochner and trans. J. Boyarin (Roslyn Harbor, New York: Solomon Gross, 1989), http://www.jewishgen.org/Yizkor/Chrazanow/chr001.html#Foreword (accessed May 7, 2010).

38. See Elaine Durbach, "Translating a Memorial Book Opens Window on Jewish History," *Welcome to the Felshtin Society*, http://www.felshtin.org (accessed March 6, 2009).

39. Jacob Solomon Berger, "The Translator's Foreward" in *Derecin Memorial Book*, a translation of *Sefer Dereczyn*, ed. Y. Raban (Tel Aviv: Deretchiners Societies in Israel and the USA. 1966), v.

40. For details about the project, see Fay Zipkowitz, "Yiddish on Demand: The Debut of the Steven Spielberg Digital Yiddish Library." Proceedings of the 37th Annual Convention of the Association of Jewish Librarians. Denver, CO (June 23–26), 2002. Also see Faith Jones and Gretta Siegel, "*Yizkor* Books as Holocaust Grey Literature," *Publishing Research Quarterly* (Spring 2006): 52–62. Jones won the 2007 RUSA ABC-CLIO Online History award for her work digitizing the collection, an award that recognizes the importance of Internet-based historical resources.

41. See *JewishGen—The Home for Jewish Genealogy*, http://www.jewishgen.org.

42. Yizker Project Digest, email to author, April 27, 2010.

43. See *Welcome to the Felshtin Society*, http://www.felshtin.org.

44. Annette Wieviorka, "On Testimony," in *Holocaust Remembrance: The Shapes of Memory*, ed. Geoffrey Hartman (Cambridge, Massachusetts: Blackwell Publishers, 1994), 24.

45. The Fellow Townsmen Association of Ritavas in Israel and Abroad, "Editorial," in A. Levite, ed., *Ritevas seyfer zikharon* (Tel Aviv: The Fellow Townsmen Association of Ritavas in Israel and Abroad, 1977), iv.

46. Dina Porat, "Foreword," in *A Yizker Book to Riteve*, eds. Dina Porat and Roni Stauber (Cape Town: Kaplan-Kushlick Foundation, 2000), 9.

47. The Yizker Book Committee of the People of Belchatow, "A Word to the Reader," *Belchatow Yizker Book*, http://www.jewishgen.org/Yizkor/Belchatow/bel002.html (accessed March 30, 2010).

2

Israel as the Cradle of Yizker Books

Michlean Amir

What was the role of the State of Israel and the Holocaust survivors who lived there in the creation of the genre known as yizker books, *yizker bikher, pinkeysim, sifre zikaron,* or simply *sefarim*? In order to attempt an answer to this question, this essay first defines yizker books, briefly describes the information that may be found in them, and discusses some new developments relevant to their use. The rest of the paper is then devoted to showing how and why — Israel and only Israel — could have been the incubator in which these books were nurtured into being.[1]

For the purpose of this essay, yizker books are defined as those volumes written about Jewish communities in Eastern Europe and published by *landsmanshaftn*. *Landsmanshaftn* are mutual aid associations, groups of people with roots in particular *shtetls*, towns, or cities, whose members painstakingly gathered evidence, including documents, photographs, stories, name lists, and much more about their locality, its history, and the fate of its population during the Holocaust. Postwar descriptions are also included in the volumes. After the materials were collected, they were edited and published in books, which became memorials for the many victims who would never have gravestones. They would document and commemorate, and thereby become "surrogate tombstones."[2] In *The Texture of Memory*, James Young states that "[f]or a murdered people without graves, without even corpses to inter, these memorial books often came to serve as symbolic tombstones."[3]

Yizker books continue a long history of written books derived from the traditional Jewish commandment to remember — *Zahor*! The word is mentioned in the Bible 169 times. The tradition began with the destruction and suffering brought on the Israelites by Amalek in biblical times and continued throughout the Middle Ages, the Crusades, and the pogroms that preceded the Holocaust. The subject of remembrance in Jewish tradition is thoroughly explored by Joseph Hayim Yerushalmi in *Zakhor, Jewish History and Jewish Memory*.[4] Yerushalmi concerned with the future of Jewish memory could not have foreseen the explosion of interest in commemorating the events of the Holocaust that occurred since the publication of his book. The memorial book dedicated to Felshtin is among the first such books written in the century. Published in 1937, the volume commemorates an event that took place on February 16, 1919, namely the pogrom perpetrated by Petlyura and his armies during which 485 of the town's 1,883 Jews were murdered. The first Holocaust-era book was written about Łódź and published in 1943.

Estimates suggest that the total number of yizker books is between 700 and 800. In actuality, though those books cover a greater number of communities than the numbers indicate. Some books cover a large town along with its surrounding *shtetls*, with each described separately. Additionally, some communities with large Jewish populations have several yizker books. For some towns, a book might be published in Israel as well as in another country, such as the United States or Argentina. At the *Yad Vashem* library, 1,421 volumes are categorized as yizker books because of a broader definition of the genre than used in this chapter.

Yizker books were not written or edited only by historians, but the first historians of the Holocaust, such as Emanuel Ringelblum, were its victims. Many survivors, including Rachel Auerbach and Israel Gutman, lived and worked in Israel after the war. They felt it their solemn responsibility to gather materials, to write, and to document — as if they could hear the great historian Simon Dubnow call out to them: "Jews, write and record!"[5] As Auerbach states:

> And if, for even one of the days of my life, I should forget how I saw you then, my people, desperate and confused, delivered over to extinction, may all knowledge of me be forgotten and my name be cursed....[6]

Auerbach's life-long goal was to remember what happened during the Holocaust. And like her, once in Israel, "the survivors played a major role in shaping and laying the groundwork of Holocaust research. They set up archives and data bases and determined the research agenda."[7] As stated by B. Shargil in his conclusion to an article in *Ayaratenu Druzhkopol*:

> They, in their silent death, commanded us to scream out their final scream to the entire world, for they were lacking the means to do so.... We believe that words that come from the heart will penetrate the hearts of the readers who will erect a monument in their souls to the martyrs of Druzhkopol ... we are ... fulfilling a double debt that we owe our martyrs.... We will never forget "that which Amalek (meaning the Nazis/Hitler) did to us."[8]

One critic notes that by 1973 over 10,000 individuals had written sections for memorial books and about 1,000 editors had helped to finalize the books.[9] But the question of veracity hovered over the books from the start. Could the works serve as a reliable basis for research on this period in Jewish history? As Jakob Shatzky concludes about yizker books: "[t]hey are for the most part gravestones, not books. As is well known, no one reads gravestones."[10] And as Beryl Mark writes: a "yizker book is neither an encyclopedia nor a totally objective study ... [it has] a different kind of value than what is found in strictly historical and ethnographic works."[11]

As a result, many historians shied away from using yizker books until the late 1970s and early 1980s when it became clear that the wealth of information in the books could make significant contributions to research. Jack Kugelmass and Jonathan Boyarin's *From a Ruined Garden*, published in 1983 and with a second edition published in 1998, is a definitive turning point for the books. Kugelmass and Boyarin argue that Shatzky is wrong. They assert that "gravestone inscriptions are read ... [and] studying the historical process by which the books were assembled ... has a great deal to teach us."[12] Since the publication of *From a Ruined Garden*, many topics covered in yizker books have been, and continue to be, studied. Papers and books continue to be written in various formats, and there are web-based articles and additional memorial books about destroyed towns. A recent bibliography of studies of yizker books and studies using them as sources contains fifty entries. The JewishGen site is home to new web-based memorial books about towns, as well as to partial or complete English translations of yizker books. In addition, some *landmanshaftn* have decided to place their books on the web. For example, the Sudilkov *landsmanshaft* put its yizker book on the Internet in 2001. Unfortunately that work is no longer accessible, which points out some of the problems with web-based, unpublished materials.

Of great importance to scholars and researchers using yizker books is the joint effort of the New York Public Library and the National Yiddish Book Center to digitize about 650 yizker books in the collection of the New York Public Library. That collection constitutes about 90 percent of the volumes listed in the bibliography compiled by Zachary Baker in the second edition of *From a Ruined Garden*. These digitized books may be read on the website of the New York Public Library, and reprints may be ordered from the National Yiddish Book Center for a fee. It is important to note that memorial books continue to be written on the history of Jewish communities and their fate during World War II. These volumes are often prepared by individuals rather than organizations, and they are not necessarily Jewish. Such is the case with many hundreds of books written about vanished Jewish communities of Germany, which are not considered yizker books as the term is defined here.

Many recurring themes may be found in yizker books, despite the fact that they were edited and published independently in various locations and with no definitive guidelines on how to write them and what information to include. The following are some of the topics found in most books: Jewish life in the hometown from the earliest days of its settlement, everyday life, market days, religious life, role of women, and relations with Christian neighbors. Also included are documents relevant to that history, such as sample birth and death registries, ownership papers, and newspaper articles. Illustrations, such as detailed maps of the town with the Jewish quarter, group photographs of meetings of various organizations, school pictures, synagogues, photographs of families, important rabbis, and community leaders, are regularly included too. Descriptions of the economic life of the Jewish population also appear in many of the books. Often there are lists of professions typical to a community, including the names associated with the professions. Poems, stories, essays, and letters may also be found in the books. An important part of every book is the description of the Holocaust period, covering dates of roundups, creation of ghettos, deportations, death marches, partisan movements, descriptions of collaborators, and details of contacts with Jewish organizations around the world. Diaries and memoirs written during the war are described and sometimes included, if they are not too long. Names of German officers who were responsible for actions in the town, as well as names of Righteous Gentiles, may be found in many yizker books. Necrologies and lists of survivors are very important features of the books because they are valuable sources of information for genealogical research. Another common feature of the books are descriptions of the activities of Zionist organizations, photographs of their activities and meetings, and details on groups preparing to make *aliyah* to *Eretz Yisrael*, often with pictures and names. More recent information found in the books are the lists and photographs of individuals from the town who fought and fell during the Israeli War of Independence, as well as lists of people from the town living in Israel and in other countries, sometimes even with their addresses at the time of publication.

With respect to the subject of this essay, my analysis of one-half of the yizker books in the collection of the New York Public Library shows that 75 percent of the 348 books examined were published in Israel, and 62 percent were published completely or partially in Hebrew. For the survivors, Yiddish would have been a more natural language in which to write. However, by using Hebrew, they ensured that the books would be accessible to their children and grandchildren whom they imagined speaking the language and living in Israel. Additionally, many yizker books editors lived in Israel, and some were involved in the editing of more than one book. For example, David Shtokfish was on the editorial team of twenty-two yizker books!

Holocaust Survivors in Israel

The number of survivors who immigrated to Israel after the war far exceeded the immigration to any other country. About 388,000 went to Israel; 105,000 went to the U.S.[13] While there were survivors drawn to the United States and other countries, often due to the fact that they had relatives already living there and wanted to be close to remaining family members, there is a general misconception about the number of survivors who came to the United States. A recent publication mistakenly states that "[t]he U.S. [was] where most Holocaust survivors fled to."[14] Ultimately, more than two-thirds of the survivors went to Israel. When the gates were opened to them, many wanted to start a new life in their historical homeland and leave behind the cursed Diaspora. In fact, Holocaust survivors constituted the first large-scale wave of immigration to the newly established State of Israel. On January 9, 1950, the *Palestine Post* reported that "345,169 immigrants had arrived in Israel since the establishment of the State."[15] Following the war, the mindset of the Jewish displaced persons (DPs) remaining in Europe was described as having an "exclusively Zionist orientation ... [and] the greatest single event in the life of the Jewish DPs was the emergence of Israel as a Jewish state."[16] The survivors as well as the events of the Holocaust were important issues in the newly established state. According to Dalia Ofer

> the Holocaust and its meaning, contrary to some scholarship, did capture the attention of Israelis, including the political leadership and intellectual elite. From the end of World War II, the Holocaust was a major topic in the discourse of the *Yishuv* and Israel.... Discussion concerning the (proper) commemoration of the Holocaust displayed its significance in the minds of individuals and leaders.[17]

The new immigrants strengthened the existing *landsmanshaftn* in Israel, as well as those in New York and elsewhere, and in many cases created new ones for the towns that did not yet have them. The survivors were mostly young because they were "chosen" by the Nazis to be used as a good and cheap labor resource. Before the war, most of them were active in youth movements, which were to a great extent inclined toward Zionism, and thus they were anxious to make *aliyah*. Among them were many contributors to the yizker books, as well as many who took part in editing them. For these immigrants, yizker books became a "source of pride and longing."[18] With the hopes of giving Jews in Israel and in the Diaspora a valuable memorial, it was written that in pre-state Israel "[t]here are two ways to commemorate the past: either by a book or by massive structures — perpetual memorials."[19]

The Place of Zion and Zionism in the Lives of Eastern European Jews

As mentioned above, most yizker books include information on the role that the longing for the Land of Israel, and later the Zionist movement, had in community life. There had always been a powerful bond between the Jews of the Diaspora and Zion. Information on the growth of Zionist sentiments and the activities of various groups in the movement is included in every yizker book. From *Bielsk Podlaski*:

> The ideological debates around various issues, Jewish problems in general, and the question of Eretz Yisrael, in particular, were frequent. This led to personal involvement, and there were many die-hards who were often ready to place their movements above all else.[20]

And the following appeal is at the end of the section in the same book:

> Let us hope that the Book of Bielsk will be more than just a memorial volume. It should help us assimilate the lessons we must learn from the Holocaust, and convince future generations ... that they cannot and must not ever depend on the hospitality of strange land.[21]

Another relevant example is this entry from *Pinkas Bendin* in which a young man's hopes to reach the Land of Israel:

> She prepared the necessary items for him for the long road and for his future life in Eretz Yisrael, as if her heart had told her that this was the correct road for her son, that his place was there in the agricultural work in the Galilee, his hope and connection to working the land that he, Menachem'ke, had often so beautifully described for her.[22]

And the following quote summarizes the historical development that changed Jewish youth into Zionists in the early part of the twentieth century. It resulted in *aliyah* from Eastern Europe and much longing by those who remained behind with the hope that their turn to "go up to Zion" would come one day. From *Pinkas Bendin*:

> How, in general, was Menachem'ke's idea to go to Eretz Yisrael born? Much youthful energy, deep feelings, clear hopes, golden dreams and joyous reports collected in the hearts of the young people in all parts of Poland. During the First World War, they came together in the Zionist union, they studied Hebrew and sang songs of Zion that were interwoven with a glowing halo of sweet longing for salvation, for redemption and they inhaled the national spirit and were seized by ideas.[23]

Another example of the same theme may be found in the Liepaja yizker book, which includes several pages describing local Zionist youth movements, such as Hashomer Hatsair, Betar, and Herzliah. Immanuel Blaushild wrote how at a Herzliah meeting in 1933

> [t]here was talk of Palestine, Hachsharah, Kibbutz. Our first Olim, Judelowitz, Lachman, Nikol, went to the land that had become the land of our dreams. Letters arrived, photographs, descriptions. I had changed entirely ... Palestine became an actuality. Still a land of palms and moonshine and romance, but also of work. In April 1934 I was among a group that went on agricultural hachsharah.... We worked hard, in rain and cold and in the hot summer. Many resigned, some fell away, and others persevered.[24]

Zionist activities from the nineteenth and twentieth centuries are mentioned in almost every yizker book. For instance, in the Svencionys memorial book, a letter from 1885 regarding a money donation for the settlement of *Eretz Yisrael* is cited. This was not an isolated act. Many communities in Eastern Europe hosted visitors from the Holy Land and sent them back with money from their meager funds. The connection between the Jews of Eastern Europe and the Land of Israel had existed for generations. Thus for the Jews of Eastern Europe, supporting those who lived in the Land of Israel, despite their own difficult circumstances, is a testament to the strong ties to Zion. This longing for Zion is mentioned repeatedly in prayers, serving hopeful souls who were certain the day would come when Jews would be able to return to their homeland.

The Hebrew Language

Teaching Hebrew was an integral part of Zionist activities in the preparation for *aliyah*. Efforts to teach children Hebrew began in towns all over Eastern Europe in the late nineteenth and early twentieth centuries. For the Jews of Czernowitz, the establishment of a Hebrew kindergarten in 1912 was a source of great pride. Hebrew was learned by children of all ages as well as by adults. Yosef Yavnai (Slep) describes reading a Hebrew book, *Shirat Ha-Zamir* [*The Song of the Nightingale*] when he was a child:

> The book was cherished by many young people in the Diaspora, and much like the hero ... they too wove their dreams of coming to Zion and working the land.... The book left a great impression on me, and got me dreaming about Eretz Yisrael.[25]

Other popular books in Hebrew were Avraham Mapu's *The Guilt of Samaria* and *Love of Zion*, the first novels written in the newly revived language. The attitude towards Hebrew, which was part of the education of many of the survivors, may be another explanation for its use in so many yizker books.

Preparations for Making Aliyah

Descriptions of preparation for and finally immigration to Palestine are found in many yizker books. In some communities there was resistance to Zionist activism from Orthodox and modern communities. But this changed almost everywhere in the 1920s. From the book to Gyor:

> In 1929, we had a special experience. A Jewish National Fund film about the Land of Israel called "Spring in Palestine" was shown. The showing took place in the biggest movie theater in the city, and this roused the Jewish community of Győr from its indifference.[26]

Through the activities of the young members of the community in various youth movements, Zionist activities prevailed. Evidence of the strong early ties of Gyor Jews to the Land of Israel was provided by the fact that when its yizker book was published about half of the survivors of town were living in Israel.

Along the same lines, the memorial book to Liepaja includes many descriptions of the youth movements, particularly Hashomer Hatsair, whose goal as Yitzhak Shmushkowitz remembers was "clearly written on its flag. Every boy and girl who joined the organization knew that there was only one way ahead: aliyah to Eretz Israel." [27]Members of various kibbutzim came to visit, and as Yitzhak Shmushkowitz also notes: they "were the first to evoke our love for the land and the wish to make it flourish."[28]

Communication Between Eastern Europe and Palestine

Contacts with family members and friends who were already living in *Eretz Yisrael* are often mentioned in memorial books. Avraham Slep notes in the Dusetos yizker book that

> in the winter of 1920 his brother, Yosef, made *Aliyah* to Erets Yisrael and from that period on we exchanged letters regularly and I would receive detailed news about the life there.[29]

In 1925, he was among the fortunate who was able to make *aliyah*. He continues: "We dreamt about the Western Wall, and here I am. I have the privilege that even the outstanding personalities for many generations have not attained."[30]

In his entry in the Liepaja book, Immanuel Blaushild describes how he became a Zionist and joined the Herzliah youth group. At meetings, members attended lectures and discussions, but they also danced the *hora* and sang

Hebrew songs. Some members made *aliyah* and joined *kibbutzim*. They wrote letters and send photographs describing the land of their dreams. Blaushild notes that he joined an urban Hachsharah, where he trained for the work that awaited him. Finally he states: "In 1936 we boarded a ship for the Land of Israel."[31]

Visitors from Palestine

There were many visitors from the Holy Land seeking donations for the impoverished Jewish communities there. Also, some famous Zionists came to cities in Eastern Europe. Chaim Weitzman, an ardent Zionist and later the first president of the newly established State of Israel, visited Czernowitz in 1928. Hayyim Nahman Bialik, considered Israel's national poet, traveled all over Eastern Europe as did Jabotinsky, the leader of the right wing nationalists. Uri Zvi Greenberg, Abraham Shlonsky, Zalman Shazar (later president of the State of Israel), and other prominent authors traveled to Easter European towns to inculcate those living in the Diaspora with Zionism. The Ha-Bimah Theater Company came from Tel-Aviv and performed the *Dybbuk* and other plays in Hebrew for those who yearned for contact with the Land of Zion.

The War of Independence in Yizker Books

Yizker books often include lists and photographs of young fighters from the town who took part in Israel's War of Independence or who fell in battle. An example of such a chapter is found in the Radoshkowitz yizker book entitled "In Memory of Those Who Fell During Illegal Immigration and the War of Independence."[32] Among those who fell was Yekutiel (Kuty) Funt who born in Petach Tikvah in 1930 and was the grandson of a Radoshkowitz rabbi. About the grandson, the writer notes:

> His parents brought him up in a pioneering spirit. He belonged to the youth movement, Hano'ar Ha'oved, where he was very active.... After graduation, he joined a youth group ... at a settlement near the Kineret ... then he trained as a squad leader, and when the War of Independence broke out his unit took part in liberating and defending Tiberias, Ramat Yochanan, Zefat.... He fell in battle on May 19, 1948.... May his memory live forever.[33]

The editors wanted to be sure that those who died and had family roots in the town would be remembered. One did not have to die during the war or in Europe to deserve a place in a yizker book. Dying in *Eretz Yisrael*, in battle or while living there, earned a *landslayt* a place on the pages of the town's memorial book.

An entry written by Yitzhak Troiba towards the end of the book to Lask is most telling. Its title is *From Slavery to Freedom*, for that is how he saw his "release" from blood-soaked Europe. After the war he made *aliyah*, fulfilling the goal of his dream to live in the Land of Israel. He writes:

> The yearning to see the defeat of the enemy and the strong desire to be privileged to make *aliyah*, saved us from all the troubles, from hunger, humiliation and endless suffering in the forced labor camps of Poland and Germany....[34]

Under the cover of darkness, Troiba was the only one of his group who managed to escape from a death march. All the others were killed during the night. He remained heart broken that all those with whom he had slaved for a long time, perished, but he admits to an enormous happiness when he realized that he was liberated from the hands of the Nazis. Eventually Troiba managed to make his way to freedom, to *Eretz Yisrael*. The symbolism of the image from the Lasker book of two hands holding a torch and an Israeli flag is an expression of the strong ties those living in the Eastern European Diaspora felt for the Land of Israel. To them, the end of the war marked their deliverance from slavery to freedom. Their goal also was to make *aliyah*, to become part of the effort to rebuild the homeland, and to fulfill the dream of Herzl. But in the process, they wanted to be certain to remember and to commemorate their loved ones who perished most cruelly at the hands of the Nazis with no gravestones as physical reminders of their lives. They also wanted to document and describe Eastern European Jewish life that vanished along with the people.[35]

Clearly, the heart, soul, and mind underlying the preparation of the majority of the Holocaust yizker books resided with the survivors who lived in Israel. The survivor/immigrants arrived in Israel with "a passionate devotion ... to the collection of historical and material data on ghetto and concentration camp life and death." In amazing ways, without the communication technologies of the twenty-first century, they managed to establish contacts with their *landslayt*, people from their town, all over the world — the United States, Canada, South America, South Africa, and Europe — in order to gather materials for the preparation of these memorial volumes of the destroyed communities of Eastern Europe. Through their writings, these immigrants fulfilled the ancient God-given commandment to REMEMBER; and as they stood on the soil of the newly established State of Israel, the country that was now the realization of thousands of years and hopes and dreams, the survivors carried out their responsibility of publishing the narrative of the greatest tragedy in the history of the Jewish people.

Notes

1. This chapter is based on a paper presented at the *Yad Vashem* conference, "The Holocaust, the Survivors, and the State of Israel," December 8–11, 2008.

2. Jack Kugelmass and Jonathan Boyarin, "*Yizker Bikher* and the Problem of Historical Veracity: An Anthropological Approach," in *The Jews of Poland Between the Two World Wars*, eds. Israel Gutman et al. (Hanover, NH: University Press of New England, 1989), 521.

3. James E. Young, *The Texture of Memory: Holocaust Memorials and Meaning* (New Haven: Yale University Press, 1993), 7.

4. See Yosef Hayim Yerushalmi, *Zakhor: Jewish History and Jewish Memory* (Seattle: University of Washington Press, 1982).

5. Simon Dubnow (1860–1941), the renowned Jewish historian who in 1891 appealed to East European Jewry to collect documentation and to study their history.

6. Rachel Auerbach, "Yizkor, 1943," in *The Literature of Destruction: Jewish Responses to Catastrophe*, ed. David G. Roskies (Philadelphia: Jewish Publication Society, 1988), 460.

7. Dalia Ofer, "The Past That Does Not Pass: Israelis and Holocaust Memory," *Israel Studies* 14:1 (Spring 2009): 6.

8. Y. Shiloni et al., eds., *Ayaratenu Druzhkopol-Divre Zikaron U-misped* (Haifa: Organization of Druzhkopol Emigres in Israel, 1958–1959), http://www.jewishgen.org/yizkor/Druzhkopol/Druzhkopol.html (accessed May 3, 2010).

9. Abraham Wein, "Memorial Books as a Source for Research into the History of Jewish Communities in Europe," *Yad Vashem Studies on the Eastern European Catastrophe and Resistance* 9 (1973): 258.

10. Jacob Shatzky, "*Yizkor bikher*," *YIVO Bleter* 39 (1955): 351.

11. Beryl Mark, "*Yizkor bikher, vos bovaynen in verk tsum kamf*," *Yidishe Kultur* 6 (1964): 27.

12. Jack Kugelmass and Jonathan Boyarin, eds. and trans., *From a Ruined Garden: The Memorial Books of Polish Jewry*. Second, expanded edition (Bloomington and Indianapolis: Indiana University Press in association with the United States Holocaust Memorial Museum, Washington D.C., 1998), 25.

13. Faith Jones and Gretta Siegel, "Yizkor Books as Holocaust Grey Literature," *Publishing Research Quarterly* (Spring 2006): 55.

14. Malcolm J. Proudfoot, *European Refugees, 1939–1952: A Study in Forced Population Movement* (Evanston, IL: Northwestern University Press, 1956), 360.

15. LM0141 Reel 4 USHMM *Palestine Post*, "345,169 Since Statehood," January 9, 1950.

16. *American Jewish Year Book*, Volume 50, 1948–1949 (Philadelphia: Jewish Publication Society, 1949), 471.

17. Dalia Ofer, "The Strength of Remembrance: Commemorating the Holocaust During the First Decade of Israel," in *Jewish Social Studies* 6:2 (Winter 2000): 25.

18. Ibid.

19. Ibid., 26.

20. H. Rabin, ed., *Bielsk Podlaski: sefer yizkor* (Tel Aviv: Bielsk Societies in Israel and the U.S., 1975), http://www.jewishgen.org/yizkor/Bielsk/Bielsk.html (accessed May 3, 2010).

21. Ibid.

22. A. Sh. Shtain, ed., *Pinkas Bendin* (Tel-Aviv: Association of Former Residents of B dzin in Israel, 1959), http://www.jewishgen.org/yizkor/bedzin/Bedzin.html (accessed May 3, 2010).

23. Ibid.

24. Immanuel Blaushild, "How I Became a Herzlianer and a Zionist," in *A Town Named Libau*, http://www.jewishgen.org/Yizkor/libau/libau.html (accessed May 4, 2010).

25. Sara Weiss-Slep, ed., *Ayarah hayetah be-Lita: Dusyat bi-re'i ha-zikhronot* (Tel Aviv: Society of Former Residents of Dusiat, 1989), http://www.jewishgen.org/yizkor/Dusetos/Dusetos.html (accessed May 3, 2010).

26. Hanna Spiegel, ed., *Le-zekher kedoshei Gyōr* (Haifa, 1978), http://www.jewishgen.org/Yizkor/Gyor/gyo010.html (accessed May 3, 2010).

27. Yitzhak Shmushkowitz, "The Hashomer Hatsair Movement in Libau," in *A Town Named Libau* http://www.jewishgen.org/Yizkor/libau/libau.html (accessed May 4, 2010).

28. Ibid.

29. Weiss-Slep, *Ayarah hayetah be-Lita.*

30. Ibid.

31. Blaushild, *A Town Named Libau.*

32. Mordekai Robinson, Rubin Yisra'el, and Betsalel Izakson, eds., *Radoshkovits: sefer zikaron* (Tel Aviv: Former Residents of Radoshkowitz in Israel, 1953), http://www.jewishgen.org/yizkor/radoshkovichi/radoshkovichi.html (accessed May 3, 2010).

33. Ibid.

34. Zev Tzurnamal, ed., *Lask: sefer zikaron* (Tel-Aviv: Association of Former Residents of Lask in Israel, 1968), 681.

35. The survivors in Israel and their desire to commemorate and remember is well described in a Hebrew article by Hanna Yablonka in *Masuah Annual* 28 (2000): 301–317.

PART II

LANDMARK ESSAYS

3

Landsmanshaftn Literature in the United States During the Past Ten Years

PHILIP FRIEDMAN

An extensive discussion has recently developed about the social responsibilities and functions of *landmanshaftn*.[1] These organizations were founded for the sake of mutual aid in general and for compatriots from the old country in particular. Recent developments have significantly reduced and even practically annulled these original functions. The economic ascent of former immigrants has made mutual aid unnecessary; the destruction of European Jewry has tragically put an end to aid directed toward the old country. Although *landsmanshaftn* are searching for new reasons for their survival, aid is still being given to small groups of survivors mostly in Israel. In part what is bringing new life to *landsmanshaftn* is a striving to eternalize the memory of their annihilated old home through various publications.

A fair number of these publications enhance and romanticize the hometown by cloaking various negative aspects of its Jewish life in an idealistic veil, understandable in light of the great catastrophe. However, the number of yizker books and monographs when compared to the number of *landsmanshaftn* in existence is not great. In New York, 1938, there were approximately 1,440 organizations (*Jewish Landsmanshftn of New York, I.L. Peretz Shrayber Farayn*, ed. I.A. Rontsh). In 1951, the United Jewish Appeal had ties to approximately 2,000 *landsmanshaftn* and 1,000 women's auxiliaries with a total of 400,000 members in New York alone. Additionally, the smaller *landsmanshaftn* in New York must also be counted, along with the significant number of *landsmanshaftn* in other cities. We estimate that the number across the country reaches several thousand.

While the last ten years have seen several dozen publications by *lands-*

manshaftn, some wealthy *landsmanshaftn* have not published anything. For example, a number of publications on the destruction of Warsaw, as well as the impressive work of Dr. Jacob Shatzky on the history of the Jews of Warsaw, were prepared without the help of any of the Warsaw *landsmanshaftn*. The same indifference to the past is demonstrated by the *landsmanshaftn* of Lemberg, Krakow, Lublin, Stanislaw, Tarnapol, Przemyl, Boryslaw, Drohobits, Kolemay, and other places. It must also not be forgotten that the literature issued by the *landsmanshaftn* of Polish and Lithuanian communities is richer than the literature issued by *landsmanshaftn* of other eastern European countries, such as the Ukraine, Russia, and Rumania and by the *landsmanshaftn* of middle and western European communities, for which there are generally no literary tombstones whatsoever in the Yiddish language.

It is true that it is not easy to write historical monographs when it is known that all archival sources, national as well as communal, have been destroyed or are now behind the Iron Curtain. Even the local periodicals and newspapers, so important to the history of previous decades, are mostly no longer in existence. We must therefore reconstruct the historical past from available fragments and rely on recollections and memoirs. Jewish historians and editors of yizker books have more than once pointed to these difficulties. Compare for example Dr. Jacob Shatzky's foreword in *Pinkes Mlave* to Dr. Refoel Mahler's foreword in *The Tshenstokhover Yidn*. As a result, the place of honor in many yizker books is not relegated to historical material, but rather to descriptions of ways of life: institutions, folklore, idioms, contemporary memoirs, biographies, various episodes and experiences of the Nazi era, and the like.

As already mentioned, the majority of these books are dedicated to Polish and Lithuanian communities. Upon first glance, the most substantial publications deal with the so-called Polish Eastern area, the border regions between Poland and Lithuania. The place of honor is occupied by publications about Białystok. The Society of the History of Białystok published A. Sh. Herschberg's historical chronology *Pinkes Bialystok* (Volume I, 1949, 512 pp.; Volume II, 1950, 380 pp., ed. Yudl Mark). Herschberg is a well-known Hebrew and Yiddish writer and journalist; his works on the second temple and the Talmud epochs are quite important. For decades, he was a community leader at the center of the Białystok economy, a textile manufacturer who led a cultural and community-oriented life. He lived through a whole range of experiences that he describes in his book. In addition, for years, he collected archival materials, such as old record registers, Talmudic laws, and similar items. Based on that, he writes extensive, lively, and detail descriptions of Białystok Jewish life from the eighteenth until after the first world war. For example, Heschberg describes city's industries and workers' movements, cultural activities, ways of life, the Jewish community, education, and other matters. The descriptions of various people, especially his close friends are written with originality and intimacy. Herschberg was not destined to see his book in print. On the eve of World War II, he sent the manuscript to New York from Białystok, where he perished at the hands of the Nazis.

Herschberg's work was continued by other Białystok writers. The director of the Białystok Historical Society Dovid Klementinovski published *Life and Death in the Bialystok Ghetto* (New York, 1946, 96 pp., illustrated.) That work is a well-written systematic overview of what occurred in Białystok from June 1941 until the liquidation of the ghetto. It also covers the liquidation in the bunkers and hideouts. The work is based of a number of testimonies. Another work based on personal experiences and richly documented materials is the exceptional monograph by Dr. Shimen Ratner, *Khurbn, Byalistok and Vicinity*. This work was initially printed in the *Bialystoker Shtime* (New York, beginning with No. 253, September-October 1946 until the present).The *Bialystoker Shtime*, published by the Białystoker Center and edited by Dovid Sohn, is the official publication of the Białystoker *landsmanshaft* in America. It is a true treasure trove of historical materials about Białystok, which uses memoirs, biographies, personal experiences of the Nazi era, literary works about Białystok, pictures, and other materials. The periodical, *Bialystoker Lebn*, in New York is also responsible for some material. A third periodical, *Der Byalistoker Fraynt*, published by A/R Branch 88, also provides support to the history of Białystok Jews in two special editions (1945, 45 pp. in English and 75 in Yiddish, ed. Yakov Krepliyak; 1950, 110 pp., eds. M. Dobish, M. Graf, H. Khabitzki, and L. Silver). The 1950 edition is much richer and provides several worthy contributions about the Białystok Jewish Workers' Movement. An important publication is the monumental picture album, *Bialystok*, edited by Dovid Sohn (New York, 1951, 386 pp.), which contains 1,200 photos, explanatory text, and introductions in Yiddish and English. A product of thirty years of collecting, this album is a true picture encyclopedia, covering virtually all facets of Białystoker Jewish life. It contains images of the countryside in the seventeenth century, including pictures of the Bronitskis, the lord landowner and his wife, who founded the town, and Itshe Zabludovsky's palace. This album contains hundreds of photographs of rabbis, clergy, scholars, Talmudists, writers, teachers, artists, merchants, manufacturers, community leaders, artisans, revolutionaries, women, doctors, community leaders, street scenes, parades, holidays, funeral processions, demonstrations, fraternities, worker organizations, strike committees, political parties, meetings, hospitals, schools, yeshivas, factories, and the 1906 tsarist and 1920 Polish pogroms. There are many family pictures. Among them is an outstanding one of a family *kapelye*, a man with his seven musical grandchildren. There are also anguishing pictures of the ghetto, partisans, and fighters. Finally there is a large section of pictures of Jewish life in the United States, in European countries, and in Israel. The album is evidence of how a systematic gathering of materials by a well-organized *landsmanshaft* with a well-functioning headquarters may provide a deeper understanding of culture and tradition.

Approximately 90 kilometers from Białystok is the city of Wolkowisk. In 1910, the city had 14,500 inhabitants, 8,000 of them Jews. In 1932, the population was about the same. The small Jewish community in Wolkowisk possesses one of the best yizker publications, the two-volume *Volkovisker yizkor bukh* (1949, 990 pp., 901 in Yiddish and 89 in English, richly illustrated, ed. Dr. Moses Einhorn). It is rare that a community is so well investigated with so much precision. Approximately twenty authors and researchers worked on this book. The most detailed pieces in the book, "The History of Wolkowisk" and "Khurbn Volkovysk and Vicinity" were written by Dr. Einhorn. The other articles contain interesting views of Jewish life, education, political life, institutions, characters, and personalities. There are descriptions of the town's neighborhoods and streets, as well as the occupations of its inhabitants. One article is a house-by-house description of what happened to each member of the household, a true biographical lexicon. This is the only work of its kind that I have seen in the current yizker literature.

Not far from Białystok is Bransk, which had a population of 7,000 before World War II. If only other communities would issue a book as fine as *Breynsk seyfer hazikorn* (Breynsker Relief Committee, New York, 1948, 440 pp.), which is splendidly illustrated and adapted by Alter Trus and Julius Cohen. The first part of the book covers Breynsker Jews from 1813 until World War I. These are short chapters based on the experiences of old city inhabitants and Breynsker community registers. Breynsker rabbis, trustees, community leaders, scholars, *hasidim*, beadles, ritual slaughterers, cantors, prayer leaders, and fellowships are extensively treated, as are events such as the revolution of 1905, plagues and fires, employment, cultural life, and emigration. By accurately rendering the distinctness of a town in its ordinariness, an aspect that is not often written about in large historical monographs, much is conveyed. The second part of the book covers the years between the two world wars. The third section is about the *khurbn* and was put together from testimonies collected by Breynsker survivors, legislative decrees, documents, and stories told by Polish neighbors.

The anthology *Toyzent yor Pinsk* is a monumental volume. Published in New York in 1941 by A/R Branch 210, the work is a 500-page, large format, illustrated volume edited by Dr. B. Hoffman, with the help of Dr. M. Kosover, Dr. Herman Frank, Z. Honig, S. Davitch, S.L. Shneiderman, Note Kozlowski, and eighteen other authors. It is impossible to briefly convey the contents of this splendid book, which contains important materials about the ship transports and transit handlers in Pinsk, the development of Jewish industry and the Jewish workforce, important statistic material, an entry by Karliner *hasidim* and their fight with the orthodox opponents of Hasidism, and a great deal about Pinsker rabbis. Additionally of importance is a description of how the Germans even during World War I ruled by means of brutal terror. Also interesting is the episode about the failed organizational experiment in Evonik. A large portion of the book is taken up with memoirs of Zionist and worker movements. The last portion of the book is a biographical lexicon and a collection of materials about Pinsker *landsmanshaftn* in America. A supplement to *Toyzent yor Pinsk* is the special anniversary issue of *Pinsk W/C Branch 210: Life in and Around Our Branch* (New York 1948, 65 pp., illustrated, edited by S. Davitch, with the help of A. Weinberg). From a historical perspective, the most important articles are Dr. Yuli Margolin's "Pinsk under Soviet Domination: 1939–1941" and L. Levin's "Khurbn Pinsk." There is also the chapter "Pinsker Memoirs" by Dr. Chaim Weizman, as well as a short history of Pinsker Branch 210 and other articles, novellas, and poems by well-known Yiddish writers. Of note is the "Open Letter to Our Children" by Aaron Weinberg written in English.

Another accomplished *landsmanshaftlekhe* publication is *Horodec, a geshikte fun a shtetl, 1142–1942* (New York, 1948, 238 pp., richly illustrated with poems, eds. E. Ben-Ezra and Yisrael Zusman). The book is beautifully edited. Horodets located in Grodno between Brisk and Pinsk shares many historical commonalities with Pinsk. Horodets was also called Little Danzig because the city developed along its waterways. Just like in Pinsk, *hasidim* and *misnogdim* fought bitterly. Economic life in the town was greatly influenced by the local military garrison. Horodets was also famous as a destination for divorces, since it is located on a river complying with Jewish divorce law. Its yizker volume is filled with folklore, folksongs, local idioms, dialects, and legends, a veritable treasure trove for folklorists and philologists. The chapter "Khurbn Hitler" is especially moving because only one Jew from the town managed to survive. The last part of the book describes the *landmanshaftn* in America and Israel.

If Vilne, the Jerusalem of Lithuania, has not been memorialized in the last ten years through a separate publication, it has not been due to a lack of cultural tradition or ambition. There is a whole list of substantial monographic works and almanacs about Vilne during the interwar period, among them, the imposing volume, *Vilne* (New York, 1935, 1,012 pp., illustrated, ed., Yefim Yeshurin). The United Vilne Relief Committee in New York published Shmerke Katsherginski's slim volume *Khurbn Vilne* (New York, 1947, 342 pp., richly illustrated). Also in print is the monumental compendium *Pinkes Lite* (ed. M. Sidarsky, over 1,000 pp.).

From more than a dozen publications dedicated to central Polish communities, three deserve mention: *Tshenstokhover yidn*, *Pinkes Mlave*, and *Grayeve*. In addition, a compendium *Tshenstokhover yidn* was issued by the Tshenstochover Relief Committee and Ladies' Auxiliary (New York, 1947, large format, richly illustrated, eds. Dr. Refoel Mahler and Dr. Volf Glicksman). In that volume, about forty authors describe the history of the relatively new Jewish settlement at the end of eighteenth century, its economic development, and its cultural, educational, and communal institutions in the nineteenth and twentieth centuries. The volume also includes Dr. Jacob Shatzky's "The History of the Jews of Czestochowa." Of the 254 pages in the essay, almost one hundred pages are devoted to the pogroms and the *churbn*. The second part of the book, which comprises memoirs and biographies, will no doubt serve as source material for historians.

Pinkes Mlave (Association of Jews from Mława, New York, 1950, 485 pp., 62 photos, ed., Dr. Jacob Shatzky, with the help of Joseph Opatoshu) presents a totally different model for a yizker book. The historical documentation on Mlave would have been lost except for Dr. Jehuda Rosental's ability to rescue some archival materials from earlier historical periods. On the basis of this preserved material, Rosental describes the history of Mlaver Jews from the sixteenth through the nineteenth centuries. Naturally, the city is proud of Joseph Opatoshu and Yakir Warshawski, its two native sons, and parts of the book consist of excerpts from their works. This book also describes a number of families in Mlava, as well as its Jewish education, ways of life, printing presses, and newspapers. Dr. Jacob Shatzky provides the interesting essay "Mlava Ten Years Ago as Depicted in the Mlave Press." Many articles cover local dialects, proverbs, nicknames, expressions, folklore, and so on. Most interesting is Opatoshu's sociological analysis of Mlaver folk lexicon and its connection to the smuggler circles of the border town. Like all yizker books *Pinkes Mlave* closes with a tragic chapter on the *churbn*. The closing words found in the lamentation essay "The Last Jew in Town" are frightfully harrowing.

Grayeve, a shtetl not far from Lomza and Białystok, is in many ways similar to Mlave. Grayeve is also a border town, which is situated about three kilometers from the Prussian border. The typical border town occupations play a significant role in the life of the Jews. The material about the smuggling of people during Czarist times is interesting, as are the facts about the tar and horse dealers and their trips to Prussia. The descriptions of the conflicts between Christian and Jewish workers in a Jewish factory deserve special attention. The chapter devoted to the *churbn* covers the negative relations between local Poles and Jews. The *Grayeve yizker bukh* (United Grayeve Aid Committee, New York, 1950, 314 pp. of Yiddish text, richly illustrated, plus

51 pp. of English text, eds. Dr. G. Gorin, Hayman Blum, and Sol Fishbayn) distinguishes itself by its beautiful appearance. Additionally, the book contains material pertaining to the annihilation of the Jews in the surrounding towns of Shtutsin, Kolna, Jedwabne, Radzilow, and others.

The United Rescue Committee for the City of Lodz published the large volume *Lodzer yizker bukh* (New York, 1943, 252 pp., plus 174 pp. and 82 pp., edited by a collaborative). The volume includes lengthy articles by Shmuel Milman and Ahron Alperin on the history of the Lodz Jews until 1939, biographies of individual Lodzers, and a rich collection of memoirs and experiences of the initial months of Nazi occupation. Informative articles about the Lodzer *landmanshaftn* in America appear at the end of the book.

Of the many towns in the Lodzer region only two have historical monographs. The Bzshezshiner Support Association in New York published *Zaml-bukh gevidmet di heylike kdoyshim fun hitler-umkum* (New York, 1946, 153 pp. in Yiddish, 47 pp. in English, illustrated, edited by Joseph Diamond and others). Aside from descriptions of the *churbn*, this book contains memoirs and descriptions of Jewish life in song, reports, and other forms.

The United Belchatower Aid Committee in New York published the small *Belchatow yizker bukh* (New York, 1950, not paginated, illustrated). The volume contains several articles about Jewish life and *churbn* Belkhatov, reworked by Zalman Pudlowski, along with articles about Belkhatover in North America and Argentina. The New York *landsmanshaft* was also very active in preparing the collection, which is now in print in Buenos Aires published by *Dos poylishe yidntum*.

Zaromb (Zaromber Relief Committee, New York, 1947, 69 pp., illustrated, and edited by Z. Dorfman) delivers a short historical overview of the town from 1687 to 1939; a work by Z. Shaykowski titled "Khurbn Zaromb" and several memoirs and poems. The Zhelekhower *landsmanshaft* in Chicago publishes the *Zhelekhover Bulletin*, in which several works about martyrology and resistance by Zhelekhover Jews during the Nazi era appear.

Lomzhe (United Lomzher Relief Committee, New York in 1946, 63 pp., in Yiddish, 27 in English, illustrated, ed. H. Sabotka) has short articles about the history and annihilation of Lomza Jews. The majority of the edition is about the community activism of Lomzher associations in America.

Lev Friedman's *Dos lebn fun di yidn in Mezritch unter der daytsher oku-patsye un zeyer umkum* (Mezritcher United Relief, New York, 1947, 30 pp.) describes the tragedy that occurred in that town. The volume *Novidvor* (Novi-Dvorer Aid Committee, Los Angeles, 1947) edited by an editorial collaborative, includes a very short historical overview of the town from 1840 to 1946, as well as several personal accounts of the Nazi times, poems, and photographs.

We have not had the opportunity to see *Tsum ondenk* (Ostrovtser Aid Committee, New York, 1946). Another noteworthy publication is the one by the Ostrovtser Aid Committee that carries a title that speaks for itself, *Di geshikhte fun di tsvey yidishe fareter fun Ostrovtse, di brider Avram un Leyb Zeyfman. der mishpet fun di fareter in New York. Di bavayzn fun lebedike eydes* [The History of the Two Jewish Traitors of Ostrovtse: The Brothers Avram and Leib Zeifman — Their Trial in New York and Testimony of Living Witnesses] (New York, 1948, 58 pp.). The anniversary book entitled *Forty yor Sokolover in Chicago* (Sokolower Independent Organization, Chicago, 1941, 204 pp. Yiddish, 60 pp. English, ed., M. Mandelboim) tells about the life and works of community members in the city. It does not contain any materials from the old country. In New York, the Sokolower *landslayt* published a yizker book edited by A.S. Lirick that is impossible to acquire.

Thanks to the initiative and support of the Krasnistover Landsmanshaft in Los Angeles, *Yizker tsum ondenk fun di kadoyshim in Krasnistov* was published (Munich, 1948, 151 pp., ed. A. Shtuntsayger). It contains historical articles about Krasnystaw at the beginning of the twentieth century, along with memoirs, biographies, and descriptions of the *churbn*.

In 1932–1933, the Federation of Polish Jews in America began publishing *Polish Jews*, an annual containing a number of interesting historical articles. As it stands, the last volume came out in 1944. From 1941 to 1944, the Federation published a monthly journal, *Polish Jew*, which is concerned with issues about Jews in Poland.

Of the Galician Jewish communities, only a few have had the honor of having their hometowns memorialized in print. David Moritz writes about three western Galician communities in *Khurbn Dinov-Sonik-Dibetsk* (New York, 1950, 156 pp., illustrated). Although this book is written with great emotion, it lacks the hand of an experienced editor who would add cohesion, correct orthography, and provide an adequate title. The chapter "Kol Nidre in the Camp" and the chapters about the partisans and their life in the forests are especially interesting.

One book from eastern Galician is *Megiles Gline* (New York, 1950, 307 pp., mimeographed). The volume is put together with much love and reverence by Henoch H. Halpern. The historical introduction has hardly any worth, but there are very valuable, interesting, and detailed descriptions of the lifestyles, rabbinics, livelihoods, and cultural and political life of the Jews in the city during the twentieth century. The statistical figures on Jews and their occupations in the surrounding rural settlements are also very interesting. Interesting details are relayed about Professor Majer Balaban's teaching career in the Gliner Baron de Hirsh school. For instance, the episode in which an orthodox Gliner throws a burning lamp into a school wiping out one of Balaban's public lectures. The description of the *churbn* is a bit chaotic. What is interesting, though, is the description of how the *Judenrat* was founded under German subjugation.

The first Yavorover Independent Association published Shmuel Druck's *Yudenshtadt Yovorov* (New York, 1950, 46 Yiddish pp., 35 English, 27 memoirs) about the *churbn*. The annual, *The Galitsyaner*, published by the *Fareynigte Galitsyaner yidn in Amerika* (New York, 1941, 37 pp. Yiddish, 75 pp. English, ed. Chone Gottesfeld) brings together journalistic articles and a few memoirs and songs.

The partisan M. Gildenman describes the Voliner community in *Khurbn Korets* (Paris, 1949, 79 pp., illustrated). The volume was published with the material and moral support of the Koretser *landslayt* in Boston and Chicago. The first part of the book conveys various facts, legends, and memories up until 1939. The second half describes the Soviet era, the years 1939–1941, and the *churbn*.

Much poorer are the *landsmanshaftlekhe* publication by Romanian Jews. A little booklet in English published by the Akkerman *Untershtitsungs gezelshaft* (New York 1950, 42 pp., illustrated) gives a short history of the Jews of Akkerman from the beginning of the twentieth century until the end of 1949. The Bessarabia Federation of American Jews has been publishing collected notebooks since 1949, which are entitled *Bessarabian yid*. This journal contains several interesting historical and literary articles, memoirs, and poems. Example are *Heft* 1, 1946, 128 pp. Yiddish, 32 pp. English, illustrated, eds. H. Zilberman and others; *Yorbukh* 2, 1941–1942, 42 pp. Yiddish, 10 pp. English, illustrated; *Yorbukh* 3, 1948, 146 pp., illustrated; and *Hefts* 2 and 3, ed. Moishe Shifris.

The following yizker books about two small Ukrainian communities are very meager in historical material: *Forty yorike yorbukh fun pliskover gmiles-khasudim farayn* (Pittsburgh, 1948, 24 pp. Yiddish, 48 pp. English) and *Dzhurnal Minkovits* (United Minkovits-Podolyer Relief, New York 1945, 112 pp.).

Dora Shulner's autobiographical chronicle, *Azoy hot es pasirt* (Radomisher Ladies Auxiliary, Chicago 1942, 108 pp.) has interesting supplementary materials on the history of the Radomishl from the beginning of the twentieth century until 1922.

From time to time, the Ukranian Farband puts out *zamlhelftn* by the name of *Der Ukrainer yid*. The richest content is contained in the 1944 *zaml-heft*, which has historical and literary articles and short monographs of various Jewish communities in the Ukraine (New York 1944, 160 pp. Yiddish, 31 pp. English, eds. William Edlin and others). In the 1949 anthology (New York, 34 pp., ed. Avram I. Bik), the article by Sholem Vasilevski, "Bibliography of Books about Towns and Cities in the Ukraine" lists the following yizker books: *Khmelnik Suavenir Dzhurnal* by M. Chazan and *Khurbn Svir* by I. Shapiro. However, we have been unable to find those volumes in any New York libraries. In 1946, the sample notebook *Pinkes Bershad* (New York 1946, 20 pp.) was issued. It contained interesting economic statistical material with articles about folklore and way of life, photographs, and a map. Unfortunately until this day it has remained a prospectus.

The Riga-Latvian Relief of American Jews issued *Yizker almanac, gevidmet dem ondenk fun Letlander kedoyshim* (New York, 1948, 44 pp.). That work contains several interesting articles about the Jewish struggle against the Nazis in Riga ghetto and the Latvian camps, as well as the role of the Latvian collaborationists and the murder of the Jews. In the last ten years, we have not managed to find any *landsmanshaftlekhe* editions about Russian Jewish communities. It is apparent that the separation in 1918 from the old hometowns has resulted in a weakening of contact between the old and new world.

Although this current article reports on the relevant literature published in the United States, it is worthwhile to mention yizker books prepared in other countries. A significant number of publications have come out of Argentina. These include books to Volin, Ostrowitz, Belchatow, Teplik, Sokolow, Plock, Stok, Czestochowa, Grodno, Miezyzec, and Pruzhany. Much of these are the publications of *Dos poylishe yidntum*, operated by M. Turkov and A. Mitelberg at *Tsentral-farband fun poylishe yidn in Argentina*. Their company has already published more than 70 books, monographs, memoirs, prose, and poetry. A number of *landmanshaft* publications are from Germany. Among these are volumes to Chrzanow, Rejowiec, Radom, Krasnystaw, Zlatshov, Podlashye, Skalat, Vilnius, Kovno, Czestochowa, Otwosk, and other places. In Israel, some *landsmanshaftn* have published editions in Hebrew to a number of hometowns, including Gline, Volkovisk, Lekhovitch, Eishyshok, Zablotow, and Stanislaw. In addition, some published bulletins, such as *Yedies Irgun olei slonim*, *Olei drutsin*, and *Olei grodne*. Books to Vilne, Korets, Levertov, and Krynki have been published by *landsmanshaftn* in Paris. Organizations in Canada, Mexico, Australia, and South Africa have also printed a few volumes.

In the final analysis, all the publications are no more than a drop in the sea. Many of the editions mentioned are nothing more than raw materials that need, first of all, to be made comprehensive and complete. Many important areas and communities have not yet found their historical *tikkun*, and there is danger that they will be completely forgotten and drowned in a sea of forgetfulness. As long as there is a generation emotionally tied to its hometown and is skilled at putting out historical tombstones there is still time to do something. There must be interest in this, and the *landsmanshaftn* must mobilize. People must help expedite this very important work, especially in America. History will be grateful to them for such succor.

Note

1. Originally published as Philip Friedman, "*Di landsmanshaftn literatur in di fareyniktn shtatn far di letstn ten yor,*" *Jewish Book Annual* Volume 10 (5712/1951–1952): 81–95. Chana Pollack and Myra Mniewski translated the article into English. Thanks to the Jewish Book Annual for permission to translate and print.

4

Review of Yizker Books — 1953

Jacob Shatzky

1. *Tshenstokhover yidn*. Ed. R. Mahler. New York: United Czestochower Relief Committee and Ladies Auxiliary, 1947.[1]
2. *Volkovisk yizker-buch*. Ed. M. Einhorn. New York, 1949.
3. *Grayeve yizker-bukh*. Ed. G. Gorin. New York: United Grayever Relief Committee, 1950.
4. *Braynsk: sefer ha-zikaron*. Eds. Alter Truss and Julius Cohen. New York: Brainsker Relief Committee of New York, 1948.
5. *Horodets; a geshikhte fun a shtetl (1142—1942)*. Ed. E. Ben-Ezra. New York: Horodetz Book Committee, 1949.
6. *Megile Gline*. Ed.Ch. Halpern. New York: Former Residents of Gline, 1950.
7. *Sefer Chrzanow*. M. Bochner. Regensburg, 1948.
8. *Zaromb — le-zikaron olam*. Eds. Z. N. Dorfman, N. Lawa, Z. Rumianek, and Moshe Shtarkman. New York: United Zaromber Relief, 1947.
9. *Dos bukh fun Lublin*. Paris: Former Residents of Lublin in Paris, 1952.
10. *Mezritsh; zamlbukh*. Ed. Y. Horn. Buenos Aires: Association of Former Residents of Mezritsh in Argentina, 1952.
11. *Sefer zikaron le-kehilat Lomza*. Ed. Y. T. Levinski. Tel Aviv: Former Residents of Lomza in Israel, 1952.
12. *Pinkes Kowel*. Ed. B. Baler. Buenos Aires: Former Residents of Kowel and Surroundings in Argentina, 1951.
13. *Belchatow yizker-bukh*. Buenos Aires: Association of Polish Jews in Argentina, 1951.
14. *Stanislaw*. Eds. D. Sadan and M. Gelerter. Jerusalem: Rabbi Kook Publishing House, 1952.
15. *Yizker kehilat Luniniec/Kozhanhorodok*. Ed. J. Zeevi. Tel Aviv: Association of Former Residents of *Luniniec/Kozhanhorodok* in Israel, 1952.
16. *De verdwenen mediene*. H. Beem. Amsterdam, 1950.

Yizker books published by individuals and compatriot associations with the goal of immortalizing the destroyed Jewish communities are an important component of Holocaust literature, which is expanding every year. The psy-

54

chological or emotional moments that gave rise to such volumes may have a positive effect on our historical perspective and on the realistic approach to the past. As a matter of course, the books are more useful as source material for history than as definite monographs. The lack of relevant literature about the destroyed cities and towns creates a disproportion between the emphasis placed on the last period and on earlier periods. Most yizker books were edited by people who had the best intentions but who were not qualified for the task. Most of the editors were not adept at dealing with the past history of their towns and villages.

The Holocaust, in a great measure, has a negative effect upon our view on the past. In the face of such a calamity, details and particulars, no matter how momentous and significant, even when new, become unimportant, small, almost unnecessary ballast for the reader of the history of his own town or village. This psychological impediment makes it difficult to conduct research and creates a situation that diminishes the worth of the described circumstantial, detailed episodes. The immediate, bewildered past overwhelmed all the bloody periods of Jewish history. It is for this reason that many of the yizker books abound with details dealing with the final chapter, the epilogue of Jewish life in the cities and towns. But the prologue and the drama called Jewish history, which spanned many generations, was relegated to an unimportant role. Therefore, the yizker books are, with small exceptions, memorial records of the last period. For that era, the books contain extremely worthy materials. One feels the sacred intention of the writers to perpetuate everything and at the least, to save for posterity the memory of their destroyed homes. In this book review, I cover only a few publications, and more specifically, only the ones that contribute to Jewish historiography and that are not just random publications. It will be the obligation of the bibliographers of Holocaust period literature to gather and list all materials published about that period.

Reviews

(1)　*Tshenstokhover yidn* is beautifully published and competently edited. The history of Czestochowa's Jews was written by this reviewer and is based in part on archival sources. The very lively and enlightening descriptions of how Czestochowa became a city were written by H.L. Schwartz. The articles about the economic life, education, political parties, and clergy are written by reliable authors and have lasting value. But the materials about the Holocaust period are already outdated because in the last few years many books were published, which present more facts about the catastrophe than were known in 1945–1946 when this yizker book was assembled. Overall though, this is one of the best yizker books published to date.

(2) *Volkovisk yizker-buch* is voluminous and monumental in scope. The introduction states that this book is "the collective creation of the Wolkovisk countrymen from all over the world." The book is illustrated with 300 pictures, which have great historical value. It is written in a folksy and almost primitive style, with little respect for language structure. Writing, for example, about a rich man in town, the editor, who authored most of the articles in the two volumes, notes: "They used to say that he can display on his desk one hundred thousand rubles in cash" (530). Additionally, the editors were not careful about giving the birthdates of prominent Wolkovisker Jews, and in many cases, no dates are given at all. For example, the article about Dr. Kadish Benjamin Einhorn should have noted that he was born in 1847 and died in 1914. However, the whole work is rich in detail about the last years, including the Holocaust period. Such an itemized list of particulars is rarely found in a yizker book. It is therefore a great pity that the history of the ancestors of Volkovisker Jews, about which there is no lack of material, is hardly mentioned. For example, the German traveler, Johann Korb, visited Volkovisk in 1698–1699 and wrote about the local Jews. The 1736 appeal by Uziel Ben Yitzhak asking for help for the economically ruined Volkovisker Jews is an available source, as is the community appeal written in Hebrew and published in 1812 by Averbuch and published in *Jewreiska Starina, 1913, 536–538.*[2] In general, there is much material available about Volkovisk in the literature of 1912 and in the correspondences of the Hebrew, Yiddish and Russian-Yiddish press.

(3) The historical section of *Grayeve yizker-bukh* is poorly edited. For instance, the editors did not use the letters of the local teacher Abraham Shatzki that were printed in the *Niedikluaya Chronika Voschoda* and describe the cultural activities and the fire in Grajewa at the end of the nineteenth century. However, Mayer Wasser's description of Jewish life is interesting; Szymon Davidowicz's memories are significant. The material about Mordecai Piurko, the only author who represented the belated Haskalah movement in Grajewa, is limited. A Jewish printing house was established in 1901 in Grajewa. Of Piurko's published works, it is worth mentioning *Bath-Yiftakh* (1833), *The Book of Letters and Articles*, and *An Anthology* (1843).[3] Other works are mentioned in the Hebrew Library Bibliography in Jerusalem (1937). A part of *Gan Sha'ashu'im*, which Piurko published in Grajewa, is the compilation *Livney Ha'neurim* (1867). It was to be a monthly journal, but only one issue was actually published. The Grayever yizker book contains important facts about the economic life at the town, articles about the labor movement, Zionism, and, naturally, the Holocaust. The fourth part of the book is dedicated to the

lives of Grajever Jews in America and to the writers and scholars Emanuel Olshwanger, Zvi Wolkowisky, and Arie Ben-Zahav, all natives of Grajewa.

(4)   *Braynsk: sefer ha-zikaron* is a written in a folksy style and is essentially a very good volume. The history of the Jews of Brainsk began around 1808. The historical part of the volume includes many interesting legends about the Cantonists and the abduction of children from poor Jewish homes. There are also many stories about the leaders of the Jewish community and how they managed to "dodge being recruited into the army." The stories about the local rabbis are very detailed and descriptive, and those about charity, folk-types, and community activities are well written. In this regard, the book is very significant and provides a fine example for other small communities. It shows how a yizker book may be written without scholarly claims and still contribute to history. The latter chapters of the book deal with many detailed and important documents of the Holocaust.

(5)   The editor of *Horodets; a geshikhte fun a shtetl* wrote part of the history of the town using many sources. His description of the town's social structure is very good. Much work was done for the biographical portrayals of the local rabbis. There is a precise listing of their publications and their works. Regarding the prominent Jews of Horodetz, there is a detailed article about Dr. Israel Michal Rabinowicz (1818–1892), the famous translator of the Talmud into French. The volume contains folk songs with sheet music, customs, and Yiddish folklore. However, legends about doctors are presented as facts. For example, there is a story on page 135 about Naftali who became medical student in Warsaw and returned home as a dentist and an oculist. But the story is not true. Nonetheless, this is a well-edited and well-compiled yizker book.

(6)   *Megile Gline* contains extensive material. The same person who collaborated on this book also wrote *Churban Glinia* in 1945. The volume is mostly based on memory, because unfortunately, there is a lack of documents about the town. In the preface, Dr. Yona Alerhand, a native of Glinia, writes: "Every writer describes his theme subjectively, more with heart than with his mind." The historic part of the book is weak, even though much could be written using Ukrainian and Polish original documents. The volume only uses Hebrew sources, such as *The Pinkas of Joseph Mordecai Leiwand* published in 1920; however the folkloristic material is excellent. The description of Purim and the Christian wedding, given on page 57, is a first-class document of the history of Purim plays. Also important is the episode about reporting for military service and the folksongs relating to it, which is on pages 116 and 117. There is one article about community leaders grabbing poor children instead of the sons of the affluent and giving them up to the military. Also interesting is the description of a tradition that lasted until 1848 that prohibited craftsmen

from wearing *shtreimels*. In the book, there is also a story about Mayer Balaban, who was in his younger years, a teacher at the local Baron Hirsh Folk School. One part of the book is dedicated to eyewitness testimonies of Holocaust survivors, the majority of them living in Israel. In sum, the book is important, interesting, and significant as a work on the sociology of a small town. However, for historical research, Asher Kurach's *Kehilath Glinia, 1473–1943 — Its Birth and Destruction* published in Jerusalem in 1950 is of much greater importance.

(7)   *Sefer Chrzanow* bestows historical preference to the town because of its introduction by the prominent countryman Dr. Yitzhak Schwartzbard. Although the material in the book is mostly compiled from memory and includes events that are already well known, the folkloric material, especially the memories of Mordecai Shore that cover a half century of Jewish life of the town, is very interesting. Unfortunately, the historical part of the collection is very slim.

(8)   The best part of *Zaromb — le-zikaron olam* is the collection of historical events written by Z. Schaikowski. The rest of the volume is no more than a collection of small, incidental, and simple articles.

(9)   *Dos bukh fun Lublin* is among the most ambitious undertakings, given its aim of perpetuating the memory of a Jewish community. The book consists of three, uneven parts: the historical; the description of Jewish life in Lublin between the two world wars; and the years of the Nazi occupation and the Holocaust. The whole publication was compiled by the Jewish folk-intelligentsia, mostly from leftist movements. The first part of the book includes articles by Meir Balaban and Bella Mandelsberg reprinted from the 1926 issue of *The Young Historian*. However, there are several new and respectable sections about Lublin's Jewish past, including J. Trunk's *Pages of the Past,* a work about the history of the Jewish community of Lublin from the oldest times until the end of the eighteenth century; B. Bialer's *The Beth Hamidrash,* a work based on material found in book form; and Bella Mandelsberg-Schildkraut's article about the blood libel trial of 1636. These three works make a contribution to the history of Jewish life in Lublin, which still needs to be written. The introductory article by Joseph Milner is full of mistakes, exaggerations, and distortions. For example, he writes that Shlomo Baruch Nisenbaum, author of *Lekorot Ha-Yehudim Be-Lublin*, a great and interesting historical work about Jewish Lublin, was printed in *Rebue des Etudes Juives*. Another problem is that the yizker book contains nothing about the Jewish community between 1794 and 1914. This is such a great omission that it is simply not understandable how one can write about the development of the Lublin Jewish community without a total picture of that period. It is possible to deal with that period by reprinting memoirs and available works of that

time, such as Joseph Kermisz's book about Lublin during the time of the Kosciuszko uprising. Likewise, A. Klainman, a native of Lublin, published two articles describing Jewish life in Lublin in the years 1862–1910 in the magazine *Yevreiskaya Lienotip* in 1923. He provides much information on the Hasidic movement, the socialist and labor movements, and cultural activities in the city. Roman Szevchin Ludnosc's *Lublina w latach 1583–1650* published in Lublin in 1947 contains much about Lublin Jews. The yizker book editors could also have translated Alexsander Cederboim's *Memorial Book* or the articles of historian David Kaufman, which include a great deal of facts about the history of Jews in Lublin in general and especially about the local scholars and doctors. The second part of the yizker book consists of small entries by many authors; the majority of whom are not professional writers. However, their writing has some historical value because of the many detailed facts and episodes and the descriptions of various institutions, social organizations, schools, important personalities, groups, and streets. This kaleidoscope of fragmented descriptions is, from the standpoint of reading material, the most interesting part of the book. Although, here and there one can feel the party bias, we must assert that all phases of Jewish life are covered in these small pieces, except for the communist movement, which was given, relatively speaking, very wide coverage. Jewish cultural activities in Lublin fragments are included, without any mention of the Yiddish printing shops and the authors of the books printed in Lublin. A chapter about these printing shops, about which so much is written, would have added much importance and significance to the book. We must correct the mistake on page 252. The author of the drama *Bustanai* was Yitzhak Overbach; the music was composed by Chone Wolfstal (1851–1914) not Helfand. Also, there is no mention of Dr. Tetz of the Jewish Hospital, even though Klainman wrote an article about him. The magazine *Perezhitoyer IV, 336* should have been mentioned. To the exaggerations, one must add the opinion that "the majority of the Jewish population of Lublin was socialistically oriented" given on page 254. Writing about the Y. L. Peretz House in Lublin, the construction of which was not completed because of the outbreak of the war in 1939, B. Kempel writes that the house on the top of Czwarta #4 looks sadly toward its fellows in misery building, the Yeshivas Chachamey Lublin. In two separate ways, the buildings were destined to spread the Torah and knowledge, and now both buildings are orphaned, like the orphaned old Jewish city of Lublin, the city of the Four Lands, the former City and Mother in Israel. To this correct statement, the editors did not agree. It was not the "official line" of the editorial board, who asserted that in the new, democratic Poland a new Jewish life would rise. The most important raw material in this part is the description of Jewish life in the city from *The Jewish Togblatt* from 1928 and 1929. These excerpts on pages

300 through 325 will be greeted by historians because the best Yiddish newspaper of the former Polish province does not exist any more. The third part of the book deals with the destruction of Lublin during the Holocaust. The most important parts are the eyewitness reports and the official minutes of the *Judenrat* for the year 1942, reproduced in the original with a Yiddish translation. Four copies of minutes, three copies of official German documents, and four posters are also included in this part. The memoirs of Ida Rappoport-Glikstein found on pages 383 though 418 are also important. The annihilation of Jews in the General-Government Area started in Lublin. There the Germans came up with the notion of a Jewish Reservation Area, and therefore it is so important to study the history of the Holocaust in Lublin and its surrounding area. Yet, the introductory materials about the Holocaust in Lublin are full of false interpretations. The authors, for instance, write: "The whole existence and the actions of the *Judenrat* helped the realization of the German plans because the *Judenrat* made it easier for the enemy to execute the bestial extermination of the Jews." The authors of the introduction present a thesis that only illegal help and actions were kosher. But there are cases that cannot be included with such an easy formula. The material should be analyzed better. For example, they write: "The evidence that the members of the *Judenrat* were former members of the Kehilah (Jewish Council) is the principle evidence for their help in the German plans" (363). The sections about the Jewish partisans and the stories about Lublin's Jews and the resistance movement in France are interesting and substantial. Some of the documents are of great importance, such as the letters of the fallen partisan, Shlomo Mitelman, found on pages 567 through 576. In general, despite the flagrant, tendentious omissions, like the lack of the biography of Henrik Erlich, the Bundist, and the dilettante editing, this yizker book is still an important work, which is beautifully printed with many important documents and interesting pictures.

(10)   *Mezritsh; zamlbukh* consists of several parts. The first one contains works of a popular nature. The only worthy material by Dr. M. Hendel was already printed in 1933 in the *Mezritzer Blatt*. The history of the Mezricz Jews is based on available documents and only goes until the period of the third partition of Poland. The volume does not record the uprisings of 1794, 1831, and 1863, even though there are many historical sources about the political history of Jewish participants in the uprisings. In general, there is no all-inclusive history about the Jews of Mezricz in the volume. The second part of the book contains substantial sources and interesting stories about the life of the town. We may say the same thing about part three, which uses quotations from Jewish sources to describe the labor movement of Mezricz and its important role in the history of the working class in Poland, especially in

the brush-production industry. Although the section on the town's institutions and organizations is edited according to the same stereotypical format of compiling random stories by countrymen, it does have folkloric value. There are a series of short pieces about the streets and alleys of Mezricz. The central part of the book is dedicated to the Holocaust in Mezricz. Among the articles are well-written essays by Faigenbaum, Keslbrenner, and Friedman, which have documentary value. Even though much space was given to Mezritshers around the world, the whole book is well-assembled and well-edited, particularly in regards to its language.

(11)   *Sefer zikaron le-kehilat Lomza* is a significant book with important information. The first section starts with the history of Lomza Jews and their life until the Holocaust. Following that, cultural institutions, leaders, rabbis, cantors, teachers, and students in different educational institutions are described in great detail. Much attention is given to the Jewish hospital, Jewish doctors, and sports clubs. There are many stories about political parties and movements as well. The chapter describing the people from the town includes a treasury of short, but content-rich, biographies of respected people in the community, such as its leaders and rabbis. There are also stories about the surrounding towns and villages and details about the Jews of Lomza who immigrated to Israel. On page 329, there is an accurate statistical list of the Jews of Lomza from the year 1826 until the Holocaust. The book ends with a report about the Lomza Jews in many countries and Israel. The logical order in which the material in the book is presented could serve as an example for other *landsmanshafn* that would like to publish a memorial book for their town. In this book, one sees the work of accomplished writers and editors. The book has more than local value and maybe of more general interest. However, the history of Lomza Jews written by Dr. Yom-Tov Loinski presents very limited new data. First there are traces of Jews settling in Lomza in 1494, but in 1556, Jews were forbidden to live there. There are many sources that indicate that Jews were present in Lomza in the eighteenth century. In 1812, a Jewish *kehillah* was officially established there. In 1863, a number of Lomza Jews played an important role in the political life of the country. The author mentions something to this effect, especially about the medical families of Edelstein. There is information in the *Pages of History* (1938), in *Social Medicine* (1936), and in the articles of Emanuel Ringelblum about Jewish doctors. In the volume, merely one chapter is dedicated to the history of Lomza Jews. A full history could have been written with available materials, such as the 1870 report by the Governor of Lomza printed in 1872 in the Polish Regional Literature. About Jews in the Lomza public schools in 1859–1869, there are detailed memorial notes in the 1927 *C'zerwony Lampas Iniebieske k£pi* written by Bronislaw Pientka. In the section on Ahavat Zion, the author printed a

Polish appeal by David Yankel Yelen, who in the year of 1863 asked the European powers to return the land of Israel to the Jews. The author refers to Dr. N. M. Gelber, who quotes this document. Presumably he did not know that the author of these lines mentioned this document many years earlier in the *YIVO Bleter*, Number 193 on page 436. Dr. Gelber was given a copy of this document. Pages 63 through 95 of the volume deal with the annihilation of the Jews of Lomza and contain important eyewitness reports of reliable testimony about the destruction. Information about cultural history is included in the article about the famous Lomza yeshiva founded in 1865. This is an excellent example on how to erect a monument to a Torah study institution and remain objective. The story of the *mashgilim* and the general atmosphere around the yeshiva is very well done. Some memoirs by Lomzer Jews are written well, such as the story by Moshe Goldin found on page 324. It is a fragment of an autobiography that received a prize from YIVO before the war. The book was scheduled to be published in Yiddish in America, but the passing of the New Yorker, Dr. Grossman, a native of Lomza, who helped a great deal in the publication of the book, but did not help with the plan to publish the Yiddish edition. It is sad and a great pity that we lost that opportunity to read the worthwhile materials. Having only a Hebrew book means that not all Lomzers could participate in the project. Although *Lomza, Monuments and Memories* was published in New York in 1946 and edited by H. Sobotko, that volume only deals with minor episodes and does not give a full picture of Lomza. In the 1952 volume, while most of the articles were written by the editor Levinsky, many Lomzers, such as Abraham Naimowich and Moshe Goldman, did help with small works. However, one can notice a professional in this magnificent book. The biographical part, list of sources, and collection of pictures were professionally edited and create a good impression. The pictures are displayed on four pages and add to the importance and tastefulness of the book. All those who helped in the publication of the Lomza book, which is filled with the holy spirit and respect for the generations of Lomza Jews who mourn the loss of their countrymen in the Holocaust, deserve a *yasher-koah*.

(12)   *Pinkes Kowel* was "written not by a professional writer or journalist, but by plain, simple people, and this was our intention. We wanted it edited and written by a native, who was known by our townspeople and who knew them too. A book not composed in literary language, but in a simple language, telling the story of the facts and happenings that really took place. And let the future historians take these stories and use them as necessary." These lines are printed as an epilogue on page 510 and signed by the editor. After reading such a statement, there is no reason to analyze a book that desires not to be of "literary quality." The book is simply written grammat-

ically and pretends not to be "historic," which implies a critical approach to the local past. The editor considered it important to open the book with his poor rhymes "Kowel, My Town." It seems he forget that "simple people" do not write rhymes about the violent destruction of a city. This is generally done by poets. Even a simple person could easily retell the history of the Kowel Jews. That could be done by translating into Yiddish the works of Rafael Mahler printed in the German-Jewish Encyclopedia on pages 354 and 355, and thereby giving his townspeople a historical view of their community, which existed from the sixteenth century. Better and often interesting are the descriptions of the town based on memories of countrymen, which are given on pages 114 through 235 and form the lengthiest part of the book. The destruction of Kowel is partly recorded from works by Melech Najsztat and Dr. Dwoziecki. Also, included are excerpts from Kowel Yiddish publications, newspapers, and journals. They are the only worthy historical materials of a local character. There are also articles about several villages in the Kowel area and a detailed report about the Kowel countrymen organization in Argentina. The book is illustrated with many pictures; some are very interesting. As a folk publication, the book is not too badly edited. Yet, as a YIZKER BOOK, this must be an example how *not to gather together such a publication.* It is too primitive and too rough. The authors could easily omit the mistakes by engaging a qualified editor, a "literary person."

(13)   *Belchatow yizker-bukh* is about a town that had 7 Jews in 1764 and over 5,000 in 1942. The town grew as a result of Jewish textile industries, and in 1925 was elevated from a town to a city. Every existing Jewish social movement had its representatives and followers in Belchatow. The town had a reputation as a dynamic center of culture, which is reflected in the pages of the book. The history of Belchatow Jewry is told by Dr. Philip Friedman on pages 19 through 60. From him, we learn that in 1859 the town had 1,100 Jewish people and large textile factories built by Jews. During the Nazi occupation, the town population grew because Jews from nearby towns and villages were transported to Belchatow. The town was annexed into the Third Reich into the province of Warteland, which was incorporated into Germany from the Western part of Poland. There was no isolated ghetto in Belcharow. Most of the members of the *Judenrat* were from the underworld. They even established the practice of whipping people for not fulfilling the orders of the *Judenrat.* Friedman's work is the central theme leading to the history and the social dynamics of the town. On pages 83 through 101, the well-known Argentinean writer P. Wald tells very interesting stories about Belchatow in the year 1898. Shlomo Zhitnitzki's memories "In Times Past There Was a Town," found on pages 218 through 244, are written with great literary zest. He won the prize for autobiographies from YIVO in Vilna for his interesting and well-

written memories and deserves special thanks. On pages 148 through 197, much historical material from the memoirs of Abraham Leib covering the years 1914–1922 is presented. Belchatow gave us one Yiddish writer Yoel Leib Goldstein. He was the author of a number of books, among them the interesting utopian romance *1960*. He is mentioned by several writers in their memoirs, specifically on pages 135 and 160–161. He is analyzed in a matter-of-fact way by Jacob Botoszanski in an impressionistic essay on pages 246 through 267. A detailed description of the destruction of the city by Leib Pudlowski on pages 391–455 strengthens his depiction of the devastation with a series of important documents obtained from the Jewish Historical Institute of Warsaw. His characterization of the *Judenrat* matches the same critical judgment of Friedman's. According to the author's estimate, only ten percent of Belchatow's Jews survived. One can find in the book a series of well-written articles about the political movements and cultural activities in Belchatow by Joseph Reich, Zalmen Pudlowski, Levi Hertzkowicz, Hersh Goldmintz, Moshe Efrati, Elimelech Pudlowski, Fishl Szmulewitz, M. Gliksman, Zainvel Przedborski, Jaakov Zingler, and J.M. Pukatch. About the destruction of Belchatow, besides Leib Pudlowski's, mentioned earlier, who contributed the central part of this chapter, there were also others, like Z. Lieberman and M. Kaufman, who added articles for this chapter. Joseph Reich closed the book with the impressive account "Belchatow Without Jews." It is important to emphasize that all the documents published in this book are of great historical importance and that these types of materials are seldom found in the yizker books currently published. The authors of this collective volume represent all ideologies of Jewish life, and each of them objectively describes specific Jewish activities. We can say that in regards to political partiality, the book is a great success. The impressive collection of photographs of individuals and institutions gives the book the distinctive character of a modern *pinkes*. Though this is a book about one town, we must assert that the colorful story of Jewish life in Belchatow and the way it is represented transforms the work into a symbolic monument for all Jewish communities in Poland. The Belchatow memorial book may serve as an example on how such a volume should be compiled. It must be read by all who would like to learn what the surviving Jews experienced as they expressed their feelings about the destruction of their town in writing.

(14) *Stanislaw* devotes more space to the history of the Jews than to the Holocaust years. The editors published a detailed and competent history of the Jewish past, which includes N. M. Gelber's *Genealogy of Stanislaw Jewry*, found on pages 9 through 67. It is the first inclusive work with many new sources from archival documents and encompasses political history, as well as cultural chronicles, such as the enlightenment movement, ideas current

at various times, and short biographies of famous Jews from the town. It is regretful that the Affair of 1848, the national conflict of Stanislaw, was hardly mentioned, despite the availability of much material on the topic. Still, the book is a solid work. Yeshayahu Halevi Ish Horowitz proficiently writes a detailed article about the local rabbis. Stanislaw was famous for its six rabbis from the same family who held the honored chair as rabbis, a fact with no comparison in rabbinical history. Dr. Mordechai Ze'ev Brode, a renowned builder of the Polish-Jewish school system between the two world wars, the spiritual leader of the Progressive Synagogue in Stanislaw during 1900–1912, and an important player in Zionist politics in Galicia, details his rabbinical years in Stanislaw on pages 98 though 165 and presents a living testimony about that stormy period when the Zionist Party in Galician participated in the election to the Austrian Parliament that brought about the creation of the first Jewish National Parliamentary Group in our history. Especially important are Dr. Brode's memories of the history of Ukrainian Jewish relations, a matter that has never been properly researched. Meir Hagish writes about Zionism from 1904–1914, and Aaron Leib Szusheim writes about the Poalei-Zion Movement. The most important, all-encompassing part of the book is written by Menachem Goldter about Jewish life in Stanislaw from 1918–1939, the years when the town belonged to Poland. There is not one important episode in the life of the Jewish community that is not mentioned, briefly or at length, in his writing. Such an all-encompassing and objective opus is rare in yizker books. The author deals with all religious groups and all cultural societies in the Jewish life in the town. He also writes about the Jewish press, theatre, the famous Goldfaden Union, and school system, and political parties. This is a monograph than spans pages 189–382, almost 200 pages. However, a few minor corrections are needed. The play *Puste Kretshme* was not written by Kobrin, but by Peretz Hirszbein (335). *Between Day and Night* was written by Ansky, not by I. L. Peretz (336). Dov Sadan describes Stanislaw authors who wrote in Hebrew, Yiddish, and Polish. While the city produced many writers, they had limited talent. What Dov Sadan wanted to accomplish with the article "Stanislaw Style" is hard to understand. A study of the sociological background of the impressive number of Jewish writers in the former East Galicia would be very interesting, but it would require more than a list of names and a few perfunctory remarks. Sadan gives only a few lines about Mayer Wajsberg, the author of the monograph about enlightenment literature in Galicia that received the Wallenberg Prize from Lemberg University in 1913 and was published, in parts, in Polish. His works were considered out of date when they were written. It is self-evident that the exaggerations do not fit here. The same may be said about many other writers that Sadan mentions; they have more local significance than historical importance. A very limited article, mostly eyewitness accounts, describes the tragic end of the old Jewish community in the town of Stanislaw, which was founded in 1654. The scant ten pages of this epilogue consist of short reports by Jewish survivors of Stanislaw. They were recorded by Menachem Gelerter and are inadequate for such an important Jewish community. But, it seems that at the time they were not able to collect enough material for the book. As a final review, though, this is a very important book. The photographs of the destroyed communities are the best part. Also, the book includes a good index of names, and in general is very nicely published, despite the lack of illustrations.

(15)   *Yizker kehilat Luniniec/Kozhanhorodok* is a narrative in Hebrew and Yiddish of the modest history of the two towns from their beginnings until their end. The town of Luniniec is located in a secluded corner of the Pinsk region and received its first Jewish settlers in the 1870s. The settlement of Kozian-Horodok is much older. In 1679, it is recorded that the "Pinsk leaders of the community, borrowed money from the Jesuits for Pinsk and surrounding area, among them also for Kozian-Horodok." In 1939, the town of Luniniec had a population of 10,000 people, 5,000 Byelorussians, 2,200 Polish, and 2,800 Jews. As Luniniec developed, Kozian-Horodek declined. The town became impoverished because of its closeness to Luliniec and the mass migration to America. Unfortunately, there is no information available on the decline of Kozian-Horodek. The majority of the volume is not the work of professional writers. One exception is the well-written and interesting essay about the history of Luliniec by Joseph Zawi. A lot of space is devoted to the history of Zionism in the two towns. It seems that every group in the Zionist movement had their representatives and conducted their own activities in the towns. The same was the case with the Socialists. There were not any great rabbis in the two towns, and the *kehilah* practiced the same rules in their societies as was done in other places. The spirit of modern culture in each city manifested itself in Hebrew. The poet Sarah Kucikowicz lived in Luliniec and perished in the Holocaust. At the age of twelve, she wrote poems that were published in Hadoar Lanoar in New York, and a large number of her poems and letters are included in the memorial volume. In general, both settlements were Zionist, genteel, and offered a number of emigration possibilities to Israel. The book describes the prayer houses, synagogues, cultural institutions, and libraries in great detail. Those descriptions will contribute to sociological studies of Jewish towns. In one case, there is a description, which is immensely significant, about the influence of the Karliner Hasidic movement on the towns of the whole region. There are stories and tales of historical value, such as the description of a Hasidic Shabbat in Luliniec on pages 147 to 152. The portraits of individuals, such as the Rabbi of Luniniec, Rabbi Alter Yehuda Zuliar by Yehuda Gurwicz, are told in a lively, appealing

way. In both parts of the book, individual Holocaust survivors tell their stories in a detailed fashion. Because of the rough, harsh way the stories are told, these eyewitness reports are mind bogging and astounding. At the end of the volume, there is a memorial section with names and photographs of some martyrs. Beside its historical value, this memorial book has importance for folklore researchers because the articles are about local traditions, customs, and ways of life. The language of the book is good. The Hebrew part is correct, and the Yiddish is without any literary embellishments. The book was nicely published by local countrymen living in America who made it possible that our Holocaust literature is enriched with an important book.

(16)   The middle of *De verdwenen mediene* is written in Dutch, and the volume is essentially a book about the lost Jewish lifestyle in the Dutch province outside Amsterdam. It sheds light on the Holocaust and the disappearance of the ancient form of Judaism that still existed rudimentarily in minor Jewish communities and in villages more distinct and vivid. The author looks like a last Mohican who warmly and intimately describes the types and characters from the old generation, namely the ritual-slaughterers, *mohels*, sextons, butchers, beggars, philosophers, and the simple market sellers, as leftovers from the past *Jodish* [Dutch-Yiddish] with which they sprinkled their dry Dutch language. For cultural historians, the book is a treasure. For Yiddish language researchers, this book is a source for studying the Jewish language in Holland in chronological order. The pictures of synagogues, rabbis, and simple folk in mannered portraits are all of great ethnographic value. It is a yizker book in the full meaning of the word. This is not a book that bemoans a city, but rather is saddened by the loss of a lifestyle that started to disappear even before the Holocaust and totally afterwards.

Notes

1. Originally published as Jacob Shatzky, "*Yisker bikher*," *YIVO Bleter* 37 (1953): 264–282. Herman Taube translated the material from Yiddish into English. Thanks to YIVO for permission to translate and print the review.

2. In *Hamelitz* (1891) #32, an important article about Wolkovisk appeared.

3. Arie Ben-Zahav was the author of a book about tar producers in Grajewa (The Dziektares) published in Hebrew in Israel and in Yiddish in Warsaw in 1939 called *Pech Yidn*. Achiever, 187 pages.

5

Review of Yizker Books — 1955

Jacob Shatzky

1. *Yizker-bukh fun Rakishok un umgegnt.* Ed. Melekh Bakalczuk-Felin. Johannesburg: Rakishker Landsmanshaft of Johannesburg, 1952.[1]
2. *Pinkas Byten.* Eds. Dodl Abramovitsh and Mordechai W. Bernshtein. Buenos Aires: Former Residents of Byten in Argentina, 1954.
3. *Churbn kehilat Shtsutsin.* Ed. Yeshayaku Skubelsky. Tel Aviv: Organization of Emigrants from Shtsutsin in Israel, 1954.
4. G. Bigil. *Meyn shtetele Berezne.* Tel Aviv, 1954.
5. *Torne.* Tel Aviv: Landsmanshaft of Jews from Torne, 1954.
6. *Pinkas Kremenits.* Ed. A. S. Stein. Tel Aviv: Former Residents of Krzemieniec in Israel, 1954.
7. *Yizker-bukh Chelm.* Ed. Melech Bakalczuk-Felin. Johannesburg: Former Residents of Chelm, 1954.
8. *Yisker-bukh Ratne.* Eds. Jacob Botoshansky and Yitkhak Yanasovitsh. Buenos Aires: Former Residents of Ratno in Argentina and the USA, 1954.
9. *Yizker-bukh fun der Zhelekhover yidishe kehilat.* Ed. A. Wolf Yosni. Chicago: Central Zhelekhover Landsmanshaft in Chicago, 1953.
10. Mikhl Grines, *Ven dos lebn hot geblit* (about Ostre, Volhynia). Buenos Aires, 1954.
11. *Fun noentn over.* New York: World Jewish Culture Congress, New York, 1955.

Reviews

(1) According to *Yizker-bukh fun Rakishok un umgegnt,* the town is "one of the oldest Jewish communities in Lithuania (29). In independent Lithuania, this city of Lubavitsher hasidim was elevated to a county capital with about 2,000 Jewish families. In the yizker book volume, nearly fifty contributors describe the city and its surroundings. The book was put together according to an already accepted style of short articles, with a lot of repetition, contradiction, and exaggeration. Several professional writers contributed to

68

the volume, namely Yaakev Leshtshinsky, Y. Blotnitzky, and Philip Friedman. The details regarding education are very interesting. Aside from various schools and a Lithuanian gymnasium, there was a progressive culture league from 1919 to 1923, Yiddish theatre, and numerous societies and institutions. Of all the towns in the surrounding area, Anushishok, where Hirsh Lekert was from, is worth mentioning. The destruction and death of Rakishtok are described on pages 383–430 in great detail based on detailed eyewitness accounts. The editor writes about the destruction in Rakishok and vicinity based on a collection of letters in an article from pages 405 through 430. Dr. Philip Friedman's bibliography of monographs of Jewish communities and cities given on pages 438 through 455 is useful, although not exhaustive. Moreover, it is positively out of place in this book. The book closes with the history of the Rakishok *landsmanshaft* in Johannesburg, with the unavoidable pictures and charts. All in all, one does not see in this book any editorial control. Everything is vague and undisciplined, such as the story of the city and its Jews.

(2)   Byten is a town in the county of Slonim with an important history. In *Pinkas Byten,* Mordechai Bernshtein notes that in the sixteen century, there were Jews already living in the town. The other articles in the volume are chiefly reminiscences. Included is an essay by Sh. Z. Vilentshik, which provides many details about lifestyle; the recollections of A. Z. Yablok, which cover the period 1900–1914; and writings by Yitzkhak Meir Rabinovitsh, M. Mishkin, and others. There are descriptions of rabbis, hasids, and a particularly interesting reportage about Byten Jews performing force labor for the Germans during the First World War. Co-editor D. Abramovitsh tells about Byten in the years 1914–1920 and the changes in the community during that period, which was a time when control of the town went from one power to another until it remained under Polish rule. The recollections of Y. L. Abramovitsh regarding the neighboring settlement of Vatsevitsh where the Germans concentrated Jews for forced labor are very interesting. It is important to point out that the Hebrew middle school is mentioned by Nahum Sokolov in his paper about the culture of the Jews, which he delivered at the 4th Zionist Congress (Minutes of the 4th Zionist Congress, Vienna, 1900, 206). From the article by Abraham Abramovsky, we learn about the role of local area Jews in the forestry and wood trades. The information regarding American support for Byten gives the assembler, who writes under the pseudonym M. Bitensky, the opportunity to document the cultural activities of the town. These reports, along with details about the local libraries and Culture League are very significant. They contain important material for the sociologist of the Yiddish shtetl between the two world wars. The most substantial part of this book is the section about the years of the last war and about the destruction. Of great

importance are the recollections of David Abramovitsh, who describes the situation of Jews in the White Russian region where the Soviets were greeted as the liberators from Polish control. First the Red Army emptied all the Jewish stores. The Soviet authority then shut down all cultural institutions, people's banks, and even charitable societies. The partisan Mayshe Pitkovsky describes in over one hundred pages how the Jewish community in Byten ceased to exist. There are startling descriptions of the Jewish Council, ghetto, mass murders, partisans, resistance, and attitude of the non–Jewish population toward the local Jews. Of more than 1,200 Jews, a total of 26 survived. Dody Abramovitsh relates interesting details regarding the anti–Semitism among the partisans. Shmuel Ostrovietsky gives details about the forced labor camp in the village of Puzevitsh. Other contributors to the rich section about the destruction of the town are Y. Yuzhelevsky, Meir Yafe, Mordechai Minkovitsh, and Yual Berkner. In the book, there are historical recollections that are really folklore. Thus, for example, Meir Yafe tells that his father, Rabbi Yakov Ben Tsion Yafe, traveled to Warsaw and came home with a certificate from the governor by whom he was successfully examined. In sum, the 300-page section on the destruction is the most substantial part of the book and is an important contribution to our literature of the destruction.

(3) *Churbn kehilat Shtsutsin* contains more pictures than text. The articles are short and really unsubstantial. Most detailed is the description of the destruction. In a twenty-page letter, Chaye Soyke Golding tells how the Jews of the shtetl were tortured to death. Documents and eyewitness accounts of the destruction that originated with the historical commission in Białystok are included. Mayshe Farborowitz and Fishl Michalsky relate their experiences during the Second World War, and Chaye Golding-Keepman writes about life in a bunker in Białystok. The end of the book lists Shtsutsiners who live in Israel.

(4) The Jews of Berezne, a shtetl in Volhynia, experienced unspeakably cruel treatment. Before the catastrophe, Berezne had 5,000 Jews. Only a small number survived. Currently, in Israel, there are about 200 people from Berezne who are organized in an association. *Meyn shtetele Berezne* consists of memoirs of compatriots from all over the world, as well as in Israel. Included are a number of eyewitness accounts and descriptions by former Jewish partisans in the Soviet army. The majority of the book originated with the editor himself, a physician and resident of Israel. The compilation has Yiddish and Hebrew sections. The Hebrew section, pages 136–182, is a summary of the Yiddish. Certain articles are reprinted from *Yalkut Volyn*. While the details about lifestyle are unoriginal and uninteresting, the details about the situation and the moods when Germany attacked the Soviet Union found on pages 84 through 112 are extremely interesting. The Ukrainians began to persecute the

Jewish population immediately. The members of the Jewish Council were designated by them. The book contains details about the ghetto, resistance, killings, and mass murder. A short article by Henekh Kaganitz describes his participation in the partisan army. The end of the book lists people from Berezne in Israel.

(5) *Torne* is an important book consisting of a series of articles presenting a fine history of its Jews from the earliest times until its fall. The book is competently edited by Dr. Avraham Khomet, the historian of the Jews of Torne, and it is one of the few yizker books edited by an historian. The editor has written a 186-page history of the Jews of Torne based on archival materials, which are no longer available. In 1903, the first historian of Torne Jewry, Dr. Yitzkhak Shippers, published a work in Polish about the history of the Torne Jews. The second part of *Torne* tells the story of the religious Jews in articles written by Avraham Kahana, Chaym Dov Friedberb, Rabbi Yehudah Creffen, and others. There is also a reprint of a chapter from the memoirs of Yosef Margoshes, may he rest in peace, which were published in New York in 1936. The economic life of Jewish Torne is covered in the third part of the volume by the editor. Torne had a reputation by virtue of the organization Yad Harutzim, an orthodox workers' institution established in 1875. There are not enough details in the volume about the Jews of Torne who excelled in science, art, literature, and journalism. Among the most distinguished are Mardechai Dovid Broshteter (1844–1928) written by Daniel Leybl and A. Chomet. Shalom Baron wrote about Bronshleter in *Hatsepirah* (1914, 94, 97); Leon Kelner (1859–1928), the famous Shakespearean scholar; Yetzklak Shipper. Mahler's article was reprinted in the YIVO *Bleter*, XXV, 1945; Maks Binenshtok; and others. Since Torne played a pioneering role in the history of Zionism in West Galicia that part of the volume is detailed and original. The monograph about Zionism spans 240 pages and was written by Chomet. It is a well-balanced article discussing the various types of Zionism based on a large number of primary sources. Missing is the important fact regarding *Admat Tsion* and the conflict with the rebbe of Tshortkev, which in its time attracted a large literary response. See *Hamagid*, Krakow, 1898, I and *Hashalah*, 1898, III. There are short, separate articles on the proletarian aspects of Zionism. Yekoshuah Landoy of Tel Aviv writes about the Jewish Socialist party, and the Bundi Urn Shposn of Montreal completes it. Other activities, such as sports, social work, and cultural institutions are described by the editor. Very interesting and even exciting are the recollections and the descriptions of unusual characters; those details have high cultural and history value. Pages 808 through 870 contain detailed descriptions of mass death. This yizker book is one of the most important in Holocaust history. Regretfully, the editor did not eliminate frequent repetitions in the biographical section or correct

certain erroneous information about living individuals who are mentioned in the book and provided less than accurate details about themselves. Nevertheless, the book is a definitive history of the Jews of Torne. The historical part is excellent and should serve as a model of how a regional monograph should be written. The great number of pictures and statistical tables enrich the book and are an important source of information and an interesting work for reading, even if one is not a Torne compatriot.

(6)   *Pinkas Kremenits* is a bi-lingual publication written in Hebrew and Yiddish. The Yiddish part is not a translation, but rather consists of original articles, except for the first that is a shortened translation of the Hebrew original history of the Jews of Kremenitz written by Etinger and Shnerak. This is a good article that even relates a few new facts and covers the history of the Jews until 1917. The most significant part of the book covers the period until 1793. The period from 1793 to 1917 is compiled on the basis of convenient materials insofar as the authors seem unfamiliar with the rich Polish literature regarding Kremenitz, such as the works of Role and others that contain many details about Jewish life. Regarding the activities of the famous Kremenitzer Reb Yitzkhak Ber Levinzon (RIB"L), the Yiddish by Volf Shnayder on pages 288 through 299 is best. Overall, the book contains a little information on many topics, but no article is substantial. Even concerning Zionism, there is no comprehensive article. The same applies to education. For example, totally absent is the role of Jews in the former Kremenitz Lyceum and the support of the local community in 1803. In connection with the activity around the purchase of the RIB"L's house in 1899, it is appropriate to emphasize the activity of Kremenitz's Rabbi Kunin. Regarding Dr. Tovyeh Hindes (1852–1910), who played a large part in Warsaw, there is a good deal of material in the diary of Ben-Avigdor (*Halzepirah*, 1917). Regarding the relations between the Jews of Kremenitz and the local Russian Orthodox seminary, it is appropriate to read *Nedelnaya Chronika Voschoda* (1896, 48). Regarding the workmen there, there is a description, in the same journal (1897, 41). Very little is told about the famous Landsberg family, one of whom, Mendl Landsberg (1786–1866) became famous as a bibliophile (Y. Shatsky, *Jews in Warsaw*, III, 331; Sh. Viner, *Koheles Moyshe*, 1898, introduction).[2] The destruction of Kremenitz is told in a few short articles. Worth mentioning are the details about the community budget of 1932–1933 and the excerpts from the local Yiddish press, which printed many historical articles about Jewish settlements in the area, such as Potshayev. Very interesting is H. Gelernt's article about An-sky's folklore expedition in Kremenitz and the section "From the Old Jewish Way of Life." In the final analysis, the book is assembled from fragments of material without any effort to synthesize them, especially considering that there is a rich literature of non–Jewish memoirs and newspaper correspondence in Rus-

sian and Hebrew about Kremenitz. A solid history of the Jews in Kremenitz, a community with a rich historic past, has yet to be written.

(7)   *Yizker-bukh Chelm* was assembled unsystematically and without much editorial guidance. The articles about the yarn of Chelm offer nothing new and simply do not belong in a book about the Holocaust. The historical introduction by Dr. Philip Friedman, "To the History of the Jews in Chelm," which spans only twenty-five pages, is far from a history. A substantial monograph about Chelm would be the best way to memorialize the city. For example, in 1816 a German officer in Chelm had a conversation with an "enlightened rabbi's wife" and that information has value towards the history of the Enlightenment.[3] Information regarding Jews from Chelm may be found in a series of official Russian publications, the report of the governor of Lublin for 1872, and in other documents in the Russian weekly *Chelm Church News*. Nevertheless, Hersh Shrshler's descriptions of charitable organizations, Torah lessons, and the press are very interesting. Nokhum Vinik writes about the Bund in Chelm during 1904–1939; Shimen Shargel writes about the left-wing Poalei Tsion. Of historical value is Yakov Beker's report about the Poalei Tsion function in the Chelm city council on pages 235–248. This is the first appearance of such content in a yizker book. The work of Yosef Milner under the name Anshei Shem is a curiosity. He includes rabbis and ordinary Jews in Chelm and people such as Peretz, Rayfman, and Avraham Yaakev Shtern, who perhaps were in Chelm once on a visit and places them among Chelm's important personages. Besides, all biographies are written in a bombastic style and contain errors. For instance, about Shtern, the author does not even know that he was Slonimsky's father-in-law. See the work of Y. Shatsky in *The Joshua Starr Memorial Volume,* 1953, 203–218). Two articles are devoted to Shmuel Mordechai (Artus) Zigelboym (1895–1943), who was not born in Chelm but spent his youth there. There is a lot of reverence in this style of writing but not much concrete biography. The same may be said of the article about Shiper written by Akiba Vinik. Some of the details are incorrect. Shiper was not Yitzkhak Grinboyn's brother-in-law (306). Moyshe Lerer was neither a founder of YIVO as A. Ayzn writes on page 312 nor a representative of "the Polish segment of Yiddish philology," the meaning of which no one understands. The section about the destruction of Chelm consists of a series of recollections and eyewitness accounts. There is very great historical value to the unique minutes of a 1942 conference on social self-help that was held in Chelm on January 25th and 26th concerning the battle against epidemics. The moral strength that exudes from the words of the doctors and community leaders presented on pages 601 through 620 belongs to the finest chapters of Jewish heroism. It is advisable for the whole world to get interested in these minutes. The bottom line of the destruction of Chelm is that of the 18,000

Jews or 60 percent of the total population who lived there in September 1939, only a few hundred were able to save themselves, most of them by accident. At the end of the book are trite, uninteresting, and insignificant descriptions of landsmanshaftn all over the world. Nearly seventy-five contributors took part in this gigantic book; some of whom had nothing to tell, and others were too wordy or were repetitious. A competent editor could cut the content in half without causing any damage; only then would this be a good yizker book. Also, what is lacking in this book is a description of Jews in light of Polish folklore, which may be found in Ascar Kolberg's two-volume collection *Chelmskie* of 1891.

(8)   *Yisker-bukh Ratne* is a large volume of more than 800 pages consisting of articles written in a hackneyed style without editorial care. Ratne, a shtetl in Volhynia, was recently memorialized in a superb book by the English-Yiddish poet Kleyn of Canada, who comes from Ratne (*The Second Scroll*, New York, 1952). That book is not mentioned in this publication. However, a poem by Kleyn is included at the end of the yizker book in the original English. A few random notes to the shtetl's history were put together by Dr. F. Fridman. Ratne belonged to Poland as early as 1366, and Jews were already in Ratne in the fifteenth century. The Russian-Jewish historian Berlin cites from the *Pinkes Shel Malakhim*, a Karaite source, an interesting fact from 1490 that is textually different from the source that Fridman cites according to Harkavy (1919, 179). In 1921, Ratne had 2,410 residents, of whom nearly 65 percent were Jews. The article, "The Beginnings of the Jewish Community in Ratne," by Fishel Held is a mixture of legends and memories, which had already come out as a brochure in 1938. From this family chronicle, one can extract a few concrete historical facts. Other contributors, such as Yudl Konishter, for example, repeat the same thing as Held. Here you find such gems as "Ratne arose when the Duchess Sangushko ruled [!]" and the like. Much better is the part where the history of Ratne in the last sixty years is described. Although here, too, one finds things that the editor should not have left in. For example, 1905 was the year in which the Enlightenment arose (83). The article occupies seventy pages and contains enough material that no more boring tracts of the type with which the book is loaded need ever be printed. L. Bayer and others write about Balachovitsh, the program-leader of the White Guard in Poland in 1920. This is a theme that was too lightly touched on. In the section about Ratne between the two world wars, one finds descriptions of organizations and parties. Very interesting, because far from just local, are the biographies of characters and images of scholars, workers, social activists, etc. In these materials, there is a contribution to the ordinary Jewish culture. Respecting the history of Yiddish literature, the articles are interesting that concern the Alitsky family and the episode about Yone Rozenfeld found on

pages 355–360. L. Bayon, a teacher in Mexico, is described in many articles. Very significant are the pre-war letters that were written to him from Ratne, in which are found details about the mental state of Jewish youth in a small shtetl between the two world wars. From a sociological perspective, this is very important material. The materials regarding the time of the destruction found on pages 483–593 are first of all rich in detail regarding the attitude of Ukrainians toward Jews. The articles about Jews from Ratne all over the world perhaps are of local interest, just as are other articles in this book. In the main, however, the history of the Jewish community in Ratne from the earliest times until the destruction is lacking. This could have been accomplished by pulling together the scattered crumbs and attempting to put together a unified history of the shtetl. But such an editorial approach requires more competence than the editors of this yizker book possess. It is therefore to be regretted that so much effort went to waste, for it is doubtful whether even compatriots from Ratne will be able to read such a big and in essence boring book.

(9)   *Yizker-bukh fun der Zhelekhover yidishe kehilat* was assembled in accordance with the same principles as other publications of this kind. First, there is a very slim article by Volf Yasni about the history of the Jews of the town that fails to bring together the existing information about the shtetl in general and its Jews in particular. It should be noted that in 1831, the famous Polish historian and revolutionary Yoachim Lelevel was the Sejim deputy from the district. In the regional Polish literature, there is enough material for writing a detailed history of the city and its Jews. On the eve of World War II, Dzhelekhov counted 5,500 Jews. During the war, the city became a center for refugees, and in 1942, the number of Jews reached 10,000. The efforts of Sholem Oshlak are very well written. The jottings of Meir Vayntsier, Yekhiel Rozenboym, and Shloyme Braynsky are interesting. Among the articles in the section "Between Two Wars," the recollections of Leybush Vaysleder are very concrete. Something new is the section "Dzhelekhov in the Mirror of Yiddish Literature." Here are found reminiscences and assessments of Itshe Meir Vaysenbug and the martyr Yechiel Lerer; the work of A. Volf Yasmi is substantial. The recollections about him by Mayshe Goldfarb, Shloyme Brayski, and Mayshe Knapheys are interesting. In the book, there are new and important biographical materials regarding Yechiel Lerer. These are the recollections of Moyshe Grosman, M. Boym, and especially Rokhl Oyerbakh (about Lerer in the Warsaw Ghetto). The years of the war and the Hitler persecutions are especially well described. First of all, the thorough and well-written article by Moyshe Borukhovitsh on pages 203–234 is important in this context. Sore Vaynberg has interesting things to tell about the Hitler era, so do Shmuel Laksman, Shmuel Hokhgelernter, et.al. There are four articles about the par-

tisans. Very interesting are the details regarding the positive attitude of Poles toward Jews provided on pages 277 and 283 and the help of peasants found on pages 243, 249, 258, 267, and 280. There is even a short article about this by Tsevie Rosental found on pages 286–288. In all, the whole section about the Holocaust is well put together. There is less about the Jewish way of life. In the journal *Yiddish Philology* (1926) there is material regarding the folklore of Dzhelikhov. There is material about Imanuel Tshizik (born 1867) who was a *badkhn* in Dzhelikhov in Z. Zilbertsvayg's *Levicon*, II, 901. A history of the Jews of Dzhelikhov remains to be written, and it will be a worthy and substantial monument. This book is richly illustrated and attractively published. It was assembled with great culture, love, and reverence.

(10)   *Ven dos lebn hot geblit*, the yizker book about the famous scholarly city of Ostre, was assembled by Mikhl Grines. While this is a positive aspect of the book, Grines was not knowledgeable about the literature of his city, and he writes in a very limited Yiddish. His description of the beginnings of the Ostre Jewish community is not correct. The earliest information about Jews in Ostre dates back to 1444. A wealthy merchant, Pesakh, from Ostre, is mentioned in 1447. Jews from Ostre were conducting business in Lemberg as early as 1502. Although Grines refers to the "writing of the historian Shimon Dubnow," (51) he has not read Dubnow's work *Jewish Antiquities of Ostre* published in *Voskhod* (1894, 10). Also he is unfamiliar with the writings of Kardoshebitsh, Yarotsky, Hrushevsky, Efimenko, and Baranovitsh. There was no convention of the Council of Four Lands in Lublir in 1648 as noted on page 57. The Hebrew print shop in Ostre was in existence from 1793 to 1837, so how is it that on page 127, there is a book published in 1733. Regarding Nosnnote Hanover, the famous chronicler, the biographical details are far from correct. He perished in Brod, Hungary, not Brod, Poland. A reproduction of his gravestone is found in David Kogfman's work about the attack on Hungary's Brod, printed in 1894. The recruitment statute came out in 1827, not in 1816 as written on page 367. Shmuel Shrayer, about whom the author writes a great deal and sympathetically, wrote an article about Ostre in the Russian-Jewish Encyclopedia. A few details regarding the debts of the Ostre community are in the second volume of the writings of the Ukranian-Jewish Concession in Kiev. The author relied too heavily on Buber's book *Memorial to the Great Men of Ostre* (published in 1907) and was unable to check it for accuracy. Respecting approvals by scholars and rabbis of Ostre, one finds substantial material in the *Index of Approvals* by Rabbi Dr. L. Levenshteyn (Frankfurt am Main, 1923). It contains fifty-five approvals until the year 1850. The history of learning in Ostre may be revised in light of these approvals. The yizker book covers the most recent time and the period of the Holocaust better and more accurately. The description of a group of types and images

of Ostre is very interesting. The bibliography is not precise; for example, what is meant by *Yivo-Shriftn, 1938*? The manner in which this yizker book was composed, albeit far from successful, deserves to be noted. Perhaps all materials sent in ought to be turned over to a professional to rework and give credit to those who contributed materials. As a result, yizker books would be smaller, but easier to read and remember. In the way in which they are put together today, they are for the most part memorials, not books. As everyone knows, people don't read gravestones.

(11)   *Fun noentn over* is a collection of papers by refugee-authors that covers topics about the recent past. In the book's introduction, Yakov Pat writes that the main objective of this collection is to perpetuate the lives of east European Jewry. The first piece, compiled by Mikhl Borvitsh, is titled "Where it was Different." These are materials and documents about Jews during the Nazi era in Sweden, Denmark, Norway, and Switzerland. They consist of memorials, eyewitness accounts, and reports translated into Yiddish. Borvitsh leads the reader into the center of the problems relating to the particular situation of the Jews in those countries and brings out the fact that the fates of the Jews there was a little different than in other countries. This collection contains twelve important reports and documents. The most interesting is Norbert Mazur's report on his meetings with Hitler. As a source for researching this geographic region, the collection makes a significant contribution. The statistical list of Jewish refugees in Switzerland found on pages 108 and 109 is very important. The materials were collected and adapted by the Research Center for the History of the Polish Jews in France. Interesting is the work of Norbert Horowits regarding the Yiddish theater given on pages 113 through 182. This is a well-documented chronicle, which is more source material than history. He states the plays, the names of the actors, the press reaction, and statistics on attendance. He also provides details on musical activities and the fate of individual players. The author writes that the builders of the Yiddish theaters and music culture "contributed to the mental health of the survivors." But when one reads of the failure of their efforts in the countries to which they emigrated, these conclusions merely invoke sad thoughts. However, this is important raw material that may at some time interest a historian of Yiddish theater. The essay "Yitzhak Shiper, His Life and Achievement" was written with great love and enthusiasm by Y. Hirshhoyt, who took on the task "of giving the reader an idea of Shiper's works." To this end, he placed "the chief emphasis on portraying the content of the works and not on their critical assessment" (184). But a comprehensive biography of a scholar without a critical approach is only half the task. Hirshhoyt's article cannot satisfy a reader who wants to know not only what Shiper wrote, but what is significant is his scientific legacy. The author accepts as valid a

series of conclusions of Shiper's that he himself subsequently withdrew. Hir-shhoyt's seventy-page monograph is not always accurate. For instance, "The History of the Jewish People," which appeared in Russian in 1914 was not published by the Russian-Yiddish Encyclopedia. During 1916, Shiper did not suffer in the army, rather he worked in the library in Vienna and collected a great deal of material about Jews in travel literature, which was later lost. Shiper's work for YIVO was not described with precision, and this could easily have been done using the systematic notes found in Vilna's *News of the Yiddish Scientific Institute*. The bibliography of Shiper's works is put together chaotically and is far from good. First, it is not organized by subject and not supported by description. Although the YIVO *Bleter* and periodicals in which Shiper took part are missing, there is nevertheless more works than Hirshhoyt lists. I want to point out several important gaps. About the history of the Yid-dish theater, Shiper wrote in the journal *The Months* (Warsaw, 1921), as well as in the almanac for the tenth anniversary of *Moment* (1921: 209–242). Shiper printed important reviews in Blokh's *Austrian Weekly* (1908). These larger and more important of his works are not mentioned at all in the bibliography: "Portraits of Jewish Intercessors (1648–1764)," a series in *Moment* 1927; regard-ing Reb Berish Mayzlsh (a series of eight articles), *Today* 1933; regarding Shi-mon Ashkenazi, *Today* 1934, 117 (4); regarding Moyshe Shor, *Today*, 1934, 113; "400 Years of The Book of Anshil," *Today*, 1934, 248; "50 Years of Zionism in Torne," *Today*, 1934, 130; regarding the Natanzon Family, *Today*, 1935 (eight articles); and the recollections of Stefan Yaratsh, *Today*, 1935, 160. Shiper also wrote remembrances of his compatriot Karl Radek. He engaged in polemics with Dr. M. Morelski about the Khazars, with Professor Balaban, and with many others. Shiper's book about the two Warsaw cemeteries was announced in the journal of the Warsaw community (July, 1939). Certain Polish-Jewish journals to which he contributed are not mentioned either. Of great importance is the work of Noakh Prilutski, "Why did Yiddish Theatre Arise So Late?" in the collection *Untervegns* (Vilna, 1940) and which also appeared in book form. This book questions Shiper's thesis about Yiddish theater and produces important insights into the problem of the historic youthfulness of Yiddish theater. On the whole not much was written about Shiper with the exception of occasional articles. Therefore, it would be appro-priate to mention the articles of Y. M. Nayman (*Today* 1934, 260); mine in the collection *Polish Jews* (New York, 1935), and the work about Jews in the Revolution of 1831 (*Historical Writings* of YIVO, II). Of the competent reviews, I want to mention those printed in *YIVO Bleter* (Yulius Brutskus, Moyshl Frenk) and those by Mark Vrshnitser, Meir Balaban, and others. Love for the subject one is researching should always go with competence. Unfortunately, one cannot say this about the present work. Shiper, a spirited and productive historian, deserves a more objective and competent assessment. To be able to carry out such a task, one must be proficient in all the problems of historical research of Jews in eastern Europe. On another note, the chapter by M. Naygreshel on modern Yiddish literature in Galicia in the period 1904–1918 found on pages 267–398 is pioneering. This is a solid monograph with new details and conclusions containing critical evaluations and thorough analyses of the writers. It is written like an essay, with emphasis on aesthetic values rather than in a dry historical and biographical style. Naygreshel's work is the first attempt at a regional monograph to encompass the period from 1890 to the Holocaust. We do not have an exact bibliography of the Yiddish literary production of Galicia. Many names of authors published in Galician publications are often unfamiliar as there is a lack of complete copies of the publications. In any case, there are not the necessary pieces of information. The most representative of the authors are, however, included in the portion of Naygreshl's monograph. Especially successful is the chapter about Shmuel Yaskev Imber. It was placed in the correct historical perspective. The artistic value of Imber's poetry reached full aesthetic expression. Informative and very rich is the chapter about Yayne Krepl (1874–1941), which is written in a literary-historical style. Thus, the monograph possesses two styles and methods — a literary-aesthetic one and a literary-historical one. A separate chapter touches on the Yiddish literature and writings on public affairs in Vienna, which had more an ephemeral character having been created on less than favorable soil. In the final analyses, this is a very interesting work. If it should be possible to analyze bibliographically the rich periodicals in Yiddish that appeared in Galicia, there will be enough source material for a history from every perspective of the Yiddish literature, and maybe also theater, in Galicia. The last section of the book, pages 401 through 451, describes the Jewish community in Melits and is written by Yekhezkl Keytlman. This is a sort of descriptive sociology written by a native of the city, which will be of value only at such time when one can gather many description of this type. The history of Melits is barely touched upon, although several regional works about the city are in existence. Interesting are the details about Jewish nobility, Jewish occupations, Talmudic scholars, and the like. In the introduction to his piece, Keytlman writes that a "Polish encyclopedias" visited Melits. It has to be a contributor to an encyclopedia, because an encyclopedist means something quite different and has a much broader connotation. All told, the piece is interesting. From Yankev Pat's introduction to the collection, we learn that this is the first volume of a series which, among other works, will also print monographs regarding the Yiddish press in Poland, reminiscences, memoirs, etc. In general, the first volume is a success. Let us hope the succeeding ones will be even better.

Notes

1. Originally published as Jacob Shatzky, "*Yisker bikher,*" YIVO *Bleter:* 39 (1955): 339–355. David Trachtenberg translated the article from Yiddish into English. Thanks to YIVO for permission to translate and print the review.

2. See P. Kojsiewicz, *Kollatajalisty,* 1844, I 86; II, 287–289. *Pamietnik Literacki,* XII, 1913, 335–340.

3. See L. Baczko, *Reise von Posen durch das Konigreich Polen,* Leipzig, 1824.

6

A Survey and Evaluation of Yizker Books

Elias Schulman

It is said that when Simon Dubnov was hurled into a truck by the Germans to be taken to an execution spot, he appealed to those who were temporarily spared that they should write down what they experienced and what they saw.[1] Although the story is probably apocryphal, it is characteristic of the anxiety of the survivors to record their experiences. Emanuel Ringelblum felt the same urgency for setting down on paper what he saw and heard. By recording what the Germans were doing, he hoped future generations would remember and avenge. As a historian, he no doubt thought he was performing a historical act by keeping a diary. But Ringelblum was not the only one in the ghettos or extermination camps who had a feeling for history. There are numerous diaries, and many more undoubtedly were lost.

The feeling for recording experiences was shared by a great many survivors. As soon as some emerged from the forest and bunkers they began to collect material to put into written form. In Poland after the liberation, a primitive printing press was established, and the first pamphlets issued described ghetto incidents. Soon after the liberation by the American armies, data were being published in the D.P. camps by the survivors. A special journal made its appearance, entirely devoted to chronicling experiences. The editors went about accumulating information, interviewing the survivors, assembling the data, and checking and rechecking. The material thus gathered served as a basis for monographs and studies.

Not only those who lived through the Holocaust, however, deemed it their duty to keep a diary. A great number who had left their native towns and cities years earlier and settled in the United States, South America, or Israel felt impelled to recount life in their former home, now that it was completely destroyed. It was an expression of nostalgia for their youth and of compassion for those who perished. They began not only to record their own lives, but also to describe the customs, mores, and everyday life in the *shtetl*. This led to the appearance of numerous yizker books published by the various *landsmanshaft* groups in different parts of the world. They usually contain recollections about life in the *shtetl*, descriptions of important people, rabbis, scholars, and community leaders. They also devote considerable attention to synagogues, Hebrew schools, and diverse self-aid and communal organizations. Special events are recorded, such as a demonstration, pogrom, fire that destroyed a large part of the town, annual draft, or important fair. Special attention is given to the economic life of the *shtetl*. The different Jewish trades and occupations are discussed, as are Jewish business and commerce. Some writers dwell on the relationship between the Jews and their non–Jewish neighbors or between the Jews and the government officials and agencies. The rise of the *haskalah* movement, the early *maskilim*, and the controversy between traditionalists and progressives are detailed. The emergence of Zionism and the Jewish labor movement, the development of revolutionary activities among the Jews, and the great migration are all there. The class struggle between Jewish manufacturers and Jewish workers is not neglected, neither is the rise of Hebraism and Yiddishism. The establishment of modern Hebrew and Yiddish language schools, public libraries, trade unions, cultural clubs, singing societies, literary societies, theatrical groups, debating societies, evening classes for adults, and political groups and parties are also enumerated. From all these descriptions a paradigm and way of life emerge in clear outline.

Special sections in each yizker book are devoted to the Holocaust. The survivors describe their experiences and, in some cases, how they managed to remain alive. Each tale is poignant, and each episode is different; their composite unity combines into a syndrome of pain, anxiety, and horror. In some books, documents are reproduced, along with German orders, photographs of mutilated bodies, and even of executions. Other books list names of all the murdered inhabitants of the *shtetl*. Some of the books contain material about those who migrated and settled in the United States and include reports about the activities of the various *landsmanshaftn* or self-aid societies.

The yizker books vary in quality. Some are edited by specialists and contain important information; others by amateurs incapable of handling the material adequately. Some have analytical essays or studies; in others there is a lack of analysis of the sources. However, even the poorly edited and weakly written works add to our knowledge about the Holocaust and about the daily life in the *shtetl*. It is astonishing that this immense source about Jewish life on the eve of the Holocaust and about the Holocaust has for the most part been ignored by writers, researchers, and historians who have written about it in the Western languages. Some authors have ignored it out of lack of knowledge, others out of snobbishness. Whatever the reason, the loss is theirs and that of Jewish historiography.

Bibliographical Material

At present, there is no bibliography of yizker books, whose number is estimated to be around 500. In 1961, an exhibit of yizker books was held in Tel Aviv, where about 150 were shown. In the *Bibliography of Yiddish Books on the Catastrophe and Heroism* published in 1962, many yizker books are listed and their contents given, but the volume has no special section for yizker books. They are interspersed with other books. Besides, since the manuscript of the volume was published, numerous new books have appeared. The late Philip Friedman published a survey of this literature in the *Jewish Book Annual* (vol. 10, 1951–1952, Yiddish section); an earlier survey by him, "One Hundred Yiddish Books on Destruction and Bravery," was published in the *Jewish Book Annual* (vols. 8 and 9, 1949–1950, 1950–1951). Some yizker books are included in that survey. An omnibus review of fifteen yizker books was published by the late Jacob Shatzky in *Yivo Bleter* (vol. XXXVII, 1953). In the same issue, there is the article "Bibliography of Books about War and Holocaust" by Dina Abramowicz, which lists some yizker books. Bibliographies about the Holocaust are included in Shlomo Shunami's *Bibliography of Jewish Bibliographies* (Jerusalem 1965). Some of these lists include yizker books. The late Beryl Mark evaluated a number of books from a leftist point of view in *Yidishe Kultur*, New York, no. 6, June–July, 1964. Yizker books have been published in Germany D.P. camps, France, Australia, South Africa, South America, the United States, and Israel. The publications outside Israel are all in Yiddish, although a few published in the United States contain English summaries or a few English articles. Those published in Israel are mostly bilingual, Hebrew and Yiddish. Some are monolingual, either all in Hebrew or all in Yiddish. The material in the bilingual books is varied. Some articles are published in both languages and some in one language only. The material in the Yiddish section is usually more folksy and popular; whereas the Hebrew section tends toward more scholarly treatment. In the Yiddish sections, articles seem inclined towards the Jewish proletarian, trade unions, libraries, and labor Zionism, while emphasis in the Hebrew sections is on Zionism and Hebrew language activities. In the main however, both areas cover the identical milieu and identical personalities and institutions.

The published volumes are devoted mostly to Jewish towns in Poland, though a few are about Jewish towns in the Ukraine and Belorussia. Polish and Galician Jews have shown more interest in their native towns than have the Russian Jews. Naturally exceptions occur. There are books about Vitebsk, Slutzk, and other Russo-Jewish cities. As has been pointed out, most of the books have been published by *landsmanshaftn,* but some were issued at the initiative of individuals. In Israel, the Encyclopedia of the Jewish Diaspora Co. Ltd. was established to publish a memorial library. A number of massive volumes have been published in Hebrew, one about Brisk (Brest) also in Yiddish. The two volumes, *Lithuania,* in Yiddish, published respectively in New York, 1951 and in Tel-Aviv, 1965, are encyclopedic in scope. A group of Ukrainian Jews began an ambitious project to publish a series about Jews in the Ukraine. The first volume appeared in New York in 1961. The continuation of the project is not certain at this writing.

Among the editors of the various books were such scholars as Raphael Mahler, I. M. Biderman, the late N. M. Gelber, and Philip Friedman. There are also such writers as Solomon Bickel, Shimshon Meltzer, and Eliezer Steinman and such political persons as Yitshak Greenbaum. But many of the books were edited or compiled by amateurs and dilettantes. Some of the memorial volumes were written completely by individual writers. Examples of such works are *Bilgori* by Moshe Teitelbaum (Jerusalem, 1955) and *Lublin* by N. Shemen (Toronto, 1951). Under the title *Arim ve-Imahot be-Yisrael,* the Rabbi Kook Institute in Jerusalem published a series of books in Hebrew about various towns. Some volumes are devoted to an individual town like Brody or Stanislav; others deal with a number of places. Some of the books in this series describe the Holocaust; others tell only about life in the cities up to the outbreak of the Second World War. These studies and essays, written by various writers and scholars, vary in value.

In 1931, the Dubnov Foundation was established to publish a general and Jewish encyclopedia in Yiddish. Unfortunately this great project was not realized. But in the series *Jews,* part of the projected encyclopedia, two volumes devoted to the Holocaust were published. The first volume published in New York in 1963 deals with the destruction of the Jews in Eastern Europe and Germany. Unfortunately, the article dealing with the extermination of Polish Jewry is replete with errors and is written haphazardly. The second volume dealing with the destruction of the Jews in Central, Western, Northern Europe, and Greece was published in 1966 and is greatly superior to the previous volume. Some of the books mentioned here may be classified technically as yizker books; the majority, however, deal not only with the destruction of European Jewry, but also with Jewish life prior to the Holocaust.

Selected Yizker Volumes

It seems that Abaham Shmuel Hershberg (1858–1943), who had devoted a lifetime to Biblical studies, had a premonition of the impending doom of Jewish life in Białystok that compelled him to abandon his previous work and concentrate on recording for posterity the life of the Jews in this great center of Jewish life. He collected and systematized vital materials which he succeeded in mailing to New York before the outbreak of World War II. The manuscript was edited by Yudel Mark and published by the Białystok Jewish Historical Society in two volumes (New York, 1949 and 1950). A more ambitious task was undertaken by Jacob Shatzky in writing a history of the Jews in Warsaw. Unfortunately Shatzky did not complete his work; only three volumes were published, which tell the story of Warsaw's Jewry up to 1896. Nonetheless this work, published in New York, 1947–1953, constitutes a major achievement in Jewish historiography. Jacob Shatzky's three volumes describe the rise and development of the greatest Jewish city in Europe. From bits and fragments, he constructed a magnificent opus. Jewish life in Warsaw in the twentieth century and its obliteration are memorialized in a number of yizker books — as in the previously mentioned series: *Encyclopedia of the Jewish Diaspora* (Hebrew). The volume about Warsaw was edited by Yitshak Greenbaum (Tel Aviv, 1953). It contains important studies by I. Greenbaum, J. Leshtsinski, Z. Turkov, R. Vulman, N. Blumenthal, R. Auerbach, J. Kermish, and others. In the series issued by the Rabbi Kook Institute, a special volume was published about Warsaw (Tel Aviv, 1948). Written by David Flinker with an introduction by Rabbi Shlomo David Kohana, the last rabbi of Warsaw, it chronicles the history of the Jewish community from the beginning to its tragic end.

A collection of encyclopedic scope about Warsaw was published in Buenos Aires in 1955. It was edited by the late essayist, Yiddish translator of Don Quixote and editor, Pinie Katz. The volume consists of 1,352 tightly set columns. Various previous studies are included, as are new monographs by a number of scholars, some with leftist sympathies. It presents a picture of this great Jewish metropolis, with emphasis on the cultural and secular life. In order to limn a sketch of what these yizker books constitute, we will delineate the contents of a few typical books in these collections. The book about Czenstochove was published in New York in 1947 and was edited by Raphael Mahler. It has a history of the city by Jacob Shatzky and numerous studies and monographs about economic, cultural, and political life. It has descriptions of Jewish institutions and personalities and a record of anti–Jewish actions and the culminating destruction by the Germans. A book about Mlave, a city in Poland, was published in New York in 1950 and was edited by Jacob

Shatzky. In it, Dr. Judah Rosenthal has a history of the Jews in the city; Dr. Z. Yonis describes the town with its houses, streets, and places; and D. Krishtol relates his recollections about life in the town. There are articles about Mlave in the revolutionary year 1905; Mlave in Yiddish literature; and a description of various institutions, the library, and the educational system. Shatzky writes about Joseph Opatoshu the Yiddish writer, who was born in that city; Opatoshu himself is represented by a few literary items. There are also excerpts from the works from another native writer, Yaki Varshovsky. One writer's description of a well-known local family offers a fine picture of Jewish social and cultural life. Dr. Shatzky fully describes Jewish life in Mlave in 1939, just before the outbreak of World War II. His article is based on reports in the local Yiddish press. The book is rounded out with a record of the destruction of the Jewish community by the Germans.

The memorial volume to Kolomey, a town in Galicia, which before the First World War was part of the Austro-Hungarian Empire and later of Poland, was published in New York in 1957 and edited by Solomon Bickel. It includes a history of the Jews in the town by N.M. Gelber, along with essays, articles, and monographs about local Zionist and socialist movements, scholars, Halutzim, educational institutions, synagogues, hasidim, and a bibliography of books published. It, too, ends with a description of the destruction of the Jewish community.

A volume about the famous Jewish town of Chelm, which in Jewish folklore is known for its fools, was published in Johannesburg, South Africa, in 1951. It is a huge tome with the standard material and an interesting section on Chelm in Yiddish literature. Another imposing volume is to Lovitch, a city in Mazovie, edited by Shayak-Tchainezn and published in Tel-Aviv in 1966. It boasts a short history of the town written in English. Besides the standard features, it has a biographical dictionary of writers and poets born in that city. Descriptions of the town by Sholem Asch, Joel Mastboym, I.J. Trunk, and Nahum Sokolov are reprinted. The book to Gostynin was edited by I.M. Biderman and published in New York in 1960. It begins with a description of the city taken from official government sources and concludes with a list of all the Jewish inhabitants murdered by the Germans.

A volume of wider range is the collection about Horodenko, edited by the poet Shimshon Meltzer and published in Tel Aviv in 1963. It is in quarto format and has 430 double column pages. It is bilingual, with a brief introduction in English. Many collaborated in its production, but the effort was worthwhile. The history of the city and its rich religious and cultural life are described. There are also essays about the various political movements, educational trends, personalities, and recollections. There is a list of all people who perished at the hands of the Germans. The late Moses Einhorn, who edited a Hebrew medical journal, also edited the impressive Wolkovisker yizker book. It was published in New York in 1949. The two volumes comprise 990 pages. Although it is a collective effort, the editor himself wrote a 344-page study about the town, its institutions, and personalities. Dr. Einhorn also included a 90-page summary in English of his monograph about his native town.

Significance of Memorial Books

From the brief summaries of the books selected and mentioned, a pattern of what these volumes constitute appears. The volumes disclose a history of the towns, although it is not always written objectively. There are recollections and aura of nostalgia in these memoirs. From the articles about everyday life in the *shtetl* and from the reports about the institutions, political, and cultural movements, one can obtain a very good impression of the way of life. For the anthropologist and the folklorist, there is a great deal of authentic information.

From the personal records of the survivors one gets a comprehensive report of what actually happened when this flourishing life was crushed and the bearers of that unique civilization were destroyed. For those historians who aim to present objective, scholarly studies about the Holocaust there is abundant material. This material, written by survivors, should be critically evaluated and utilized for further studies. For the professional historian, many of the accounts may seem contradictory, but essentially they are not. The murder of the Jews was carried out in various ways and by many methods, and in the same town, various modes were employed. The honest and objective historian cannot afford to ignore this rich source of information. Thus far the histories of the Holocaust are of poor quality because this source material has not been adequately utilized. The conflicting accounts should in no way prevent the historian from making use of them and from arriving at an objective appraisal of the events. Preparatory to a final evaluation of Jewish behavior in the ghettos and concentration camps, the historian is duty bound to read the books written mostly by simple folk who led a simple life and died like martyrs.

Finally, a few words are in order about Dr. N.M. Gelber who died in Jerusalem on September 23, 1966, at the age of 75. Dr. Gelber was a historian of note who wrote extensively about the Jewish past in Poland. He wrote his doctoral dissertation at the University of Vienna about the Jewish participation in the Polish Uprising of 1863. His last years were devoted to recording the history of the Jews in the various towns in Poland. His studies were penned exclusively for yizker books, about twenty-five were enriched by his excellent monographs.

Note

1. Originally published as Elias Schulman, "A Survey and Evaluation of Yizkor Books," *Jewish Book Annual* 25 (5728/1967–1968): 184–191. Thanks to the Jewish Book Annual for permission to reprint the original.

7

"Memorial Books" as a Source for Research into the History of Jewish Communities in Europe

Abraham Wein

Ever since the war years (1939–1945), European Jews viewed the commemoration of the past as a task of great importance in the struggle of the Jewish people to survive.[1] The aspiration to leave behind some sort of memorial evidence for future generations found its expression during the period of the Holocaust in the collections of documentary material, the underground archives of Ringelblum and his associates in the Warsaw Ghetto, the underground archives of Mersik-Tenenbaum in the Białystok Ghetto, various research projects, the diaries of everyday life, and the poems, songs, and stories that express the feelings of those facing destruction. All this activity continued and expanded after the liberation. Historical committees were set up in Lodz, Munich, and other places to gather the documentary material and collect the evidence and testimonies of the survivors themselves; these committees also published material relating to the Holocaust period. Survivors and emigrants from the destroyed communities in all parts of the world met together with the purpose of attempting to perpetuate the memory of the past. They continued the age-old tradition of concluding an era by recording its history; this was done for the sake of preserving the cultural and national value of the past, as well as transmitting its lessons to future generations.

This role, which had been performed in earlier periods by various chroniclers and scholars, was now an enterprise in which thousands from all classes and strata of the nation participated from political leaders and intellectuals to ordinary people having some sort of knowledge of their community and its past. They felt very deeply that professional historians in their analytic and synthetical research would not be able to encompass the problem in its enormity; meanwhile, their contemporaries whose own memory was an invaluable source of rich information would gradually pass away. As a result of this commemoration project, approximately 400 memorial books for different European communities, mainly to Eastern Europe, were published between 1945 and 1972. Survivors from the communities of Western Europe, especially Germany, continued the local tradition of Jewish historiography and have published approximately 70 memorial books, mainly monographs or anthologies written in European languages, mostly German, and in most cases, the work of one author.[2] Those works will not be dealt with in this article.

This survey will discuss memorial books of a special type, namely those prepared by editors and writers, who in the majority of instances were not professionals but rather were members of *landsmanshafn*, emigrants' organizations in Israel and the Diaspora.[3] Since there has not yet appeared a general bibliography of memorial books, we have seen the need to gather data on such books and publish them separately.[4] Scattered in newspapers and magazines are short reviews of memorial books, which usually only examine the contents and pay attention to the editors and publishers and do not provide actual criticism. Among the few critical articles to have appeared, it is worthwhile to single out the articles by Jacob Shatzky on 27 memorial books.[5] He used comparative material, and as an experienced historian who was well versed in Jewish historical bibliography, he has been able to take a quite critical approach as well as to point out overlooked material. In his introduction, he writes:

> A number of memorial books are rather detailed in regard to the last period, the epilogue of Jewish life in different cities and towns; the prologue, however, and the earlier scenes in the permanent drama of Jewish history which sometimes lasted entire generations are neglected and discarded to a forgotten corner.... The majority of memorial books therefore are in fact chronicles of the final period. It is there that they abound in a wide range of material. The sacred desire to perpetuate the memory of each figure and each thing in order that at least a shadow of immortality will remain seems to burst forth from these pages.[6]

Sometimes, however, due to lack of space or perhaps haste, Shatzky simply jots down marks of good or bad in evaluating the books. Shatzky did, however, devote a deep and inclusive review to N. M. Gelber's *History of the Jews of Brody 1584–1943* (Jerusalem, 1955) and to *Pinkes Warsaw* (Buenos Aires, 1955).[7]

A different category of critical review is found in Sara Neshamit's "The Story of the Partisans in Memorial Books."[8] In that article, she explores specifically what the memorial books to the communities of Lublin, Bilgoraj, Sherpts,

Kurow, Markuszow, Miedzyrzec, and Zelechow contribute to the documentation on Jewish participation in the partisan movement. As stated above, only a few critical reviews have actually appeared on the subject of memorial books, and it is regrettable that historians and professional writers, as well as ethnologists, sociologists, and folklorists have not given their critical observations, which could have prevented many of the mistakes and defects. The first memorial book appeared during the very crucial time of the Holocaust in 1943.[9] However, it seems that the volume in memory of the martyrs of Felshteen published in 1937 set the example for the present pattern of memorial books.[10] A unique memorial book was published in a displaced persons camp in Munich, 1947 in memory of the destroyed community of Sherpts; although written in Yiddish, it was printed in Latin letters.

According to geographical distribution,[11] the vast majority of memorial books are dedicated to communities of East European Jewry, Poland, the U.S.S.R., Rumania, Lithuania, Czechoslovakia, Hungary, and Latvia; only a few are dedicated to the Jewish communities of southeastern Europe, Yugoslavia, Greece, and Bulgaria. The books also contain chapters to approximately 230 smaller communities, giving the history of each settlement from its beginnings to its destruction. A single, uniform index to the approximately 150,000 printed pages, covering their tables of contents, persons, and places, has not yet been worked out.

Approximately 7,000–8,000 writers and 1,000 editors participated in the writing and editing of these memorial books. Committee members and contributors also number in the thousands. Sometimes the editors decided from the outset that the memorial books were designed solely for members of the emigrants' society of their city and the material used to portray the history of their community was chosen to suit their emotional concepts of the past. With no intention of depreciating the value and contribution of the memorial books to the research of the history of East European Jewry, it has to be admitted that some of the shortcomings of the books lower their general value.

Within the framework of this article it will be impossible to exhaust the topics raised in these books in their entirety. Various subjects, such as ways of life, folklore, cultural life, religious life, demography, economics, and social and political life preceding the period of the Holocaust, may only be hinted at here, although the books are extremely abundant in material of this type. The topics under discussion in this article deal with the Holocaust years and the period after it, specifically, the resistance movement and the uprisings, collaborators with the Germans from among the conquered peoples, the righteous gentiles who helped to save Jews, concentration and forced labour camps that are not well-known to the general public, the fate of the refugees from Poland, Lithuania, and other countries who fled to the U.S.S.R., the history of the communities re-established after World War II, both the legal and illegal immigration to Palestine, and Holocaust survivors in the struggles and war for Israel's independence. Various questions on methodology will be discussed, such as editing, language, recording of testimony, choice of material, and other topics.

The editing of the memorial books was usually assigned to members of the community who may have had some previous experience in writing. However, some editors were historians, professional writers, or social scientists. In those cases, the memorial books reach the level of a historical monograph, as is the case for Nowy Sącz, Rzeszow, Otwock, Piotrkow, and others. Noteworthy contributions were made by some important people who recorded their reminiscences. For instance, the book to Stolpce was honored by the article "My Stolpce" written by Z. Shazar, President of the State of Israel; the book to Plonsk includes an article by David Ben-Gurion called "My Youth in Plonsk." A series of articles dealing with the history of Sarny was written by the eminent contemporary Jewish historian, B.Z. Dinur. Other memorial books have reprinted, and thus made accessible to a larger number of readers, articles by these great Jewish historians of Poland: M. Balaban, I. Shipper, M. Shorr, and E. Ringelblum. Among other the important historians who dedicated much effort to perpetuating the memories of various communities are J. Shatzky, P. Friedman, and N.M. Gelber. Gelber's body of work is quite extensive. Examples of his publications are *History of the Jews in Stanislawow, History of the Jews of Brody 1584–1943, History of the Jews of Rohatyn, Annals of the Jews of Rzeszow, History of the Jews of Zolkiew, History of the Jews of Kalisz, History of the Jews of Zloczew, History of the Jews of Lwow, History of the Jews of Tarnopol from the End of the Nineteenth Century, History of the Jews of Lutsk,* and others.

Memorial books are enriched by the comprehensive research articles of a number of historians who were contemporaries of the Warsaw group *Yung Historiker* [Young Historians]. These include R. Mahler's penetrating and exhaustive monograph on the history of the Jews of Nowy Sącz and his article "On the Hassidim of Sacz"; I. Trunk's *History of the Plotsk Community From the Mid-Seventeenth Century Until the First World War* and *History of the Jews of Lublin*; N. Blumenthal's *On the Holocaust of Lublin*; J. Kermish's *Plotsk Jewry under the Nazi Rule*; and A. Homet's *On the History of the Jews of Tarnow*. It is also worthwhile to mention Sh. Ettinger and Ch. Schmeruk's *On the History of the Jews of Krzemieniec* and Y. Goldberg's *History of the Jews in Wielun* and *History of the Jews in Zdunska Wola*.[12]

Sometimes historians concentrated their research on a specific area of community life. M. Sh. Geshuri wrote many articles on the lives of rabbis and hasidim, on liturgical music, and on religious life in Lwow and Cracow.

Similarly, due to his expertise, Dawidowicz contributed well-researched materials on the synagogues in Lancut and Krasnobrod.

Not all the books, however, reached such a high standard. It is astonishing that some editors took upon themselves the task of editing books from widely-scattered communities. For instance, D. Shtokfish edited books on Kazimierz, Kutno in central Poland, Rohatyn in Podolia, and others; and A. Sh. Stein edited books on Krzemieniec, located on the eastern border of Poland, on Radom in central Poland, and on Bedzin near the western border. The qualitative difference between articles is another matter. In the book to Krzemieniec, the important work of Sh. Ettinger and Ch. Shmeruk is placed next to articles and accounts of inferior value by authors who did not even bother to use the rich material accessible in the Jewish, Polish, and Russian press. In several instances, the sloppiness of the editing is very blatant, and there are signs of carelessness in the handling of documents. For example, in the book to Zoludek and Orlowa there are extracts from Baruch Levin's diary in Yiddish, along with a Hebrew translation. The Hebrew translation, "edited and supplemented," differs completely from the Yiddish. The following is an extract from the Yiddish diary with a literal translation into Hebrew, and then the Hebrew translation.

> In Yiddish: "I left my escorts standing about 100 meters from the railroad track. Mishka and Dimka were covering me. I left Vanka Trubach to keep a watch on the railway that passed above. I began digging underneath the tracks. At the height of the digging Vanka Trubach turned to me and said, "Baruch, the train is coming closer."[13]

> In Hebrew: "I had my two escorts stand to my right and left, each one watching in one direction which led into the distance. I began digging with much fervor, as if my hands were performing some sacred task. It seemed to me as if not only my heart but my digging hands were re-living, in those minutes, the memory of the town which had been wiped out, the memory of my daughters, of my wife and my father. While I was still in the midst of digging, and mediating on mourning and revenge, I suddenly heard Trubach calling to me: "Baruch, I see that a train's coming in the distance."[14]

The book to Wisniowiec was edited with needless haste and carelessness.[15] It contains speeches given at various occasions, eulogies, and even the homework of pupils from the school in Israel that adopted this community. Why did the editor include the speech of the Binyamina school principal at the adoption ceremony[16] and the schoolchildren's compositions?[17] Additionally, the section commemorating those survivors who died in Israel includes a rather banal eulogy delivered at the graveside of Sarah, the daughter of David Roynik.[18] Also, the last chapter of the book includes the speech by A. Auerbuch under the heading "Survivors of Wisniowiec in Israel and America (Reflections

During a Party in my Honor, Tel-Aviv, 1969)." And finally, a considerable portion of the book is comprised of articles, reviews, and memoirs printed in Hebrew and Yiddish.

Most memorial books were edited by functionaries among the community's survivors. It should be noted that in the majority of cases, they used the popular and traditional style of the genre. Nevertheless, they followed good editing practices, placed the articles in chronological order, and included suitable illustrative material. For example, in 1954 the survivors of Troki published a memorial book, which included memoirs, short articles on the community's life and history, institutions and personalities, a step-by-step description of the persecution and destruction, and a list of martyrs. The book, only 79 pages long, is modest and concise. Lacking more material or more authors willing to make contributions, the editors did not try to include irrelevant material.

More than once, however, a book has been printed without any distinction between factual material and articles that speak only of grief and agony. The yearning for the past may cause the writers to see everything in glowing colors; persons and figures are taken out of their natural context and presented to suit descriptions of Jewish tradition and way of life. Instead of emphasizing and accentuating the specific detail or person, the books are full of longing for mother's Sabbath, stereotyped figures like the water carrier, the village fool and the entertainer, and related topics. Out of a desire to give those who survived a distinguished and well-presented memorial book anything that comes to hand is included, sometimes due to pressure exerted by people making a financial contribution to the book's publication. The rules for the use of documents, memoirs, testimonies, and evidence are not always followed. Even a rather casual perusal of a bibliography could have prevented mistakes and filled in gaps. Note that the contents and value of a memorial book as a source for research into a community's life and history is not determined by the community's importance or by the size of the survivor organization but rather by the views of those who directed its editing and publishing. A glaring example of inferior editing is *Pinkes Warsaw.*[19]

An exceptionally fine memorial book written in Dutch and only 125 pages long is the volume dedicated to the Jews of the Netherlands.[20] Shatzky writes in his review:

> This is a memorial book in the full sense of the word. This is not a book which bemoans a city, but rather mourns the loss of a special style of life, a special form of Jewish community that had already begun to decline before the Holocaust and disappeared completely only after the great destruction.[21]

The memory of Belchatow, a small town in Poland within the district of Lodz, has been perpetuated in one of the most becoming memorial books in terms of its contents and quality of editing. In contrast, the book dedicated to Lask, a town in the same district, a "mother of Israel" with a splendid past and many rabbis and scholars, is weak in content and quite poor in external appearance. The editor did not even use the rich material on Lask and its well-known figures that is found in P.Z. Glicksman's book.[22]

Frequently editors faced obstacles that could not be overcome. In the foreword to the memorial book of Olkieniki, the editor, Sh. Farber, writes:

> It must be pointed out from the outset that we have no delusion of giving a scientific, historical evaluation of our small town, nor are we presenting to the public distinguished literary material. Most of the material comes from the painful hearts and soul-yearning of the older generation who witnessed the Holocaust and desired to erect some kind of memorial to their city.[23]

A similar feeling is expressed in *Pinkes Kowel* in the closing words of the editor-in-chief, B. Baler:

> We decided from the outset that this chronicle was not to be written by a professional writer or journalist, but instead by an ordinary member of the community. We wanted the chronicle to be written by someone who personally knew the town and its people, to be written not in a literary style but in a simple language telling the facts and events which really did occur. Afterwards the historian may come and extract from this book the information that he needs.[24]

A rather strange, but typical approach of publishers and editors, is illustrated by the remarks of L. Markowitz in his article "Yosef Tennenbaum" in the book to Tomaszow-Mazowiecki:

> The memorial book committee decided in one of its sessions not to write about the poor behavior of certain Jews in Tomaszow toward those who lived in the ghetto or toward camp prisoners. But we would be in error were we not to speak of those who tried to help the Jews, and of their good and kind deeds which sometimes endangered their lives. To this category of people belongs Yosef Tennenbaum.[25]

In the introduction to the second volume of the book to Pinsk, the editor, B. Tamir-Mirsky, writes:

> Unlike the first volume, which was the work of historians, in this volume we have tried to illustrate the last fifty years of the community's life, based not on objective research, but rather on testimonies, impressions, memoirs, and the recollection of actual experiences.[26]

The above shows that many editors of memorial books tried hard to distinguish between "objective" historical research and the sources for historical research. However, there were many cases in which writers and editors did not distinguish between different types of sources or did not handle them properly from the perspective of methodology or editing. Sometimes differences between memoir and article are not distinguished; testimonies and evidence were reworded and rewritten; literary works were presented to the reader as memoirs, and original sources such as diaries, letters, or documents were printed without proper editing.

Below are a number of examples of defects in the editing or the preparation of materials. In the book to Radoshkowitz, within the section "From Bygone Days," a summary of the book of memoirs of a Lithuanian rabbi from the year 5548 (1788) is included erroneously.[27] As the historian I. Halperin points out: "The editors did not realize that this book, which came out in Paris (1950), is not a book of memoirs but rather a story in the form of memoirs."[28]

Another curious example is that as a result of a misunderstanding or neglect to clarify material before it was sent to the printers, the distribution of the book to Tarnogrod was delayed for about six years. The book was printed in 1966 and distributed in 1972. The reason seems to lie in the criticism of the former chairman of the *Judenrat*, Sinai Groyer, who was active in the emigrants' society in New York. Pasted to an article by N. Krummerkopf, also active in the emigrants' society, regarding the activity of the *Judenrat* chairman Sinai Groyer that reads: "It is spoken of with much bitterness," there is a typewritten note dated May 2, 1972, which states among other things: "We have no direct or indirect knowledge of any kind of information that would throw suspicion on the personality of Sinai Groyer."[29] A longer and more detailed explanation is found on three additional typewritten pages appended to the book.[30] Apparently N. Krummerkopf's article and S. Groyer's protest caused a scandal in the emigrants' society. The dispute was brought to a *bet din* [rabbinical court] of justice and peace of the Board of Rabbis of Boro Park, Brooklyn, N.Y., whose ruling of 1967, as well as the declarations of several survivors of Tarnogrod who were saved by S. Groyer, are printed in the appendix to this book for some reason.

The articles selected for the book to Cieszanow cause some astonishment.[31] Apart from some rather doubtful chapters of memoirs and verse, the book also carries an article by T. Friedman who tries to give an historical evaluation of the Holocaust period. A similar article by M. Kaufman is entitled "How Many Traitors Does the Jewish State Need?" This is a review of the latest book by Uri Avneri. Surely a platform other than a book dedicated to the memory of the community of Cieszanow could have been found for polemics of this kind.

A lack of discrimination in quality of material and inadequate classification, as well as a tendency to embellish books by pompous and pretentious phrasing, disturb the discerning reader. In the book to Hrubieshov,[32] the section captioned "Memoirs" stands out even though the caption's meaning is not readily understood given that most of the other sections are basically memoirs too. Another section in the book is dedicated to "Hassidism, Legends and Tales, and Poems." The book to Zablotow[33] contains the pompous title, "The City and the Dead — Zablotow, the Populous and the Destroyed." The book's main article that spans pages 9–100 and discusses the history of the town and its inhabitants during the last 150 years bears the title "In the Streets of the City." Incidentally, it is worthwhile to note that this article is reprinted almost in its entirety in Yiddish as well.

The main article in the book to Zinkow is "The Geographical Setting of Zinkov and its Public Life."[34] It is difficult to understand how the author can handle a combination of two such unrelated topics. In the foreword to the book to Kosow Poleski, the editors note: "Herein is given the scroll of agony of the community and its sons ... details are related by Meir Kolishevsky."[35] It is clear that anyone wishing to use the book as a source will find difficulty in separating the details from the narration.

Memorial books are as a rule written in Hebrew and Yiddish, but it is impossible not to note needless trouble in printing the same material in the same book in the two languages, sometimes in an inferior or unfaithful translation.[36] The argument that there are readers who know only one of the languages is not reasonable. It should be pointed out that linguists and lovers of Yiddish may find much of interest in the different varieties of style and working of the articles, some of them replete with the idioms of a provincial Yiddish.

Despite all the faults, mistakes, and deficiencies in the writing and editing of these books, it must be emphasized that the memorial books contain more information and data on the life of East European Jewish communities than all other publications in this field that have so far been published.

Memoirs and testimonies printed in the memorial books hold a very important place as source material for research into the history of the communities and the characteristic ways of Jewish life in Eastern Europe. These memoirs and testimonies are the life of Eastern Europe. These memoirs and testimonies are the records of Holocaust survivors themselves or of Jews who emigrated from their hometowns. Their value as source material depends on the ability of the authors to distinguish between the relevant from the irrelevant as well their general orientation and erudition in the period concerned.

The testimony gathered from survivors of the Holocaust immediately after the war by Jewish historical committees set up in Cracow and Munich, as well as in other places, have vital documentary value. This work continued through the 1950s and through today by the Testimony Department of *Yad*

Vashem; the memorial books have published much of this. This material encompasses a period of over seventy years; it supplements other sources for the study of the history of Jewish community life between the two world wars. The material also fills in our knowledge of what took place in smaller towns and villages during the Holocaust since the books contain information on the process of extermination, Jewish resistance and the organization of cultural life within the ghettos and small settlements, forced labor camps, and the participation of the Jews of the small towns and settlements in the armed struggle.

Memorial books include original documents that were originally in archives or private collections. For example, the book to Jampol contains extracts from the Register of the Burial Society from 1746 to 1753, which had been in the hands of the society's treasurer, Sh. Lerner. The book to Wegrow has documents from the court's register from the end of the eighteenth century; and the diary of Rabbi Jerushalimsky written during World War I is printed in the book to Kielce. In the book to Cracow, there are extracts from a diary dealing with Jewish self-defense in the city during 1918–1919; and the records of the communal council from 1919 appear in the book to Sokolka.

Diaries written during the Holocaust appear in a number of memorial books. The book to Lesko and Ustrik contains Hinda Schwarz's diary; the book to Mizocz contains several pages from Yitzhak Berg's diary; the book to Czortkow includes a chapter from Gerta Hollander's diary; the book to Wlodzimierz has Moshe Margalit's and Shmuel Shatz's diaries; the book to Rubiezewicze has the diary that Sara Fishkin's kept from July 22, 1941 until May, 16th, 1942; and the book to Radomsko includes the diary that Miriam Roshtchewitzky began writing at the age of 16 in 1941 and stopped on October 17, 1942.

Another type of document found in memorial books is the correspondence between public organizations and between individuals during the Holocaust period. For example, the correspondence between the *Judenrat*, the "Joint," and the public assistance organization is printed in the book to Falenica. The book to Zolkiew contains the letters of Yosef Rosenberg written in the city's ghetto and the Janowsky camp near Lwow; the last letter of Ben-Zion HaCohen Rappoport to his only son appears in the book to Nowy Sącz. Letters from the Jews of Plotsk sent from deportation and found in the Ringelblum Archives are reprinted in the book to Plotsk. The book to Kowel contains the sentences that the town's Jews wrote on the synagogue wall before being led to their deaths. Many books include documents from the archives of *Yad Vashem* or the Jewish Historical Institute in Warsaw.

Useful and good work was performed by the editors of the Sącz, Pinsk, Stolpce, Plotsk, and other books who took pains to find and reprint rare items from newspapers. Among these are articles that appeared in *Hatzefirah*, *Hamelitz*, and *Hatzofeh*, as well as in the world-wide Jewish press during the Second World War.

Illustrative material occupies an important place in memorial books. Sometimes there are hundreds of photographs, maps, sketches, and other types of illustrations in a single book. That material complements the written word, capturing the general atmosphere of the town, its synagogues, institutions, and organizations, and personalities and types that characterized East European Jewry. It is regrettable that in more than a few cases, editors reproduce photographs of individuals or families who contributed financially to the book's publication. This transforms the memorial book, or part of it, into some kind of album. This is also true for the obituary sections, where sometimes too much space is assigned to generous donors. At times, words of praise are added for relatives who hold important positions in the emigrants' organization.

Poems also appear in memorial books. Among the poems are the writings of known poets, as well as amateurs; some poems are reproduced from earlier publications. Researchers will be interested, however, only in those poems actually written during the Holocaust, offering a type of evidence about the mood and state of mind of the victims of the Holocaust. Sometimes poems describe actual events. Examples are the poem by Lusia Fuks, a girl of 15, written in the Sborov ghetto in 1943 and printed in the book to Jezierna or the poem by T. Trushinky written in Uzbekistan in 1943 and published in the book to Krzemieniec. Literary critics, ethnologists, and folklorists will find much of interest in the stories and accounts of traditional Jewish atmosphere and modes of life.

The basic value of memorial books resides in the rich factual material of which they are woven. Moreover, researchers will find a great deal of data and information likely to contribute to the elucidation of important topics in the historiography of the Holocaust period. Several such topics are touched upon here.

Jewish participation in the armed struggle against the Nazis and their collaborators

Nearly every memorial book discusses Jewish resistance and armed struggle. One can classify the articles, testimonies, evidence, and memoirs on this subject into several groups. First, there is much factual material on the revolts in the ghettos and camps and on the resistance of individuals and groups. These are some examples: in the book to Rubiezewicze, Yehiel Segalowitch's "How We Revolted"; in the book to Rzeszow, B. Lazar-Stein's "The Daughter of Rzeszow Rebels"; in the book to Lukow, Sh. Rubinstein's "Resistance in the Lukow Ghetto" and Sh. Huberman's "The Jews of Lukow Fight"; an entire series of articles on the uprising in the ghetto in the book to Lachwa; in the book to Latvia, Y. Kaplan's "Arms in the Riga Ghetto"; in the book to Lutsk, Sh. Shilo's "The Uprising on the Eve of the Liquidation of the Camp in Lutsk"; in the book to Janow, A. Apelbaum's "The Heroism of Lazar Ratnalski"; in the book to Tarnow, H, Hornstein's "Memories of the Revolt in the Tarnow Ghetto" and Y. Kener's "How Miriam Korn Died a Hero's Death"; and in the book to Cracow, A. Bauminger's "Insurgents in the Cracow Ghetto." Some books contain material on the participation of fellow townspeople in the revolts in the Warsaw, Białystok, and other ghettoes, as well as in camps.

The richest and most detailed material deals with Jews who fought with partisans. There is no memorial book for any community in eastern Poland, Byelorussia, Lithuania, the western Ukraine, or the region of Lublin, Kielce, and Warsaw that does not include a section or several chapters on Jewish fighters in partisan units. At times, there is also material on the participation of Polish Jews in the French Partisan movement. Examples from the book to Wieruszow are A. Lusner's "Listings of Jewish Partisans in France" and E. Ne'eman's "Facts from the Period of the Resistance in France." The book to Kazimierz includes Sh. Rosenberg's "Story of a Partisan in the French Resistance Movement."

A third category of material deals with the Jewish soldiers in the Soviet, Polish, French, and Czechoslovakian armies. For example, the book to Subcarpathian Ruthenia contains the article "The Jews of Subcarpathian Ruthenia and the Czech Legion"; the book to Lowicz includes a list of Jewish soldiers from Lowicz who fell in the ranks of the French Army. In the book to Lutsk, there is M. Schuldner's "On the Jews of Lutsk in the Soviet Army," and in the book to Rakow, there is Sh. Avni's "In Russian Captivity and in the Polish Army." These testimonies and articles carry information of great value on the difficulties encountered by Jews and on the anti–Semitism of their comrades-in-arms. That material is not contained in official documents and publications. There is also information on Jewish fighters who hid their Jewish identity by adopting a Polish, Czech, or other name.

The fate of Jews in the extermination, concentration, and forced-labor camps

In addition to material on the large camps on which much has been written, such as Auschwitz, Maidanek, Treblinka, Chelmno, Buchenwald, and Stuttfhof, memorial books abound with information on minor labor camps, which were set up alongside the cities and small towns of Poland, Lithuania, and the Soviet Union and which have not yet been described in monographs or in research studies. Examples include the Rozwadov work-camp, Lysa Gora near Cracow, Stopki, Amsee near Poznan, Pole Tomaszowskie near Koziniec, Konin in the Poznan district, Smolensk, Mogilew, and Minsk-U.S.S.R.

The attitude of the non–Jewish population to the Jews; righteous gentiles who helped and saved Jews

Nearly every description of the expulsion and the extermination of daily life in the ghettos and camps and of attempts to escape to the forests and to the Aryan side contains remarks on the attitude of the local population, namely, Polish, Ukrainian, Russian, Lithuanian, German, and others, towards the Jews. Facts on collaboration with the Germans and indifference to the tragedy engulfing their Jewish neighbors are noted; incidents are also related when local people helped to save Jews, and in some these books reminiscences of righteous gentiles are found. For example, the memorial books of Chorostkow, Krynki, Krzemieniec, Kamien Koszyrski, Pinsk, and Tluste describe how Poles and Ukrainians plundered and looted the Jews and handed them over to the murderers, as well as stories of Jews who escaped from the ghettos or the transports to the death camps. Next to these narratives are found stories of gentiles aiding Jews and of the self-sacrifice, at times at the risk of their lives, of individuals and even of entire groups trying to save Jews. In the book to Frampol, Stanislaw Sobczak relates how he hid and saved twelve Jews; in the book to Zloczew, a German named Joseph Mayer, the official in charge of the city's supply and agriculture, tells how he saved Jews; a Polish woman, and the book to Kozienice records how a German Dr. Neumann saved many Jewish lives.

The position of the Jews in the cities of the Western Ukraine and Byelorussia (Polish territory until 1939) under Soviet rule (1939–1941); the fate of Jewish refugees throughout the U.S.S.R. during World War II

The memorial books carry important source material, for instance, testimonies, diaries, and memoirs, as well as articles and reviews on Jewish life and events in the areas annexed to the Soviet Union in September 1939. That type of material may be found in the books to Kowel, Przemysl, Rokitna, Lida, Wysotsk, Krzemieniec, Rohatyn, and Latvia. Among other material, articles on the Zionist underground and illegal immigration to Palestine during the period of Soviet rule appear in the books to Ciechanowiec and Lida. Most fascinating are the recollections of refugees who fled into Russia and provide first-hand information on the work camps and the life of Jewish prisoners in Siberian exile, the Ural mountains, and Central Asia. Some examples are as follows: in the book to Chmielnik, Y. Weiman's "In the Soviet Camps"; in the book to Jezierna, L. Fischer's "A Wanderer in an Alien Land"; in the book to Lida, Y. Gnuzowicz's "Pages from the Expulsion (Exile to Siberia in 1940)"; in the book to Latvia, "Latvian Jews in Siberian Exile"; in the book to Wyszogrod, E. Holländer's "Martyrdom in Moscow"; in the book to Kolno, H.T. Grabowicz's "From the Nazi Snare to the Soviet Snare"; in the book to Radzyn, Sh. Ahikam-Fein's "With My father, Rabbi Fein, in Russia"; and in the book to Tomaszow Lubelski, Ch. Y. Lerer's "The Saved Remnant in Russia." Information on the fate of Polish refugees in the U.S.S.R. may be found in the memoirs and recollections of soldiers in the Red Army and in the Polish Army organized within the Soviet Union.

Immigration (legal and illegal) to Palestine and survivors who fell in the battle for Israel's freedom and independence

Much may be found on the Zionist movement and immigration to Palestine until the Holocaust period relating to the *aliyah* movement and to the *kibbutzim* and pre-*aliyah* preparation centers located throughout Poland. In addition, most memorial books carry lists of survivors who arrived in Palestine, participated in the underground, and fell fighting for Israel's independence.

History of the community after the Holocaust

Some memorial books contain articles on the post-war years. In the book to Plotsk, there is the article "Attempts at Rebuilding the Saved Remnant"; in the book to Subcarpathian Ruthenia, there is Sh. Y. Freilich's "The Jews of Subcarpathian Ruthenia after World War II"; in the book to Kielce, there are articles and newspaper reports on the pogrom and slaughter of June 1946; and in the book to Cluj, there is a review of the community's position following the liberation from the Nazi occupation. There are memorial books that give information on the fate of the survivors and on those institutions and historic monuments remaining in the community.

The project of commemorating the Jewish communities of Eastern Europe still continues. It may be assumed that the increased immigration from the U.S.S.R. will widen our knowledge on all areas of the Soviet Union and will help to fill the gaps in Soviet Jewish history. Complete and detailed bibliography of all memorial books due to appear within the series of the bibliographical project of Hebrew books will certainly contribute to research in this field.[37]

Notes

1. Originally published as Abraham Wein, "'Memorial Books' as a Source for Research into the History of Jewish Communities in Europe," *Yad Vashem Studies on the Eastern European Catastrophe and Resistance* 9 (1973): 255–272. Reproduced by permission of Yad Vashem Publications.

2. For critical reviews of books on Jewish communities in Germany, see G. Lowenthal, "In the Shadow of Doom, Post-War Publications on Jewish Communal History in Germany," *Year Book XI*, Publications of the Leo Baeck Institute, Jerusalem, New York (1966): 306–333; *Year Book XV*, 1970: 223–245.

3. This article, as well as the bibliographical list, are based upon memorial books found in the Yad Vashem Library and the National and University Library in Jerusalem.

4. David Bass, "List of Memorial Books Published in the Years 1943–1972," *Yad Vashem Studies on the Eastern European Catastrophe and Resistance* 9 (1973): 273–321.

5. J. Shatzky, *"Yizker Bikher,"* YIVO Bleter (Yiddish) Vol. 37 (1953): 264–282 and Vol. 39 (1955): 339–355.

6. Shatzky, *Yizker Bikher,* Vol. 39: 266.

7. J. Shatzky, *"Yiddishe Kehiles un Yishuvim — Referaten un Rezensies"* [Jewish Communities and Settlement — Reports and Reviews], *YIVO Bleter* (Yiddish) Vol. 40 (1956): 238–254

8. *Yedioth,* Ghetto-Fighters' House, Kibbutz Lohamei Hagetaot, (Hebrew), Nos. 1–2 (18–19) April 1957: 35–43.

9. *Lodzer Yiskor Book*—"Memorial Book of Lodz" (Yiddish), NY, 1943.

10. *Felshteen zamelbuch zum andenk fun die Felshteener kdoshim* [The Felshteen Volume in Memory of the Martyrs of Felshteen], edited by the Book Committee of the Association of Felshteen (Yiddish) New York, 1937.

11. Acording to the borders of 1939; in the case of Czechoslovakia—1938.

12. We do not list the names of all the authors and their articles.

13. *The Book of Zeludok and Orlowa, A Living Memorial* (Hebrew, Yiddish), Tel Aviv, 1967.

14. Ibid., 184.

15. *Wisniowiec Memorial Book* (Hebrew, Yiddish), Tel Aviv (year unknown).

16. Ibid., 33.

17. Ibid., 34–38.

18. Ibid., 232–234.

19. *Pinkes Varshe* [Warsaw Memorial Book] Buenos-Aires, 1955 (Yiddish). Shatzky wrote a depreciatory critical review of this book.

20. H. Beem, *De verdwenen mediene, This Holy Community* (Dutch), Amsterdam, 1950.

21. Shatzky, *"Yizker Bikher,"* Vol. 37: 282.

22. P.Z. Gliksman, *Ir Lask Vehachameha* [The Town of Lask and Its Sages] Lodz, 1926, (Hebrew).

23. *Olkieniki in Flames,* A Memorial Book (Hebrew, Yiddish), Tel-Aviv, 1962.

24. *Pinkes Kowel* [Kowel Memorial Book] Buenos-Aires, 1951 (Yiddish), 510.

25. Note: No reference was given by Wien in the original essay.

26. Note: No reference was given by Wien in the original essay.

27. *Radoshkowitz, A Memorial Book* (Hebrew), Tel-Aviv, 1953.

28. I. Halpern, *Eastern European Jewry, Historical Studies* (Hebrew), The Magnes Press, Hebrew University, Jerusalem, 1968, 325 (Note 62).

29. *Memorial Book—Tarogrod* (Hebrew, Yiddish), Tel-Aviv, 1966, 318.

30. Ibid., 490–491.

31. *Cieszanow Memorial Book* (Hebrew, Yiddish), Tel-Aviv, 1970.

32. *Pinkas Hrubieshov, Memorial to a Jewish Community in Poland* (Hebrew, Yiddish, Polish, English), Tel-Aviv, 1962.

33. *The Town and Its Martyrs—Zablotow Alive and Destroyed* (Hebrew, Yiddish), Tel-Aviv, 1949.

34. *Zinkover Memorial Book* (Hebrew, Yiddish, English), Tel-Aviv and New York, 1966.

35. *Memorial Book of the Kosow Poleski Martyrs* (Hebrew), Jerusaleum, 1950.

36. Some of the books were written in German, Hungarian, and Dutch. See the bibliographical list on pages 273–321 of this volume of *Yad Vashem Studies*.

37. Our thanks are due to Mr. M. Piekarz for his advice and help and for his readiness to place at our disposal the bibliographical list of memorial books to be published within the Bibliographical Series Project of Yad Vashem.

PART III

STUDIES OF YIZKER BOOKS

8

Reception of Memorial Books in Poland

MONIKA ADAMCZYK-GARBOWSKA

Recognizing the Genre in Poland

Nachman Blumenthal in the Lublin yizker book of 1952 recalls his dreams from the partly liberated Poland when he and his colleagues from the newly established Jewish Committee of Jews in Poland hoped that it would be possible to rebuild the Jewish community on a relatively large scale. They estimated that a quarter of a million Jews would return from the Soviet Union, at least one hundred thousand would emerge from the Aryan side that was still under the Nazis, and at least another one hundred thousand would be liberated from German concentration camps. At the time, Blumenthal and his colleagues did not yet know about the destruction of the Lodz ghetto, so they thought that there were still a number of Jews living there. Altogether then there would be a half million large Jewish community. That meant in ten or fifteen years there would be one million Jews in Poland, and "so life will go on contrary to the wishes of enemies!"[1]

But all this did not happen due to various factors, among them progressive Stalinization and the dissolving of all Jewish political parties, as well as anti–Semitism, the major manifestation of which was the pogrom in Kielce of 1946. If Blumenthal's dreams and hopes had turned out to be true, probably survivors after settling down again in their home cities and towns would have in time come up with their own memorial books created with the financial and editorial help from various *landsmanshaftn* scattered all over the world. But due to the political and economic situation only two memorial books were published in Poland, specifically to Vilno and to Łuków, both published in Lodz in 1947.[2] Later there were only some contacts between *landsmanshaft* associations and organizations and/or individuals in Poland. For example, Ber Mark, the director of the Jewish Historical Institute in Warsaw in the years 1949–1966, contributed to a number of volumes and reviewed them for American Yiddish press.[3] In the Frampol memorial book, there is a testimony from a Pole who rescued several Jews and remained in friendly correspondence with them after the war.[4] There are also Polish articles in the memorial books dedicated to Wieliczka, Ostrog, Wiślica, Skarżysko-Kamienna, Busko, Konin, and Hrubieszów.

But for many years, except to a few specialists, yizker books were almost unknown in Poland. One of the main obstacles was certainly the linguistic barrier, but even books in English or partially in English were hardly accessible. In Polish historical monographs and other works on Jewish topics, especially those concerning regional history, published in the 1980s and 1990s, there are references to yizker books. Sometimes regional historians would go to the Jewish Historical Institute in Warsaw and search through the books with the help of librarians. The late Adam Bielecki, who worked there for many years until his death in 2001, deserves kudos in this respect as he would translate or summarize parts of them on a voluntary basis.

As far as the availability of the volumes, the Jewish Historical Institute has the largest collection of original books. In 2000, a collection of books, both originals and reprints, devoted to communities from the Lublin region was developed at the Center for Jewish Studies of Maria Curie–Skłodowska University, and in 2008, the Institute for Strategic Studies in Krakow established a collection of 247 reprints.

Some articles published within the last years in Polish have drawn readers' attention to memorial books. The first scholar to write extensively about yizker books in Polish was the Polish-Israeli ethnographer Olga Goldberg-Mulkiewicz.[5] Additionally, there are some more general and popular publications by Sylwia Bojczuk, Monika Adamczyk-Garbowska, and Aleksander Klugman.[6] A special edition of the cultural quarterly *Akcent* based in Lublin contained information about and a selection from two Biłgoraj volumes.[7] Also, some specialized articles and bibliographical guides have been published.[8] So far, two complete Polish editions of yizker books have been published in the country, along with an anthology from various books. There are also some works in which authors use some parts of yizker books, for instance, Kazimierz Dolny or Pruszkow.[9] The genre became better known to the general public after the publication of Jan Tomasz Gross's book on the pogrom at Jedwabne of July 1941, because Gross refers to the Jedwabne memorial book.[10]

Ostrołęka, or Reaching the Consciousness of Poles

Sefer kehilat Ostrolenka, originally issued in Tel Aviv in 1963 by the town's *landsmanshaft* in Israel, was the first full edition of a yizker book translated into Polish and published as a joint initiative of two local societies, namely Towarzystwo Przyjaciół Ostrołęki [Society of the Friends of Ostrołęka] and Ostrołęckie Towarzystwo Naukowe im. Adama Chętnika [Adam Chętnik Academic Society of Ostrołęka], in cooperation with the Ostrołęka *landsmanshaft* in Israel. The project was largely financed by Dr. Zalman Drezner, born in Ostrołęka, who treated it as a gift to his hometown.

Apart from the original text, the Polish edition contains additional prefaces by representatives of the Polish and Israeli sides, postscripts, and a glossary of Hebrew and Yiddish terms. The Polish editors stress that they tried to make the translation as faithful as possible with regards to the content, as well as the linguistic and stylistic aspects. They admit that a number of texts might be perceived as controversial or very subjective, often dictated by bitter feelings, but the editors decided to leave them to the readers to judge. They state that the book documents various examples of cooperation between Poles and Jews, manifestations of philo– and anti–Semitism, as well as various attitudes of Jews towards Poles, specifically, a lot of positive feelings but also resentment and even enmity. It includes the image of Polish behavior during the war as it was remembered in the memory of survivors. Furthermore, the editors state that various views and opinions expressed in the book show both human virtues and vices. Poles may be proud reading some parts and ashamed reading others. The editors emphasize the fact that the Polish edition was prepared with a multifold purpose: to serve as a source for the study of the town and the region, to educate young generations of Poles to bring Poles and Jews together, and to teach tolerance and respect for the common past and warn against dangers.[11] They also emphasize the role Dr. Drezner played in the fulfillment of this project:

> He presented us with a unique story of everyday existence of our former co-citizens, the Jewish inhabitants of the town of his childhood. Dr. Drezner's work is a result of genuine love for Ostrołęka. Such an effort can be undertaken only by those who are able to speak with the language of the heart and understand difficult things, who cherished the places where they were born, who know how to teach others how to overcome prejudices, those who are very fond of Poles.[12]

All these explanations, which might seem Polonocentric to the Western reader, testify to the delicate nature of Polish-Jewish relations and the editors' concern for the proper understanding of the whole undertaking. It is interesting to juxtapose the words of the Polish editors with those of the project's main initiator and sponsor who apart from presenting the book in detail and thanking a number of people for their help and hospitality during his half year stay in Ostrołęka finds it necessary to declare:

> Perhaps the Republic of Poland and the State of Israel, the countries to the development of which Polish Jews contributed so much, will be an example of humane and civilized relations between the states and nations.... I consider it proper and necessary to state at this point that in spite of all things that my nation has experienced on the Polish land in the recent decades I still believe in a genuine and noble Poland. I was strengthened in my conviction due to my contacts with institutions and individuals of present day Ostrołęka and the fact that three Polish families from the Ostrołęka district were awarded the title of the Righteous among Nations. All this was the main stimulus to undertake the translation of the Book into Polish. I want to believe with all my heart that the Polish edition of the yizker book will be an honorable work to commemorate the Ostrołęka Jews of Blessed Memory and will reach the consciousness of many Poles so that in Polish homes they will eventually think with warmth and fondness about the living and the murdered, who like Christians were created in God's likeness and image.[13]

These words show the emotional tenor of the writer and prove how important for survivors is the awareness that their communities, which cannot be revived, will at least be duly commemorated in the place that they had flourished for many years before they met their tragic end.

Biłgoraj, or the Paradoxes of Genealogical Search

The Biłgoraj volume was published on the initiative of the Isaac Bashevis Singer Association, which is active in the town. For this purpose, members of the association contacted the Center for Jewish Studies at Maria Curie-Skłodowska University in Lublin and the association of Jews of Biłgoraj in Israel. This cooperation permitted maintaining the high standard of the edition. The translation is supported with numerous notes and a glossary of Jewish terms, as well as with additional archival photographs. There are also indexes of proper names and places. In contrast to the Ostrołęka volume, the project was fully subsidized by Polish sources, the funds supplied by Janusz Palikot, a businessman and politician born in Biłgoraj, and academic institutions including the Committee for Academic Research [Komitet Badań Naukowych] and the Foundation for Polish Science. The Polish edition is accompanied by four short prefaces: by the representative of the Singer Association; by *landsmanshaft* members, including one former inhabitant and a second generation representative; and by translator's and editor's note. Nothing was changed or omitted from the original, but occasionally, when there was a need, clarifications were added. It is interesting that even before the book was published, the translation evoked some interest beyond Biłgoraj. For example, it was thanks to the Polish translation that an American diplomat Daniel Gedacht discovered his cousin in Israel. Since he does not know Hebrew and the original does not contain an index, it would have been very difficult for him to search through the original edition. Although he does not know Polish, the translation in the electronic version enabled him to find the needed data very quickly. This is what he writes about his discovery:

> Others will write about the historical value of this book from a Jewish perspective, or from a Polish standpoint, or from a Biłgoraj point of view. I'd like to add another: the personal perspective. My grandfather was born in Biłgoraj in 1909, immigrated to the United States 6 months later, and never looked back. He died before I was born, so I never heard anything about the old country. I always assumed that my entire family had left Poland about the same time as my grandfather, in the first quarter of the twentieth century. Ellis Island's website confirmed this, showing that a six-month old Kalman (later Charles) Gedacht arrived in the United States in 1910 with his mother and siblings, one year after his father, Isaac Meir Gedacht. Subsequent cousins arrived in 1921. And that, I thought, was that. My surname is rare and all Gedachts in the United States are related. As far as I knew, beyond us no others existed. Upon receiving the Polish translation of this book, the first thing I did was search for my surname, expecting no results. Seeing "Isaac Gedacht" among other names being lined up in the square in 1940 to march off to a labor camp made me do a double take. Isaac Gedacht? My great-grandfather had left thirty years earlier! Who was this other Isaac? His mere presence in Poland in 1940 meant that perhaps other Gedachts had stayed ... and survived? Did I have cousins I knew nothing about? Searches in online archives like JRI-Poland and Biłgoraj's Civil Records Office told me that yes, there were others. What had become of them? Did they all perish in the Shoah? Did he survive? Did he have children? I visited the Jewish Historical Institute in Warsaw to see their archives. The only record of a survivor Gedacht turned out to be Kielman, who registered with the Central Committee of Polish Jews in Lodz in 1946. What happened to him after that? Through the help of Biłgoraj residents who are active in commemorating the town's Jewish past, I learned that there is a group of Biłgoraj survivors and descendants in Israel. I sent this organization an e-mail, and immediately received a response that he personally knew this Kielman Gedacht in the 1960s, when they both lived in Netanya, Israel. Further communication told me that Kielman had children, who currently live in Jerusalem. I *did* have cousins! Finally, in January 2007 I went to Israel to meet my cousin Moty Gedacht. Moty's father, Kielman, was the aforementioned Isaac's brother and the nephew of Kalman (my grandfather), although they never met. Kielman had survived the war hiding in Ukraine and Russia, then in the late 1940s made his way to Argentina, where he had a family, including Moty. They immigrated to Israel in the early 1960s. Three months earlier I hadn't even known of his existence, and there I was

hugging my cousin. We even have a certain family resemblance. And this was all started by a passing reference to a man, just one among many, in the journal from Biłgoraj in 1940. They say that each of the six million victims has his or her own individual story. Isaac Gedacht helped reunite cousins, more than sixty years after his death.[14]

For Israel Bar-On, whose father Shmuel Bron came from Biłgoraj and contributed largely to the original volume edited by Abraham Kronenberg, writing the preface to the Polish edition was "an opportunity to publicly honor the memory of a community of Jews that also happen to be [his] roots," as he writes in his reflections, "Infected by the Obsession to Cultivate the Memorial for Those Who Are Gone."[15]

Until July 2007, Bar-On had never been to Biłgoraj, as he was born when the war already ended, but he was exposed to the stories about the town through his father's memories. He states that after establishing his life in Israel, his father

> like many others, never considered the possibility of visiting Poland again and particularly Biłgoraj. Nothing could convince him to do so. The most obvious reason was that he could not set foot on the ground that symbolized for him the cataclysm and the most terrible, most cruel Jewish disaster in human history. Another, more touching and personal reason, was that the Biłgoraj of old does not exist anymore ... it was totally wiped out along with the Jewish congregation, and he wanted to remember it until his last day like it used to be.[16]

He admits that his involvement with the Biłgoraj of the past and today manifested by his active participation with the survivors' organization ended with being "infected" in order to

> cultivate a memorial for those who are gone, for those who once lived there, for those whom their parents could not open up and tell the painful past, and for our children who may ask questions and need to get honest answers.[17]

Bar-On also sees that this task is important not only for Jews, but also for

> the non–Jewish population of Poland who should know about the Jewish people who lived along with them, who worked, contributed and developed important cultural milestones before they lost their lives by a human systematic murder machine.[18]

Time will tell how the book will be received by the present Polish inhabitants of Biłgoraj. Undoubtedly they will enjoy reading nostalgic pieces in which Jewish authors recall with love their hometown or will learn with curiosity and amazement of various personages, including famous rabbis on the one hand and eccentrics and *meshugeners* on the other, but they might not be too happy to read that "Biłgoraj was a Jewish town" or object to some bitter comments about Poles' behavior during the Holocaust, the more so that some names are mentioned of people who denounced Jews and whose descendants might still live in the town of today. Some may also read the fragments and interpret them to support their prejudices that the "Jews ruled Poland." Statements like "all trade was in Jewish hands" may be interpreted differently when it is a reflection of pride of the survivors that they were so important for the development of their town and by some Poles with anti–Semitic sentiments who will read them as proof of former Jewish dominance.

Pruszków, or Commemorating Abel

An excellent example how material from yizker books may be incorporated into new books is a monograph about the Jews of Pruszków written by Marian Skwara and published by the local library. This is a work by an amateur historian who through this volume wanted to commemorate the Jewish population of his hometown. He considers this a moral imperative for he is convinced that a sense of humanity obliges present Polish inhabitants to openly face the tragedy that befell a large group of their co-citizens. To support his claim he quotes from the famous essay by the eminent literary critic Jan Błoński (1931–2009), published in the liberal Catholic weekly *Tygodnik Powszechny* in January 1987, which was a breakthrough in Polish Jewish relations and stimulated a number of important discussions:

> To purify after Cain means, above all, to remember Abel. This particular Abel was not alone: he shared our home, lived on our soil. His blood has remained in the walls, seeped into the soil. It has also entered into ourselves, into our memory. So we must cleanse ourselves, and this means we must see ourselves in the light of truth. Without such an insight, our home, our soil, we ourselves, will remain tainted.[19]

Skwara states that *Sefer Prushkov, Nadazhin ve-ha-sevivah*, published in Israel in 1966, was the richest source for his monograph. He admits that this is the only publication that gives both a general idea and many details about the life of the prewar Jewish community of Pruszków. He found an interesting formula of incorporating into his own text large fragments from the yizker book in smaller print marked as if with commemorative frames. Moreover, he often refers to the yizker volume in his commentary. This is what the distinguished Polish literary historian and writer Michał Głowiński, himself a Holocaust survivor, originally from Pruszków, states:

> I think with gratitude about Marian Skwara's initiative, who decided to write a documented history of the Jews of Pruszków. Pruszków was not a traditional *shtetl*, nevertheless Jews constituted several percent of the town's inhabitants.

They lived their own lives, worked, many of them struggled with poverty, prayed, had all kinds of problems, some of them emigrated. The book tells us about everyday Jewish life, worries and customs, points at places important for this community, the community which was almost completely annihilated. Marian Skwara with both a sense of engagement and diligence tells us about this community and brings it back to memory, preserves the traces. He deserves a lot of credit for this![20]

Kazimierz on the Vistula, or Getting to Know the Jewish Community from the Inside

An anthology of texts about Kazimierz on the Vistula was my first more serious encounter with yizker books.[21] The idea of the anthology is to show how the picturesque place was represented in Polish and Jewish literature in various languages. A great deal of information about the life of the Jewish community of Kazimierz may be found in *Pinkas Kuzmir*, the 700-page yizker book published by the Kuzmir *landsmanshaft* in Israel in 1970 and edited by Dovid Shtokfish with much help from Kazimierz born Shmuel Leib Shneiderman, a Yiddish journalist who also wrote a separate book on the town. This also served as a guide to literary sources as the literary section is especially rich in this yizker book because of the fact that the town attracted so many writers. Altogether more than a dozen texts or their fragments translated from Hebrew and Yiddish were taken from the yizker book, covering a larger area of themes, including poems by Zusman Segalovitsh; memories by Pola Ilon Shenderovitsh, Tova Liberman-Shor, and Pnina Herzog (Pola Rubin); an article by Avu Pnina's about painter Israel Shmuel Wodnicki; a whole plethora of Kazimierz Jews presented by Shimen Chelmish (Shlaferman) and Sara Chelmish-Vizenberg; and dramatic reports about returns after the war by Naftali Fayerstein or Mordecai Tsanin. Not to mention that a number of other texts by well-known Yiddish writers like Leyb Rashkin, Yakov Glatstein, Y. Y. Trunk, and Shneiderman himself were tracked down to some extent thanks to the information contained in the book. For contemporary Polish readers, this opens a completely new perspective and lets them see the Jewish community from the inside. So far Polish readers would mainly learn about Kazimierz Jews from works by Polish authors, especially Maria Kuncewiczowa, who although very positively inclined towards Jews before the war and expressing her grief after the Holocaust, nonetheless maintained the typical outsider's look at the community, which she perceived as exotic and foreign, especially the Jewish religious customs. As Eugenia Prokop-Janiec rightly observes

> the Jewish porters, boatmen, and merchants in [Kuncewiczowa's work] are seen from the Polish perspective, and mostly in the context of their contacts

with Poles.... The Polish perspective is particularly noticeable in the presentation of Jewish culture and the "estrangement has an obviously religious character." ... The contrast between the synagogue and the church is the contrast between the Old and the New Testament, between the impatience of waiting and the joy connected with the fulfillment of the messianic prophecies.[22]

By contrast, *Pinkas Kuzmir* permits the reader to know the Jewish perspective, which often varies dramatically from the Polish and Christian one.

Introducing Yizker Books En Masse

My work on the Kazimierz anthology led me to another much larger project, which was conducted with my colleagues, the historian Adam Kopciowski and the art historian Andrzej Trzciński. Together we amassed an anthology of more than 160 texts from approximately eighty yizker books.[23] A few texts were written originally in Polish, but most of them were translated into Polish from Yiddish, Hebrew, and English. The aim of the anthology was to create a large panorama of yizker books and supply a tool for researchers, to stimulate interest in yizker books throughout Poland, and last but not least, to create a readable book. The anthology was prepared within a research project of the Polish Scientific Committee (KBN) under the title *Jewish Memorial Books (Yizker Bikher) as a Source of Knowledge on the History, Culture, and the Holocaust of Polish Jews,* conducted at the Center for Jewish Studies of Maria Curie-Skłodowska University in Lublin. Its publication was preceded by the separate publication of the bibliography whose updated version is included in the anthology.[24]

The anthology consists of an introduction, a rich selection of texts, a bibliography of yizker books, a bibliography about yizker books, a glossary of Jewish terms, and indexes to places and names. The texts were divided into the following sections: "Instead of a Matzevah," "My Shtetl," "Everyday Life," "Cultural Life," "Around the Synagogue," "Characteristic Figures," "Traditions versus Modernity," "They Have Achieved Fame in the World," "With Poles for Better and Worse," "At Turning Points in History," "Between the Legend and the Truth," "At the Threshold of World War II," "The Holocaust," and "Returns and Farewells." Each section contains seven to twenty texts. The anthology is richly illustrated with images taken from the memorial books in which the selected texts were originally published, as well as from other sources. It also contains a map especially prepared for this purpose with all the towns, villages, and cities within the borders of the Second Polish Republic that possess yizker books marked on it. This is the first map of this kind that has been created to date. Originally we planned to include approximately 350 texts from around 110 books. Eventually, we published less than half of the selected texts from two-thirds of the selected books.

Although our volume was to some extent inspired by Jack Kugelmass and Jonathan Boyarin's English-language anthology, we show not only towns and villages but also large cities including Warsaw, Krakow, or Lviv and political, social, and cultural life, much of the everyday existence of small towns and their individual peculiarities. Since it was prepared with the Polish reader in mind, it naturally contains some texts on Polish-Jewish relations and also pieces that we considered particularly interesting for Polish readers, for example, showing them a different perspective. And thus we included a text on Szczebrzeszyn in which the author explains the Hebrew etymology of the name of the town, which although legendary, shows the deep ties of Jews to Poland, as well as Chelm stories, so well known in Yiddish folklore and practically unknown in Poland. It also includes a rich selection of texts on postwar visits of survivors to places bereft of Jews, sometimes containing very dramatic and bitter comments. So far the anthology has met with much interest and positive response; time will show whether it will bear fruit in the form of subsequent publications. Ideally, each Polish city or town that has a yizker book could adopt it, or them, as some possess more than one book, and translate and publish either the entire book or at least some parts. Such a publication is being prepared in Lublin now concerning the Lublin yizker book from 1952.

Delayed Polish Memorial Books

Yizker books have already played an inspirational role. The best examples in the West are Theo Richmond's *Konin: A Quest* about Konin; Yaffa Eliach's *There Was a World* about Ejszyszki; and Eva Hoffman's *Shtetl* about Brańsk.[25] Richmond, whose family originated from Konin, learned Yiddish and Hebrew in order to read the memorial book from his ancestral hometown, along with other materials. As he explains, his own book constitutes a return to the place where he had never been and about which he knew very little; he only knew that his family originated from the place. However, while living in London, he felt more and more that in a sense he was a former inhabitant of Konin:

> that other town [i.e. Konin], also set on a river, has always coexisted alongside [London] — its unofficial twin. I felt that I was in some way an ex-citizen of that town, an exile. What I did not know was that one day it would in a sense, reclaim me and that its pull would be irresistible.[26]

Responding to the pull, he spent more than ten years collecting materials for his work, which at the same time constitutes a new memorial book of the town and a journey in search of his identity.

In Poland, a number of decades have passed before a new phenomenon appeared resulting in publications that may be called delayed memorial books. They are results of searches of individual authors or groups of people, usually of the postwar generation, who began to discover the genuine, multidimensional history of their hometowns and realize that those places were very different before the war. Sometimes these publications are inspired by Jewish memorial books and their aim is to supplement and/or even shape the memory. For instance, Jerzy Bojarski, who initiated such a publication in Lublin, explains his aim as follows:

> We, the inhabitants of Lublin must not forget that here in Wieniawa, Podzamcze, Kalinowszczyzna, and Piaski [parts of Lublin — author's note] there lived a large Jewish community with its culture, religion, and customs. The streets of Szeroka, Krawiecka, or Jateczna no longer exist but it is our duty to remember about the Jewish Town.[27]

Bojarski, a historian by education, was a member of the City Council at the time of the book's preparation so in a sense acted from a position similar to that of many Jewish editors of memorial books. Like many of them, for his project, he recruited a number of journalists, academics as well as other people, both Jews and Christians, who still remembered Jewish Lublin. And thus, with his sense of duty and a moral imperative to commemorate the people and places that perished, he resembles the editors of Jewish memorial books or authors like Richmond, but his situation is somehow the reverse. Living in London, Richmond had close contact with the community where the memories of Jewish Konin were very vivid, but he himself had never been there. The authors of the Lublin book edited by Bojarski (the title in English translation is *Paths of Memory*) were born and raised in that concrete place where earlier Jewish life had flourished for centuries, but they did not know anything about that past because to a large degree it had been erased.

Searches of this kind may also lead to more personal reflections. For instance, in a moving essay commemorating the Jewish inhabitants of his native town, Arkadiusz Pacholski, born in Kalisz, formulated a thought that could be applied to various other places:

> I am looking at my Kalisz through the window and I am asking myself a question: which Kalisz is real, the one from before September 1939 or the one of today? If the former one, then other questions arise which boggle the mind. Where are the 27 thousand Jewish inhabitants of Kalisz? Is the contemporary Kalisz an illusion? Is it possible that my life — which is undoubtedly real — is taking place in some fictitious theatrical scenery? And if today's Kalisz is real after all, then were the 27 thousand Jews living here 60 years ago merely a hallucination?[28]

And all those reflections were inspired by the images from the Kalish memorial book that someone sent to him from Israel.

We might hope that each town or city already commemorated in a yizker book finds at least one follower like Richmond or Bojarski. Such publications are often loaded with emotion, but also contain some meticulous research and in a sense respond with a delay to the call of the survivors who by publishing their volumes wanted to leave a testimony, fulfill their duty to commemorate the dead, and leave something that would document both the Holocaust and the world before. Thus, considering what we already know about yizker books, we may look at them from different points of views.

For the authors, their families and *landsmanshaftn* they were (and still are because some books are still being compiled) a way of commemorating their relatives and communities as a whole. Some of them were written with more personal intentions, to leave something for the children and grandchildren (e.g. we often encounter comments from the editors that this particular volume should be part of the home library of the people from a town or city), others had an awareness of the historical significance of their undertakings. For instance, in one of the prefaces to *Khurbn Biłgoraj* we read that by his work, the editor Abraham Kronenberg added a "stone to the future monument which Jewish historians [would] erect in the future describing with a pen the sufferings of Jews in the days of Nazi gloom."[29]

From the modern American or Israeli point of view, yizker books serve as sources of information about the communities for research or personal interests. But the books are also very important for the Polish audience, both the academic and general ones. Although most memorial books focus on the Jewish life, and in some you get an impression that almost no Gentiles lived in those cities and towns, or even if they lived there, they are regarded as unimportant. For example, the Biłgoraj book mentions that one did not feel anti–Semitism in the town because the town was Jewish, but we also find out that Jews constituted sixty-five percent of the population. This means that there was still a sizeable Polish minority about which almost nothing is mentioned. By contrast, some volumes do have separate chapters on Jewish-Christian relations. And in general it is interesting to juxtapose these accounts with the Polish ones from the 1960s and 1970s when Jews are barely mentioned, even if they constituted the majority. Not to mention the reasons I have already mentioned in the contexts of the Polish books on Jewish Lublin and Jewish Kalisz.

Last but not least, yizker books and later volumes inspired by them are definitely important from an educational point of view, no matter in which country. I cannot think of other sources that in a relatively condensed form give such a comprehensive multidimensional account of the Holocaust and the life before. Many educators increasingly emphasize the fact that Holocaust cannot be taught in separation from the earlier history. When you see the richness of the Jewish life, the more you see the scope of its destruction and this is exactly the message most yizker books do convey.

To partly answer the question about the significance of yizker books, let me quote the remarks Elias Schulman made in his 1968 article "Survey and Evaluation of *Yizker* Books." Since that time some substantial research has been done, of course, but there is still a great deal of reserve and prejudice against yizker books, so I think his words have not lost their validity:

> The yizker books vary in quality. Some are better edited by specialists and contain important information; others by amateurs who are incapable of handling the material adequately. Some have analytical essays or studies; in others there is a lack of analysis of the sources. However, even the poorly edited and weakly written works add to our knowledge about the Holocaust and about the daily life in the *shtetl* (I would add city as well — author's note). It is astonishing that this immense source about Jewish life on the eve of the Holocaust and about the Holocaust has for the most part been ignored by writers, researchers and historians who have written about it in the Western languages. Some authors have ignored it out of lack of knowledge, others out of snobbishness (or both — author's note). Whatever the reason, the loss is theirs, and that of Jewish historiography.[30]

One could add that not only Jewish historiography, but historiography of the twentieth century in general, and from my point of view, definitely a loss for Polish historiography. Fortunately, in recent years there has been more and more interest in this genre. Apart from the examples given above, I am aware of translation projects concerning the books of Sierpc, Zgierz, Pińczów, and Szczekociny. In the documentary *Po-lin: Okruchy pamięci* [Polin: Scraps of Memory] by Jolanta Dylewska released in November 2008, the director uses a number of fragments from yizker books for her commentary of archival photos incorporated into fragments of prewar documentary footage about Jewish life in various regions of Poland. Altogether the viewer receives a kind of collective yizker book in motion. The Museum of the History of Polish Jews that is currently being built in Warsaw makes use of yizker books for its web page (see especially www.sztetl.org.pl) and planned exhibitions. We can hope then that gradually Jewish memorial books and their Polish supplements will become a permanent part of the landscape of memory in contemporary Poland.

Notes

1. Nakhman Blumental, "Lublin nokh der tsveyter velt-milkhome," in *Dos bukh fun Lublin* (Paris: Parizer Komitet fun Shafn a Monografye vegn Yidishn Yishev in Lublin, 1952), 595.

2. See *Bleter vegn Vilne: zamlbukh*, ed. L. Ran and L. Koriski (Łódź: Farband fun Vilner

Yidn in Poyln bay der Tsentraler Yidisher Historisher Komisye, 1947) and *Lukover kdoyshim un heldn: yizker oysgabe*, ed. Moyshe Tirman (Łódź: Algemayne Komitet fun Lukover Yidn bay der Tsentraler Yidisher Historisher Komisye in Poyln, 1947).

3. See Beryl Mark, "Yizker-bikher, vos baveynen un vekn tsum kampf," *Yidishe Kultur* 6 (1964): 25–29.

4. See Stanisław Sobczak, "Vi azoy kh'hob oysbahaltn tsvelf Yidn," in *Sefer Frampol*, ed. David Shtokfish (Tel Aviv: Vaad ha-Sefer, 1966), 304–307.

5. See "Itineraria miasteczek żydowskich," in *The Jews in Poland*, ed. Andrzej K. Paluch (Kraków 1992), 387–395; "Księgi pamięci ("Memorbuecher") a mit żydowskiego miasteczka," *Etnografia Polska* 2 (1991): 187–199; "Miejsce i dom w zbiorowej pamięci Żydów polskich," in *Budownictwo i budowniczowie w przeszłości*, ed. Andrzej Abramowicz and Jerzy Maik (Łódź: Instytut Archeologii i Etnologii PAN, 2002): 515–521; "Miejsce, którego już nie ma," in *Stara i nowa ojczyzna. Ślady kultury Żydów polskich, Łódzkie Studia Etnograficzne* XLII (2003): 55–85; "Stara ojczyzna w nowej ojczyźnie. Pojęcie ojczystego miejsca w tradycji polskich Żydów," in *Stara i nowa ojczyzna. Ślady kultury Żydów polskich, Łódzkie Studia Etnograficzne* XLII (2003): 17–43.

6. See Sylwia Bojczuk, "Księgi Pamięci — geneza i charakterystyka," *Scriptores — Pamięć-Miejsce-Obecność* 1 (2003): 73–75. See for example, Monika Adamczyk-Garbowska, "Żydowskie księgi pamięci i ich współczesne kontynuacje," in *Odcienie tożsamości — literatura żydowska jako zjawisko wielojęzyczne* (Lublin: Wydawnictwo UMCS, 2004): 106–121. An earlier version of this article was published in the *Akcent* quarterly (see note 7). See Aleksander Klugman, "Pomniki z papieru," *Karta* 38 (2003), 140–145. See Sylwia Bojczuk, "Księgi Pamięci — geneza i charakterystyka," *Scriptores — Pamięć-Miejsce-Obecność* 1 (2003): 73–75.

7. See *Akcent* 93, 3 (2003), a special issue devoted to the town of Biłgoraj and the Singer family.

8. See Anna Dobranowska, "Teren nieistniejącego," *Forum Europejskie* [Instytut Europeistyki UJ, Kraków] 14 (2007), 50–62; Joanna Lisek, "Problematyka kobieca w księgach pamięci (Na przykładzie Pińczowa)," *Literatura Ludowa* 4–5 (2008): 53–62. Also see Alina Skibińska in cooperation with Monika Polit, "Księgi pamięci," in her *Źródła do badań nad zagładą Żydów na okupowanych ziemiach polskich. Przewodnik archiwalno-biblioteczny* (Warszawa: Centrum Badań nad Zagładą Żydów, Wydawnictwo Cyklady, 2007): 370–377; *Księgi pamięci gmin żydowskich — bibliografia/A Bibliography of Jewish Memorial Books*, ed. Adam Kopciowski (Lublin: Maria Curie-Skłodowska University Press, 2008).

9. Marian Marian, *Pruszkowscy Żydzi. Sześć dekad zamkniętych Zagładą* (Pruszków: Powiatowa i Miejska Biblioteka Publiczna im. Henryka Sienkiewicza w Pruszkowie, 2007).

10. See Jan Tomasz Gross, *S siedzi: historia zagłady żydowskiego miasteczka* (Sejny: Pogranicze 2000) and its American edition, *Neighbors: The Destruction of the Jewish Community in Jedwabne, Poland* (Princeton: Princeton University Press 2001).

11. See Janusz Gołota and Jadwiga Nowicka, "Przedmowa do wydania polskiego," in *Księga Żydów ostrołęckich*, ed. Icchak Iwri et al., translated into Polish by Anna Ćwiakowska, Zalman (Zenek) Drezner, and Szoszana Raczyńska (Ostrołęka-Tel Aviv: Ostrołęckie Towarzystwo Naukowe im. Adama Chętnika, Towarzystwo Przyjaciół Ostrołęki, Ziomkostwo Ostrołęckie w Izraelu, 2002), 21.

12. Ibid., 22.

13. Zalman (Zenek) Drezner, "Wstęp do wydania polskiego," in *Księga Żydów ostrołęckich*, 27.

14. Daniel Gedacht, unpublished note, 2007.

15. See Israel Bar-On, "Owładnięty obsesją zachowania pamięci," in *Zagłada Biłgoraja — księga pamięci*, ed. Abraham Kronenberg (Gdańsk: słowo/obraz terytoria, 2009), 7–8.

16. Ibid., 7.

17. Ibid., 8.

18. Ibid.

19. Skwara, 11. For the full English version of Błoński's article, see Jan Błoński, "The Poor Poles Look at the Ghetto," *Polin* 2 (1987): 321–336.

20. See Skwara — book back cover.

21. See *Kazimierz vel Kuzmir: Miasteczko różnych* snów, ed. Monika Adamczyk-Garbowska (Lublin: Wydawnictwo UMCS, 2006).

22. Eugenia Prokop-Janiec, "Kazimierz on the Vistula: Polish Literary Portrayals of the Shtetl," *Polin: Studies in Polish Jewry,* 17 (2004): 236.

23. See *Tam był kiedyś mój dom... Księgi pamięci gmin żydowskich,* ed. Monika Adamczyk-Garbowska, Adam Kopciowski, and Andrzej Trzciński (Lublin: Wydawnictwo UMCS 2009).

24. See *Księgi pamięci gmin żydowskich — bibliografia/A Bibliography of Jewish Memorial Books.*

25. Theo Richmond, *Konin: A Quest* (New York: Pantheon Books, 1995); Yaffa Eliach, *There Once Was a World. A Nine-Hundred-Year Chronicle of the Shtetl of Eishyshok* (Boston: Little, Brown, 1998); and Eva Hoffman, *Shtetl: The Life and Death of a Small Town and the World of Polish Jews* (Boston: Houghton Mifflin, 1997).

26. Richmond, *Konin,* xvii–xviii.

27. Jerzy Jacek Bojarski, "Owoce spotkań," in *Ścieżki pamięci. Żydowskie miasto w Lublinie — losy, miejsca, historia,* ed. Jerzy Jacek Bojarski (Lublin-Rishon LeZion: Norbertinum, 2001): 14.

28. Arkadiusz Pacholski, *Krajobraz z czerwonym słońcem* (Kalisz: Sztuka i Rynek, 2001): 24–25.

29. Y. D. Mitlpunkt, "Hakdome," in *Khurbn Bilgoray,* ed. Abraham Kronenberg (Tel Aviv: no publisher given, 1956), II.

30. Elias Schulman, "A Survey and Evaluation of *Yizker* Books," *Jewish Book Annual* 25 (1968): 185–6.

9

"To Hold Our Own
Against Silence"[1]

ADINA CIMET

The yizker book is the generic name for a text that in Jewish culture is designated to remember people, places, and events. The contemporary versions of these books written by survivors of the Holocaust began appearing immediately after World War II. They have continued to emerge since then; some estimates suggest that hundreds of places have been memorialized in approximately one thousand books. When the survivors of Eastern European communities regrouped in new locations, they wanted the publications to commemorate those who were murdered, as well as to re-capture a vanished way of life.

Narratives written in remembrance of destroyed communities have a precedent within Jewish culture and history. Those from the Middle Ages are in response to the attacks on Jewish communities in the Rhine region; those from the turn of the twentieth century are in response to the pogroms in Russia. Reading and writing has always been a valued form of expression among Jews, and as groups migrated, their texts were a portable commodity and a precious sustaining force. Nevertheless, one cannot help but be amazed by the variety of yizker books produced and the scope of the outpouring after the Holocaust. While only a few libraries worldwide house comprehensive collections, namely Yad Vashem in Jerusalem, the YIVO Institute for Jewish Research in New York City, and the New York Public Library in New York City, these collections or parts of the collections are mainly known to specialists. Initially, critical reaction to the books was lukewarm. Some researchers dismissed the historical value of the books because the books were created by survivors who had no pretensions that they were historians or ethnographers.[2] However complete a book may have seemed to its creators, others could always read it as biased or incomplete. Yet, survivor groups kept organizing themselves for the task at hand. The task of memorializing a destroyed people, its history, and its physical and social communities could be overwhelming. Much of what was produced inevitably fell short of the goals and expectations of many. However, the last few decades have witnessed a growing recognition of the richness and importance of the books as source documents by a number of scholars who have focused on the books, rescuing them from oblivion. Additionally, translation and digitalization efforts have expanded the audience for the works. Prior critiques have begun to fade.[3]

What are these books? Do they acquire added value when seen collectively? Yizker books are not booklets, diaries, or hand-written notebooks. In fact, even the earliest versions, which date from the 1940s, appeared as formal books. The books vary in length and other characteristics and range from two hundred pages to multiple volumes.[4] By the 1950s, dozens of books had already been published. During that period, writers and historians reviewing the books recognized the achievement but focused on the shortcomings, primarily the historical inconsistencies in the books and the amateurish quality of the books.[5] A few books were shaped by professional historians of the region, survivors who had a solid knowledge of the past of their region and the writing and editing ability to attempt such a project. However, most volumes were written by people who simply qualified for the job by having survived. The books were very slow to gain professional recognition, but over time, a consensus emerged that these materials are not only rich primary sources but are also treasures for an analysis of communal Jewish history. Narratives that reflect on other traumatic historical events of other ethnic groups do exist, but they are not common. However, Jewish survivors of Holocaust seem to have thrown themselves into producing narrative in such quantities as to make these memorials extraordinary in and of themselves.[6]

Yizker books encompass such a variety of material that they are a vast source of information on many subjects. This essay, in particular, examines some of the intended and unintended messages of the books. Given that the goal of each book varies, as does its expression, the books still share sufficient commonality to constitute a genre. But, over time, the issues that they raised and explored became more complex, varied, and broader in scope, elaborating and amplifying the messages that they deliver. For this essay, I examine forty-six books from 1946 to 1987, generally selecting two books in each year. I chose the cut-off date of 1987 because it marks the proximate year when Yiddish began to be supplemented or complemented by other languages and completely replaced by Hebrew and other languages, primarily English. In looking at the goals and *raison d'être* of the books, I identify a variety of cultural and philosophical messages that seem worthy of further analysis and present the most complex and innovative examples of a collective voice sustaining the moral compass of the world for the post–Holocaust centuries.

One Medium and Its Many Messages

Lomze; momentn un zikhroynes, issued in 1946, takes a stanza from the poet Avraham Liesin as its motto: "The Eternal Jew." The motto is the central tenet of the book itself: "I live and I live, and I will still go on living."[7] The introduction ends with an analogous thought, which is the desire to create an "eternal memory." This is a defiant chant from people who were almost annihilated and who were hardly able to confront the fact that they were not meant to live. This line takes cognizance of the fact that the goal of the Nazis was almost achieved regarding Eastern European Jews. This book also attempts to review the historical past of the community, describe the war as it was experienced in that place, and identify survivors of Lomza and contextualize their new existence. The stated goal is to reconstruct the Jewish past, capturing the war period and the resettling of survivors. While all yizker books are based on the same historical period and tragedy, the books have diverse goals. It is their collective statements that evolved into a sharp and elaborate consciousness for social and political redress for the victims.

The 1946 volume *Mayn khorev shtẹtl Sokolow* includes a historical presentation of its past, though there are few primary sources on that subject as most were destroyed. The book states that its goal is to create a "monument for a village *not* disappeared."[8] Thus, with a bold rejection of reality and the use of irony, the authors underline the persistence of memory in the face of the physical reality of the village's destruction. These survivors want to make sure that erasure is not achieved. They point out that there had been an especially lengthy historical coexistence of the locals and Jews. For Jewish readers, the book has cultural resonance insofar as the volume is introduced with a sentence from the haggadah: "*Vekhol marbim lesaper vegn undzere kedoyshim harei ze musubakh.*" This echoes the haggadic injunction to tell and retell the stories of the lives of the martyrs of the Holocaust as Jews retell of the story of slavery and freedom from Egypt. The mixture of Yiddish and Hebrew renders the sentence immediately recognizable and familiar to any reader of the group. The book is meant to become consecrated and used as a haggadah. The metaphor of the *matzeyve* [tombstone] is also evoked. The book is a surrogate monument required for traditional memorializing. It therefore recognizes the killed and martyred Jews who do not have a *matzeyve*, which is the way all Jews are recognized and remembered when buried. Reading and rereading the book will be a mental pilgrimage similar to the custom of visiting the *kever avot* [the burial places of ancestors]. The readings return the reader to a place that is no more. The authors acknowledge the humiliation of what has happened to their space: the "earth that had bones of generations of Jews is today the ground for cows."[9]

Each group of survivors struggles with what it wants to achieve with its book. *Tshenstokhover yidn*, published in 1947, rejects the possibility of creating a memorial with the book itself. For Czestochowers, the book must also be a *seyfer ha chaim* [book of life], a book about their *yikhus* [lineage]. The book is the measure of who they were and where they came from. They do not just want to describe or to relate what others did to them and to what they were reduced. Rather, they want to state who and where they come from as a people, and, as a corollary who they still are. They recognize that the information about their identity and their existential identity fills a crucial gap; without it, who were they? They poignantly ask themselves and others that question. Their goal is "a rebuilding of the Jewish remnants of the war."[10] They are reconstituting themselves as a community to affirm and sustain continuity, the same continuity that was threatened. The history of their Jewish community, its economy, its culture, its idiosyncrasies, and its distinctions should be a source of wonder to all because of the great achievements and value of their cultural output. Rebuilding and reconstruction will make possible a re-birth of sorts.

In their 1947 volume *Khurbn Levartov*, survivors seek to memorialize individuals, the actual people who perished or were killed. They concentrate on names, photographs, and material evidence in order to evoke those who had a life and culture before they were uselessly and unjustifiably murdered. They mention that three years after the war, the last Jew of Lubartow left the town, finally accepting the overwhelming reality of destruction. They mock the "great" goals of the German people. While Germans and Nazis described their aims as progress and civilization, the survivors refer to them only as the Amalek of modern times, alluding to the biblical people who became the symbol of Jewish enemies for all times.

Braynsk; sefer ha-zikaron of 1948 describes the process of its gestation. While every book project was the result of complex negotiations among the members, some projects had more resources and support from earlier emigrants. Bransk had only forty-two survivors, and most helped create the book. This was not always the case; often survivors were strong-headed in their opinions, and the book projects were frequently a source of confrontation and disagreements. Bransk survivors agreed on goals and on how they wanted to be formally represented in their book. Branskers who settled in Sweden helped out. In the process, people realized how much they needed to reinvent themselves to accomplish the job. In the case of the Bransk book, a former millinery worker from Bransk became the editor of the project. This was a grassroots effort in the finest sense of the word. The editor used his scant memory of the *pinkes* housed in his home. A *pinkes* and its documents often went back hundreds of years as a record of the management of the communal structure of a particular place and some important events of that group. The editor's description is a combination of simple and sophisticated sources; his memory is obviously imperfect for the task. He managed, at the very least, to offer an idealized version of the *pinkes*. By comparison, *Lakhovitz, sefer zikaron* of 1948 drew on supporters from a number of countries where Jews from the hometown settled. These included South Africa, Argentina, Mexico, New Zealand, the United States, Israel, Cuba, Canada, and China. This combined effort offered members the possibility for expression in a shared language of concepts, imagery, and meanings.

The two-volume Białystok yizker book issued between 1949 and 1950 is the first of a series of three publications devoted to the city. The second one was published in 1951 and the third in 1982; all the books emerged in different languages and places.[11] The initial group of survivors wanted to tackle the whole of Jewish history. For them, historical knowledge would remain incomplete if their specific piece was lost. While they never claim to have produced an exhaustive text, they feel that, at the very least, they offer a partial historical description and information that may be used for the reconstruction and understanding of a larger, more conclusive Jewish history. Theirs is an effort against historical obliteration. With it, they claim to be offering ways to retain and build upon Jewish "cultural national meanings." This is a national effort with wider objectives but stated in an objective/academic framework.

Those who published *Ostrovtse; geheylikt dem ondenk fun Ostrovtse, Apt* in 1949 conceived of their effort as a "paper memorial." For them, little could be done to salvage the destruction imposed on them. But if nothing else, the evidence of their living and dying could be memorialized on paper. That would be at least evidence of historical passage. They recognize the enormity of the project and their limited capacity to undertake such an objective; yet, despite that, they assume that any contribution, small or large, however imperfect, would serve as a bulwark against forgetfulness and complacency. Inexperience in such an endeavor is not an obstacle; the book is their authentic way of paying tribute to the murdered. The fact that they see themselves as simple people who came together to produce a memorial volume is not to be dismissed or berated. They speak their minds through their own memories and in their own voices as they remember and memorialize their murdered townspeople.

Interestingly, by the end of the 1940s, yizker books began including translations of parts of their text. People were becoming aware that their compatriots might be the only readers and that their offspring might be linguistically excluded from access to the texts. Moreover, issues described and argued there would be limited to Jewish circles. Including a non–Jewish language in their text, without waiting for translators, made their messages available to a completely new set of readers. But choosing or including a foreign language was not an easy choice, as if the foreignness of it struck a strange chord affecting how it would be read and understood. For those who raised this as an issue, the choice of language created some tension. In part, the ensuing political debate had a well-trod history. Once the choice of Yiddish and/or Hebrew was discussed, the outcome was often dictated by the writers themselves. Yiddish dominated for a few decades, but Hebrew increasingly became the dominant medium of expression of the texts, especially when those organizing the projects were in Israel. On occasion, other languages were used as the books took on a more future-oriented goal. English, French, and German are among the languages mostly used, but also Hungarian and others. Reaching new potential audiences, prior to translating the books themselves, signaled that the books' goals and messages were going to be expanded.

Yizker books cover a range of topics. Some have comprehensive overviews that include historical descriptions, memory maps that Jews created to recreate the destroyed buildings and streets of their given sites, descriptions of specific personalities and leaders, economic developments, accomplishments, education, institutions, rabbinic luminaries, chronicles, and memoirs. Like scrapbooks, the books preserve descriptions, photographs, newspaper articles, and rosters of inhabitants. From their desire to achieve meaning and take a stand to the consciousness of the need for remembrance, continuity, and history, survivors saw themselves as advocates and protesters refusing to accept their imposed fate as continued destiny. Their multiple goals therefore modify or expand the contents and formats of the yizker books.

Megiles Gline, issued in 1950, states that although the initial efforts were aimed at themselves, the survivors eventually included materials for their children. Their goal of the book was to leave a "shield of paper" for their offspring, something stronger than stone and sword. Their motto "*netzakh Israel lo yshaker*" [Jewish victory/survival will not be denied] was taken from biblical language.[12] That was their way to affirm being alive and celebrating their aliveness individually and existentially as a group. The Nazi mission was not achieved. Writers understood, as did most of the lesser-trained editors, that their book could not compete with materials produced by formal historians. Their books, by definition, were incomplete. But even historians do not know their own period, they claimed. Scholars also need time and perspective to analyze history. Survivors' voices, their argument goes, are testimonials of first-hand observers. As such, these observers have the duty and commitment to fight against the logic that Nazis and their supporters and collaborators imposed on them. The exchange of "a kilogram of salt for a Jewish head"[13] was the value they had been accorded by the victimizers. But the survivors could not accept such an exchange for the survival of any human being, let alone themselves. They were exposing the perverse evil as expressed in a market value that had overtaken what defined itself as "the reigning civilization" of the world, a world and a system that de-valued life and humanity. The survivors' aim was to prove the enemy wrong and to identify their political and philosophical goals as perverse.

The voices of survivors were therefore worth preserving, and for others, worth listening to. This consciousness of the mutual interdependencies between themselves and the others needed to understand the war and its meanings led the survivors to believe that Jews needed to speak up and remember and never allow themselves or others to forget. Jews needed to be understood. This was their way of affirming themselves and their philosophical entity. Without pointing out the actions and the actors that created such an evil state of affairs, the account of any historian would be faulty. Each book, through these testimonials, uses the language of the survivors as a new indictment. Authors were not just searching for meaning or for a way to respect and recognize the martyred dead. They were, above all, confronting the other, the criminal. They were offering readers, historians, statesmen, politicians, and others a way to understand and recognize the facts that Nazis and their sympathizers and collaborators tried to dismiss or distort. "The mark of Cain should be placed on the murderers; they earned it."[14]

After the war, there was no expectation that these efforts would be promoted or encouraged. Could masses of criminals be punished in cold blood? Could the innocent, the decent, and the victim behave like the criminal in order to mete out justice? In fact, during the war there were few possibilities, only some extraordinary exceptions by those who kept records and diaries that survived, to record the fate and treatment of those who suffered,[15] let alone a mechanism to confront the enemy and demand accountability and justice. Jews were exiled people and orphaned human beings.

Jews involved in the book projects after the war sought the possibility of a commitment between the survivors and those who supported them, a pledge against the political totalitarian systems of life and death. To legitimize their cultural perspective and present it as a start rather than a full-fledged achievement, they quoted the *Ethics of the Fathers* on the ongoing commitment required of each member: "It is not up to you to complete the work, but neither are you free to desist from it" (Pirkei Avot, 2:21). The books tried to plant a new beginning, rejecting totalitarianism and its logic. In them, we find the seeds for the flourishing of justice and decency, lest they be forgotten from the consciousness of humanity.

Some yizker narratives are aimed at an international audience; others delve deeper into ways of reconstructing the patterns of mourning and remembrance. For instance, in the 1950 volume *Grayeve yisker-bukh*, Jews portray themselves as permanent mourners; their collected memories are a way of eulogizing and elegizing the martyred and murdered Jews. While they never dismiss group tragedy, they focus on personal tragedy because they experienced living in a "no man's land" bereft of any support or protection. Their forced unprotected status allowed them to confront their own effacement from the social structures of the world. After the war, when they "could find neither the living nor the dead" upon returning to their old country — an irony that is not meant as a poetic expression of loss — they began to understand the absolute rootlessness. Slowly, they came to understand that reconstructing the past and their tragic end was a natural way to mourn. Unexpectedly, however, they also realized that the mourning process, especially as unique a process as theirs, could ensure a future with continuity of meanings and purpose for their own surviving children. In this future, the old vision of hope of *beacharit hayamim*, the messianic future depicted in the Isaiah prophecies, takes hold of their amorphous dreams and shapes them into the concepts of social justice, freedom for all, and peace as requirements for a viable human future.

Some of the survivors found it difficult to organize their texts and memories. In those cases, lack of resources and conflicts between personalities and philosophies thwarted success. Moreover, not all survivors were fully committed to this process. Some showed disinterest; others were unable to deliver materials, recall events, or write about them. In the case of the 1951 *Kobryn; zamlbukh*, the survivors who settled in Israel parted ways with those of the same town who went to the United States. Each group decided to create its own project. Their aim was to reproduce the former *pinkes* by recreating a communal diary. The volume was intended to highlight the lineage of each community and provide the documentary evidence of its aliveness. Their frustration in achieving the impossible reconstruction is expressed in the damning cry: *imach shemam* [erased should be their name], a curse on those who forced them to reconstruct from memory who they were and who they are. Although the injunction expresses the desire to forget the evil and horror of the crimes and the criminal used in conjunction with the name of the criminals, it is actually a systematic way of remembering and blaming the evildoers. Each Nazi was a criminal whose name "should be blotted out," but who should nevertheless be remembered for what he or she was. Again, the approach is to follow a moral compass that underscores the distinction between criminals and victims.

In many books, such as *Dos bukh fun Lublin* from 1952, writers attempt to develop the historical content and perspective as best they could by extending their descriptions as far back as possible despite the paucity of materials. This is, of course, an elaborate and deliberate strategy to deny and preempt the characterization of their being outsiders to the land from which they were ousted. The need to develop *yirat hakavod* [spiritual fear and solemnity], but applied to the past, is to secure hope for the future. The book must strengthen the forces of life. In cultural terms, their book is a *ner tomid* [an eternal light], in other words, a beacon of steadfast spiritual light.

Expanding Goals and Readers

The language and terminology of yizker books evolved along with their goals and narratives. While the book to Lublin is meant to be useful for the future for the group and its offspring, it contains pledges and recommendations that seek to reach the broader world. The testimonies describing the tragedy are the voices and words of those who faced the horror of a changed world. They promise never to forget Maidanek, the death camp next to Lublin, a symbol of all Nazi death camps, or its builders. They indict those responsible for the crimes committed. Their book is not just a memorial for lost lives, but also a call to the living who are forging a future, a future that cannot allow the criminals to have the last word.

This desire to accuse the criminal is evident in *Yisker-bukh fun Rakishok un umgegnt*, also published in 1952. That book aims to be a volume "that will rob the killers peace in their lives and prevent their nightly slumber."[16] There is a desire to avenge the victims. Some books, for instance the 1954 *Yisker-bukh Chelm*, achieve more accuracy in identifying individuals through rosters of accurate historical information. These include names, dates, descriptions of death marches, descriptions of erratic killings, deportations, and more.

Along other lines, some books, like the 1958 volume *Brisk de-Lita*, document the impressive internal leadership of the community, such as the great rabbinic personalities and families dating to old times and the world-renowned three generations of Soloveichik rabbis of the Mir yeshiva. That book includes photographs, documents, memories, and descriptions of individuals, activists, leaders, the intelligentsia, distinguished women, fighters, rabbinic judges, cantors, and heads of yeshivas. The point is to identify the losses and the killed.

Some books set out a code of behavior for survivors. *Khurbn Glubok*, which came out in 1956, for example, includes a description of a new code of behavior that is prescribed for all survivors and the children of survivors, and even all Jews. Writers refer to the poem *Yerushalaim de-Lita: in kamf un umkum* [Jerusalem of Lithuania: In struggle and death]. This reference is found in other yizker books. If memorializing and the memorial itself are really to be a *kos tanjumim* [cup of consolation],[17] remembrance should be accompanied by a new code of behavior in a changed world. This is expressed in a set of commandments that should define the [new] humanity at its core. These new injunctions anchor the present in the experiences of the past and link the act of remembering to quotidian life. Thus the statements combining the past and the present:

> Remember the *churbn*;
> May the memory of it all be there while you eat and in your blood.
> Clasp your teeth and remember;
> When you eat, remember;
> When you drink, remember;
> When you hear a song, remember,
> When the sun is shining, remember;
> When the night arrives, remember;
> When you build a house, break a wall in it and remember;
> If you plant a field, make a mountain of stones, let them be a witness
>   and memorial for those that did not get a burial;
> When you walk your child to the *chuppah,* remember;
> May the dead and the living be one, as are united those that were
>   murdered with the remnants of Israel.
> Listen.... and say,
> Amen.[18]

Although the term *churbn* most often refers to the destruction of the Jewish Temple, it also describes the Nazi destruction of Jewry. The format of the above commandments embeds the memory of the *churbn* with a consciousness and connectedness, thereby sustaining the logic of the memory in the same way that the loss of the Temple has remained in Jewish consciousness as a marker of seminal historical change. In presenting these rules as religious pre-scriptions, the writers seek the symbolic sanctity and anchoring that comes only from religion itself.

The Logistics of Creation

Yizker books differ in how long they took from conception to realization. Some were prepared in less than twelve months; others took more than ten years. In general, the more distant from the events of the war, the more difficult it was to form committees, obtain editors, gather and approve resources, coor-dinate other survivors, but, most of all, achieve consensus on content and sat-isfy the multiple expectations concerning what the book should be. For instance, Pabianice was a typical village that no mapmaker would bother to mark.[19] But in Jewish memory, this place had a particular content and style. Because it was a small settlement, no historian would spend time researching the history of such a seemingly insignificant place. Yet, Jews lived there, died there, and led a Jewish cultural life there; they were murdered for being who they were. Why should such a place not be remembered? How should survivors memorialize a place like this, given the meager documents that recorded anything of importance? No Jewish encyclopedia refers to this community. No monographs describe it. Pabianice had a textile industry, and its importance lay in the commerce between this region and Russia, China, and Siberia. The writers of the 1956 memorial book *Sefer Pabianice* tried to reconstruct its Jewish history, but that task proved to be daunting. Yet, with whatever they had, with their own memories, they succeeded in putting together their yizker book which, in all its modesty, marks the existence of Jewish life in a place that otherwise would have been unaware of it.

Some towns with Jewish settlements that were ruthlessly destroyed and pillaged had survivors who could prepare a book after the war because the Jews from the place emigrated before the destruction. People from the ancestral hometown assumed the task of creating a book for their loved ones. Issues of language surfaced once again. The decision to use Yiddish, Hebrew, English, German, French, Hungarian, or Polish arose along with the need to connect to younger generations. The language issue was a struggle in itself. Survivors debated how they could or should express themselves concerning actions that had never happened before and had therefore never before been expressed in any language. The fact that most of the human and financial resources came from a specific place influenced the choice of language. In most cases, no translations were kept. Where materials had been translated, they often covered only part of the texts. The emphasis was on the audience's ability to read the books.

The 1964 volume *Yisker-bukh Palawy* stresses that it is an enterprise in which many took part. The writers state that the work was a gravestone for those that perished. But in a strong, new voice, the text is also meant as "an arming for the offensive against the Nazis and their collaborators, facilitators, and allies."[20] The expression of this aspiration stresses that there is a need not only to remember one's own, but also "to prosecute the guilty" and hold the world accountable for having kept, to a large degree, silent. Jews should have, they claim, a voice "providing testimony and indictment" regarding what happened in that destruction, and their book is part of that effort. It attempts to stir the participants who enabled the catastrophe to occur. For the surviving majority, words are the only tool available.

Often the goals of the books are loftier than their contents. But nobody else raised the issue of consequences to be faced by survivors, indirect victims, and societies that dismiss the past as a sad chapter of history without further action. Herein is the novelty: the need to question the horrendous events because they were man-made and the need to grasp and confront that it was done by humans.

Di kehile fun Horodlo recognizes that memorial books were "a new type of literature for the People of the Book." The genre claimed a special space by sheer quantity and uniqueness. The writers saw their function as articulating a critique and indicting the dormant masses of humanity: "Woe to you, blind and deaf humanity ... how did you allow yourself to stand and watch how the Jewish people were exterminated?!" In almost the same breath, the book proposes a pledge to adopt and sustain a new code of commandments to remember this history and destruction. As indicated earlier, the writers of many yizker books recognize themselves as amateurs, but also as keepers of memory. They therefore scold those who have not been part of the enterprise. They ask:

> Who would have ever imagined that simple folk would be destined to write, memorialize and fight for the continuity of their people? Who would have ever imagined that "warning" and "demanding" would be our way of assuring continuous enlightenment [*ner tomid*] so that ethical and just thinking does not disappear?[21]

The books are thus recognized by the survivors as a source of knowledge and a spur to memories that would otherwise be forgotten. For some, surely these books were a source of consolation. Their aim is mostly to create a path of sanity amidst the political and philosophical madness in which they found themselves rooted by the Nazi war.

Regaining Language, Restoring Community, and New Messages

Yizker books refract different ways in which groups of surviving Jews reacted to the trauma inflicted on them. They are a massive social response to the Holocaust. Not all survivors joined in these projects or even supported them. Not everyone understood the multiple functions of such an effort. For some, it was too little and too ephemeral. For others, any effort to memorialize the Holocaust and its victims seemed inappropriate and inconsequential. But for those who gathered strength from this effort and saw it as a response to what had been inflicted on them, yizker books were invaluable. After the Holocaust, many survivors described that what they felt was a tension between *speech* and *silence* for themselves and their listeners. They felt few wanted to hear about what happened to the individual. Who wanted to hear of the horror? And, given such a reception, who could force others to listen to what had happened? If the Holocaust consumed people, names, identities, property, and existence, it also swallowed language itself.[22] The crisis was followed by the void of silence. Within Jewish culture and tradition, there is an awareness of the power of language and of the failure that ensues when language is absent. A crisis of language, which is when one does not know how to speak, what to say, or whom to address, is a reflection of trauma in itself. The biblical story of Moses, the paradigmatic Jewish teacher, leader, and speaker, is suffused with issues of trauma and language. Moses changed languages, and almost lost the capacity to speak altogether when his tongue was burned in childhood. Yet he became the quintessential leader who spoke to and for his people. Although he suffered diverse traumas that affected language, it was with language that he sustained his role and vision and forged the future of his group. Undoubtedly, the Holocaust was an enormous social trauma inflicted on Jews. Moreover, and even more frighteningly, the crisis it unleashed generated the post-traumatic disarray not just of the victims but of the world itself. Because of the totalitarian destruction that distorted values and justice, the whole world community of people was stripped of the values and principles needed to uphold social decency. The story of Moses may serve as a Jewish parable and cultural paradigm of the need for speech and the right speech and for the creation of text and narrative after the *churbn*. The difficulty of finding to whom to speak, along with what to say and how should not deter anyone from bearing witness to the events that shaped so many lives and threatened human coexistence. A resistance to speech, oral or written, was described by many survivors. This was accompanied by the reciprocal inability of others to hear and to listen. The condition of exile in which the word was trapped, displaced geographically, politically, philosophically, and humanely after such massive destruction obliterated the communication of the victims. Language isolated the traumatized and the events they witnessed in a silence that confused reality with acquiescence and illegitimacy with destiny. George Steiner alludes to this conundrum by suggesting that language is essential to humans. Moreover, those who are denied speech in any form are really stripped of their humanity. As a result, survivors of the Holocaust, saved from the intended fate of death, remain as witnesses to carry and bear the accumulated weight of the silenced world destroyed. They are also the only voices that, by their very existence, can challenge the legality and power structure that otherwise elude indictment.[23] Further, denied that capacity to speak, victims are condemned once again to destruction and oblivion. Survivors hesitate to speak for fear of encountering an unbearable deafness in the outside world. Conversely, writing and speaking is their protest against the horrors to which they were subjected. They reject their imposed past, their treatment, and their status. They also reject the unchallenged power of others over them. In the exile condition they find themselves after the war, they grieve and complain of the forgetfulness of others that perpetuates their existential silencing. That silencing accepts and tolerates what is unacceptable and intolerable.

We may hypothesize that the Mosaic paradigm of speech, the fight against all odds for ethical rectitude in an amoral world, is a backdrop to the choices made by Jewish survivors and their decision to speak and write to ensure the existence of listeners. Speech and texts are thus adopted as a way to create narratives that demand to be heard. *Lemaan tesaper* [and *You* may retell the story] ... is the traditional Biblical injunction to tell and retell from generation to generation what is basic for the shared group memory.[24] The imperative to tell the story expresses the refusal to accept the world as is, as it has become. The Moses story, decomposed into the images of the Sinai moment where there is a need for ongoing witnessing to sustain its messages, along with the burning bush episode, which illustrates the difficulty of speaking to sustain the messages, offer cultural linkages to the challenges that faced survivors. These are dealt with in yizker books. The burden needs to be passed on to others; the spoken message neither consumes nor is consumed, as the burning bush story shows. The message remains essential for the grounding of consciousness for the living.

Two types of generic categories of narratives appear in yizker books. One highlights the past social achievements and contributions of the group. That narrative intends to formalize Jewish history along a unique and often tortuous trajectory, yielding continuity and successes. The other highlights protest. It describes the unparalleled and undeserved suffering to which victims were subjected during the Holocaust and is a narrative that vents anger and identifies the blameworthy and guilty. It is a purposeful narrative that expresses new goals as it clamors against the silenced and therefore ignored realities sustained by victims and survivors. Their fight requires disinterring the past. Their stories need to be told, much as the stories in ancient Jewish history need to be told and retold in order to shape identity, sustain an ethos and an ethic, and build hope. Of course, the historical reconstruction may never be a perfect reconstruction of the past, never complete or final. But the effort to recapture the past and its obliterated subjects, coupled with the meticulous descriptions of the defaced Jewish urban landscape of the towns and cities that housed them for hundreds and hundreds of years, are safeguards against the blurring of human memory. For a people so conscious of the importance of memory and group activity, the gaps in reconstructing the past are eloquent evidence of the destruction and disorder that befell them and the world. Thus reconstruction and a text narrative are tools to approach the truth; they are the voice of the witness who remembers what *humanity* looked like or should be.[25] Despite their original intentions, their fight was not just for themselves, but for the disappearing humanity of the world as well.

The unsolicited narratives in yizker books have generated meaning and raised issues for their own constituency by recapturing lost meanings and stating the moral tone of what is right and wrong. They retain historical connectedness and, in so doing, sustain continuity.[26] However, these books also present a destabilizing effect in much the same way that the narratives of survivors did immediately after the end of the war: they confront others with a reality most wanted to ignore.

European Jews were evacuated from a region in which they had lived for a thousand years in settled communities, and the vacuum, silence, and disappearance remained dissonant. But from that void and silence emerged speech and narratives. These narratives of memory are the voice of the world's superego; they scream *No!* to established ways. The texts neither complain to God nor pose metaphysical questions.[27] There is no pleading to find out *why?* The statements in these books are more tragic because they are more human. And they are more compelling because they address only the physical, which is that something *was* here and *is* no more. If they echo Jewish concepts *yesh* [there is] and *ayin* [there is not][28] of the narratives of creation, they also echo man's destructive capacities saying "yes, there was, creation, even God's creation; but you, man, have created nothingness, void." There is in that no sense of wonder and awe; there is only revulsion for the destructiveness. These actions defy all sense of right and wrong. From the encounter with the man-made horrors, there emerges some human honor. The texts are not just for those who suffered and survived; they are meant for all insofar as they replace silence, forgetfulness, avoidance, and abyss with words, memory, confrontation, and humanity. There is a fiercely clear intent to make murder and social murder something one cannot overcome.

By repossessing the survivors' voices with integrity, we acknowledge their testimony as a re-emerging source of truth. These truths serve history, even when they are not complete, perfect, absolute, or precise enough to function in a court of law. The quixotic effort of the books and the witnessing experience they enact is not about "whole truth;" it is about bearing witness to refute the accepted death as unjust.[29] In the words of Hannah Arendt: "whatever happened or was done within [that world of Shoah, is ensured not to] perish with the life of the doer or endurer; but [to] live on in the memory of future generations."[30]

While no penalty is commensurate with the crimes of the Holocaust, the books are nonetheless a plea for making the acts punishable. They include thoughts of revenge and not requests for reconciliation or forgiveness. The plea for a penalty is also a way to recapture a lost language of morality. Right and wrong are clearly recognized in all texts.[31] Yizker books empower the readers to say *we*. They re-invent the content of the association of the reconfigured group, while rejecting the definition of *group* (Jews), which had been imposed on them during the war.[32] The creators of the books reconstitute their collective identity for others and make clear their demand for understanding and facing human obligations. These include obligations to each other as Jews, but also, and no less so, obligations to each other as people. One may therefore argue that if Nazism intended to control who belonged to Europe and elsewhere and who should live or die, then these texts and their narrative of protest stress the ethics of survival, continuity, past, and history, thus undermining the grounding principles that reigned for years.

A reading of yizker books that concentrates on the historicity of events, their accuracy, the sequence of events that memory and forgetfulness may or may not recall, their literary qualities, or the archeology of communal living as expressed in the narratives may easily miss the profound issues these books collectively raise. The books represent a long-term effort to regain lost paths of decency, humanity, and accountability. Having been banned from the public arena, Jews enter the public debate uninvited, bringing up judicial and ethical issues that must be engraved in all our consciousnesses. The unprecedented level of violence of the twentieth century was unleashed by bending and modifying rules and by disavowing rights. The right to have rights remains the central demand of the books. The books are also an indictment of those who have denied the rights of others. The fact that the books deal in claims, specifically who may claim, who deserves to claim what, and who owes what to the claimants, brings to the forefront the problem of social living. How do we live together with our differences? And, by acting on behalf of the victims, the books offer a chance to recast who we want to be in the future. Yizker books are displaced texts of displaced people. From their exile, these writers created an island of sanity for themselves. To whom but to themselves could they write at first? From whom could they seek echo and understanding after the experience of oblivion and dejection? The survivors understood these projects survived in a no man's land; their absorption to new states was slow and complex and a separate issue. At first, they wrote primarily in Yiddish and Hebrew, and only years later started the addition of local languages to the texts. The narratives they created were and are for themselves. Their purpose is to heal and confront their own traumas, their pain, and their shared memories, thereby satisfying some of their internal demands. Their language, rejected and displaced from the languages of the world, is their tool. It is an affront to the intellectual rejections and the best way to express their feelings and thoughts.

Survivors never claimed martyrdom for themselves, but only for their dead. Their words, the unfinished memories, histories, reminiscences, diaries, chronicles, and analyses are the most important evidence of the age we have entered. They witness and remember and they sustain and clarify the most extreme despair that our society has inflicted on one another. Theirs is a text for an endless protest against death, limitless power, powerlessness, and the destructive ideology of group hatred. Theirs is piercing cry to reject the deaths and killing, to protest the treatment and make it a permanent international issue, and to request that such behavior be made universally unacceptable in order to maintain that the world is still inhabited by humans. Their task is neither small nor insignificant. To read yizker books in depth, grasping the themes and the requests as real, is to be aligned with the writers of the most revolutionizing of ethical revolts of the twentieth and twenty-first centuries. The writers refuse to accept the destruction of people and culture; they also refuse the status of victim without forging changes in the world as they experienced it. Languages, at first their own languages, but later all languages become a vessel for their thinking, the medium to connect and correct the world. Murder is to be seen as unacceptable and unforgivable.

Yizker books represent an extraordinary effort against oblivion. Their goals and functions are many, not just historical. The books collapse time and space, combine and compress events and visions, and merge past and present. The original and most significant aim for Jews was to confer dignity and meaning to the dead and to ward against forgetfulness and obliteration. But the books also build step-by-step arguments that challenge the thinking world to a sustainable future by recovering and repairing the lost moral compass of the last tortuous and abysmal century.

Yizker Books Reviewed for This Essay

Lomza
    Lomze; momentn un zikhroynes. Ed. H. Sabatka. New York: United Lomzer Relief Committee, 1946.
Sokolow
    Mayn khorev shtetl Sokolow; shilderungen, bilder un portretn fun a shtot umgekumene yidn. P. Granatshtein. Buenos Aires: Union of Polish Jews in Argentina, 1946.
Czestochowa
    Tshenstokhover yidn. Ed. R. Mahler. New York: United Czestochower Relief Committee and Ladies Auxiliary, 1947.
Lubartow
    Khurbn Levartov. Ed. B. Tshubinski. Paris: Association of Lubartow, 1947.
Lakhovits
    Lakhovitz, sefer zikaron. Eds. I. Rubin, N. Tuksinsky, and A. Lev. Tel Aviv: Igud Yotzei Lehevich, 1948.

Bransk
  Braynsk; sefer ha-zikaron. A. Trus and J. Cohen. New York: Brainsker Relief Committee of New York, 1948.
Białystok
  Pinkes Bialystok. Ed. Y. Mark. Volume 1, *Geshikhte fun di yidn in Bialystoker un rayon.* New York: Białystok Jewish Historical Association, 1949.
Ostrowiec
  Ostrovtse; geheylikt dem ondenk fun Ostrovtse, Apt. Buenos Aires: Former Residents of Ostrovtse in Argentina, 1949.
Wolkowysk
  Volkovisker yisker-bukh. Ed. M. Einhorn. New York, 1949.
Gliniany
  Megiles Gline. Ed. H. Halpern. New York: Former Residents of Gline, 1950.
Grajewo
  Grayeve yisker-bukh. Ed. G. Gorin. New York: United Grayever Relief Committee, 1950.
Białystok
  Bialystok; bilder album. Ed. D. Sohn. New York: Białystoker Album Committee, 1951.
Kobryn
  Kobryn; zamlbukh. Ed. M. Glotzer. Buenos Aires: Kobryn Book Committee, 1951.
Lublin
  Dos bukh fun Lublin. Paris: Former Residents of Lublin in Paris, 1952.
Rokiskis
  Yisker-bukh fun Rakishok un umgegnt. Ed. M. Bakalczuk-Felin. Johannesburg: Rakishker Landsmanshaft of Johannesburg, 1952.
Byten
  Pinkas Byten. Eds. D. Abramovich and M.W. Bernstein. Buenos Aires: Former Residents of Byten in Argentina, 1954.
Chelm
  Yisker-bukh Chelm. Ed. M. Bakalczuk-Felin. Johannesburg: Former Residents of Chelm, 1954.
Glebokie
  Khurbn Glubok, Sharkoystsene, Dunilovitsh, Postav, Droye, Koziany. Eds. M. and Z. Rajak. Buenos Aires: Former Residents' Association in Argentina, 1956.
Pobianice
  Sefer Pabianice. Ed. A. W. Yassni. Tel Aviv: Former Residents of Pobianice in Israel, 1956.
Brzesc nad Bugiem
  Brisk de-Lita. Ed. E. Steinman. Jerusalem: Encyclopedia of the Jewish Diaspora, 1958.
Czestochowa
  Tshenstokhov; nayer tsugob-material tsum bukh "Tshenstokhover yidn." Ed. S. D. Singer. New York: United Relief Committee in New York, 1958.
Klobucko
  Sefer Klobutsk. Tel Aviv: Former Residents of Klobucko in Israel, 1960.
Gostynin
  Pinkes Gostynin; yisker-bukh. Ed. J. M. Biderman. New York: Gostynin Memorial Book Committees, 1960.
Ciechanow
  Yisker-bukh fun der Tshekhanover yiddisher kehile; sefer yizker le-kehilat Ciechanow. Ed. A. W. Yassni. Tel Aviv: Former Residents of Ciechenow in Israel and the USA, 1962.
Hrubieszow
  Pinkas Hrubieszow. Ed. B. Kaplinsky. Tel Aviv: Hrubiesov Associations in Israel and the USA, 1962.
Horodlo
  Di kehile fun Horodlo, yizker bukh. Ed. Y. Ch. Zawidowitch. Tel Aviv: Former Residents of Horodlo in Israel, 1962.

Baranowicze
Baranovitsh in umkum un vidershtand. Ed. Y. Fuksman. New York: Baranowicher Farband of America, 1964.
Pulawy
Yisker-bukh Palawy. Ed. M. W. Bernstein. New York: Pulawer Yiskor Book Committee, 1964.
Czestochowa
Tshenstokhover landsmanshaft in Montreal. Ed. B. Orenstein. Montreal: Czenstochover Society in Montreal, 1966.
Czestochowa
Tshenstokhov; naye tsugob-material tsum bukh Tshenstokhover Yidn; Czenstochov; A New Supplement to the Book *Czenstochover Yidn*. Ed. S. D. Singer. New York, 1958.
Chorostkow
Sefer Chorostkow. Ed. D. Shtokfish. Tel Aviv: Former Residents of Chorostkow in Israel, 1968.
Husiantyn
Husiantyn; Podoler Gubernye. Ed. B. Diamond. New York: Former Residents of Husiantyn in America, 1968.
Kazimierz
Pinkas Kuzmir. Ed. D. Shtokfish. Tel Aviv: Former Residents of Kazimierz in Israel and the Diaspora, 1970.
Nowy Sącz
Sefer Sants. Ed. R. Mahler. New York: Former Residents of Sants in New York, 1970.
Rawa Ruska
Sefer zikaron le-kehilat Rawa-Ruska ve-ha-sevivah. Eds. A.M. Ringel and I.Z. Rubin. Tel Aviv: Rawa Ruska Society, 1973.
Lithuania
Bleter fun yidish Lite. Ed. J. Rabinovitch. Tel Aviv: Hamenora, 1974.
Nieswiez
Sefer Nieswiez. Ed. D. Shtokfish. Tel Aviv: Nieswiez Societies in Israel and the Diaspora, 1976.
Warka
Vurka; sefer zikaron. Tel Aviv: Vurka Societies in Israel, France, Argentina, England, and the United States, 1976.
Mielic
Melitser yidn. S. Klagsbrun. Tel Aviv: Nay-Lebn, 1979.
Sasow
Mayn shtetl Sasow. M. Rafael. Jerusalem, 1979.
Białystok
Der Bialystoker yizker-bukh. Ed. I. Shmulewitz. New York: Białystoker Center, 1982.
Zwolen
Zvoliner yisker-bukh. Ed. B. Kahan. New York: Zwolen Society, 1982.
Ostrow-Lubelski
Sefer yizker Ostrow-Lubelski. Ed. D. Shtokfish. Tel Aviv: Former Residents of Ostrow-Lubelski in Israel and the Diaspora, 1987.

Notes

1. Edmond Jabès, *The Book of Shares* (Chicago: University of Chicago Press, 1989), 82.
2. See Jacob Shatzky, "*Yizker bikher*," YIVO *Bleter* 37 (1953): 264–282; Jacob Shatzky, "*Yizker bikher*," YIVO *Bleter* 39 (1955): 339–355; and Leybush Lehrer, "*A yizker bukh vos is andersh*," YIVO *Bleter* Vol. 39 (1955): 355–359.

3. Jack Kugelmass and Jonathan Boyarin, eds. and trans., *From a Ruined Garden: The Memorial Books of Polish Jewry* (New York: Schocken Books, 1983).

4. Kugelmass and Boyarin estimate there are approximately 400 of these books from 1943, which includes around 1,000 editors and close to 10,000 writers.

5. See for instance Jacob Shatzky's *"Yizker bikher,"* *YIVO Bleter* 39 (1955): 339–355.

6. For a short review on the types of Jewish narratives regarding memorial books, see Rosemary Horowitz, *Literacy and Cultural Transmission in the Reading, Writing, and Rewriting of Jewish Memorial Books* (San Francisco: Austin & Winfield, 1998). This study looks at differences between first and second generation survivors, historians, and literary critics.

7. H. Sabatka, ed., *Lomze; momentn un zikhroynes* (New York: United Lomzer Relief Committee, 1946), 4.

8. P. Granatshtein, *Mayn khorev shtetl Sokolow; shilderungen, bilder un portretn fun a shtot umgekumene yidn* (Buenos Aires: Union of Polish Jews in Argentina, 1946), 2–4.

9. Ibid., 2.

10. R. Mahler, ed., *Tshenstokhover yidn* (New York: United Czestochower Relief Committee and Ladies Auxiliary, 1947), v–vi.

11. See Horowitz, *Literacy and Cultural Transmission,* 72–75. Chapters 6 and 7 review the diverse contributions of the first and second generation in preparing these books. The first edition, a two volume set, is a compilation written by the historian and biblical scholar Abraham Shmuel Hershberg and edited by Yudl Mark. The second book, in Yiddish and English, edited by David Sohn, is mostly a collection of photographs of life before, during, and after the Holocaust. The 1982 volume is a *landmanshaft* production. Horowitz follows the diverse opinions and disagreements around the formatting and editing of the books.

12. H. Halpern, ed., *Megiles Gline* (New York: Former Residents of Gline, 1950), 1.

13. Ibid., 5.

14. Yoan Alerhard, "Introduction," in *Megiles Gline,* ed. H. Halpern (New York: Former Residents of Gline, 1950), 6.

15. See for instance, the ghetto diaries from Warsaw, Kovno, and Lodz. See the drawings made at the time, for instance, of the Kovno Ghetto by Esther Luria. Also, see Samuel Kassow, *Who Will Write Our History? Rediscovering a Hidden Archive from Warsaw Ghetto* (New York: Vintage Books, 2009).

16. M. Bakalczuk-Felin, ed., *Yisker-bukh fun Rakishok un umgegnt* (Johannesburg: Rakishker Landsmanshaft of Johannesburg, 1952), 5.

17. Jeremiah 16:7, cup of consolation: served at first meal of the family after interment at a cemetery [*seuda havraah*], in which mourner drinks a cup, presumably of wine.

18. Mark Dvorzetsky, *"Yerushalaim de-Lita: in kamf un umkum,"* in *Khurbn Glubok, Sharkoystsene, Dunilovitsh, Postav, Droye, Koziany,* ed. M. and Z. Rajak (Buenos Aires: Former Residents' Association in Argentina, 1956).

19. Many yizker books have what are called memory maps, maps made from memory localizing Jewish markers. Since so many of the cities or town were razed or modified, and many of the Jewish institutions converted into something else to destroyed, these maps are really memory maps of towns as Jews left them when they lived in them.

20. M. W. Bernstein, ed., *Yisker-bukh Palawy* (New York: Pulawer Yiskor Book Committee, 1964), 7.

21. D. Shtokfish, ed., *Pinkas Kuzmir* (Tel Aviv: Former Residents of Kazimierz in Israel and the Diaspora, 1970), 7.

22. Avivah G. Zornberg, *The Particulars of Rapture: Reflections on Exodus* (New York: Doubleday, 2001), 343.

23. Ibid., 118.

24. The sentence comes from Exodus chapter 10:2: "And that you may tell in the ears of your son and of your son's son...." It is used as a permanent expectation of communication between the generations about history and group memory.

25. See chapters 1, 2, 3, and 7 in Shoshana Felman and Dori Laub, *Testimony: Crises of Witnessing in Literature, Psychoanalysis, and History* (New York: Routledge, 1992).

26. Zornberg, *The Particulars of Rapture*, 189.

27. It is important to notice that the post Holocaust Yiddish literature is full of complaints and dialogues with God. The yizker literature is completely silent on that.

28. Zornberg, *The Particulars of Rapture*, 237.

29. Felman and Laub, *Testimony*, 15.

30. Hannah Arendt, "The Great Tradition: Law and Power," *Social Review*, Vol.74, No. 3 (2007): 717.

31. Ibid., 929. Totalitarianism created an abysmal alienation at multiple levels: social, internal, cultural, political, and more. Again, Arendt clarifies that the totalitarian system sustained violence, hiding, and injecting it covertly in three forms:

    a. Making the victim carry out the horror as though he subscribed to it;

    b. The prohibition to speak of the horror; using rumors, lies, distortions, etc.

    c. With the above rule imposed, all participants — including victims — become "absent" from the situation, as they were forbidden and unable to construct narratives/testimonies of the evil that was inflicted on them.

32. Cathleen Kantner, "Collective Identity as Shared Ethical Self-Understanding: The Case of the Emerging European Identity," *European Journal of Social Theory* Vol. 9, No. 4 (Nov. 2006): 508.

10

"Write This as a Memorial in the Book"—A Jewish Pattern for Memory

Roni Kochavi-Nehab

The production of a book to commemorate an event is a typical Jewish reaction, and examples of that practice abound. The event might be negative, for instance, a disaster, war, or death; or the event might be positive, for instance, a holiday or major achievement. This is the context for the production of memorializing and perpetuating books, such as yizker books and jubilee books. Those books are based on the biblical commandment of *zakhor* [remember], a commandment that imparts a traditional schema for the creation of Jewish collective memory and its retention. Although this is a very common popular cultural occurrence, it has not yet been fully researched. To that end, this chapter examines aspects of two cultural phenomena. Specifically, it focuses on two genres of community memorial books, the yizker books of the Holocaust and the jubilee books of the kibbutz.[1]

A comparison between yizker books and jubilee books may appear suspicious at first. The reader may ask the question: "What has one to do with the other?" This suspicion may be amplified by the necessarily sensitive nature of any appraisal of Holocaust memorials. The onus is undeniably on the researcher to explain the basis of the comparison. Jubilee books are dedicated to living Jewish communities in Israel; whereas yizker books are dedicated to destroyed Jewish communities in the diaspora. Jubilee books celebrate the creation of communities; yizker books mourn the loss of communities. While jubilee books, especially those from the latter decades of the twentieth century, are colorful, cheerful, and entertaining, yizker books are somber, printed in black and gray, and tend to use obituary linguistic and visual constructions of destruction and mourning.

Tradition sees the relationship between the people of Israel and God as conditioned by obedience to the biblical commandment of *zakhor*, which crystallizes a personal and collective identity for Jews throughout the ages. In *Zakhor*, Y. H. Yerushalmi traces the Jewish perception of memory and discusses the paradoxical relations between the *zakhor* commandment and its traditional interpretation. He writes:

> Judaism throughout the ages has never stopped reflecting on the meaning of history; but historiography itself has always played a marginal part at best, and often no part at all; and so, while the remembrance of things past has always been central to Jewish experience, the historian has never been its primary keeper.[2]

Additionally, Yerushalmi counts at least 172 appearances of the verbal root *z-k-r* (in the context of memory) in the Hebrew Bible. This is the starting point for his discussion of the changing meaning of the commandment *zakhor* from biblical to modern times. The univocal commitment to remember and remind creates unique modes of memory, which have apparently blocked the development of a Western-style Jewish historiography since the end of biblical days. Instead, a set pattern of relations was established between the people of Israel and God; this pattern based in the biblical events that are read as the essence of national-historic memory is the paradigm for all future events. The cycle is known in advance. God chooses Israel; Israel sins against him; Israel is punished by destruction and exile and then temporarily rescued, as in the Passover haggadah. Total divine salvation is promised at the end of days.[3]

This collective memory, which defines a Jewish national ethos, is determined and upheld by texts such as the haggadah, the parchment scrolls ensconced in phylacteries and *mezuzah*, and of course the texts of prayer.[4] In this covenant of memory, God joins Israel in committing Himself to remembering the covenant: "I remember the devotion of your youth" (Jeremiah 2:2).

In this chapter, I argue that the urge to document an unusual event reflects the commandment of *zakhor* as defined in the Bible and as interpreted by every generation. In the last few centuries, as communication media became more sophisticated and widespread, the possibilities of documentation have grown. Memory, until recently the instrument of the ruling elite in furthering its own power, has become a popular tool of many groups. This process is the "democratization of memory" in Jacques Le Goff's terms.[5] The promise to remember is no longer made only by the leadership; it is no longer the sole responsibility of leaders. On the contrary, it is a gesture made by people from all parts of society. Those behind commemorative projects may be individuals or official entities, such as archives, monuments, museums, and the like.[6] I argue that the producers of yizker books and jubilee books rely on the same thought-schema and use the same patterns of passing on tradition, consciously or not, as part of an inherited and constructed Jewish cultural framework. The new contents are poured into old vessels, which have throughout the ages been used to create the cultural canon. In our case, the preferred form is the anthology. Since the Bible, the majority of canonical and holy texts in Jewish culture have been in the form of anthologies.[7]

The universal urge to provide the documentation with a historical, national, and ethical context is parallel to the reaction to these retroactive documentation projects and serves the needs of the present. We may find examples of the need for a historical mythos in the service of the new Jewish identity in high literature, as well as in the Zionist anthological projects. For example, at the time of its publication, the short story "The Sermon" by Haim Hazaz made waves by virtue of the provocative text put in the mouth of its hero Yudke:

> We have no history of our own that belongs to us, do we? It's clear! That's why I'm against it, I don't recognize it. It doesn't exist for me! ... Simply put, Jewish history is boring and uninteresting. It includes no great feats or sagas, no world-conquering heroes, no rulers and men of action, lords of action; only a gathering of faded and drifting men, moaners and weepers and beggars for mercy. You will agree that this is not interesting. To say the least: uninteresting. I would forbid the teaching of Jewish history to our children. Why the hell should we teach them the shame of their fathers? I would tell them: fellows! We have no history! From the day we were exiled from our land, we have been a people without history. You are hereby exempted. Go play football.[8]

This role of inventing myths was first played in Zionist-Israeli culture by the publication of the booklet *Yizker* in 1911. This document was important in fortifying the status of the Hashomer organization and the immigrants of the Second Aliyah, those with the right to determine the values of the Zionist ethos. It is interesting that this publication, produced in response to the deaths on duty of guards in various Jewish settlements, became a cult book for generations of youth.[9]

As Jewish society became more secular in the eighteenth century, a modern Jewish historiography developed along the lines of *Wissenschaft des Judentums* ideology. The biblical historical model no longer fit the spirit of the times. But while the model lost validity among sections of the Jewish community, the commandment *zakhor* maintains its centrality and vitality in Jewish cultural consciousness, especially since the Holocaust. Two kinds of commemorative books produced by communities in response to historical events in medieval Europe provided models for this Jewish response. These are the *memorbucher* [memory books] in the communities of Ashkenazi Jewry and the *pinkeysim* [community registers] in Eastern European Jewish communities. These two kinds of community books are differentiated by their function. *Memorbucher* had a religious use; *pinkeysim* had an administrative one.

Books for murdered individuals and destroyed communities appeared for the first time in response to the atrocities of 1096 in the Rhineland. They began as prayers in the synagogues that mentioned the names of victims of the crusades from the communities of Speyer, Worms, Cologne, and Mainz. The lamentable recurrence of similar calamities in these areas created the necessity for institutionalizing the ceremonies of commemoration and mourning, thus guaranteeing admiration for the valor of the martyrs who died for *kiddush hashem* [sanctification of God], not only to preceding generations but also beyond the communities directly involved. Thus, beside the prayers said in synagogues, lists of names appeared in some communities. With time, memorial books became an accepted, even a mandatory, response to catastrophe.

The first research on *memorbucher* was published at the end of the nineteenth century by Sigmund Salfeld, who studied the 1296 book of the Mainz community by Yitzhak ben Shmuel of Meiningen.[10] Salfeld found that prior to acquiring a standardized name, these books were called variously *sefer zikkaron* [book of remembrance] after Malachi 3:16; *sefer zikhronot* [book of memorable deeds] after Esther 6:1; or *sefer hazkarat neshamot* [book of remembrance of souls]. The latter was the most common. Occasionally the books were called *pinkeysim*. Dr. Magnus Weinberg, who was the rabbi of Sulzbürg/Oberpfalz between 1895 and 1935 and also served as the last rabbi of Würzburg (1935–1943), studied the history of the Jews of the Rhineland.[11] He dedicated much of his research to the memorial books that came out after the Middle Ages. Weinberg claimed that the pattern for this tradition was set by the Maharil (Rabbi Yaakov Levi) on the first anniversary after the first crusade, Sunday 3 Sivan 4857 (May 23, 1097), when it was announced the names of the victims would be read out on those two Sabbaths of the year in which tradition mandates the remembrance of tragic historical occurrences. These are the Sabbath before Shavuot, the last of the *omer* [first harvest after Pesach] and the Sabbath before the Ninth of Av, when the destruction of the Temple is lamented. Over time, names were recorded in other communities as well, and the tradition of the yizker prayer was established. As the lists of names grew longer, it became customary to read them in parts, according to a predetermined plan on every Sabbath, except those on which mourning is prohibited. The growing length of the lists eventually made it impossible to read all the names. The names of destroyed communities replaced the names of individuals. From then, individuals, when mentioned at all, were leaders, rab-

bis, or historical and mythical figures, such as the patriarchs or the sages of
the Middle Ages whose deaths were not always related to the relevant historical
events. The custom of memorial books spread through the communities of
Germany with the calamities. Every community administered its own *mem-
orbuch*, which was dedicated to the place and its surroundings.

The *pinkes* is a later, but parallel, form of community book. It is an
administrative document, initially intended for the autonomous management
of Jewish life on behalf of the rulers primarily for taxation purposes. The
word *pinkes* appears in Hebrew for the first time during the period of the Second Temple. It is found in the Jerusalem Talmud, which describes the books
opened in heaven on the eve of Rosh Hashanah when the deeds of man are
discussed. The passage reads: "even deeds which are not sins are written on
one's *pinkes* (Talmud Yerushalmi, Hagigah 2). Another passage states: "the
pinkes is open and the hand is writing" (Aboth, 3:16). This is the origin of
the term *pinkes*, a reference to an individual's account book, as well as to the
Jewish community's account book. The most famous community *pinkeysim*
are those of the Council of Four Lands in Poland and Russia created in 1520
by Sigismund I for the purpose of administering the life of the community
and its responsibility to the central authority. The Council existed for two
centuries as an executive and judicial authority. Its regulations were noted in
the *pinkes* kept in the Lublin synagogue, which was subsequently burnt or
lost. *Pinkeysim* were kept by every community, and even by community organizations and institutions, such as the *hevrah kadisha* and *gemilut hasadim*.
Only a few *pinkeysim* have survived to this day, but those that have are an
important source for the study of Jewish life in the diaspora. The *pinkeysim*
intended for certain well-defined purposes eventually became chronicles documenting the central events of community life, including meetings, laws, lists
of public officers, lists of fines and punishments, trials, extraordinary historical
events, and other details of community life.[12]

The *memorbucher* and *pinkeysim* are the old vessels into which new contents, specifically yizker books and jubilee books, were poured. The dominant
features of yizker books include visual and symbolic elements and the lists of
victims' names, which derive from *memorbucher*; whereas jubilee books are
mainly influenced by *pinkeysim*. Nonetheless, each genre reflects these biblical
verses:

- Write this as a memorial in a book (Ex. 17:14);
- You shall tell your son (Ex. 13:8); and
- These words that I command you today shall be on your heart. You shall
  teach them diligently to your children, and shall talk of them when you
  sit in your house, and when you walk by the way, and when you lie

down, and when you rise. You shall bind them as a sign on your hand, and they shall be as frontlets between your eyes. You shall write them on the doorposts of your house and on your gates (Deut. 6:6–9).

The French historian Pierre Nora describes the relation between memory and history as one between history and its reconstruction when he writes:

> Memory is life. It is always borne by living groups and as such is always developing, open to the dialectic of remembering and forgetting, sensitive to all uses and manipulations; it knows long periods of dormancy and sudden bursts of vitality. History is the problematic and always partial reconstruction of what is no longer.[13]

According to Nora, the process by which memory becomes history is twofold. The first relates to the distance from the event or *lieux de memoire* [the living environment of memory]. That exists so long as the impression of events lives in the consciousness of those who have lived through them; they do not appear to need any artificial tool to remind them or to guarantee the continuation of this memory in the future. At that point, collective memory has no uniformity; it creates a Rashomon effect.[14] The second is the creation of *milieux de memoire* [the sites of memory]. This refers to the cultural institutions that determine the collective memory of a social, ethnic, or religious group. The institutionalization of memory occurs constantly. Memorial ceremonies are sometimes instituted quite quickly after an event. Examples are the memorial days for Israel's wars or the prayers inserted into prayer books following these wars. However, so long as memory and the status of the group that has heretofore been the elite are endangered, whether following the disappearance of the remembering group or changes in the spirit of the times, these efforts become more intensive and more territories of memory are created. Those include museums, monuments, and commemorative books. Nora further notes:

> The territories of memory are born from the feeling that there is no spontaneous memory.... Without their demands to "remember!" history would erase them quickly enough. These are the fortifications, but if the thing they are defending were not threatened, there would be no need for them.[15]

The creation of various territories of memory reconstructs and retains, and in fact *creates*, the authorized narrative, retrospectively fitting the past to the ideology of the social or political group doing the remembering according to its needs in the present. In Barry Schwartz's words: "remembering means enlisting bits of the past in the service of the needs and conceptions of the present."[16] Additionally, the commandment *zakhor* might be one source for Martin Buber's assertion that memory is the legislating principle, constructing and establishing the Jewish identity as people, which he calls a "community of memory."[17]

A variety of cultural instruments and institutions were conceived to guarantee collective memory before and, with redoubled efforts, after World War II. These include monuments, museums, ceremonies, prayers, and books. Regarding yizker books, in particular, almost a thousand have been published to date. The exact number of books is difficult to know due to the popular and local nature of the books, as well as the differing definitions of the genre. Regardless, over the last few years interest in them has grown as the events themselves become more distant. This interest is also a function of the possibility of going to the places themselves. As frontiers opened in Eastern Europe in the early 1990s, it became easier to visit Poland, Lithuania, the Ukraine, and Russia. Also, a number of bibliographies and catalogs of yizker books have been published in the last few decades. As a result, what was once the province of few besides the survivors of the communities is now more widely available.[18]

Pinkeysim *and Yizker Books*

The perception that documenting the horrors of World War II was an important task in the fight for the life and future of the people took root with some Jews even while the war was raging. Historians, such as Emanuel Ringelblum, who created the *Oyneg Shabbos* archive in the Warsaw Ghetto, Zvi Marsik and Mordecai Tannenbaum, who compiled the clandestine archive of the Białystok Ghetto,[19] and many others, understood the tremendous importance of keeping diaries and documenting events for future generations.[20] An immense desire to tell, write, and testify was characteristic of many survivors, but the world with which they would have to deal sometimes silenced them. This conflict, between the need to document and retell the experiences of the Holocaust and the paralysis and muteness forced on the survivors by the understanding that it would be impossible, even immoral, as Adorno said, to write about it, deserves another discussion. In any case, yizker books created to commemorate communities destroyed in the Holocaust are a response to that need to write and document, despite hardships and lack of sources.

While the creation of yizker books for the destroyed communities was an immediate response to the end of the Holocaust, some books were actually published earlier in the century. An example is the 1937 *Felshtin: zamlbukh lekoved tsum ondenk fun di Felstiner kdoyshim*, a memorial book dedicated to Felshtin, a community destroyed in a 1920 pogrom. The first yizker book for a community destroyed in the Holocaust is the *Lodzher yisker-buch*, which was published in 1943 in New York. At the end of World War II, numerous survivors and their organizations started collecting materials and testimonies for their own books. Most of the books were published in Israel; the others were printed in the United States, Argentina, France, and elsewhere. Most of the texts are in Hebrew, Yiddish, or English; a few are in other languages. The titles of the books reflect the different motivations behind these efforts. Among these are the following:

- **to sanctify.** Many books are called *The Book of* followed by the name of the community. Examples include *The Book of Lutzk*, *The Book of Ludvipol*, and *The Book of Sosnoviets*. This naming convention links the books to the Bible, whose parts are named in a similar fashion.
- **to mourn.** Some books are entitled yizker in Yiddish or *sefer yizker* in Hebrew. *Sefer yizker Rozwadow* is an example. The term alludes to the Jewish memorial service.
- **to chronicle.** Some books are called *pinkes*. Examples are *Pinkes Bendin* and *Pinkes Kozmir de Lublin*. This suggests that the books continue the town's chronicling tradition.
- **to memorialize.** Some titles include the term *yad* [memorial] Examples are *Yad le-Ataki* and *Yad le-Yedinits*. This means that the book acts a tombstone for the victims.

The need to memorialize the dead and to name them was a desperate task of the remnant of Jewish people dispersed after the war because millions of Jews were not buried, and as a result, they did not have their names etched on a tombstone. Yizker books explicitly or implicitly aspire to provide a tombstone as the fulfillment of an obligation to the dead. Just as monuments demand to be read so do the books. They are shrines to the memory of the victims demanding to be visited.[21] Two commandments merge and are metaphorically fulfilled in yizker books. These are *zakhor* and *khessed shel emeth* [true grace or sincere mourning]. The various lists and texts are compiled by members of the community who left the hometown before the Holocaust and emigrated to Israel or other countries or by those who survived and found themselves in one of these countries. The task of editing was sometimes given to a literary figure from the hometown or to a professional or otherwise well-known figure in the field of editing and representation. In other cases, the editor was a member of the organization. Editors decided what to include or exclude.[22]

Only a few Holocaust yizker books appeared before 1953. After that, books appeared more frequently. Between the Six Day and Yom Kippur Wars (1967–1973), an average of eighteen books appeared every year. In 1974, there was a forty percent increase. From then, the number of new books declined every year until 1984, in which only four books appeared.[23] Yet, new books continue to appear even now. Sometimes they are expanded versions of older books or translations for those readers who do not speak Yiddish or Hebrew. One example is the book to Zelwa, which appeared in English;[24] other examples are the books to Luboml, Piotrkov-Trybunalski, and Białystok, which were translated to English from Hebrew or Yiddish.[25] These new editions and English translations help to ensure the continuation of the cultural pattern of passing on traditions to the next generations, especially as the geographical and linguistic spread of Jews makes Hebrew and Yiddish less useful as communicating languages. The large Jewish community in the United States and the emergence of English as an international language contribute to the changes in yizker books. These changes benefit third and fourth generations of Jews who are seeking to solidify their identity on a basis of knowledge of the past.

Due to the democratization of memory, personal memoirs and journals have proliferated, filling the empty space of memory and sometimes replacing community yizker books.[26] As the witnesses grow older, documentation and testimonial projects using all forms of media are underway. A sense of urgency is ever-present because testimony must be available to fulfill the *zakhor* commandment, as expressed by the prophet Joel (1:2–3):

> Hear this, you elders; give ear, all inhabitants of the land! Has such a thing happened in your days, or in the days of your fathers? Tell your children of it, and let your children tell their children, and their children to another generation.

Memorial Books as a Twentieth-Century Genre

Although memorial books are found in Jewish and non–Jewish communities, the books written in non–Jewish communities may be distinguished from those written in Jewish communities by their intention. Yizker books are nationally oriented, sometimes with nostalgic aura, but mainly are written as a religious reaction to a loss. By comparison, books by people in other communities are mainly political. They aim to establish a written legacy and a claim by refugees of rights to the places from which they where expelled by wars or other circumstances. Susan Slyomovics suggests that the genre of invented local history is a twentieth-century innovation to the century's expulsions and ethnic- and national-cleansings. Her claim is problematic. Expulsions and ethnic- and national-cleansings of communities are not new, especially in Jewish communities. I hold that the reason for this genre's broad distribution in the twentieth century has to do with the distribution of literacy and the exposure of the Jewish custom of memorial books to other cultures.

This may be the case with the Palestinian project that stands at the center of her work. As an introduction to her discussion, Slyomovics combines all the traumatic events of the twentieth century that produced commemoration books. She includes the Armenian genocide of 1915–1919, the Jewish Holocaust of 1939–1945, the destruction and expulsion of German communities after the defeat at World War II, the destruction and expulsion of Palestinian villages followed the 1948 war, and the destruction and expulsion of Bosnian communities from Yugoslavia after the civil war in the 1980s and 1990s. Specifically, she focuses on two narratives, the Palestinian village Ein-Houd and the Israeli village Ein-Hod. In the prologue to her book, Slyomovics devotes short passages to the yizker books and compares interviews made for her family's native town Maramorosh with interviews conducted during the Palestinian commemoration project initiated by the Bir-Zeit University for the 400 deserted or destroyed places in 1948. She claims that while the documentation of Palestinian historical memory deals with the villages in the past as autonomous entities and in the present as resettled by Israelis, yizker books document their community history until its destruction. She writes:

> In their nostalgic yet anguished backward glances, these two groups maintain diametrically opposed attitudes toward the possibility — or impossibility — of an eventual return.[27]

Slyomovics concludes that the former inhabitants of Ein-Houd keep nourishing their hope of returning to their village, and they do so by compiling a commemoration book and engaging in other activities. For that goal, a process of reinventing and reconstructing the local geography takes place in accordance with the preserved memory of the exiled villagers and the next generations. The geography does not fit the physical one. The book assists in creating a tangible focus for the refugees' yearning for their place. The manner in which this collective memory is created or actually invented among the exiled villagers fixes the community members' identity.[28] These types of commemorative books are characterized by a political and declarative dimension behind which stands a real intention, even if based upon an illusion, which is to return, rebuild, and resettle their old communities or to gain recognition in their rights as refugees to be compensated for their lost property. By comparison, yizker books lack any concrete political dimension, except by their reflection on the community's political identities before its destruction. Jews did come back to their hometowns, but not to resettle in them. They did not claim rights. Rather, they wanted to renovate destroyed holy places, synagogues, and graveyards, as well as to erect memorial monuments.

Jubilee Books of Kibbutzim — Documenting a Living Community

Jubilee books are a type of *lieux des memoire*. They are produced in the physical sphere as sites of memory. Due to the characteristic of rural settlements in Israel, jubilee books resemble each other. They have features that are different from other books. The most significant is the process of production, which is similar in many ways to the folk literature production process. This is a circular communication process, where the addressers and addressees change places constantly. It contains the four functions of folklore as described by Bascom.[29] A jubilee book's production depends on the formal approval by the community's establishment, and every stage is held inside the intimate community of kibbutz members. It is never the only event to celebrate a special date in the life of the kibbutz. Moreover, sometimes it is postponed due to the complexity of such a project. Nevertheless, the books are always published in the context of the date of beginning of the kibbutz. The date is usually printed on the front cover. There is no rule stating when they should be published, and they may not necessarily have a connection to the jubilee in its biblical sense, namely the fiftieth anniversary.[30] Rarely, does a kibbutz produce a book in its first year. Usually one is produced for a particular anniversary, such as the fifth, tenth, or twentieth year of the kibbutz. The main goal of the book is to tell the history of the place and its people from its first day.

My research identified 261 jubilee books published before the year 2000 that fit the definition of the genre. Counting the books by decade shows that between the years 1932 and 1969 sixty books were issued. And then in each of the following decades, over sixty books were published. In the first decade of the twenty-first century, no more than twenty jubilee books were issued. That figure is based on a survey of the kibbutz movement archives. This low number might reflect the deep crisis in which the kibbutz movement finds itself and the progression of privatization, which affects all communal activities. But, books are being produced despite that, though in small numbers. Officially, jubilee books are made to gather, revive, and preserve the local legacy for the present and future. This legacy is molded from the reservoir of local knowledge, which includes archives and testimonies. The awareness of the importance of the archives is generated from the increasing distance from the beginning of the kibbutz and the desire to create a collective memory for a generation that never knew its origin. In the jubilee book, a local and seemingly insignificant narrative is expressed, reflecting the Zionist meta-narrative, an organ of the rural-collective Israeli settlement's ideology. A reader of many jubilee books could not avoid finding a resemblance between them. Similarities appear in the structure, themes, pictures, and other features. Differences appear in the format and subgenre. Some are thin brochures that contain local legends, legends of origin, and anecdotes; others contain statistics and chronicles, prospectus, and diagrams. Some are multi-page and multi-photo books, which I call encyclopedic, aiming to describe all aspects of kibbutz life, usually as a coherent-chronological narrative. Among them, mainly in last decades, there are encyclopedic books edited as lexicons in which the story of the kibbutz becomes a list of themes, mosaic-like, sometimes accompanied by photos. There are jubilee books lacking any adornments, and there are books edited like photograph albums. The common denominator for all jubilee books is the aesthetic effort invested to reach the goal of a distinctive and respectful publication. All readers of the books are defined, even when the book is published by a commercial publishing house. Readers include kibbutz members, as well as ex-members, children who left home, friends, and ideological partners home and abroad.

Yizker Books and Jubilee Books — A Comparison of Memory and History

The most frequent criticism of yizker books and jubilee books concerns their untrustworthiness. This criticism is raised because sometimes editors intentionally made concessions to objectivity by choosing a personal tone rather than an academic one for the books. But mainly it is because the materials in the books are provided from community people rather than from professional people, even though some yizker books include contributions by professionals, such as Mahler, Tronek, Shatzky, Ringelblum, Schipper, Schmeruk, Dubnov, and Dinu. In general though, yizker books and jubilee books are grassroots projects. About yizker books in particular, Abraham Wein estimates that more than ten thousand writers and one thousand editors contributed to the yizker books.[31] There are no comparable statistics for jubilee books.

I argue that the phenomenon of writing these books is folkloric and ritualistic. The books are destined to fortify and approve the individual's identification with the group. The editors invest a great deal of effort in reconstructing the community's history, along with "formatting the authenticity," a term borrowed from Moocky Tsur concerning the jubilee books, in accordance with a social and ethical wide consensus supposed to satisfy all community members.

Regarding the original community, especially in pre-war times, there were controversies and rival groups striving for objective truth. As a result, yizker book editors seek solidarity since ultimately townspeople all suffered the same fate. The same goes for the history of kibbutzim. Rivals and crises are hardly mentioned in jubilee books.[32] Other attitudes take the place of truth. There are concerns that no one should be offended by negative information or by details contrasting the positive image of the place. This helps to explain why certain issues are omitted or glossed over; whereas others are emphasized and glorified. The narrative expressed in community books is subjective and carefully presented, sometimes embellished and sometimes vague. The available is enslaved to the desirable. Without admitting it, and maybe without being conscious to it, readers of their own community's yizker book or jubilee book give up objectivity from the start. They want to find their own concept of their community, as well as to confirm what they know and widen their knowledge. Disappointment is a frequent reaction when a gap exists between the individual's image of the community and the image reflected in the book. When there are no contradicting images, people feel like they belong; their bonds to the community are strengthened.

Apart from their differing motivations, jubilee books and yizker books are defined by the nature and identity of the community described and the processes of creating the books. The kibbutz as a living community is documenting itself; whereas the ancestral hometown as a destroyed community is documented by its heirs and successors and its survivors and their children. Both books are marked by a ceremonial festivity. Jubilee books serve as rituals of passage in communal life; yizker books serve as rituals of mourning. Like all local community books, each genre thrives to glorify and heighten life. However, unlike jubilee books, yizker books glorify and heighten the past. However, if the books did not have any goal in the present, then they would not been compiled in the first place.

The two genres share a number of features. Both are local histories made by people for their own interests. Both are marked by the same paradox. Despite the fact that the books often serve as primary sources for historians and culture researchers, they are hardly ever examined as a cultural phenomenon or subgenre of Jewish local literature. Until recently, little attention was given to yizker books, and until my own research, no attention at all was given to jubilee books. [33] This lack of attention stems from the fact that scholars and others often doubt the reliability of these genres due to their folkloristic nature.

Discussions of the value of yizker books as historical sources are found in the works of Elias Schulman, as well as in those of Jack Kugelmass and Jonathan Boyarin. These writers claim that the books contain a richness of materials. Moreover, they hold that the books are actually the only valid source for information about the everyday life prior to the war. They further claim that ignoring this rich source is a great loss for historical research and

Jewish historiography.[34] Kugelmass and Boyarin's anthology in particular introduces the yizker books to the general audience. The material in the anthology is grouped into these sections: "Our Towns," "Townspeople," "Lifeways," "Events," "Legends and Folklore," "Holocaust," "Return," and "The Townspeople Abroad." Each section represents a wide spectrum of cultural and ideological sectors to which authors and editors of yizker books belonged. Some researchers of yizker books trace the birth of a new community out of an imagined community by focusing on the inner conflicts occurring during a book's production. Miriam Hoffman's in-depth study of the Zwolen book is an example.[35] Some scholars have studied the books from an anthropological point of view. An example of that approach is Olga Goldberg's "The Memory Book and the Myth of a Jewish Little Town." Goldberg claims that the yizker books create myth more than history. She notes that this myth is different from the myth created by great writers like Mendele Mocher Sforim or Shalom Aleichem since in the center of this myth stands the institutionalized activities of the cultural organizations that existed between the two world wars.[36]

In comparison to yizker books, jubilee books mainly cover the kibbutz history and economy, the ideology of the kibbutz, the landscape of the kibbutz, the family life on the kibbutz, and yizker in that order. The section on kibbutz history sometimes includes descriptions of the personal history of kibbutz members before they settled down. The family life section includes discussions of education, ways of life, culture, and anecdotes. The yizker section is usually a list of names, sometimes with portraits of deceased members and fallen soldiers.

Despite the crucial difference between the two genres of community books that are derived from their different motivations and nature, their similarity is obvious and expressed in many ways. Similarities are seen in format, in some stages of production, in the attitude towards the past, and above all, in the orientation as a means of constructing a self and collective identity. Both genres are different kinds of local history. Both strive to revive literally and retrospectively a full picture of the Jewish community in its past. One of the main goals is to establish a local collective memory for future generations. In both types of books, the final product is a verbal and sometimes a visual reconstruction of the past, which becomes a myth.

Although the impulse for compiling these books is the desire to construct a historical consciousness, the picture generated is somehow embellished and glorified. It shows the existence of a community built upon the ideals and myth of its origin from which everything that does not fit the collective positive self image or consensus is ignored or omitted. It is a common convention that this is the argument used to exempt yizker books from scientific examination. Perhaps that is also the explanation for the lack of research into jubilee books. I claim that both genres are based on a folkloristic collective creation formulated inside a community. In the case of the jubilee book, the community is real. In the case of the yizker book, the community is "imagined," in Benedict Anderson's terms,[37] until the stage of producing the yizker book, when it becomes a real community too. Usually people involved in a yizker book project become a group. Even if lacking mutual connections or personal knowledge of each other, they are connected by the ceremonial activity and the awareness of being part of this community. It is interesting to note that during the making of the book, people get to know each other. Despite geographical distances, differences in languages, and generational differences, a real community is born and functions. The community begins with individual survivors searching for people from the hometown. As time passes, they become a substitute family, which replaces their lost one. Making the book unites locals with an international community.

In many ways, the similarities between jubilee books and yizker books are more obvious than the differences. Both are mostly bound and respectful volumes, telling the story of the place, either fully or partially, with preference for the time that serves as the motive for their production. Jubilee books tend to describe the early days of the settlement; yizker books tend to emphasize the years of the Holocaust. Preparing these books requires a variety of materials, such as historical reviews, statistics, figures, sketches, maps, literature, everyday episodes and anecdotes, and folkloristic episodes and anecdotes. Preparing these books also takes the efforts of many people. Books require graphic design and artistic editing resources too. Similarities are found in the process of producing the books. The dependence on funding resources is obvious and influences the final physical and social-cultural format or shape. Additionally, the editorial approaches show a resemblance. Editors ask readers to understand the editor's limits in describing the place. Editors apologize for their inability to portray the whole picture and for the limited view they have due to the distance in time from the subject. Both genres are based upon oral and written documentation, relying on the living or reconstructed memory of the first generation and others. Both genres are written after a period of years. Sometimes efforts are hampered by a lack of documentation. Documents may have disappeared during the Holocaust or may be unavailable due to a lack of awareness during the first decades of the kibbutz.

Community Books as a Folkloristic Phenomenon

Susan Slyomovics suggests an explanation for the increasing interest in memorial books by folklorists from different cultures and societies when she states:

Memorial books engage scholarly interest because each volume combines and codifies the best of folklore's many subjects: oral literature, folk history, vernacular architecture, community photography and sociocultural anthropology.[38]

The same may be said about jubilee books. At first, using traditional definitions of folklore, which insist on oral transmission, it seems that the books have nothing to do with folklore. However, newer definitions broaden the scope of transmission and distribution and define folklore as a message, formulated artistically, not necessarily orally. The message is created and transmitted within a community of people who share mutual interests and exhibit multiple existences.[39] There are three more characteristics:

- Only what is adopted by the community can be considered as folklore.
- The folkloric work is non-personal, and its transmitter displays his or her talents by artistic means to satisfy the audience. This satisfaction is due to the text being inside the community's conventions and moral consensus. The piece of folklore must go through social censorship, therefore it reflects the community's scale of values and dictates what will be saved and what will be erased.
- The artist aims to pass the social censorship so he or she does not express his or her own observations but a communal ideology. The art represents collective conventions.[40]

These definitions support my claim that despite their unique attributes, both genres must be examined as folklore artifacts. Like folk narratives, they are created inside an intimate community, exhibit multiple existences, pass communal censorship, and reflect collective values.

Jubilee books and yizker books are in most cases collective projects and not the work of individuals. Like folklore, their main object is to transmit knowledge to future generations. Both genres are read and kept as long as they are relevant to the readers. In rare occasions, these books are edited and printed in new editions. In those cases, the present generation dictates what materials will be omitted and what new texts will be added. Unlike the claim that folklore has no moment of birth and its creators are unknown, yizker books and jubilee books do have origination dates. Their creators are often mentioned by name or initials. However, this does not annul the many virtues of placing them in the domain of artifacts. The last point relates to the context of the books. The context is a folk activity whose aim is to establish a collective memory and protect a conventional narrative that is accepted and agreed upon by the community and replace the formal history as a local database for the community's narrative.

As stated before, both genres are ceremonial by nature. Many yizker books are introduced during memorial ceremonies. The wish that a book should be used in the yearly gathering ceremony of the organization or that the book should serve as a replacement for the missing tombstone or funeral is expressed in many yizker books. In a similar way, jubilee books are handed over to the kibbutz members during one of the many celebrations held during the jubilee year. Jubilee books are always written in the context of the jubilee. Later if they are well received by their audience, they may be given as a present or as a collective identity card to newcomers or official guests.

The approval of a book stems from its relevance to the times, fit into the community image, and ability to deliver the message to the following generations. A dissonance is felt when this is not so. For instance, in his review of *Lomza Yizker Book*, Chaim Shapiro complains that he does not find his hometown truly represented in the book and wonders why there are hardly any descriptions of the rich religious life and the different types of Jews in the town.[41] Interestingly, disapproval is rarely published. Rather it is expressed orally. In the case of the jubilee books, the most common way to recompense a dissatisfied group is to produce another, usually smaller, jubilee book, in which the dissatisfied group will be central.

To conclude, I suggest seeing the community books as ceremonial texts, in which any reading is by definition a kind of a ritual activity toward which a kind of preparation must be invested. It is not like reading other texts. This ritual activity often takes place within the individual sphere, either among an intimate group of people or by oneself. Individuals know and are aware of the existence of other group members who share the same motivation to learn and pass on their legacy to the next generations. Doing this creates a collective identity and provides a sense of belonging. The imagined community of yizker books readers and the real community of jubilee books readers are similar to Anderson's description of the morning newspaper reading ceremony. That activity is done in silent privacy by individuals, but each knows that there are many readers who are performing the same ceremony more or less at the same time.[42] A difference is that reading the paper is a routine and everyday activity; while reading a yizker or a jubilee book is an occasional one done at certain dates. The newspaper is relevant for a day; the books are meant for posterity. What is common, though, is that readers belong to a greater community of people who share a mutual interest.

"Write This as a Memorial in the Book"

Two main issues, pivotal to this article, are hinted in Exodus 17: 14: "Then The Lord said to Moses, write **this** for a memorial in the **book** and

recount it in the hearing of Joshua."[43] First, memory is a means of establishing a national-religious identity, which is crucial in ensuring its covenant with God. Second, delivering the message from one generation to the next is a divine command. Memory is therefore the legislative principle establishing Jewish identity. This is why Buber saw the Jewish people as a "congregation of memory." This is a good explanation for why they are also called the "People of the Book." Yizker books of the Holocaust and jubilee books of the kibbutz are anthologies in which one may find co-existing texts of different kinds. Even in a generation that abandoned its faith in God, the community depicted is undoubtedly a Jewish community with its values and institutions. Jubilee books, celebrating a flourishing life and success, and yizker books, mourning the vanished communities, are written in the name of the living and for the living. Both projects are also for the sake of the next generations and their everlasting memory.

Notes

1. I wish to thank my friends Mooli Brog, Yonat Rotbain, and Rina Ben-Ari for their helpful remarks on the manuscript. Thanks to the Central Archives for the History of the Jewish People for assisting my research. Thanks also to Matan Kaminer for his help with the English version of this paper. For English citations of biblical phrases, see English Standard Version at http://www.gospelhall.org. See my book, *Sites in the Realm of Memory: Books Celebrating Jubilee of Kibbutzim* (Hebrew) (Yad Tabenkin and Yad Yaari, 2006). The comparison suggested here deals with these two genres as representatives of local literature and local history in general.

2. Yosef Hayim Yerushalmi, *Zakhor: Jewish History and Jewish Memory* (Tel-Aviv: The Samuel and Althea Stroum Lectures in Jewish Studies, 1982/1988), [pages fit the Hebrew edition], 16.

3. See Yerushalmi, *Zakhor*, chapter four. Also see, Amos Funkenstein, *Perception and Historical Awareness* (Hebrew) (Tel Aviv: Am Oved, 1991), 13–30, 232–242, and the endnotes [English version *Perceptions of Jewish History* (Los Angeles, 1993)].

4. Exodus 13:1–16; Deuteronomy 6:4–9; 11:13–21. This pattern is exemplified in Deuteronomy 26: 5–9.

5. Jacques Le Goff, *History and Memory: European Perspectives*, trans. Steven Rendall and Elizabeth Claman (New York: Columbia University Press, 1992), 86–90. Le Goff outlines five stages in the production of collective memory. The fourth is the democratic, which is expressed in popular media, such as photographs and recordings, which create private archives, containing unlimited information. The historian has to choose carefully.

6. This is a very frequently discussed subject in Israel since the 1980s. See Judy Tidor Baumel, "For Eternal Memory: Commemoration of the Holocaust by Individuals and Community," (Hebrew) *Iyunim Bitkumat Yisrael* 5 (2005); Mooli Brog, "Landscape of Memory: Monuments for the Shoah and Heroism in Yad Vashem"(Hebrew) *Ariel* 170 (2005); "A Stone Will Cry Out From the Wall: Monumental Commemoration of the Shoah in the Landscape of Israel" (Hebrew) *Massuah* 33, (2005); Maoz Azaryahu, *State Cults: Celebrating Independence and Commemorating the Fallen in Israel 1948–1956* (Hebrew) (Sde Boker: Ben-Gurion University of the Negev Press, 1995); and Sivan Emanuel, *1948 Generation: Myth, Profile, Memory* (Hebrew) (Tel Aviv: Ma'arakhot — Misrad Habitakhon, 1991).

7. The subject of the anthological imagination in Jewish literature was the focus of an

academic conference held in Tel Aviv in 1995, which generated two volumes of *Prooftext*, edited by David Stern, who contributed two seminal forewords from which I borrowed these ideas, specifically *Prooftext* 17 (1997) and *Prooftext* 19 (1999).

8. Haim Hazaz, "The Sermon," *Boiling Stones* (Hebrew) (Tel Aviv: Dvir, 1943).

9. On ways that Zionist myths were established, see Yonathan Frenkel "The 1911 Book *Yizker*: Remarks on National Myths in the Time of Second Alyia," (Hebrew) *Yahadut Zemanenu* 40/4 (1988): 64–96. Also see, Zeev Tsahor, "David Ben-Gurion as a Myth Creator," (Hebrew) in *Myth and Memory*, eds. Robert S. Wistrich and David Ohana (Tel Aviv: Van-Leer Institute and HaKibutz Hameuchad, 1996), 136–155.

10. Siegmond Salfeld, *Quellen zur Geschichte der Juden in Deutschland: Das Mart6yrologium des Nuernberger Memorbuchs* (Berlin: Verlag von Leonard Simion, 1898).

11. Rabbi Magnus Weinberg was murdered in Theresienstadt on December 2, 1943.

12. See *"Pinkas,"* in *Encyclopedia Judaica* 13, 537; and "Autonomy Kehila," in *Encyclopedia Ivri* (Hebrew Encyclopedia) Vol. 29, 184.

13. Pierre Nora, "Between Memory and History: *Les Lieux de Memoire*," *Representations* 26 (1989) or *Realms of Memory* (New York: Columbia University Press) [Hebrew translation by Rivka Spivak] *Zemanim* 45 (1993), 6.

14. The Rashomon effect refers to the subjectivity of perception on recollection by which observers of an event are able to produce substantially different but equally plausible accounts. It borrows the name from Akira Korasawa's film *Rashomon*.

15. Nora, "Between Memory and History," 8.

16. Barry Schwartz, "The Social Context of Commemoration: A Study in Collective Memory," *Social Forces* 61 (1982): 374–402.

17. Martin M. Buber, "Talmud Tora — How Come?" (Hebrew) *Darko shel Mikra* (Jerusalem: Mossad Bialik, 1964), 359.

18. See Zachary Baker, "Bibliography of Eastern European Memorial Books," in *From a Ruined Garden: The Memorial Books of Polish Jewry*, eds. Jack Kugelmass and Jonathan Boyarin. Second expanded edition (Bloomingdale and Indianapolis: Indiana University Press, 1998), 273–339; and Cyril Fox and Saul Issroff, *Jewish Memorial (Yizker) Books in the United Kingdom: Destroyed European Communities* (London: JGDGB Publications, 2006).

19. B. Klibansky, "The Archives of the Bialystok Ghetto, founded by Tennenbaum and Marsik," *Yad Vashem* 2 (1958).

20. Abraham Wein, "Memorial Books as a Source for Research into the History of Jewish Communities in Europe," *Yad Vashem* 9 (1973): 209. See also Rosemary Horowitz, "Reading and Writing During the Holocaust as Described in *Yizker* Books" in *The Holocaust and the Book*, ed. Jonathan Rose (Amherst: University of Massachusetts Press, 2001), 128–142.

21. See Tidor-Baumel, "For Eternal Memory," 368. For the missing-grave syndrome, see Kugelmass and Boyarin, *From a Ruined Garden*, 34.

22. See Jack Kugelmass and Jonathan Boyarin, "*Yizker Bikher* and the Problem of Historical Veracity: An Anthropological Approach," in *The Jews of Poland Between Two World Wars*, eds. I. Gutman, et al. (Waltham, MA: Brandeis University Press, 1992), 519–536.

23. Tidor-Baumel, "For Eternal Memory," 371.

24. Kugelmass and Boyarin, *From a Ruined Garden*, 36.

25. See Rosemary Horowitz, *Literacy and Cultural Transmission in the Reading, Writing, and Rewriting of Jewish Memorial Books* (Dissertation) (San Francisco-London-Bethesda: Austin & Winfield, 1998).

26. Nathan Wachtel, "Remember and Never Forget," *History and Anthropology* 2/2 (1986): 307–335. Wachtel compares collective and individual memory in yizker books. He mentions many essays and books assembled by individuals for the purpose of telling the community's historical narrative and claims that those efforts were made to replace an unpublished yizker book.

27. Susan Slyomovics, *The Object of Memory: Arab and Jew Narrate the Palestinian Village* (Philadelphia: University of Pennsylvania Press, 1998), xiii.

28. Eric Hobsbawm, *The Invention of Tradition* (Cambridge: Cambridge University Press, 1983).

29. William Bascom, "Four Functions of Folklore," *Journal of American Folklore* 67 (1954): 333–349.

30. The English word *jubilee* comes from the biblical Hebrew *yovel*, which originally means a ram. Its meaning derives from second temple time-counting system and its associated rituals. According to this system, every seventh year is a sabbatical, called *shmita*, a year of remission, in which the land is not cultivated due to a divine demand. Seven times *shmita* is 49 years. The 50th is the *yovel*. See "Sabbatical Year and Jubilee," *Enyclopedia Judaica* (Hebrew). Today, *yovel* means mainly an important date in one's life or in a community's existence. For the purposes of this essay, *yovel* refers to the festive celebrations of the settling of the kibbutz.

31. Abraham Wein, "Memorial Books for the Holocaust Destroyed Communities," (Hebrew) *Encyclopedia for the Holocaust*, chief editor Yisrael Gutmann (Jerusalem: Yad Vashem and Sifriat Poalim, 1990), 893–894.

32. In jubilee books, issues such as political or personal rivalries, the expulsion of Arabs as a result of the 1948 war, gender equality, or emancipation for women are subjects rarely mentioned, and if they do appear they are dealt with special care.

33. The list of academic works dealing with yizker book is less than ten. Jubilee books of the Israeli moshava are dealt in the M.A. thesis by Orit Manor entitled *Jubilee Books of the Galilee Moshavo as a Reflection of Collective Memory and Identity* (Haifa University, 2000).

34. Kugelmass and Boyarin, *From a Ruined Garden*; Elias Schulman, "A Survey and Evaluation of Yizkor Books," *Jewish Book Annual* Vol. 25 (1967–1968): 184–190.

35. Miriam Hoffman, *Memory and Memorial: An Investigation into the Making of the Zwolen Memorial Book* (M.A thesis) (New York: Columbia University, 1983).

36. Olga Goldberg-Mulkiewicz, "Księga Pamięci A Mit Żydowskiego Miasteczka," *Etnografia Polska* 35: 187–199. I wish to thank my friend Dr. Rina Benari for the Hebrew translation.

37. Benedict Anderson, *Imagined Communities: Reflections on the Origin and Spread of Nationalism* (London: Verso, 1983). Although Anderson deals with nationalism as a factor in molding a collective identity, his definitions may be used for other identity-groups as well.

38. Slyomovics, *The Object of Memory*, xiii.

39. Allen Dundes, ed., "What Is Folklore?" in *The Study of Folklore* (Englewood Cliffs, NJ: Prentice Hall, 1965), 1–3; Allan Dundes, *International Folkloristics — Classic Contributions by the Founders of Folklore* (USA: Rowman & Littlefield, 1999), vii–viii.

40. Roman Jacobson and Peter Bogatyrev, "On the Boundary Between Studies of Folklore and Literature," in *Readings in Russian Poetics: Formalist and Structuralist Views*, eds. Ladislav Matejka and Krystyna Pomorska (Cambridge, MA: MIT Press, 1971), 91–93.

41. Chaim Shapiro, "How Not to Write a *Yizker* Book," *Jewish Observer* 14/8 (1980): 18–25.

42. See Anderson, *Imagined Communities*.

43. My emphasis.

11

Blood Ties: Leib Rochman's Yiddish War Diary

JAN SCHWARZ

> "...the historical analysis of the Holocaust and the Jews should focus on texts, broadly conceived, and they should be studied as cultural expressions of the conditions of those who experienced the Holocaust."—*Amos Goldberg*[1]

> "We, the very few left of Eastern European Jewry are mostly people who have no graves left behind. Everything has been completely destroyed. We seek them constantly on the earth. Wherever we are, we step on and are pulled to a source. As if we were still bound to the graves. Everywhere, we are propelled to visit our ancestors' graves from our old lives."—*Leib Rochman*[2]

Those who shaped Jewish memory of the Holocaust were primarily Jewish writers who had survived in Poland, Lithuania, and the Soviet Union. Following the war, they edited and published their wartime diaries, poetry, memoirs, and songs. The transformation of the diaries and chronicles into public testimonies took place in the DP camps, the courtroom, historical commissions, commemorations of the *landsmanshaftn*, and the Jewish mass media.[3] The Yiddish press in New York, Paris, and Buenos Aires were particularly important in disseminating testimonies and diaries written during the war, and for those who survived, reworked in its aftermath. What set Yiddish literary testimonies apart from testimonies in non–Jewish languages was the existence of a world wide Yiddish mass media and readership that commissioned, published and discussed Jewish witness accounts from the war.[4] After the war, Yiddish mass media continued to make *belle-lettres* and testimonies about the Holocaust a centerpiece of Yiddish culture.[5] Unlike testimonies in non–Jewish languages, which functioned in specific national and ideological contexts and which were, largely, marginalized and suppressed

until the 1960s, the Yiddish cultural world addressed the repercussions of the
Holocaust continuously and immediately after 1945. This took several forms,
including journalistic accounts of trips to the destroyed Jewish communities
in Eastern Europe; serialized novels and memoirs, some of which were based
on diaries kept during the war; yizker books about Jewish towns and cities;
and publications of historical and personal documents written in the ghettos,
camps, and in hiding.

Yiddish testimonies gave voice to Jewish survivors, some of whom became
consumers of and contributors to Yiddish mass media world wide. Historical
and literary issues related to the publication of original Jewish documents
written during the war were hotly debated in the Yiddish press. These public
debates anticipated discussions that would take place decades later in the field
of Holocaust Studies on issues such as the "limits of representation" and what
it meant to write "poetry after *der khurbn*" [the Yiddish word for the Holo-
caust]. In addition to young Yiddish literary talents some of whom came of
age in the ghettos, in hiding, and in the concentration camps, historians and
editorial boards of yizker books sponsored by *landsmanshaftn* compiled the
history of destroyed Jewish towns. Rescued material from the ghettos, such
as the Ringelblum archive and diaries of cultural and political figures and
ordinary people were edited for publication in the Yiddish book series *Dos
poylishe yidntum* in Buenos Aires.[6] The diary, in particular, became a template
that authenticated the testimonial account of a specific time and place. In the
words of Sara Horowitz, "implicit in the chronicles and diaries is the vision
of a posterity resembling the writers'."[7] Imagining a postwar world is a central
theme in posthumously published diaries of the Holocaust (e.g. Anne Frank
and Herman Kruk). For surviving writers, the act of addressing a specific
readership and shaping public memory determined how they transformed
their wartime diaries into testimonial literature.

The Yiddish writer Leib Rochman (1918–1978) kept a diary beginning
on February 17, 1942, three months after he went into hiding with his wife,
his wife's sister and brother-in-law, and a friend. It ended with the liberation
by the Red Army on August 8, 1944. The five Jews survived in hiding with a
Polish family in a village in the vicinity of their hometown Minsk-Mazowieck,
thirty-five kilometers from Warsaw. In the final months of the war, the group
was hidden by another Polish family in the same area. A comparison of the
original diary (located in the Yad Vashem archives), the serialized version of
the diary in the New York daily *Der tog* and the Buenos Aires daily *Yidishe
tsaytung*, and the 1949 book sponsored by the Paris *landsmanshaft* of Minsk-
Mazowieck, indicate how the original diary was reworked by the author for
publication in different venues. The various versions of the diary — the diary
manuscript, the serialized version in the Yiddish press, the Yiddish book and

the English translation — highlight the cultural transmission that took place in regard to genre and publication venue.[8] Particularly important was the author's decision to use a yizker format for the publication of his diary. This article delineates the genre, narrative style, and themes of Rochman's *Un in dayn blut zolstu lebn (togbukh 1943–1944)* [And in Your Blood You Shall Live (Diary 1943–1944)] published in 1949 and translated into English in a shortened version as *The Pit and The Trap: A Survivor's Chronicle* in 1983. It also examines how Rochman's war diary was conceived and framed as a yizker book.

Published in minor languages, only two years separates the publication of Anne Frank's diary in 1947 and Rochman's in 1949. The English translation of Anne Frank's diary published in 1952 catapulted it to international bestseller status. Soon it would rank second only to the Bible in popularity. Rochman's diary was not published in English translation until 1983 under the auspices of the Holocaust Library with the assistance of Zachor: Holocaust Resource Center, which arranged for the "the translation and editing of this neglected classic." Prominent survivors such Elie Wiesel and Hadassah Rosensaft were on the advisory board of the Holocaust Library, the purpose of which "is to offer to the reading public authentic material, not readily available, and to preserve the memory of our martyrs and heroes untainted by arbitrary or inadvertent distortions." The English version was published with an introduction by the Israeli survivor writer Aharon Appelfeld and remains almost completely unknown, even among Holocaust studies scholars.[9] Appelfeld's introduction to the English version lends literary gravitas to the book indicating its artistic importance:

> Leib Rochman was a Yiddish writer, someone with whom I became very close. At his home I heard a different kind of Yiddish. A small group of us would get together frequently, and he would read aloud from Yiddish poetry and prose.... Rochman had grown up in a Hasidic household and been educated at the home of the Rabbi of Prusof. Unlike other members of his generation, he kept faith with his Hasidic heritage. His vocabulary and his expressions were completely Hasidic, although his lifestyle was not.[10]

The English translation changed the title to *The Pit and the Trap*, a quote from Isaiah 24:17–18. It is shorter (261 pp.) than the Yiddish book (361 pp.) and does not include the yizker section of the Yiddish book. Instead, a map of the Minsk-Mazowieck area is inserted at the end of the book without explanation. The English version leaves out some paragraphs of the original, while adding text not found in there. A particularly striking example is this one: on the last page of the English version, a biblical reference has been included, "We had seen God's face and lived," which does not appear in the Yiddish book. Instead, the Yiddish reads "*s'geyt oyf a morgnshtern*" [a morning star rose]. Thus, the religious sentiment of the English translation is re-enforced and has replaced the image of rebirth and renewal.

The comparison between Anne Frank and Rochman brings into focus a number of reasons for the erasure of Rochman's work from the field of Holocaust literature. The story of how Elie Wiesel's Yiddish memoir *Un di velt hot geshvign,* published as Volume 117 in the Yiddish book series *Dos poylishe yidntum* and redacted into *La Nuit* in 1958 and *Night* in 1960 has by now been thoroughly mapped.[11] In the case of Rochman's war diary, it was not only the lack of translation into a major language until 1983 that made the work invisible outside the Yiddish world. Other reasons for its exclusion even after 1983 are these: the book is too religiously, culturally, and linguistically Jewish; it depicts a complex relationship between Poles and Jews while giving a realistic account of widespread Polish anti–Semitism; it describes the Holocaust as a local affair of German and Polish collaboration killing Jews at close range by shooting and burning; it depicts the Jewish will to survive in a non-heroic way; and it offers a Zionist religious vision of Jewish redemption as the main lesson of the war. In short, Rochman's diary goes against the grain of what today is generally considered Holocaust literature in English translation as exemplified by Anne Frank's *The Diary of a Young Girl* and Elie Wiesel's *Night.* These two works center on Auschwitz. Readings of Anne Frank's *The Diary of a Young Girl,* which closed with her deportation in the summer of 1944, is universally informed by her death in Auschwitz a few months later. The historian Timothy Snyder argues that

> Auschwitz as symbol of the Holocaust excludes those who were at the center of the historical event. The largest group of Holocaust victims — religiously Orthodox and Yiddish-speaking Jews of Poland, or, in the slightly contemptuous German term, *Ostjuden*— were culturally alien from West Europeans, including West Europeans Jews. To some degree, they continue to be marginalized from the memory of the Holocaust.[12]

Instead of Auschwitz, Snyder situates the Nazi Operation Reinhardt at the center of the Holocaust. Operation Reinhardt led to the creation of the extermination camps Treblinka, Belzec, Majdanek, and Sobibor, where the majority of the victims of the Holocaust, Polish and Soviet Jews were killed. Many were also killed by bullets fired over death pits. Two-thirds of the Jews killed during the war were already dead by the end of 1942.

The myth of the innocent childhood and adolescence that characterizes the self depiction in Frank and Wiesel is very different from the young man who narrates Rochman's diary. He is in his early twenties, intellectually and emotionally mature, and newly married to Ester who survives in hiding together with him and three other Jews. Frank's and Wiesel's works are shaped by the war, without which it is questionable whether they would have become writers. In contrast, Rochman worked as a professional journalist for the Yiddish press in Poland in the 1930s. He belongs to a small group of Yiddish and Hebrew writers who came of age in interwar Poland, survived the war, and continued to write prolifically. The group includes Chaim Grade, Avrom Sutzkever, and Shmerke Katcherginsky, survivors of the Vilna ghetto; the Yiddish actor Jonas Turkov, survivor of the Warsaw ghetto; Isaiah Shpiegl and Chava Rosenfarb, survivors of the Lodz ghetto; K.Zetnik, survivor of Auschwitz; and Mordechai Shtrigler, survivor of multiple concentration camps.[13] Unlike younger Yiddish writers such as Eliezer Wiesel (born in 1928), their "approach to art, reality, and history determined their responses to Hitler" and had been crystallized prior to the war.[14] This group has been less favored by Holocaust scholars, who are primarily interested in writers who were fundamentally shaped by their wartime experiences. As a result, the emphasis in scholarship about Jewish Holocaust literature has been on rupture and catastrophic transformation.

Rochman's biography may be divided into four phases, indicating the continuity between his prewar and postwar life:

- **the prewar period.** Rochman first studied with *melamdim* and then in a yeshiva in Warsaw, which combined secular and religious subjects. He became a follower of the Porisover Rebbe in Warsaw and Otvotsk. He then left the hasidic environment and became a journalist for the daily Yiddish newspaper *Varshever radio*.
- **the war period.** He spent the first part of the war in the Minsk-Maszowieck ghetto. After it was liquidated in August, 1942, he was sent to a nearby work camp. In December 1942, he went into hiding with his wife and three other Jews sheltered by a Polish family in a small village near Minsk-Maszowieck. He survived the final months in hiding with another Polish family in the same area.
- **the immediate postwar period.** He became a contributor to the journal *Naye lebn* in Lodz from 1944 to 1945 and then left Poland for Switzerland at the end of 1945. He published his first book *Un in dayn blut zolstu lebn* (1949) in Paris and settled in Israel in 1950.
- **the new life.** Rochman worked in Israel as a journalist for the daily *Forverts* and other publications. He published several books based on his war and postwar experiences, including the 600-plus page novel *Mit blinde trit iber der erd* (1968).[15] The novel is a grand modernistic work depicting the immediate aftermath of the Holocaust in various European cities. Rochman died in 1978 after being awarded the Israel Prize in 1975.

Rochman's artistic biography is typical of Yiddish writers of his generation who started out in interwar Eastern Europe as young writers and wrote
prolifically during the war in the ghetto, in hiding, or in exile in the Soviet
Union. In the aftermath of the war, they published literary testimonies in
various genres, including epic poems, memoirs, and fiction, during their brief
sojourn in the Soviet Union, Poland, Switzerland, Germany, or France. They
continued to write prolifically after they emigrated to New York, Tel Aviv,
Montreal, or Buenos Aires in the 1940s and 1950s. During the last phase of
their artistic careers, they published works that depicted their experiences of
the Holocaust from multiple generic, stylistic, and narrative perspectives. An
increasing turn to their childhood and youth in pre–Holocaust Eastern European became a prominent theme of their late work, such as Chaim Grade's
and Chava Rosenfarb's novels about interwar Vilna and Lodz.[16]

In the 1970s, Rochman published several chapters of an unfinished autobiographical novel about his childhood and youth in a Polish hasidic family,
which is typical of the "late style" of surviving Yiddish writers.[17] The trajectory
of Rochman's artistic career from testimony to modernist apocalyptic visions
of the war and its aftermath and accounts of the world prior to the war is
characteristic not only of surviving Yiddish writers, but also of Yiddish writers
who lived in the Americas, Australia, and South Africa during World War II.
The artistic careers of Yiddish writers after the Holocaust have many features
in common with the yizker books. The yizker book typically begins with the
historical documentation of the writers' home towns and ends with testimonies
about how the Jews were killed by the Nazis and their collaborators. In some
cases, including that of Rochman's, Yiddish writers contributed to and edited
the yizker books about their hometowns.

The yizker book format is the most distinctive feature of Rochman's
diary. A section following the diary describes the history and destruction of
Minsk-Mazowieck, Jewish resistance fighters, and the memorial to the murdered Jews in the cemetery *Banye* in Paris (including a photograph). These
features — the narrative sequence of before, during, and after the destruction
of a particular town emphasizing its commemorative mode — are modeled on
the yizker book. Rochman's diary is presented in the framework of a yizker
book documenting how the Jews of the town were murdered and how fewer
than a hundred survived out of the prewar Jewish population of over five
thousand. The yizker book's retrospective focus on the collective history of
the town creates an interpretive framework for the diary. The final section of
the book, "Our Memorials" [*Undzere denkmeler*], stresses the diary's commemorative and redemptive qualities:

> In your blood shall you live — that's the name of the book by our *landsman*
> that survived through a thousand miracles, the young writer, Leyb Rochman,

which we bring to the reader as a memorial of our town. Live in your blood — the outpouring of blood will strengthen our people to a new life and a renewed life![18]

The title of the diary, *And in your blood shall you live*, is from Ezekiel chapter 16: 6–7. In that chapter, the prophet admonishes the people of Israel for their transgressions. Blood signifies a state of impurity resulting from the rejection of God's commandments exemplified by the inhabitants of Sodom and Gomorah whom Ezekiel mentions in the above section. Jewish ritual laws such as dietary rules, the separation of men and women, and observance of the Sabbath and holidays have been abolished among the Jews in hiding in order to survive. They have no choice but to eat the *treyf* food served by their Polish helpers. The extremely close quarters behind a screen in the hayloft makes modesty impossible to maintain; opportunities to observe Jewish ritual time are rare. However, the impurity of blood that defines the condition under which the five Jews must live is never viewed through the traditionally biblical scheme of reward and punishment. Rather, it is presented by the diarist as an inexplicable curse that has been forced on them. Obviously, blood also refers to the slaughter of the Jews' family and *landslayt* in their hometown that they witnessed while hiding out in the nearby fields before being taken to their hiding place by an old Polish woman, Auntie. Their relationship with their Polish helpers, Auntie and her brother Felek, becomes a blood tie that binds them together in life and death. The Jews and their Polish helpers are dependent on each other for survival; the latter constantly threatens to denounce the former to the Germans.

At the end of the diary, in an entry from June 25, 1944, Rochman depicts the Polish fields, ripe for a rich harvest of wheat and corn:

> We looked at the surrounding fields — and indeed — and indeed everything is bursting and overripe. The long stalks are bent almost to the ground heavy with produce. A big riddle on God's earth! Man has giving the earth so much blood to drink — so now they receive its reward: fat stalks will be fed not one but several years.... Underneath, under the earth is a rebellion, a rebellion of blood, which can not congeal, it sparkles, simmers, boils and tear apart and will yet shoot to the heavens like a volcano, an earthquake, worse than in Korekhs times. The earth and man will jointly turn into dust![19]

The "rebellion of blood" [*bunt fun blut*] under the earth reflects a primordial universe worse than the biblical Korekh's rebellion against the leadership of Moses and Aaron in the desert (Exodus 6:21). The blood simmers under the earth, a sign of the total anarchy that has swallowed the last traces of Jewish existence. This apocalyptic image subverts the seasonal transformation of the Polish landscape, highlighting the irreversible rupture of natural and moral laws that has turned Poland into a blood soaked land of nameless graves.

Unlike a typical diary written and kept privately by an individual, Rochman's diary is conceived as a collective project, a vehicle for the discussions taking place among the five Jews. Thus, the first person plural is frequently used. In the cases when the first person singular appears, it is usually a disguised representation of the collective. Only rarely does Rochman describe the individuality of the four other Jews who are depicted as being part of a common communal entity. Like war diaries in general, the diarist is imagining a future readership and organizing to hide the manuscript and securing its publication after liberation. These issues are discussed among the Jews in hiding:

> "Keep a diary!" Froiman (one of the hiding Jews, JS) advises me to mail what I've written to a Christian acquaintance and ask him to hand it over to Jews after the war. That way I can bequeath to the world, after I'm gone; interesting descriptions, "sensational" material, maybe even literature. My teachers and friends, people after the war! I know that you will not bring any laurels to my grave, and while reading my account you will be indulging in luxury. At night you will go to the theater in order to regain your courage — you will not know my grave just like I don't know the graves of my mother, sister, brother and all my relatives and my whole people whose graves fill the fields and gardens. Grass already grow there, fruits blossom and young couples who believe in Jesus Christ are talking indecently and conducting lewd acts on the graves — on the forgotten from both worlds. No, I am afraid of this kind of writing. I fear that I diminish the memory of the forgotten martyrs, who in ten, or perhaps less than ten years, won't be remembered by anybody, neither they nor the fearful cataclysm. No, my friend Froiman, I won't ask any Christian to hide my writing! If God will grant me life, then my writing will survive, and if not, God forbid — nobody shall know about me and my writing. Let them quietly eat from their fleshpots. Why interrupt the humor of the post-war couples who would rather go to the theater ... to idle away with the rest of the world after the war. And my poor scribbles, I read them in the meantime to my four friends in hiding, condemned to death.[20]

This remarkable entry from the beginning of the diary (February 1943), written six months after the German annihilation of the diarist's community in August 1942 and three months after they went into hiding, affords the reader a glimpse into the inner debate that takes place in the diarist's mind and among the five Jews in hiding. For Rochman, it is pertinent to maintain his agency in shaping postwar memory of the cataclysm. As a result, he vows that only if he stays alive will he publish his diary. Only his survival will enable him to control the way in which the diary is presented to the reading public and to prevent being exploited for sensationalist purposes. The survivor's fear of his friends' and teachers' lack of understanding and, in particular, the indifferent hostility of the Polish bystander to the German genocide of the Jews is viewed as a threat to his agency in creating Jewish memory of the Holocaust. Without his authority as witness and survivor, Rochman fears that his words will be misrepresented. At the same time, the intended readership of "brothers and sisters" overseas in the United States and the *yishuv* in Palestine provides hope for the Jews in hiding:

> It is for sure Tishe b'av in every Jewish home in the world! Oh, if we could only see a Yiddish newspaper from over there! How bitter and painful must be the articles by Jewish writers. Everything is surely published in a big black frame. Is there still humor among Jews? Is Yiddish theater still being performed in the world? ... And you brothers and sisters in the Land of Israel, we imagine your quiet pain and intense sufferings! Our arms reach out to you![21]

Rochman skillfully intertwines two time frames: the sequence of the systematic murder of the Jews of Minsk-Masowieck in August 1942 as recollected from Rochman's perch in hiding and the group's daily tribulations to stay alive, recorded chronologically from February 1943 to liberation August 8, 1944. The literary shaping of the diary is particularly visible in the suspenseful dialogue sections, such as the depiction of Rochman's encounter with an SS officer.[22] In his review of the book in the literary journal *Di goldene keyt*, Avrom Lis compared Rochman's diary to literary works of Avrom Sutzkever and Yitkshok Katsenelson.[23] Similarly, in *Forverts*, Yitskhok Varshavski (a pen name of Isaac Bashevis Singer) praised the work's excellent language and that it reads "like good belletristic."[24] In *Der tog*, Shmuel Niger characterized the book as being "not only a chronicle, not a collection of 'episodes' ... it is, if you will, a novel."[25]

Like other Jewish diarists during the second half of the war in Eastern Europe, Rochman witnessed the systematic murder of his town and had no illusion about the scope of the German genocide of the Jewish population. The diarist's accounts of the various phases of mass murder and deportation become a way of confronting his traumatic pain and loss. The diary combines multiple genres — lamentation, memoir, confession, *journal intime*, and witness account — that fashions a memorial to the destruction of a whole community.[26] The five Jews in hiding are depicted with almost no prewar history through their responses to German assaults and their daily tribulations. They belong to a new breed of Jews, the survivors, marked by the blood ties of suffering and breakdown of Jewish normative behavior. Their new identities erase their pasts, which only appear sporadically in formulaic ways, such as the reciting of Psalms and the *Shema* in moments of danger.

Surviving Yiddish writers utilized a variety of literary styles and genres to reach a readership with the full force of their chronicles of survival. As long as the author anchored the narrative in a specific locale and at a specific point in the German extermination process, the Yiddish readership was willing to accept a great deal of poetic license. Yiddish testimonies were typically less concerned with who had done what to whom than with employing the full range of literary techniques to recreate the inner experience of Jewish life under Nazi rule. In his review of Yehuda Elberg's first book of short stories from the war, *Unter kuperne himln* [Under Copper Skies, 1952], Shmuel Niger pointed out that "like Mordechai Strigler, Elberg is not concerned with telling us exactly what happened to Hitler's victims. He touches the deep dimension and the main dimension of their tragic experiences."[27]

Maydanek, the first volume of Mordechai Strigler *Oysgebrente likht*, prompted the Yiddish critic, Y. Rappaport in Melbourne, Australia, to reflect upon the thorny issues related to creating art about the extermination camps. Many of the concerns raised in his review would be rehashed several decades later in the field of Holocaust Studies. Rappoport states that "because the human language has no words for what took place in Madaynek, its most appropriate expression is perhaps stuttering."[28] Rappaport argues that Strigler's artistic perspective in the aftermath of the war was already fully developed in *Madaynek*: "Of course, Strigler wrote the book as a free man, but the artistic perspective ... Strigler [...] accomplished in the camp. Otherwise, he wouldn't have been able to convey it with such plasticity and deep psychological feeling."[29]

Rochman's diary closes with the liberation by the Red Army July on August 8, 1944 and was published five years later. The book is informed by Rochman's immediate postwar experiences in Poland, where he wrote for the Yiddish newspaper *Dos naye lebn* and his retrospective view while rewriting it in Switzerland and Paris. As documented by Jan Gross, the period right after the war was particularly dangerous for Jews returning to their home towns and reclaiming their property.[30] The transformation of Polish social and economic life that resulted from the German annihilation of almost the entire Jewish population contributed to the onset of anti–Semitic murderous attacks on Jews who returned home in the aftermath of the war. This led to the mass immigration of most of the Polish Jewish survivors following the Kielche pogrom in the summer 1946. By spring 1947 before the consolidation of the new communist regime in Poland, the following year only 90,000 Jews were left in the country.

Obviously, these dramatic changes in Polish life informed Rochman's editing and rewriting of his diary. It was impossible for him to publish the work in Poland, where the topics of Polish collaboration with the Germans and continued postwar anti–Semitic assaults on Jews were highly contentious issues regulated by censorship in the increasingly tightly controlled communist Poland. Paris became a way station for many surviving Yiddish writers in the late 1940s and early 1950s, and most of them later immigrated to the United States, Argentina, or Israel. Rochman found economic sponsorship from his *landsmanshaft* in Paris to publish his book. This secured him a world-wide Yiddish readership and reviews in major Yiddish journals and newspapers.

On May 7, 1944, Rochman expresses his desperate sense of being rootless, displaced, and without relatives: *"O, mame, mameshi, mitamol hob ikh zikh derfilt naket, on vortslen, vi an eynzam farvorfn bletl in vint."* [Oh, mother, dear mother, suddenly I felt naked, without roots, like a lonely abandoned leaf in the wind.][31] The social and economic ties between the Jews in hiding and their Polish helpers occupy a central part of the diary. The Jews' only bargaining power is to exchange goods and money, some of which have been entrusted with Polish friends. Their survival is contingent upon them being able to cash in their belongings, such as clothing, jewelry, furniture and the like, by using their Polish helpers to claim their property from the debtors. Their ability to stay alive derives in part from their ingenuity in inventing stories that allow them to put pressure on their Polish debtors. They spread the word that Jewish partisans will take revenge on their Polish debtors if they do not follow through on their word and return the Jews' property. They shrewdly enforce the anti–Semitic stereotypes of the Polish farmers who believe that a Jewish conspiracy controls the Allied forces and the Red Army and will reward the hidden Jews' Polish helpers after liberation. At the same time, the diary provides ample evidence of the lawlessness and brutality of the Polish population, graphically depicting how Poles exploited Jews and stole their property. Jews were routinely handed over to be shot by the Germans. Polish farmers and their families were mostly hostile to the Jews and at best they were indifferent to the life and death struggle of Jews. In many cases, Poles killed Jews for no apparent reason, vividly depicted in the diary.

In Aaron Appelfeld's introductory words to the English translation of the diary, "the essence of the book ... lies in the unwilling dialogue between the old woman who offers protection and the young people who are condemned to death."[32] The Jews' protectors, Auntie, an old whore, and her brother Felek, a small time criminal, are looking out for their own interests. But Auntie and Felek are also generous and risk their lives to save the Jews, repeatedly invoking the sixth commandment. The book's depiction of the bond between these two Polish outcasts, who despite their flaws, are willing to sacrifice their lives to save these Jews, is a tribute to the small number of Polish righteous gentiles.[33]

Published Yiddish, Hebrew, and Polish literary testimonies initiated the mourning process and commemoration in a public Jewish context. This enabled the survivors to openly discuss their war experiences without any kind of censorship.[34] In contrast, according to Jan Gross, the Polish inability to mourn the loss of their Jewish neighbors had fatal consequences:

Wherever Jews had been plundered, denounced, betrayed, or killed by their neighbors, their reappearance after the war evoked this dual sense of shame and contempt, which could be overcome only by mourning. And as long as Polish society was unable to mourn its Jewish neighbors' deaths, it had either to purge them or to live in infamy.[35]

Jews who fled Poland after the war, on the other hand, "for the most part successfully resumed their lives in Israel, Canada, United States, Australia, and various countries in Western Europe and South America — certainly a lucky denouement by twentieth century criteria."[36]

From the very beginning of his diary, Rochman expresses the belief that Jewish life in Poland will never be the same again. In a particularly striking depiction of an imagined postwar Poland without Jews, dated February 17, 1943, Rochman presents a catalogue of religious books, objects, and dresses that have been appropriated by the peasants after their original owners have disappeared:

> Farm girls wear elegant blouses and skirts made out of prayer-shawls; bonnets made of the black velvet hats worn by Hasidim; and fur scarves made out of the Hasidic *shtrayml*. Farmers' tables are set with silver Kiddush cups and spice boxes, and their dressers and buffets decorated with silver Torah plates, Torah pointers and Sabbath candlesticks. The wind sweeps across the countryside scattering thousands of pages torn from *Pentateuchs*, the Talmud, commentaries, books of *Musar* (ethics) and Hasidism, the *Tsena Ur'na*, chapbooks, classical and modern Jewish literature, scientific and philosophical works. These pages are tightly piled in the peasants' outhouses; then sold in the shops as wastepaper by the pound and kilogram; used for wrapping ham, herring, and the like. The leather bindings are worked over into useful items such as handbags and wallets.[37]

Not only has the Jewish religious and culture heritage been eradicated in the war, but its artifacts are stolen by the Polish population. Jewish traces remain everywhere in the form of items that look absurdly out of place among the Polish families. Delineating how the Polish robbery of Jewish property begins immediately following the Jews' deportation is part of the diarist's documentation of the injustice and greed of his Polish neighbors. Rochman conceives his war diary as a yizker book by recollecting the social, cultural, and religious features of his community, whose sudden absence has left a void in the Polish landscape and social fabric. *Un in dayn blut zolstu lebn* demonstrates that the diary as eyewitness account of atrocities committed against the Jews was informed by the diarist's realization that Jewish life in Polish had been terminated. This initiated the diarist's mourning process in the yizker book mode, which in the absence of actual gravestones for the gassed, shot, and burned victims, could serve as a symbolic "substitute gravestone." Rochman went beyond Ringelblum's directive to a member of the *Oyneg shabes* archive to document and "collect as much as possible — they can sort it out after the war."[38] In addition to Rochman's retrospective literary shaping of what had happened to his community during and after its annihilation, he recorded his experience of belonging to the last Jews on Polish soil. As a (former) religious Jew writing in Yiddish, Rochman had access to the various biblical archetypes of Jewish responses to catastrophe. In an entry dated May 9, 1944, the diarist addresses "*rebeynu shel oylem*" [God of the Universe] in an outpouring of pain and desolation, quoting from the Psalms. This entry is prefaced by the diarist's brief depiction of the circumstances of his diary writing:

> I wrote for two days. I lay outstretched in the stall on the ground, under a crack in the foundation, and wrote. Ester stood guard up above. She is already tired. Today, five in the morning, I had to take on my guard duty. I look out and the images from those days [*yene teg*] float in front of my eyes.[39]

The yizker book's recreation of "*yene teg*" [those days] is reflected through Rochman's literary style and careful editing, a process he began in the middle of the cataclysm and completed as a free man in his West European exile. Rochman's war diary partakes in the collective Jewish effort to create memorials to the destroyed Jewish communities. In 1977, one year before his premature death at the age of sixty, Rochman contributed to the publication of *Seyfer Minsk-Mazowieck.* He was both a contributor and a member of the editorial committee.[40]

Unlike Jewish diarists writing in non–Jewish languages, who "often kept in their heads the image of an audience of strangers from the outside world reading their diaries,"[41] Rochman's imagined readership was no stranger. He perceived his readers as "sisters and brothers," representing the hope for a return to normalcy that would entail resuming reading and writing in the Eastern European Jewish mother tongue. The act of rewriting begins in the extreme circumstances of hiding during the war while the diarist is still in mortal danger. On May 19, 1944, the diarist requests that Janek, one of the Poles sheltering the group, retrieve his writings which lie buried in a container in the field. He tells Janek:

> "I need them to look for something. In a few days I will return them to you." He has already buried several notebooks. When I finish a notebook — I give it to him and he buries it with the earlier notebooks. I remind him constantly, that one day he will be rewarded.[42]

Although the Yiddish critics of Rochman's diary stressed the active Polish participation in killing Jews, some also mentioned the book's path breaking depiction of the Polish farmers. Beyond the anti–Semitic stereotypes of Polish farmers, Rochman portrays the Jewish rescuers Auntie, Felek, Janek, and

Szhube in ways that enable the reader to sympathize with the difficult choices these Poles had to make in order to shelter the Jews in hiding. In a 1949 review of the book, Yitskhok Yanasovitsh points out that Rochman's realistic depiction of the Polish village is a departure from Yiddish literature in the interwar period. The intimate portrait of a non–Jewish Polish peasant society is made possible by the position of the Jews as *roye veeyne-nire* [they see but are not seen]. Yanasovitsh praises Rochman's artistic objectivity which despite "his despondent Jewish heart does not lead him to make quick conclusions."[43] Despite the diary's overwhelming documentation of Polish hostility and murderous desire to get rid of the Jews, Rochman's artistic skill in depicting the mundane details of daily life of the Polish peasants makes the diary an important historical and artistic document:

> Particularly interesting from a general human point of view are Auntie and Felek whom the author paints with deep understanding of the complexity of their characters. A lot could be written about why the Gentile criminal Felek is almost the only representative of humanity and how the human inclinations come to expression in his character. Much could also be written about Auntie and her contradictory character and the same about Szhube and his mix of fear and avarice.[44]

Rochman's masterpiece fell through the cracks of the dominant paradigms that in the early 1950s had crystallized in the creation of a Holocaust literary canon. First and foremost, Rochman's war diary was not admitted to this canon because it did not have the good fortune of finding an English translator in the 1950s. Other barriers included its being too Jewish, its not being Auschwitz centered, and its depiction of passive, non-heroic Jewish victims in complicated relationships with the Poles who sheltered them. The publication of the English translation in 1983 came at a time of increased popular and scholarly interest in the Holocaust, but suffered the fate of being "drowned out" by the growing number of published war testimonies by Jewish survivors.

Only by recovering Rochman's diary as part of a vibrant post–Holocaust Yiddish culture does it become possible to describe a set of responses and literary strategies which to a large extent have not yet found expression in English translation. Rochman and other Yiddish writers attempted as objectively as possible to grapple with the complexity of the choices the Poles and Jews had to make during the extremity of the war.[45] A crucial life sustaining factor for the Yiddish diarists was their knowledge of a worldwide Yiddish readership that would be interested in reading authentic accounts of Polish-Jewish relations during the war. This gave Rochman's war diary a glimmer of hope, a point Aharon Appelfeld made in his introduction to the English translation:

The literature of the Holocaust is extremely diversified. One sometimes feels that here's a hidden competition: who can tell the more horrible tale. No wonder that the ears and eyes balk at hearing and reading any more. It is difficult to absorb a terror that knows no bounds. In this respect Rochman's book is different. Though it stays scrupulously close to the facts, complete with accurate names and dates, it is a book of hope. Not of facile hope or of saccharine optimism but of a tempered faith in humankind.[46]

Unlike Emanuel Ringelblum, the initiator of the *Oyneg shabes* archive who viewed "history as an antidote to a memory of catastrophe," Rochman embedded his literary testimonial in Jewish collective memory that drew on age-old religious archetypes, as well as Yiddish literary realism. Ringelblum, in the Warsaw Ghetto and in hiding on the Aryan side, fashioned a usable past out of Polish Jewry's death throes, recorded with meticulous commitment to historical objectivity. However, he did not survive to see the publication of his war writings. Rochman, a Yiddish survivor writer, was able to maintain agency over his war diary, which he reworked for publication after the war by fusing fictional styles, documentary testimony, and scriptural antecedents.

Notes

1. Amos Goldberg, "The Victim's Voice and Melodramatic Aesthetics in History," *History and Theory* 48 (October 2009): 236.

2. Leib Rochman, "*Af keyver oves,*" *Yerushalayimer almanakh* 6–7 (1976): 116.

3. David Roskies, "What Is Holocaust Literature?" *Studies in Contemporary Jewry* Vol. 21 (2005), 172–173. This is a seminal article.

4. Literary testimonies in Hebrew and the Hebrew cultural context are not addressed in this article.

5. See Anita Norich, *Discovering Exile: Yiddish and Jewish American Culture During the Holocaust* (Palo Alto, CA: Stanford University Press, 2008).

6. See my article, "A Library of Hope and Destruction: The Yiddish Book Series *Dos Poylishe Yidntum,* 1946–1966," and "Appendix: List of 175 Volumes of *Dos poylishe yidntum,*" *POLIN 20: Studies in Polish Jewry* (2007): 173–196. Edited by Gabriel N. Finder, Natalia Aleksiun, Antony Polonsky, and Jan Schwarz, this volume of POLIN is devoted to the theme "Making Holocaust Memory."

7. Sara Horowitz, "Voices from the Killing Ground," in *Holocaust Remembrance: The Shapes of Memory,* ed. Geoffrey H. Hartman (Oxford, UK, and Cambridge, MA: Blackwell, 1994), 50.

8. Rochman's original diary is located in the Yad Vashem archive. I have seen an excerpt of this manuscript, which is legible and easy to read. It is the most important source for examining the process of editing and rewriting which Rochman conducted in hiding during and after the war. A study of the manuscript which would include a comparison with the published version is a desideratum.

9. Saul Friedlander's *The Years of Extermination* (New York: HarperCollins, 2007) uses a rich sample of Jewish diaries and does not include or even reference Rochman's war diary.

10. Aharon Appelfeld, *The Story of a Life* (New York: Schocken Books, 2004), 115.

11. Naomi Seidman, *Faithful Renderings: Jewish-Christian Difference and the Politics of Translation* (Chicago: University of Chicago Press, 2006), 216–236; and Jan Schwarz, "The

Original Yiddish Text and Context of Night," *MLA Teaching Approaches to Elie Wiesel's Night,* ed. Alan Rosen (2007), 52–58.

12. Timothy Snyder, "Holocaust: The Ignored Reality," *The New York Review of Books,* July 16, 2009: 14. For a similar point, Alexandra Garbarini, in *Numbered Days: Diaries and the Holocaust* (Yale University Press 2006), points to the importance of Yiddish diaries because they "may illuminate other segments of the Polish Jewish population during these years — those who were older or were politically engaged with the Bund or were Hasidic" (xii).

13. Yekhiel Sheyntukh at the Hebrew University is the foremost scholar of Yiddish and Hebrew testimonial writing and has edited Yiddish and Hebrew works by survivor writers Isaiah Shpiegl, K.Zetnik, Yitskhok Katzenelson, and Aaron Zeitlin. He is working on an edition of Yiddish survivor writer Mordechai Strigler's correspondence during his Paris sojourn 1946–1953. See Yechiel Szeintuch, "The Corpus of Yiddish and Hebrew Literature from Ghettos and Concentration Camps and its Relevance for Holocaust Studies," *Studies in Yiddish Literature and Folklore* (Jerusalem 1986): 186–207.

14. Roskies, "Holocaust Literature," 62.

15. Rochman's critically appraised 1966 novel like his war diary has been translated into Hebrew and requires a study of its own. See Dan Miron, "Yiddish Prose" in *The YIVO Encyclopedia of Jews in Eastern Europe*: "Leyb Rokhman (1918–1978) was perhaps the only Yiddish writer of fiction who understood the need for innovative tonality in writing on the Holocaust. His works, *Un in dayn blut zolstu lebn* [And in Your Blood You Shall Live, 1949] and *Mit blinde trit iber der erd* [With Blind Steps Over the Earth, 1966] are the most rewarding texts of Yiddish prose fiction written on the unspeakable topic." Also see David Roskies, *Yiddishlands: A Memoir* (Detroit: Wayne State University Press, 2008): "I alone helped Leybl [Rokhman, JS] proofread the galleys of his novel *With Blind Steps Over the Earth*, about survivors who journey in several simultaneous time frames, a huge work that would have changed the face of Holocaust literature if only enough people had survived in the world who still read Yiddish" (150).

16. See Jan Schwarz, "Confrontation and Elegy in the Novels of Chaim Grade," in *The Multiple Voices of Modern Yiddish Culture,* ed. Shlomo Berger *Studia Rosenthaliana* (Amsterdam, 2007), 30–55.

17. See Edward Said, *On Late Style: Music and Literature Against the Grain* (New York: Vintage Books, 2006).

18. Rochman, *Un in dayn blut,* 380. The term "substitute gravestones" was first suggested by eds. Jonathan Boyarin and Jack Kugelmass in *From a Ruined Garden: The Memorial Books of Polish Jewry* (Bloomington and Indianapolis: Indiana University Press, 1998), 34.

19. Yiddish, 302; English, 227.

20. Yiddish, 18; English, 22. The hostile quip at Christianity in the second section of the quote has been excluded from the English translation.

21. Yiddish, 141; excluded in the English translation.

22. Yiddish, 223 and 224; English, 176.

23. Avrom Lis's review appeared in *Di goldene keyt* 7 (1951): 210–213.

24. Yitskhok Varshavski, Review of *Un in dayn blut zolstu lebn, "Tsvey vikhtike bikher fun yunge yidishe shrayber"* [Two Important Books of Young Yiddish Writers], *Forverts,* October 9, 1949.

25. "Leyb Rokhman," *Leksikon fun der nayer yidisher literatur* Vol. 8.

26. See Alexandra Garbarini, *Numbered Days*: "During the war, diaries became sites and vehicles for Jews to re-conceptualize different versions of the religious, to employ a range of cultural practices, and to cling to familial and increasingly Jewish national frameworks" (12).

27. Shmuel Niger, "Farbrekhn un shtrof," *Der tog* December 30, 1951. Reprinted in *Yehuda Elberg: Eseyen vegn zayn literarishn shafn,* ed. Gershon Viner (Ramat Gan: Bar Ilan University, 1990), 68.

28. Y. Rappoport, *Zoymen in vint* (Buenos Aires: *Opteyl fun altveltlekhn yidishn kulturkongres,* 1961), 484.

29. Ibid. For a similar point, see James E. Young, *Writing and Rewriting the Holocaust: Narrative and the Consequences of Interpretation* (Bloomington and Indianapolis: Indiana Uni-

versity Press, 1988): "This is to suggest that the events of the Holocaust are not only shaped *post factum* in their narration, but that they were initially determined as they unfolded by the schematic ways in which they were apprehended, expressed and then acted upon" (338).

30. Jan Gross, *Fear: Anti-Semitism in Poland After Auschwitz. An Essay in Historical Interpretation* (New York: Random House, 2006).

31. Yiddish, 207; English, 160.

32. Aharon Appelfeld, "Introduction," *The Pit and the Trap* (New York: Holocaust Library, 1983), 9.

33. See Wladyslaw Bartoszewski, *The Samaritans: Heroes of the Holocaust* (New York: Twayne Press, 1970).

34. In *Numbered Days*, Garbarini examines a sample of one hundred unpublished Jewish diaries written in German, French and Polish: "Those written in Polish constitute the largest single language group of diaries, numbering slightly more than those in Yiddish" (xii). See also Zoe Vania Waxman: "Between 1945 and 1949, seventy five [Jewish Holocaust] memoirs were published in a variety of languages [the figure provided by Yad Vashem]: fifteen in Yiddish, thirteen in Hebrew, and twelve in Polish." *Writing the Holocaust: Identity, Testimony, Representation* (Oxford: Oxford University Press, 2006), 100.

35. Gross, *Fear*, 258.

36. Ibid.

37. Yiddish, 21–22; English, 25.

38. The member was Hersh Wasser, one of three surviving members of the *Oyneg shabes* archive, quoted in Kassow, *Who Will Write Our History: Emanuel Ringelblum, the Warsaw Ghetto, and the Oyneg Shabes Archive* (Bloomington and Indianapolis: Indiana University Press, 2007), 13.

39. Yiddish, 229; English, 182.

40. S. Even-Shushan, ed., *Seyfer Minsk-Mazowieck: yizker bukh nokh der khorev-gevorener kehile* (Jerusalem: Minsk-Mazowiecki Societies in Israel and Abroad, 1977). The yizker book includes several articles by Leib Rochman.

41. Garbarini, *Numbered Days*, 163.

42. Yiddish, 267; English, 206.

43. Yitskhok Yanasovitsh, *Penimer un nemen, band tsvey: yidishe prozaikers un zeyere verk fun nokh der tsveyter velt-milkhome* (Buenos Aires: *Farlag Kiem*, 1985), 299.

44. Ibid.

45. Mordechai Shtrigler is another overlooked Yiddish writer of the Holocaust. He published six volumes of literary testimonies *Oysgebrente likht* [Extinguished Lights] in the Yiddish book series *Dos poylishe yidntum: Maydanek* (1947) vol. 20; *In di fabrikn fun toyt* (1948) vol. 32; *Verk 'ce'* (1950) vols. 64–65; and *Goyroles* (1952) vols. 85–86. See Mordechai Shtrigler *"Tsu aykh shvester un brider bafrayte: nokhmilkhome-problemen fun yidishn folk,"* New York (1945); *"Zamoshtser brentsh 375, Arbeter ring: Bukhnvald. Dokumentn fun undzere teg,"* *Tsukunft* August 1945:493–500; and *"Araynfir tsum bukh."* In *di fabrikn fun toyt. Dos poylishe yidntum* vol. 32 (1948):7–67. Yehiel Szeintuch, *"Mavo leheker yezirato shel mordechai shtrigler beyidish vebeivtz,"* *Chuliot* 9 (August 2005):223–237; *"Mordkhe shtrigler afn sheydveg nokh bukhnvald,"* *Forverts* 28–5.2004:11 and 4.6.2004:16; and *"Opgetseylte verter vegn mordkhe shtriglers veg in der yidisher literatur un prese,"* *Forverts* 10.5.2002:17.

46. Appelfeld, *The Pit and the Trap*, 9.

PART IV

STUDIES USING YIZKER BOOKS

12

Authenticating the Historical Fiction of Uri Orlev

ROSEMARY HOROWITZ

Considering that Jews lived in Poland for over eight hundred years, the ongoing interest in the relations between Jews and Poles is understandable. Even in hiding on the Aryan side of the Warsaw ghetto, Emanuel Ringelblum wrote on the subject. Much has been written about it since then. While a variety of materials have been used to investigate the topic, yizker books still remain relatively underappreciated, especially by public school teachers. Although Jared Stark discusses yizker books as sources for classroom use, he does not fully describe how the books may be used in student research projects.[1]

With the increasing popularity of historical fiction, especially in the study of the Holocaust, there is growing interest among teachers for works that deal with the subject in an accurate and sensitive manner. The work of Uri Orlev meets the criteria of accurate and sensitive writing about the Holocaust. Born Jerzy Henryk Orlowski in Warsaw in 1931, Orlev, along with his family, were moved into the ghetto in 1939 when the Nazis invaded Poland. Later, he was sent to Bergen-Belsen concentration camp in Germany. During that period, his mother was killed, and his father was captured by the Russians. Orlev, his brother, and his aunt survived Bergen-Belsen. At the end of the war, the two boys went to Palestine, where they were eventually reunited with their father. Orlev, who started writing in the 1950s, is an author of over thirty books. He writes in Hebrew, and his work has been translated into thirty-eight languages. His corpus for young adult readers includes *The Island on Bird Street*; *The Man from the Other Side*; *Run, Boy, Run*; *Lydia, Queen of Palestine*; and *The Lady in the Red Hat*. For those works, he has received the Mildred L. Batchelder Award, the American Library Association Best Book for Young Adults, the Hans Christian Andersen award, and the National Jewish Book Award.[2]

To date, *The Man from the Other Side* and *The Island on Bird Street* have received the most attention from teachers, so those works provide my examples in this chapter.[3] Social studies educators Eric Groce and Robin Groce argue that authentication projects, which are assignments that use nonfiction sources to validate the facts in historical fiction, may help students increase communication abilities, improve research skills, understand literature and history better, and become more engaged in learning.[4] Robin Groce details one project related to Holocaust fiction in her study of Lois Lowry's *Number the Stars*.[5] Building on the work of Eric Groce, Robin Groce and Jared Stark, my aim in this chapter is to explore ways in which high school teachers may use yizker books for authentication projects.[6] Given Orlev's life, my particular focus is on the portrayal of Polish-Jewish relations in the two texts. Regardless of their focus, authentication projects help teachers achieve the goals of language arts and social studies curricula, as well as meet state and national standards.

The Novels

In *The Man from the Other Side*, Marek, the protagonist, is a fourteen-year old boy living in Warsaw, Poland. One day he and two other boys steal money from a Jewish man. Marek confesses to his mother and then decides to atone by giving the money to another Jew. At that point, Marek's mother tells him that he is half–Jewish himself because her first husband was Jewish. Her second husband, Antony, is an employee of Warsaw's department of sanitation, who smuggles food and arms through the city sewer system to members of the Jewish underground. He also transports people, including Jewish babies, from the ghetto. Pan Jozek is the Jewish man who Marek befriends and who hides on the Aryan side of the ghetto for a time with Marek's help. When word about the Warsaw ghetto uprising spreads, Pan Jozek decides that he wants to join the resistance and asks Marek to lead them through the sewers into the ghetto.

Alex, the hero of *The Island on Bird Street*, is an eleven-year-old boy living alone in an abandoned building in the ghetto waiting for his father to return. Although Alex despairs over his lonely situation, he remains hopeful that his father will come back someday. During his five months in hiding, Alex manages to find food and shelter. He sees looters steal from the vacant apartments in the building and soldiers force people out of hiding. He is helped by Boruch, an old Jewish worker, as well as by Bolek, a Polish resistance worker. He, in turn, helps Freddy and Henryk, two Jewish partisans. Other people and other activities also help him during his time in hiding. Eventually, his father returns and takes Alex to the forest and the partisans.

Like all good fiction, the two novels yield insights into human behavior and its consequences. Read together with yizker books, the novels provide a way for students to explore the theme that individuals are fundamentally responsible for their own actions.

Perpetrators

In the study of the Holocaust as it relates to the Jews, the perpetrator is the one who implements or who carries out the anti–Jewish policy. Perpetrators may be classified by type and motivation. For example, in *Perpetrators Victims Bystanders: The Jewish Catastrophe, 1933–1945*, Raul Hilberg identifies various types of perpetrators: German civil servants, military officials, business leaders, educators, Nazi party members, doctors, lawyers, zealots, sadists, as well as non–German governmental bodies and individuals. In addition, Hilberg identifies psychological, sociological, demographic, historical, professional, religious, organizational, regional, and other variables that influenced anti–Jewish behavior. Not surprisingly, Orlev incorporates numerous kinds of perpetrators in his novels.

In *The Man from the Other Side* and *The Island on Bird Street*, the Jews are living under the effect of Nazi policies, such as the deportations, ghettos, and shootings. On the streets, the Jews encounter bullies, punks, and informers. To an extent, the bully, punk, and informer reinforce the Nazi policy.

An early scene in *The Man from the Other Side* describes how Wacek and Janek, Marek's acquaintances, rob the Jewish man:

> At first they talked to him nicely to keep from arousing the suspicions of any passers-by who might want a share of the loot. Then they took him into a doorway, shook him down, and cleared out.[7]

Wacek and Janek have developed a system for stealing from the Jews, and during this particular episode, Marek gets his first-hand view into their actions. Later, he regrets his actions, which end up changing his life.

Bullies also play a role in *The Island on Bird Street*. At one point, Alex looks out from his hiding place and recognizes the

> bully who used to throw stones at us in the days before the transports. He still threw them at everything that moved, dogs, cats, and small children, and called everyone a "stinking kike." He knew lots of other swear words too, but those were his favorite.[8]

This passage links the bully's actions to his view of Jews. The bully's anti-Semitic tendencies drive his behavior during the war as they did beforehand. He did not change.

The willingness by some to betray their relatives, neighbors, co-workers, classmates, and others is a sad fact of life. In *The Man from the Other Side* and *The Island on Bird Street*, the boys refer to those people who inform on others as "rats." In *The Man from the Other Side*, Marek learns about betrayal one night in the sewers when he and Anthony are accosted by Pan Krol, one of Anthony's co-workers:

> That's when I first understood why Anthony had told my mother that first night that he couldn't trust anyone, not even my uncle. But that's what wartime is like: suddenly you find out that everything you've thought about your friends, or your neighbors, or your relatives is wrong. Anyone at all can inform on you and get you into hot water, because when someone is frightened, or hungry, or desperate for money, he's no longer the same person.[9]

Likewise in *The Island on Bird Street*, Alex learns how people turn on one another. One day leaving Bolek's house, he hears loud voices:

> "What happened, Pani?" Bolek asked a woman.
> "We found some kikes hiding with the landlord and turned them in. The bastard jeopardized our life. Raising the rent wasn't enough for him."
> Bolek spit angrily on the ground. The woman must have thought it was on account of the Jews, but I knew it was on account of her.[10]

Just like Orlev's characters are subject to the actions of various kinds of perpetrators so too were the Jews of Poland.

On an individual and a societal level, Jews were at the mercy of perpetrators. Yizker book writers want their readers to know and to remember that. Consequently, the books provide many details about the various experiences of Jews during the Nazi era. All books contain information about the actions of perpetrators in the ghettoes, camps, countryside, and other places. In *Sefer yizkor Goniadz*, Tuviah Ivri recalls criminal activities in the Goniondz ghetto. He describes what he remembers:

> Bands of Poles had started to roam the streets with clubs in their hands. They collected Jews in a wagon and threw some bodies into it. The wagon, with eight live persons and a number of dead began to move. The Poles beat the people in the wagon. At the market, a huge band of them surrounded the wagon. They chased one man and tied him up. They beat him without letup. They walked away with Jewish goods on their shoulders.[11]

In *Sefer zikaron le-kehilat Rozan*, Minna Mlinek-Magnushever recounts what happened to her:

> When we reached the village of Shlon near Ostrolenka, some Poles betrayed us. They sent a boy of theirs to fetch the Germans and to deliver us into their

hands. In the meanwhile they surrounded us lest we slip off. They were rejoicing at the idea of seeing Jewish blood. The others, refugees from Wlotzlavek and Plotzk, got away and only I and those I had rescued were left as prisoners in their hands. They robbed us, took our garments and handed us over to the Germans, who first of all beat us up and then searched us thoroughly and took whatever they found. I had nothing left but a heavy heart. I had not rescued my parents, had abandoned my children, as a burden, which my husband would have to carry, and which might make it impossible for him to reach safety.[12]

In these passages, Ivri and Mlinek — Magnushever are blunt about their experiences. In addition to the details about what occurred in the city or countryside, Abraham Wein finds that yizker books are good sources of information about the treatment of Jews in the minor labor camps, about which not much information is available.[13] He mentions that *Sefer kehilat yehudei Dąbrowa Górnicza ve-hurbanah*, for instance, contains an article about the work camp Grünberg/Schlesien in Silesia.

Although the recollections in yizker books cover a range of Polish-Jewish encounters, the balance between negative and positive accounts is generally skewed toward the negative. Gabriel Finder makes that same point:

> Many memorial books of Jewish communities in Poland contain ... Polish Jews' recollections not only of their deadly confrontation with the Germans but also, with obvious bitterness, their negative — and likewise, occasionally deadly — encounters with Poles. It was not uncommon for the same account to contrast such encounters with the courageous assistance of select righteous individuals in the Polish population, but in the collective consciousness of survivors, the negative aspects of Polish behavior outweighed the positive by far.[14]

Regarding the question of balance, it is noteworthy to remember that yizker book writers were primarily accountable to their compatriots, and those affiliations shaped the content of the books. An awareness of the organizational sponsorship of yizker book projects should inform any authentication project.

Victims

While Roma, homosexuals, Poles, Jehovah's Witnesses, communists, criminals, and others were all targets of Nazi policy, the annihilation of the Jews was the ultimate aim of the Third Reich. In *Unequal Victims*, Gutman and Krakowski estimate that by the end of 1942, Nazis had killed the majority of the Jews of Poland. Since the two novels feature child protagonists, students who want to focus on Jewish children in particular have access to numerous texts. Regarding children in particular, examples of collections include Wiktoria Sliwowska's *The Last Eyewitness*, Alexandra Zapruder's *Salvaged Pages*, Laurel Holiday's *Children in the Holocaust and World War II: Their Secret Diaries*, and Martin Ira Glassner and Robert Krell's *And Life Is Changed Forever*. Given the Nazi policy and his own experiences, Orlev highlights the campaign against the Jews and the suffering of the Jews in his writing.

In *The Man from the Other Side*, Marek starts to understand the plight of the Jews when he is caught in the ghetto. As he looks around the crowded bunker, he sees:

> old men and women, families with babies, mothers with children of all ages, even people who looked educated and distinguished. For the first time, I grasped concretely what the liquidation of the ghetto ... actually meant.[15]

By blurring the distinctions between the people in the bunker, Orlev allows Marek to see that all the Jews would share the same fate.

The fate of the Jews is central to *The Island on Bird Street* too. One of its most disturbing scenes is the discovery of the Jewish hiding place, which signals the death of the inhabitants. Orlev describes how one day Alex hears

> a sharp explosion. Plaster fell on me from above. For a panicky moment I though the whole top floor would collapse on me. Then there was silence. And then a sound of screaming and wailing that seemed to come from deep in the earth. Followed by shots, which sounded near. I prayed that they were just warning shots fired outside the bunker. No one was screaming anymore. The children just cried and some of the grown ups moaned.[16]

The alternating silence and noise create a sense of uncertainty for Alex. In addition, his description of the crying and moaning of the people trapped under the rubble point out their helplessness.

Yizker books are the products of survivor organizations, so they are naturally written from a Jewish perspective. The partial or complete testimonies, diaries, memoirs, reportage, letters, and other materials printed in the books function as source documents of what happened to individuals. The following examples illustrate what the books reveal about Jewish victims. In *Mlawa ha-yehudit*, Moshe Peles recalls his experiences:

> The "Judenrat" received an order to deliver 100 people to the Germans. They chose 50 young people and 50 old ones. The old people dug the pit and the young ones were shot. I wanted to run away but it was impossible. Still I decided to try, as there was nothing to lose. The moment the German guard turned his back in the yard, I ran. There were bars on the windows and Jewish ghetto guards. In the adjoining yard, there was a large carpentry shop that worked for the Germans. The shop was owned by a friend of mine and I knew that if I could reach it, there was a chance that I would survive. A policeman named Purman who now lives in Israel was on guard. He was mar-

ried to the daughter of my uncle's brother. He saw me attempting to escape and looked the other way. Jewish policemen searched for me later, particularly Haskel Alter, who used to live in Israel. I hid until the end of the action.[17]

From *Pinkas Kolbishov*:

When I walked on the ghetto streets for the last time, I saw broken doors and windows everywhere, while feathers floated in the air. Saturday morning I took my bag with the most essential things and went to the bet-midrash where we all gathered. A number of wagons were waiting. We put our things in and, accompanied by German and Polish police, left the ghetto. We walked all the way to Rzeszow on foot, like the evacuated Jews who had preceded us. At noon we reached the city. The ghetto area looked like hell-on-earth. Into the 12,000 Jews who had been crowded together in the little narrow alleys, an equal number had now been added. People were lying in streets, yards, cellars; it was impossible to cross a street without stepping on someone. People were searching for relatives in this mass, quarrels and fights broke out, and tears shouts and curses expressed the general despair at their grim fare. Whole families sat stunned, without a crumb of food, the parents having been shot to death on the way.[18]

This type of rich description provides details from people, who despite the passage of time, recall their actions, thoughts, and feelings rather clearly. Their accounts offer much information about the attitudes of people, the chances they took, the despair they felt, the confusion they saw, and other matters related to their particular situation. The specificity of the recollections provides students with concrete details to consider in research projects.

Bystanders

The number of bystanders is impossible to calculate because inaction reflects a very complicated reality. Some people were unable to help; others were unwilling to help. Still others were pressured not to help. Some were afraid to help. Others were glad not to help. Not surprisingly, there are few primary accounts of bystanders. One exception is *Ponary Diary, 1941–1943: A Bystander's Account of a Mass Murder*, whose author Kazimierz Sakowicz, records the atrocities taking place him. Besides Hilberg's work, Steven K. Baum's *The Psychology of Genocide: Perpetrators, Bystanders, and Rescuers;* and Victoria Barnett's *Bystanders: Conscience and Complicity During the Holocaust* also examine the phenomenon of the bystander. The attitude of survivors towards bystanders is understandably critical, as is seen in Orlev's works.

In *The Man from the Other Side*, Marek coming upon a crowd that has gathered to watch soldiers shoot into the ghetto asks an onlooker what is going on. One man answers:

> "They're finishing off the Jews," an old man says to me.
> "It's about time, said a young one. He laughed.
> Before my mother caught me with the Jew's money and before meeting Pan Jozek, I would have felt the same way.
> "What do you think," asked someone, "will they give us back the Jews' houses?
> "Why shouldn't they?' said someone else. Didn't they do it in the Little Ghetto?"
> "What's all this talk about 'giving back'?" asked a woman who seemed very brave to me. "Those houses belong to the Jews." Everyone looked at her suspiciously and a man sniggered and said, "She must be a Jew herself."[19]

Laughter at the Jews, desire for their property, and pressure to comply are some of the factors influencing the crowd in this scene. Marek recognizes that his views about Jews have changed since he met Jozek, and Marek also understands that the woman who questions the others about the Jewish property is taking a chance by going against the crowd.

The Island on Bird Street describes how Alex observes from his hideout, the routines of the Polish people who live outside the wall. He sees the policeman, mailman, pharmacist, grocer, barber, doctor, doorman, and others at work. Additionally, he sees children playing and women shopping and cleaning. By juxtaposing the life outside the ghetto with the life inside the ghetto, Orlev suggests that the city residents chose to ignore what was going on around them.

Although studying the subject of the bystander is difficult because few individuals willingly admit to inaction, yizker books may be used to explore the attitudes of survivors towards bystanders, as well as the attitudes of helpers towards bystanders. In some books, survivors describe the indifference of their neighbors or co-workers; in others, helpers describe their motivations not to be a bystander.

From *Sefer Frampol*:

> Placing my own life and the lives of my family in danger, I took these people in — not for the sake of profit, but because my conscience wouldn't permit me to leave these poor unfortunates in the murders' hands.[20]

In his chapter, Stanislow Sobczak recalls his decision to help the Jews of Frampol. He is very aware that his actions place himself and family in danger, yet he chooses to protect the Jews nevertheless. Interestingly, as part of his evaluation of yizker books, Wein notes that the volumes are valuable for exploring the topic of attitude. In addition to the book to Frampol, Wein finds accounts of helpers in the books to Zloczwe and Kozienice. Ultimately however, authentication projects must be grounded in the fact that few people actually helped the Jews.

Helpers

Discerning the number of Poles who helped Jews is difficult. Gutman estimates that about one percent of the Polish population actually provided aid to Jews, and Krakowski estimates that about 30,000 Jews were saved by members of underground organizations, even though Jewish fighters were seldom accepted into the organizations when they applied.[21] Krakowski also estimates that about 300,000 Jews escaped from the ghettos and camps to the countryside, where their fate depended on the attitudes of the locals. Various Polish relief organizations, such as Zegota, also helped Jews. Details about an individual helper may be found in the personal account of Irene Gut Opdyke's *In My hands: Memories of a Holocaust Rescuer*, for example. Others accounts are given in works such as Nechama Tec's *When Light Pierced the Darkness: Christian Rescue of Jews in Nazi-occupied Poland.*

Recognizing the role of the helper in the survival of some Jews, Orlev depicts circumstances in which Jews are aided by non–Jews. In one book, it is a priest; in the other, it is a member of the Polish underground. In *The Man from the Other Side*, Pan Jozek explains to Marek what the priest has been doing:

> "And today, I have to move out of the apartment where I've been staying."
> "You mean the priest's place?"
> He didn't answer.
> "I've seen you in that church every Monday."
> "Yes," he said. "Every Monday his sister comes from the village with a package of food for him. And she insists on arranging it in the pantry by herself."
> I didn't get it.
> "And that's where he has been hiding me during the day."[22]

In *The Island on Bird Street*, people from the underground play a role in the story. Alex asks Freddy and Henryk if they took part in the ghetto uprising. They reply:

> We tried reaching it. A Pole in the underground got us into the ghetto, and we were on our way to the fighting when we ran into a patrol. There were ten of us. Not all of us were armed.[23]

Many survivors recall with gratitude the help they received from individuals or from groups, and as a result, descriptions of helpers may be found in numerous yizker books. Of course, the degree and duration of help varied greatly. For some, help came in the form of a single encounter. This was the situation for Chaim Krystal, who recalls in *Sefer kehilat yehudei Dąbrowa Górnicza ve-hurbanah*:

> We approached the house with but one prayer on our lips: that the inhabitants would have pity on us and let us in. Though it may sound strange [now], we

had lost all faith in mankind. I cautiously approached the door. When it opened, a scrawny woman appeared. Her face went all pale when she looked at us, as she cried: "Dear God — Holy Mother!" and let us in. She didn't ask us any questions. She realized who we were, refugees from across the border. She added wood to her stove. The warmth from the stove restored us both physically and mentally. She also gave us clothes to change into and something hot to drink. We certainly reaped motivation from the kind behavior of this Christian woman. She also told us how hard it was these days to cross the border, and that on a daily basis people who attempted to cross were killed. After a day we parted from the woman offering our profuse thanks and continued on our way.[24]

By contrast, help was more extensive for others. That was the case for Esther Kimch. In *Sefer Zloczew*, she recalls her time living with a Christian family:

Following the Polish uprising in Warsaw, the city lacked food and to a certain extent water, but I hardly felt it as I was provided by the savior family with the necessary needs. Since I did not attend school for fear of being exposed, the daughters of the family taught me how to read and write. They also escorted me to church and instructed me how to pray. Sometimes I joined the church choir. I was always escorted by one of the girls when I visited the priest at the church and he always stressed the importance of religion and adherence to it. As for myself, I was still rather young to understand the importance of religion. The home atmosphere however was one of warmth and reception. I received and gave gifts, participated in family celebrations, and felt as though I belonged to the family.[25]

The issue of paying for help is a complex matter. For example, *Yad Vashem* honors non–Jews who risked their lives for Jews with the title *Righteous Among the Nations*. In considering a person for that honor, *Yad Vashem* judges the candidate's behavior in terms of the active involvement by the rescuer, the risk to the rescuer, and level of altruism of the rescuer. However, not all yizker books writers are so rigorous in their definition; they appreciate help in all its forms. For instance, when a rescuer asked to be paid, survivors understand the request. Albert Greenbaum makes that point in the Gombiner yizker book:

The condition for my staying on, naturally, was bound up with my paying him a large sum of money. But this was not the worst of it. My staying at Grabarek's was bound up with other difficulties that were growing more complex every day.... Until now, I had been able to show my face before people under the guise of a Pole who ran away from the "Reich." But from now on I was forced to hide and not be seen by strange eyes. It meant that outside Grabarek, his wife, their children and the two elderly Poles, nobody in the village must know of my presence. It became necessary to find a hiding place.[26]

Greenbaum's use of the word *naturally* shows that his judgment on the helpers is not necessarily the same as *Yad Vashem*'s. Regardless of their small number, helpers are worthy of praise because they endangered themselves and others by their efforts. Projects designed around the subject will stimulate lively discussions about the responsibility of individuals.

Resisters

Resistance may be classified as active or passive. Active resistance refers to blowing up railroad lines, sabotaging factories, or taking up arms. Passive resistance refers to activities such as keeping a diary, writing literature, reading books, teaching school, conducting religious services, holding cultural events, distributing materials, printing underground newspapers, and other activities. Details about armed resistance in the Warsaw ghetto, for instance, may be found in primary sources, such as Abraham Lewin's *A Cup of Tears* and in secondary sources, such as Israel Gutman's *Resistance: The Warsaw Ghetto Uprising*. Active resistance also occurred in the Vilna, Minsk, Lodz, Krakow, and Białystok ghettoes, as well as in the Auschwitz, Treblinka, and Sobibor camps. Not unexpectedly, as a native of Warsaw, Orlev incorporates the Warsaw ghetto uprising into his writing.

When Jozek, in *The Man from the Other Side*, learns about the uprising, he decides that he wants to join and asks Marek to lead him through the sewers into the ghetto. Regarding the Jewish fighters in the uprising, Marek recalls that Pan Jozek says:

> "But no less important, and perhaps even more so, is their having saved Jewish honor for the Jews! The Jewish people," he declared fervently," have begun to fight back against the Germans.
>
> I was infected by his enthusiasm. "My uncle says that you're thinking of going back into the ghetto."
>
> "I'm not thinking of it. I'm going. Tonight."[27]

Although *The Island on Bird Street* is set in an unspecified place, the story also features ghetto fighters and partisans. At one point, Freddy tells Alex:

> "Now that I have a rifle and bullets, I'll join the uprising tonight. But Henryk will stay with you…. [Our] liaison will help both of you to reach the resistance in the forests."[28]

Survivors are proud of their actions against perpetrators, and Wein finds that almost every yizker book contains details of active resistance. He classifies the descriptions of armed resistance found in the volumes into three categories: accounts of resistance in the ghettoes and camps, accounts of partisan activities, and accounts of Jewish soldiers in various armies.[29] In *Sefer Kielce*, Pincas Cytron recalls partisan activity:

There was an attempt by several young men who left the ghetto to join the Polish leftist underground, which was hiding in the forests around the city ... this underground saved several people here and there when the ghetto was liquidated; but due to informers from the right wing Polish underground, they were captured by the Gestapo in the end and murdered.[30]

In *Yizker-bukh Koriv*, Nekhemye Vurman also recalls the partisans:

I went to the Christian who was the messenger between me and my family. Several days later he directed me to a partisan detail in the forests outside of Ostrovtse. Among the partisans, I sensed strong anti–Semitism, even though the group included several Jews along with Poles and Russians. The Jews were given the most dangerous assignments, and had no choice but to carry them out. Despite everything, we were glad for the chance to take revenge.[31]

While accounts of resistance like Cytron's and Vurmans's are found in yizker books and should be lauded, teachers should not overemphasize active resistance. Doing so creates a false impression of what was actually possible to accomplish. Passive resistance is a contested category because it raises questions about what counts a resistance. Even though Orlev does not focus on passive resistance, details about those types of activities are found in yizker books. For example, *Der Bialystoker yizker bukh* contains information about the ghetto archives of Mordechai Tenenbaum-Tamarof and Hersz Mersik; *The Kalish Book* contains a description of the illegal publishing activities of an underground press.

Smugglers

Smugglers were crucial in the ghettoes and camps. According to Emanuel Ringelblum smuggling took place through the ghetto walls, gates, tunnels, sewers, and border homes. Additionally, organizations outside the ghetto smuggled information, arms, ammunition, food, medicine, literature, letters, and other goods. Much is known about smuggling in the Warsaw ghetto from works such as *To Live with Honor and Die with Honor* edited by Joseph Kermish, *Notes from the Warsaw Ghetto: The Journal of Emanuel Ringelblum* by Emanuel Ringelblum, and *Who Will Write Our History* by Samuel Kassow. Given the importance of smuggling in the ghetto, not surprisingly Orlev incorporates details about smugglers in the two works.

The Man from the Other Side describes the procedures by which Antony carries his merchandise through the city sewers of Warsaw. Not trusting anyone else, Antony brings Marek into the business. In the following exchange,

Marek explains the enterprise. When Marek arrives in the ghetto with Pan Jozek, the men who often receive goods from Antony remark:

> "Why, it's Marek, Pan Antony's son," he said pointing at me.
> "But they haven't brought anything," someone said disappointedly.
> It seemed that Antony had promised to bring some "candy" that day....
> "Candy," by the way, was our code word for bullets. "Food parcels" were guns, "eggs" were hand grenades, and "sausages" were pistols.[32]

The Island on Bird Street suggests that looting, like smuggling, could be a positive activity. For instance, looters who gather items to smuggle on behalf of an underground group could be considered resisters. Orlev suggests that in the scene where Alex starts to understand why Bolek stole the coats.

Since smuggled goods provided a lifeline for some people, numerous yizker book writers reminisce about smugglers. A number of books contain descriptions of smuggling in the ghettoes. In *Bielsk-Podlaski; Sefer Zikaron*, Meir Peker writes about the Bielsk ghetto:

There were also non–Jews who would enter the ghetto in some mysterious way

> and arrange on-the-spot exchange. Some brought leather to shoe-makers or cloth to tailors in order to get shoes or clothes in return. There were no craftsmen apart from the Jews of Bielsk to serve the local non–Jews, and the devastation which was brought upon the Jews caused these Gentiles much discomfort. Formerly they had accused the Jews of living off others, but now, seeing that the Jews were laboring only to survive, they went into the Ghetto to seek them out.[33]

Similarly, Ben Giladi writes about smuggling in the Piotrkow ghetto:

> In order to stay alive, many people started to smuggle food into the ghetto in exchange for money, clothes and other valuable items. Very few bakeries were functioning legally. To supply the pressing demand for daily bread, dozens of little, illegal bakeries came into existence. The butchers, despite strict prohibiting orders, were supplying meat. Such activities were punishable by death; many paid the price of being arrested and deported, among them shochet Yehoshua Lerner and butcher Berek Pudlowski, who was caught when bringing a cow (live) up flights of stairs for slaughter.[34]

The *Belchatow yizker-bukh* describes incidents of bribery and smuggling in the ghetto also. Smuggling also took place in the camps. In *Pinkes Bedzin*, David Liwer writes about a number of people from Bedzin who smuggled guns into Auschwitz. While smuggling is not usually considered an activity to be studied, the role of Jews and non–Jews in bringing goods into the ghettoes, camps, and other places was so vital that writers such as Rachel Auerbach, a chronicler of the Warsaw ghetto, praised them publically.

Conclusion

Yizker books represent the collected memories of survivors, which according to Annette Wievorka is part of what makes the books an exceptional corpus.[35] Authentication projects designed around Uri Orlev's novels and yizker books give students a means of using first-hand accounts to examine specific behavior during the Holocaust. Yizker books allow students to examine sources created by Holocaust victims. The books also help students to place the Holocaust within the context of Jewish history since the books describe the hometowns before and after the war. Depending on curricular goals, authentication projects may be extended to countries other than Poland. Those projects would be useful for exploring the ways in which the Holocaust against the Jews was not the same everywhere. Projects could also be extended to non–Jews. In all cases, projects should adhere to the guidelines of the United States Holocaust Memorial Museum for teaching about the Holocaust.[36]

Selected Resources for Classroom Use

Arad, Yitzhak, Israel Gutman, and Abraham Margaliot. *Documents on the Holocaust: Selected Sources on the Destruction of the Jews of Germany and Austria, Poland, and the Soviet Union.* Eighth edition. Lincoln: University of Nebraska Press; Jerusalem: Yad Vashem, 1999.

Barnett, Victoria. *Bystanders: Conscience and Complicity During the Holocaust.* Westport, CT: Greenwood Press, 1999.

Baum, Steven K. *The Psychology of Genocide: Perpetrators, Bystanders, and Rescuers.* Cambridge and New York: Cambridge University Press, 2008.

Glassner, Martin Ira, and Robert Krell, eds. *And Life Is Changed Forever.* Detroit: Wayne State University Press, 2010.

Groce, Eric, and Robin Groce. "Authenticating Historical Fiction: Rationale and Process," *Education Research and Perspectives,* Volume 32, Number 1, 2005: 99–119.

Groce, Robin. "Authenticating *Number the Stars* Using Nonfiction Resources," *Social Studies and the Young Learner,* Volume 21, Number 3, 2009, 6–9.

Gutman, Israel. *Resistance: The Warsaw Ghetto Uprising.* Boston: Houghton Mifflin in association with the United States Holocaust Memorial Museum, 1994.

_____, and Shmuel Krakowski. *Unequal Victims: Poles and Jews During World War Two.* New York: Holocaust Library, 1986.

Holiday, Laurel. *Children in the Holocaust and World War II: Their Secret Diaries.* New York: Pocket Books, 1995.

Hilberg, Raul. *Perpetrators Victims Bystanders: The Jewish Catastrophe, 1933–1945.* New York: Harper Perennial, 1992.

Jordan, Sarah. "Educating Without Overwhelming: Authorial Strategies in Children's Holocaust Literature," *Children's Literature in Education,* Volume 35, Number 3, September 2004, 199–218.

Kassow, Samuel D. *Who Will Write Our History? Emanuel Ringelblum, the Warsaw Ghetto, and the Oyneg Shabes Archive.* Bloomington: Indiana University Press, 2007.

Kermish Joseph, ed. *To Live with Honor and Die with Honor! Selected Documents from the Warsaw Ghetto Underground Archives.* Jerusalem: Yad Vashem, 1986.

Lewin, Abraham. *A Cup of Tears: A Diary of the Warsaw Ghetto.* Antony Polonsky, ed., and Christopher Hutton, trans. Oxford and New York: Basil Blackwell, in association with the Institute for Polish-Jewish Studies, Oxford, 1988.

Opdyke, Irene Gut, with Jennifer Armstrong. *In My Hands: Memories of a Holocaust Rescuer.* New York: Knopf, 1999.

Orlev, Uri. *The Man from the Other Side.* New York: Penguin Books, 1989.

_____. *The Island on Bird Street.* Boston: Houghton Mifflin, 1984.

Ringelblum, Emanuel. *Notes from the Warsaw Ghetto: The Journal of Emanuel Ringelblum.* New York: Schocken Books, 1974.

_____, Joseph Kermish, and Shmuel Krakowski. *Polish-Jewish Relations During the Second World War.* Evanston, IL: Northwestern University Press, 1992.

Sakowicz, Kazimierz. *Ponary Diary, 1941–1943: A Bystander's Account of a Mass Murder,* ed. Arad Yitzhak. New Haven, CT: Yale University Press, 2005.

Shawn, Karen. "Virtual Community, Real-Life Connections: A Study of *The Island on Bird Street* via an International Reading Project," in Samuel Totten, ed. *Teaching Literature of the Holocaust.* Boston: Allyn and Bacon, 2001.

Sliwowska, Wiktoria, ed. *The Last Eyewitness.* Chicago: Northwestern University Press, 1998.

Tec, Nechama. *When Light Pierced the Darkness: Christian Rescue of Jews in Nazi Occupied Poland.* New York: Oxford University Press, 1986.

Zapruder, Alexandra, ed. *Salvaged Pages: Young Writers' Diaries of the Holocaust.* New Haven, CT: Yale University Press, 2002.

Notes

1. Jared Stark, "Broken Records: Holocaust Diaries, Memoirs, and Memorial Books," in *Teaching the Representation of the Holocaust,* eds. Marianne Hirsch and Irene Kacandes (New York: Modern Language Association of America, 2004), 191–204.

2. Biographical material is distilled from "Contemporary Authors Online." (Detroit: Gale, 2004) Literature Resource Center. Appalachian State University, Boone, NC.

3. Karen Shawn describes one classroom project in "Virtual Community, Real-Life Connections: A Study of *The Island on Bird Street* via an International Reading Project;" in *Teaching Literature of the Holocaust,* ed. Samuel Totten (Boston: Allyn and Bacon, 2001), 103–124; Sarah Jordan discusses *The Island on Bird Street* and *The Man from the Other Side* in "Educating Without Overwhelming: Authorial Strategies in Children's Holocaust Literature," *Children's Literature in Education* Volume 35, Number 3 (September 2004): 199–218.

4. See Eric Groce and Robin Groce, "Authenticating Historical Fiction: Rationale and Process," *Education Research and Perspectives* Volume 32, Number 1 (2005): 99–119.

5. See Robin Groce, "Authenticating *Number the Stars* Using Nonfiction Resources," *Social Studies and the Young Learner* Volume 21, Number 3 (2009): 6–9.

6. English translations of yizker books may be found at Jewishgen.org or in the English section of specific yizker books. For yizker books that have English sections, check Zachary Baker's bibliography in *From a Ruined Garden: The Memorial Books of Polish Jewry,* ed. and trans. Jack Kugelmass and Jonathan Boyarin, Second, expanded edition (Bloomington: Indiana University Press in association with the United States Holocaust Memorial Museum, 1998), 273–339.

7. Uri Orlev, *The Man from the Other Side* (New York: Penguin Books, 1989), 25.

8. Uri Orlev, *The Island on Bird Street* (Boston: Houghton Mifflin Company, 1984), 90.

9. Orlev, *The Man from the Other Side,* 10.

10. Orlev, *The Island on Bird Street,* 129–130.

11. Tuviah Ivri, "The Destruction of Goniondz," in *Sefer yizkor Goniadz,* ed. J. Ben-Meir (Tel-Aviv: The Committee of Goniondz Association in the USA and in Israel, 1960), http://www.jewishgen.org/Yizkor/goniadz/Goniadz.html (accessed May 5, 2010).

12. Minna Mlinek-Magnushever, "Troubles and Horrors at the Beginning of the War," in *Sefer zikaron le-kehilat Rozan*, ed. Benjamin Halevy (Tel Aviv: Rozhan Societies in Israel and the USA, 1977), 65.

13. Abraham Wein, "'Memorial Books' as a Source for Research into the History of Jewish Communities in Europe," *Yad Vashem Studies on the Eastern European Catastrophe and Resistance* 9 (1973): 255–272.

14. Gabriel Finder, "Introduction," *Polin Studies in Polish Jewry* Volume 20 (2008): 26.

15. Orlev, *The Man from the Other Side*, 157.

16. Orlev, *The Island on Bird Street*, 81.

17. Moshe Peles, "Jews and 'Goyim' Together," in *Mlawa ha-yehudit; koroteha, hitpathuta, kilayona-di yidishe Mlawe; geshikte, nyfshtand, unkum*, ed. David Shtokfish (Tel Aviv: Mława Societies in Israel and in the Diaspora, 1984), http://www.jewishgen.org/yizkor/mlawa/mla584. html (accessed May 5, 2010).

18. Naftali Salsitz, "The Holocaust in Kolbuszowa," in *Pinkas Kolbishov*, ed. I. M. Biderman (New York: United Kolbushover, 1971), http://www.jewishgen.org/yizkor/kolbuszowa/ko 1055e.html (accessed May 5, 2010).

19. Orlev, *The Man from the Other Side*, 122.

20. Stanislaw Sobczak, "How I Hid Twelve Jews," in *Sefer Frampol*, ed. D. Shtkfish (Tel Aviv: Book Committee, 1966). Reprinted in *From a Ruined Garden: The Memorial Books of Polish Jewry*, ed. and trans. Jack Kugelmass and Jonathan Boyarin. Second, expanded edition (Bloomington: Indiana University Press in association with the United States Holocaust Memorial Museum, 1998), 203.

21. See Israel Gutman and Shmuel Krakowski, *Unequal Victims: Poles and Jews During World War Two*. (New York: Holocaust Library, 1986).

22. Orlev, *The Man from the Other Side*, 62.

23. Orlev, *The Island on Bird Street*, 100.

24. Chaim Krystal, "The Struggle for Life in the Nazi Inferno," in *Sefer kehilat yehudei Dąbrowa Górnicza ve-hurbanah*, ed. N. Gelbart, et al. (Tel Aviv: Former Residents of D browa Górnitza, 1971), http://www.jewishgen.org/yizkor/dabrowa/Dabrowa.html (accessed May 5, 2010).

25. Esther Kimch, "Due to the Merits of the Righteous of the World," in *Sefer Zloczew* (Tel Aviv: Committee of the Association of Former Residents of Zloczew, 1971), http://www.jew-ishgen.org/yizkor/Zloczew/Zloczew.html (accessed May 5, 2010).

26. Albert Greenbaum, "Saved by a Peasant Family," in *Gombin: dos lebn un umkum fun a yidish shtetl in Poyln*, ed. Jack Ziklin, et al. (New York: Gombiner Landsmanshaft in America, 1969), 60.

27. Orlev, *The Man from the Other Side*, 129.

28. Orlev, *The Island on Bird Street*, 102.

29. Wein, "Memorial Books as a Source," 269.

30. Pinchas Cytron, "The Story of the Ghetto and Liquidation," *Sefer Kielce: toldot kehilat Kielce*, ed. Pinchas Cytron (Tel Aviv: Former Residents of Kielce in Israel, 1957), http://www.jewishgen.org/Yizkor/kielce/Kie226.html#Page237 (accessed May 5, 2010).

31. Nekhemye Vurman, "I Was a German Soldier," in *Yisker-bukh Koriv*, ed. M. Grossman (Tel Aviv: Former Residents of Kurow in Israel, 1955). Reprinted in *From a Ruined Garden: The Memorial Books of Polish Jewry*, ed. and trans. Jack Kugelmass and Jonathan Boyarin, Second, expanded edition (Bloomington: Indiana University Press in association with the United States Holocaust Memorial Museum, 1998), 223.

32. Orlev, *The Man from the Other Side*, 146.

33. Meir Peker, "In the Bielsk Ghetto & the Camps," in *Bielsk-Podlaski; Sefer Zikaron*, ed. H. Rabin (Tel Aviv: Bielsk Immigrants' Societies of Israel and the United States of America, 1975), http://www.jewishgen.org/Yizkor/Bielsk/Bie002.html#Ghetto (accessed May 5, 2010).

34. Ben Giladi, "The Topic of Resistance," in *A Tale of One City*, ed. Ben Giladi (Shengold Publishers in cooperation with the Piotrkow Trybunalski Relief Association, New York, 1991), 202.

35. Annette Wievorka, *The Era of the Witness*, trans. Jared Stark (Ithaca: Cornell University Press, 2006), 29.

36. Follow the link for teachers under the heading "Education," on the website of the United States Holocaust Memorial Museum, http://www.ushmm.org.

13

Yizker Books and Photographic Form

Daniel Magilow

Yizker Books and Iconic Memory

Recent scholarship on visual culture and genocide has stressed that the photographs used in well-known Holocaust memorials often create as many interpretive problems as they ostensibly solve. Specifically, the issue pertains to the way that widely circulated images tend to divorce memory from history. Cornelia Brink has labeled as "secular icons" the photographs of the boy led from the Warsaw Ghetto at gunpoint, Margaret Bourke-White's shocking images of liberated prisoners at Buchenwald, the portrait of a smiling Anne Frank, and other oft-reproduced photographs that have taken on a quasi-religious character. According to Brink, secular icons

> mostly impress themselves on our sentiments and conjure up a threatening, mute and nameless sense of "once upon a time." Then as now they set off strong emotional reactions, of shock and terror, of compassion as well as rejection. Usually the pictures are accepted as straightforward and unambiguous reality, not as a specific photographic rendering of that reality open to analysis. More than other photographs they make a moral claim to be accepted without questioning.[1]

When they concentrate complex events into easily consumable visual packages, secular icons enable historical amnesia. They encourage us to smooth out the rough edges of history and to remember the past as we want it to have been. Consider, for instance, the iconic photograph of the boy led from the Warsaw ghetto at gunpoint. It begs the question how a child could possibly have posed such a threat as to warrant being led away at gunpoint and, *mutatis mutandis*, how Europe's Jews could possibly have threatened Germany to the extent that it would divert critical resources from its war effort to deport and exterminate them. Because it humanizes atrocity, this photograph has become one of the Holocaust's most famous symbols. The pathos and tragedy in the boy's frightened face concentrate genocide's fundamental senselessness, tragedy, and absurdity into one discrete image.

But for all of its rhetorical ability to generate *pathos*, a troubling ethical dilemma surrounds this secular icon and others like it. Like many important Holocaust photographs, it was created by a perpetrator. It first appeared in the photographic appendix of the Stroop Report, the bureaucratic document that SS Major-General Jürgen Stroop sent to Berlin as proof that his soldiers had successfully suppressed the Warsaw ghetto uprising. It was never intended as a protest against genocide. In fact, the original caption *Aus Bunkern mit Gewalt hervorgeholt* [Forcibly Taken from Bunkers] leads one to think that the boy is himself the threat.[2] Photographs like this one force viewers into the ethically awkward subject position as perpetrators of genocide. And all the while, the proximate history and context in which the image was produced and consumed remain relatively obscure.

The overrepresentation of perpetrator photographs in the Holocaust's visual archive begs important questions: Do photographic representations made by and for victimized Jewish communities and their descendants differ from those intended primarily for larger audiences of non–Jewish spectators? And how do these representations situate the Holocaust within the larger, complex, and irreducible fabric of Jewish history? How do they articulate the relationship of history and memory, and do they do so in a way that avoids the tendency of iconic photographs to objectify victims in the undifferentiated categories of *The Jews* or *The Six Million*?[3]

One approach to these question lies in the study of the photographs in yizker books, the memorial compendia that survivors of specific localities produced after the Holocaust to memorialize their destroyed hometowns.[4] To examine the relationship of yizker books, photography, and memory in more detail, this essay presents a reading of *The Kalish Book*, an English language yizker book for the Polish town of Kalisz.[5] *The Kalish Book* suggests a different relationship of photography and memory than do universalizing secular icons, although this relationship brings its own problems and complexities. In the ways it invokes the traditions and organizing principles of family photography, both with literal photographs and with textual forms that evoke photography, it creates a coherent and totalizing narrative of Jewish life and history in Kalisz. Paradoxically, however, these same photographs and photographically-inflected forms concurrently undo *The Kalish Book*'s drive towards establishing a timeless image of Kalisz and its Jews. In their formal and thematic specifics, the texts and photographs betray their creators' biases, grow obscure, and ultimately foreground memory's fragility and impermanence.

A Brief History of Kalisz and The Kalish Book

A brief essay about Kalisz's yizker book cannot do justice to the town and its rich history. Nevertheless, a reading of *The Kalish Book* demands at least a cursory sketch of the community that its yizker book concerns.[6] Kalisz can stake a claim as one of Poland's oldest continuous settlements. Located in a frontier region that over the centuries variously fell under German, Polish, and Russian administration, Kalisz benefitted economically over the centuries from its location on the Amber Road, a trade route that connected the Baltic and Adriatic seas. In the nineteenth century, Kalisz expanded as a center of textile production and in particular of lace manufacture, a point of civic pride that figures significantly in the visual iconography of *The Kalish Book*. According to the 1931 census, 15,300 Jews lived in Kalisz, which at the time amounted to approximately 30 percent of the population. When World War II broke out in 1939, the town's total population totaled 89,000, with an estimated 20,000 Jews.[7]

According to some sources, Kalisz's Jewish community traces its history to the Jews who fled Crusaders in the Rhineland in the early twelfth century.[8] Nevertheless, Kalisz owes its lasting importance in Jewish history and myth primarily as the namesake of the Statute of Kalisz of 1264. Through this statue, the Polish king Bolesław the Pious ostensibly affirmed certain key civil liberties and economic rights for Jews. It stipulated, for instance, that a Jew be allowed to call Jewish witnesses to testify in support of his case if a Christian accused him of an offense. The Statute of Kalisz also established a right of Jewish settlement that persisted until Poland's Third Partition in 1795. It is sometimes called the Jewish Magna Charta. Like the frequent visual allusions to lacework, artistic renderings of the Statue of Kalisz also run through *The Kalish Book* as a *leitmotif*. Many are the work of Arthur Szyk, the prominent illustrator and political cartoonist who emigrated from Poland to the United States before World War II.

By the time World War II and the Holocaust began, Jewish life in Kalisz had already been in a state of tremendous flux. The city suffered heavily during World War I, and immediately thereafter, during the Polish independence movement of 1919, nationalist Poles perpetrated a deadly pogrom.[9] Unsurprisingly, the early 1920s witnessed significant emigration of Kalisz's Jews, who nevertheless retained firm ties to their hometown.[10] Around the world and in particular in the United States, expatriate former Jewish residents of Kalisz, or Kalishers, formed immigrant aid societies to help their compatriots, those newly arrived to the United States and those still in Poland. Particularly in the 1930s, the *landsmanshaftn* based in America undertook philanthropic endeavors to help Kalisz's remaining Jewish community in the face of institutionalized anti–Semitism. They funded schools and soup kitchens and even sent food parcels to help needy families at Passover.[11]

The broad outlines of the Holocaust in Kalisz, which *The Kalish Book* expands upon in far greater detail, are tragically familiar. They resemble those of many Polish cities in German-occupied areas. Kalisz came under German occupation in October 1939. The occupiers quickly formed a *Judenrat* to consolidate their control. Through this proxy government, they disenfranchised Jews and segregated them into their own institutions, such as hospitals, factories, and work camps. Many Jews were conscripted into forced labor as textile workers in the service of the Reich. Through deprivation, deportation, and outright murder, Kalisz's Jewish population quickly eroded. Many Jews were deported to labor camps elsewhere in Poland or to the ghetto in nearby Lodz. The final transport from occupied Kalisz took place on July, 9th 1942.[12] No substantive Jewish community survived the war; no significant one exists today.

Members of the Kalisz *landsmanshaftn* continued their work after the Holocaust with added urgency. In the immediate aftermath, they raised money for displaced persons. In the 1950s, they kept working to support fellow Kalishers, but with the decline in immigration and the absence of Jews in Kalisz itself, they shifted their time and resources towards memorializing their murdered *landslayt*. To this end, the Kalish *landsmanshaftn* encouraged and funded three main memorial activities: the establishment of a Kalish House in Tel Aviv that would "contain books, pictures, documents and anything pertaining to the Kalish Kehilla"; the planting of trees in Israel to create The Forest of the Kalish Martyrs; and the publication of a yizker book.[13]

This third project began in the late 1950s as the result of joint efforts of *landsmanshaftn* around the globe. *The Kalish Book*'s title page refers to these groups corporately as The Societies of Former Residents of Kalish and the Vicinity in Israel and U.S.A. According to a section about the book's genesis:

> The initiative for the project came from Polish and French Kalish folk. Yehiel Grinspan of Paris and Itzhak Kleichewsky began to collect material, pictures and documents and wrote articles on the social institutions of the town. Grinspan contacted members in the United States, and was assisted by the members Saltzman, Makowsky, and others. In 1957, joint steps were taken by the Kalish Societies and Israel and the United States. The Committee organized activities, held meetings and gatherings, maintained constant contact with Book Committees in Canada, France, Brazzaville, Uruguay, Australia, and in particular with the Israel Committee.[14]

The first volume of *The Kalish* book appeared in Hebrew and Yiddish in 1964 in connection with the 700th anniversary of the Statute of Kalisz. The second volume went to press during the Six-Day War in 1967. The two volumes were translated into English in 1968.

Compared to other yizker books, particularly the Yiddish language books of the immediate postwar period, the volumes the Kalish *landsmanshaftn* published stand out as materially extravagant tomes. The very fact that *The Kalish Book* appeared in different translations, for instance, points to the relatively significant resources at its authors' disposal. *The Kalish Book* also includes more texts, photographs, plates, drawings, and maps than most yizker books; its production values, while at times still amateurish, are still of relatively high quality. Although this lavishness may make *The Kalish Book* atypical compared to other yizker books, it brings advantages from an interpretive standpoint. The large amount of material in different visual and textual media creates a rich network of significations that coalesces solely around the space, idea, and memory of a real and imagined community, the once and future Kalisz, or more precisely, Kalish. The diversity of forms transforms the reading experience into a series of cinematic cuts between dissimilar texts and images. As disorienting as the reading experience may be, the heterogeneous mix of genres render explicit certain protocols of memory that in other yizker books must remain implicit or confined to the written word.

The Kalish Book *as a Memory Text*

What exactly are these memory protocols, and how does this yizker book fulfill them? With its profoundly visual character, *The Kalish Book* evinces cultural theorist Annette Kuhn's claim in *Family Secrets: Acts of Memory and Imagination* that "the language of memory does seem to be above all a language of images."[15] Yizker books are "memory texts," to use Kuhn's locution, which she defines as "cultural productions across a range of media [that] are in effect secondary revisions of the source materials of memory."[16] "Secondary revision" alludes to Sigmund Freud, who described this process in his *New Introductory Lectures on Psychoanalysis* as a "rationalizing [activity that] at best provides the dream with a smooth façade that cannot fit its true content."[17] Freud cautioned against mimetic readings of image narratives because intentional and unintentional forces shape their form and content. The finished memory text is replete with meaningful gaps, biases, and distortions. Although we shall see later how certain photographs manifest this secondary revision and inadvertently detour from *The Kalish Book*'s self-appointed task to create a memorial of the town using place-specific texts and photographs, it is first necessary to examine what those tasks are and why the secondary revision occurs.

The revision takes place when the source texts that *The Kalish Book* uses to narrate Kalisz's Jewish history do not mesh cleanly with the memorializing mandate it establishes for itself. Kuhn concludes *Family Secrets* with six theses about memory and memory texts, all of which in varying degrees characterize the memorial aspirations of yizker books in general and *The Kalish Book* in particular. Four of these theses describe memory itself. Memory, Kuhn argues, shapes our inner worlds, is an active production of meanings, embodies both union and fragmentation, and is formative of communities of nationhood. Kuhn submits two related theses about represented memory, that is, "memory texts." These texts "have their own formal conventions" and "voice a collective imagination."[18] To greater and lesser degrees, all of the drawings, maps, chronicles, anecdotes, vignettes, memoirs, obituaries, poems, local histories, diaries, and reminiscences in *The Kalish Book* support Kuhn's claims about memory.

If any single text synthesizes these aims of memory, it is one of its opening documents: the initial yizker prayer. This text appears among several other prefaces and introductory texts that establish a serious, memorial, and religiously inflected tone. In Jewish liturgy, the yizker is the traditional prayer that mourners recite for the departed after the Torah reading on the last day of Passover, on the second day of Shavuot, on Shemini Atzeret, and on Yom Kippur. The grammatical inflection of yizker, literally "He will remember," presupposes the very communicative situation of public memorializing. The speaker who says "He will remember" tells a listener that a third person, "He," presumably God, will remember. In this regard, the yizker prayer organizes *The Kalish Book* as a space of memorial discourse, where memory is to be both produced and consumed. As it tells readers how Kalisz's Jews suffered and why they deserve a memorial, this yizker prayer performs the tasks that Kuhn stipulates. (See figure 1.) It condenses centuries of Kalisz's Jewish history into several paragraphs. It presents Kalishers as a group unified across time in spite of political and religious differences that existed among this population of 30,000. It presents Kalisz's physical destruction as violent and total, although Kalish persists in memory and in exile and remains metaphysically significant and worth remembering. The prayer's florid, religiously tinged diction "shapes readers' inner worlds" and actively produces meanings when it situates Kalisz's Jewish history within the broader narratives of Jewish suffering and the diaspora. The opening line "Jewry, remember the City and Mother in Israel cut down with her children" equates the life and death Kalisz with Jewish history's paradigmatic catastrophe: the destruction of Jerusalem and its temple. Rhetorically, the sentence is an apostrophe, which in addressing "Jewry" as a unified group, creates in word if not in fact the unified, transhistorical community that forms both its subject matter and audience.

With its idiosyncratic visual layout, this yizker prayer furthermore embodies Kuhn's claim that memory texts have their own unique forms. For-

יזכור

Jewry, remember the City and Mother in Israel cut down with her children. The city remains as it had been, untouched.

The houses rise high, the gardens blossom, the River Prosna twines as of old, with banks that are now paved with tombstones out of the Jewish graveyard.

Yet the thirty thousand Jews of Kalish have been cut down one and all; never brought to a Jewish grave. Their ashes are part of the ashes of millions burnt, their bones flung afar in alien fields, all they had was left behind in the city where aliens batten upon it.

Seven hundred years ago and more they arrived in the city and at once became the yeast in the dough; they minted coins for the king, they toiled and they traded. Swiftly they spread beyond the narrow bounds of the Jewish callings of those times and engaged in crafts and commerce.
Skilfully, wisely they laboured until they made their city into a leader in all embroidery and lace-making work.

This was a city of Jews, a Jewish city, a city of merchants and craftsmen, the city of the learned "Magen Abraham" and "Nefesh Haya"; the city of Revolutionaries in 1905 and of Ghetto Fighters who came from Youth Movements, went to their brethren all over the country and with their blood wrote pages of valour in the Record of Polish Jewry; city of pioneer Halutzim who went ahead to show the way to the Homeland; city of All-the-year-round Jews who filled synagogues and stieblech with the chanting of prayer and the study of Torah; city of youngsters in many a party contending together, their hearts full of the Love of Israel, flaming with zeal for the Honour of Israel; city of Erect Jewish Workers with skilful hands who were honoured at home among their own people, and in the eyes of their Gentile comrades.

But the murderers came like robbers at noon, encompassing them with deceit and trickery, and brought them to the flames before they could utter their prayer, before they could lift up their hands.

See them go to the Market Building, to the railway waggons, with little bundles and huge eyes, sad Jewish eyes. For seven hundred years they had contended here with hostile, envious neighbours who drove them away and oppressed them; sevenfold they fell and sevenfold rose; their right to eat and pray to God they purchased with anguish, yearning, intercession and money. Here or there the hand of a Jew was raised to repay murderers their deserts. So it went on day after day, century on century. Read the tale of their chronicles in the city and you will know what brought the sad sheen to their eyes.

Women pass clutching the babes to their breast, running naked to gas chambers, some stumbling and perishing. Children pass; and their wise eyes know the whole of the naked truth. The old folk pass with their hands clutching their prayerbooks. Men pass along and their backs are bowed with the burden of seven hundred years. Lads leap from the waggons and smash against the stone permanent way. The hopes of the people pass, and ironshod jackboots trample them underfoot in the sun.

Remember and Never Forget

LET THE PEOPLE REMEMBER THEIR OFFSPRING
AND WRITE THEIR NAMES LARGE
AND HALLOW THEIR MEMORY.
YOU WHO WERE BORN IN THIS CITY
OR WHOSE FATHERS AND MOTHERS WHERE BORN THERE,
REPEAT AND REPEAT TO YOUR CHILDREN:
YOUR FATHERS BEFORE YOU WERE PURE IN THEIR LIVES
AND WERE MARTYRS IN DEATH,
AND THEIR SOULS ARE BOUND UP FOREVER
IN THE BUNDLE OF LIFE.

Figure 1. Opening *yizker* prayer in *The Kalish Book* (Tel Aviv: 1967).

mally, the prayer stands out for its highly stylized quality, which persists throughout *The Kalish Book*. Multiple visual elements construct this yizker prayer as a ceremonial text evocative of Torah scrolls, a Haggadah, or an annotated Talmud: the centered Hebrew "יזכור" (yizker) at the top, the narrow, scroll-like column layout, the enlarged uppercase letters at the beginning of each paragraph, the more-widely typeset and bold lettered imperative to "REMEMBER AND NEVER FORGET," and the concluding demand in uppercase letters to make the work of memory a perpetual one.

This text announces *The Kalish Book*'s intention to memorialize Kalisz not for the world at large, but for its Jewish residents. It explicitly names its readers as "You who were born in this city or whose fathers and mothers where [*sic*] born there."[19] The prayer commands survivors to remember the history of Kalisz's murdered Jews and to repeat this history to their children. The book should become a family heirloom to be passed on and explained to future generations. Although this prayer ends with the oft-repeated call to "never forget" that imperative resonates differently because it consciously addresses a limited audience. Rather than resound like a vague, universalizing, and sacralizing platitude, this "never forget" stipulates in much greater detail what survivors and their descendants should remember. The subsequent table of contents for *The Kalish Book* inventories those memories. It organizes the town's history comprehensively through sections titled "The History of the Jews in Kalish," "The Men of the City," "Society and Culture," "A Decade," "The Final Years," "Organizations and Institutions," "The Holocaust," and "Those Who Fought Back." These chapters aspire to detail with encyclopedic thoroughness Kalish's history, its important individuals, the activities of the *kehilla* (Jewish community), and, the experience of the Holocaust.

To unify Kalish and its history across space and time, *The Kalish Book* also relies on recurrent visual *leitmotifs* that lend continuity to a disparate collection of source texts. The framing emblems at either end of *The Kalish Book* underscore this effort to confer a sense of continuity and permanence to a project designed to reanimate and reunite a destroyed community. Except for their inscriptions, the emblems are identical. The first inscription reads "The History of the Jews in Kalish." At the end, that caption changes to "The Tale of Kalish Jewry Closes Here, Unended." The details in these images represent visually the importance of everyday activities specific to Kalisz, and because of their placement at opposite ends of the yizker book create the sense of a closed, unified narrative. The emblem montages material from across the centuries: it includes a bracteate (a medieval coin) with Kalisz written in Hebrew, which alludes to the long history of Jews in Western Poland. The strip of lace again evokes Kalisz's importance in the textile industry. (See figures 2 and 3).

The stern looking religious figure reappears in the yizker book in one of the many illuminated manuscripts by Arthur Szyk, the prominent illustrator and political cartoonist who emigrated from Poland to the United States before World War II. In the late 1920s, Szyk created a series of forty-five plates called *The Statute of Kalisz*, which as Steven Luckert notes depict the Polish-Jewish relationship not with reference to the rights and benefits it bestowed upon Jews, but rather through examples of how Jews have helped increase the prosperity and security of Poland.[20] Szyk's images are consciously anachronistic. They conflate disparate moments in the history of Jewish Kalisz. The uneven margins in one of Szyk's drawing of the statue invoke the visual layout of the Talmud, yet the statute's text is in Yiddish, not the original Latin. This temporal layering supports the intended narrative of *The Kalish Book*, namely that a Jewish Kalisz persisted long before — and will persist long after — the Holocaust. Unlike Kalisz, which still exists in Poland, Kalish exists independently of space and time as a space in memory and representation. The Holo-

Figure 2 (left) and figure 3 (right): Frontispiece (left) and almost identical page at the end of *The Kalish Book* (Tel Aviv: 1967).

caust represents only one aspect of the history of Kalishers, albeit a significant one. Jewish Kalisz existed long before the Nazis arrived, and as the yizker book implies will continue to thrive.

The Kalish Book *as Photo Album*

The formal and thematic idiosyncrasies of the initial yizker prayer, the framing emblems, and Arthur Szyk's drawings of the *Statute of Kalisz* all draw attention to *The Kalish Book*'s memorial aims and the profoundly visual character of this memory text. But as much as any discourse, family photography, both literally and figuratively, shapes this yizker book's memorial project. On the literal, material level, *The Kalish Book* includes both captioned and uncaptioned photographs of the city, its residents, organizations, congregations, events, and the like. Almost all come from private collections. These photographs alternate with the wide variety of other genres that provide "figurative snapshots" of a lost world, including chronicles, anecdotes, poems, and prayers, as well as maps, drawings, and newspaper clippings. In tandem, the texts and images generate a personalized scrapbook, yearbook, or photo album that targets a very specific audience, specifically those Jews who feel a sense of kinship with the geographical space of Kalisz, the town in Poland, and Kalish, its destroyed Jewish community.

However much the constant switching between text and images may disorient a reader, the diversity of media serves a purpose with regard to the photographs. As critic John Berger argues in *About Looking*:

> There is never a single approach to something remembered...Words, comparisons, signs need to create a context for a printed photograph in a comparable way; that is to say, they must mark and leave open diverse approaches. A radial system has to be constructed around the photograph so that it may be seen in terms which are simultaneously personal, political, economic, dramatic, everyday and historic.[21]

With its prayers, chronicles, anecdotes, death announcements, maps, drawings, and other visual and textual *leitmotifs*, *The Kalish Book* creates just such a network of significations necessary to give meaning to obscure images. The entire book is, in one sense, an extended caption for photographs that are ostensibly so personal and so specific that they often mean little even to those who know that space well.

The creation of this network of signification aligns *The Kalish Book* with another important form for structuring memories, namely the photo album and the oral tradition, real or imagined, that photo albums trigger. In *Suspended Conversations: The Afterlife of Memory in the Photographic Album*, Martha Langford considers photo albums not merely as physical artifacts, but as narrative devices and figures of relationships to the past. Langford suggests that oral tradition structures albums like an invisible scaffolding. The silent, illegible or only partially legible images on each album leaf demand, "reactivation through spectatorial performance."[22] In *The Kalish Book*, vaguely captioned photographs such as "A Family," "A Young Couple," "Family Festivities and Social Gatherings," "Age and Youth in the Park," and "Jews in and Out of Procession" all depend on an implied oral tradition.[23] The images mean little to those not privy to a specific oral history that is almost exclusively for Kalishers and their descendants. *The Kalish Book* presupposes insider knowledge of certain geographies, traditions, people, and histories because this knowledge is the condition of possibility for the materials of the yizker book to communicate effectively. Several photographs have fake photo mounts drawn at their corners. (See figure 4 for an example.) These simulated mounts explicitly acknowledge the formal affinities between this yizker book and a photo album. In one example, three images of class photos, captioned together simply "School Children," zigzag across the page in a casual, wavy curve. Like a signature or a marginal inscription, the layout suggests the individual authorial presence behind a private photo album.[24] Together with the simulated

Figure 4. Pictures of unidentified school children in *The Kalish Book* (Tel Aviv: 1967).

photo mounts and gray background, the vague caption lends *The Kalish Book* a personal touch and alludes to private stories about these school children to which not all are privy.

The use of personal photographs in *The Kalish Book* has important cultural and theological ramifications. In presupposing an oral tradition, this yizker book honors the importance of oral tradition in Jewish culture, epitomized in the annual retelling of the Passover story. Moreover, it articulates a model for redemption specific to Jewish culture and history. Describing this understanding of redemption, Arthur A. Cohen has noted that a characteristic signature of the classical rabbinic style is

> its interweaving of various theological motifs and preoccupations, its refusal to separate out high arguments from examples drawn from the most mundane events of life, its continuous care for using simple fidelities and loyalty to the *halakhah* as occasions for promising large redemptions.[25]

The montage of private photographs and reminiscences with more public texts about war and genocide in a scrapbook-like form exemplifies this interweaving of low and high. The photographs enable readers to use them as prompts to reanimate this destroyed past. These images encourage a specific segment of posterity, Kalishers and their descendants, to remember their *landslayt* as active historical agents whose lives held meaning aside from the violent ways in which they died. For those seeking to redeem the fundamentally irredeemable mass murder of the Holocaust, this multimedia form would seem to offer just such an opportunity. But such is not always the case.

Undoing the Claims of Memory

In an essay that compares yizker books with the photographically illustrated fiction of the late German author W.G. Sebald, Katharina Hall notes that the frequent use of photographs in yizker books "give[s] readers a feeling of immediacy, a sense that they are directly accessing the past."[26] When it invokes the forms and traditions of family photography, *The Kalish Book* generates this sense of more direct access to Kalisz and its history. Photography plays a key role in its project to establish the memory of Kalisz as perpetual. But this project periodically runs aground when certain images and photographs draw attention to memory as both historically determined and ephemeral. Rather than create direct, unmediated links to the past, such images sanitize, normalize, and even erase the past.

This yizker book's very first page is a case in point. (See figure 5.) One sees simply a list of empty lines and in Hebrew, Yiddish, and English the

משפחתי
מיין משפחה
My Family

Figure 5. Inscription page from *The Kalish Book* (Tel Aviv: 1967).

words "my family." This page aims to involve a reader in the memorial project through recourse to the traditions of family scrapbooks and local history. On one level, these lines are simply a blank space, like the title page of a yearbook or photo album that owners use to name, dedicate, and personalize their copies of this yizker book. To write one's name is a speech act that connects oneself and one's family to a lineage of Kalishers, past, present, and future. Here *The Kalish Book* also introduces another visual icon, the *yahrzeit* candle that persists throughout this yizker book and doubles as the letter *i* in the word Kalish on the cover. The act of inscribing one's name under this memorial image establishes historical continuity because it evokes earlier memory book traditions, notably the *pinkas kehilot*, the local record books used to document Jewish community life. More relevant in the context of a yizker book, the blank lines evoke the pre–Holocaust *memorbücher* used to record the names of victims of anti–Jewish violence. More broadly, they echo the myriad other forms of archival lists connected to the deportation, murder, and in rare cases, rescue of Jews.[27]

But at the same time as this inscription page seeks to solidify and stabilize the memory of Kalish across time, space, and exile, it also points to its erasure. The blank lines imply that for every person who has survived the Holocaust and can write a name, many others exist only as blank spaces, either because they died, because there is no way to find out any information about them, or because they have simply been forgotten. This dedicatory page radically, if unintentionally, points to the fact that in many cases, emptiness is all that remains of "my family," a point that this page's status as the first one of a Holocaust memorial book reinforces. Since a *yahrzeit* candle burns not perpetually, but only for twenty-four hours once a year, this motif also suggests a time limit on the act of mourning. As it pursues the goal of making the memory of Kalish permanent, this image paradoxically points to its fleeting character.

The periodic use of avant-garde photographic techniques in *The Kalish Book* also highlights how the use of family photography to make memory specific and personal backfires. One exemplary photomontage captioned "The Older Generation" presents the portraits of six older but unnamed Kalishers, three men and women who stand against an ashen grey background. (See figure 6). The image appears in an extensive photographic section that documents everyday events and social groups in Kalisz. Its caption suggests a sense of historical continuity with its comparative adjective *older*, which complements an earlier set of images about "The Younger Generation." The image is marked by its crudeness: the outlines where the headshots were cut from their original contexts are still evident. Erasures or possibly excess glue around the pasted-in caption underscore the photomontage's homemade and constructed quality. As it prompts readers to remember older Kalishers, this photomontage concurrently draws attention to its own constructedness, contingency, and historicity. It reunites the older generation in a way that both betrays its authors' biases and hauntingly evokes the Holocaust. For one, the gendered understanding of Kalisz's Jewish community becomes immedi-

The Older Generation

Figure 6. A group of unidentified men and women in *The Kalish Book* (Tel Aviv: 1967).

ately apparent. Appearing as it does in a yizker book whose title page lists men alone as authors, this photomontage arranges the men and women along a vertical axis that forms an invisible *mechitza*, the partition that separates men and women in a synagogue. Two of the three men wear beards and hats that mark them as religious against the women with distinctively secular hair-cuts. For all of their gendered differences, however, the image implies that they shared a similar fate. The six men and women stare powerfully at the reader from the oblivion of a decontextualized grey background. Only the caption and reader who reanimate them anchor this image to any referent. Even as "The Older Generation" points to the implied oral tradition of yizker books passed down through generations, it is again a reminder, to cite the second word of Martha Langford's title *Suspended Conversations*, that the conversation that occurs in albums and in yizker books becomes suspended without qualified interpreters. As time claims those whom gas chambers did not, photographic memory texts and images like this photomontage become increasingly illegible. The sterile background in "The Older Generation" powerfully evinces Roland Barthes's claim that photographs carry with them the time of the future anterior, the sense that "this will have been."[28] To see the image of living people with the knowledge that they very likely died horrifically just a few years later positions an observer in a troubling but helpless relationship to catastrophe. The stories that *The Kalish Book* narrates are not simply the stories of one central European town. Rather, they are the stories of small central European towns whose Jewish residents were massacred. Because of the knowledge that hindsight affords post–Holocaust readers, the photographs of regular people in *The Kalish Book* take on an added severity, tragedy, and emptiness. They "cut" us, to use Susan Sontag's famous description of her first encounter with a Holocaust photograph.[29]

Conclusion: The Return to the Iconic

The frequent use of family photography in *The Kalish Book* marks this yizker book as a memory text that tries to avoid the de-historicizing pitfalls of iconic photographs. Rather than communicate a rich history in the overly generalized and universalizing mode of a great many post–Holocaust forms, particularly mass cultural secular icons, it instead seeks to focus attention on the specific events, spaces, and institutions of Kalisz and its Jewish community over the centuries, not just on Jewish death during the Holocaust. Indeed, as is often the case with yizker books, the forty-five page section on the destruction of Kalisz's Jews begins on page 250 and does not monopolize this yizker book, even as its shadow looms heavily. The focus is instead on the familiar. Detailed essays and photographs tell of the local rowing club, the old bridge over the river Prosna, pre-war café culture, election results for the town's Jewish council, and other everyday people and activities. These details may seem exceedingly mundane to the outsider, particularly one versed in the tropes of harrowing Holocaust testimonies. Yet to Kalish's former residents, this yizker book's intended audience, such fragments symbolize tradition, comfort, and normalcy, like cherished family photographs. The Holocaust may constitute a defining historical period in Jewish history, but it is not represented as the *sine qua non* of Jewish Kalisz. Through this focus on the everyday, *The Kalish Book* would appear to articulate a redemptive model of Holocaust memory drawn not from the externally imposed moralizing paradigms of mass cultural Holocaust representations, but immanently, from the details of a specific Jewish history and tradition.

But at several key points in *The Kalish Book*, the model of specific redemptive memory drawn from the details of Jewish life reverts to the more familiar model of universalizing iconic photographs. The subtle inclusion of several images by Roman Vishniac suggests an anxiety about relying exclusively on private photography as a medium of memory that *The Kalish Book* ultimately does not overcome. These images are poorly attributed and not easily distinguishable from photographs of Kalish. They come from the archive of images that Vishniac produced in the mid–1930s, as traditional Jewish life in East Central Europe was disappearing under the pressures of anti–Semitism, emigration, and modernity in general. Years later, in an introduction to one of the many volumes of his photographs, Vishniac hyperbolically claimed that he "knew that Hitler had made it his mission to exterminate all Jews, especially the children and the women who could bear children in the future" and that he therefore made it his mission to save their memory.[30] Vishniac's famous, melancholic and in many ways stereotypical images have become the defining and iconic images of Ashkenazi Jewry on the brink, leading Elie Wiesel to refer to the mythic pre-war time and space of Eastern European Jewry as "The Time of Vishniac."[31] Ever the voice of moral authority related to the Holocaust, Wiesel reinforced the iconic status of these photographs when he called Vishniac a "supreme witness."[32]

One of the iconic Vishniac photographs appears on the title page of the section "Kalish Jewry Day by Day." The image has been cropped and framed within the recurrent lace motif that reiterates the sense of Kalisz's importance in the textile industry. In the photograph (shown in figure 7), a bushy-bearded old man sits with his hand on his tired forehead, suggesting perhaps the toil of daily existence. The original photograph, however, had nothing to do with Kalisz. Vishniac's caption describes the man as "An elder of the village. Vrchni (Upper) Apša, Carpathian Ruthenia, 1938." His further commentary reads:

> It was 1938, but warmth and light were provided in the dwellings of the village of Upper Apša by burning branches and logs. I remember so well the firelight illuminating the hands and face of this village elder, whose advice was sought by members of his community. How wise and comforting a man he seemed to be.[33]

Figure 7. Uncredited Vishniac image of a man in *The Kalish Book* (Tel Aviv: 1967).

The mystical and metaphysical tone of Vishniac's commentary, combined with the fact that the photograph lacks any immediate relevance to Kalisz, retreats from a memory specific to Kalish and into the realm of the general and universal. Particularly because it does not mention its origins in Roman Vishniac's *oeuvre*, this image runs against the grain of the rest of *The Kalish Book*. Rather than stress what made Kalish unique to Kalishers, it instead repeats a gesture common to many mass cultural Holocaust representations. It constructs Europe's Jews as an undifferentiated mass and implicitly subsumes Kalish's history under it.

Figure 8. Uncredited Vishinac images of children in *The Kalish Book* (Tel Aviv: 1967).

A similarly excerpted photograph, also by Roman Vishniac, depicts young school children, but like the village elder montage, obscures its provenance. (See figure 8.) It appears as the top image in an uncaptioned, zigzag layout along with two group pictures. The adjacent page is captioned "Children" and implies that all of the children in the photographs are Kalishers, when in fact Vishniac's photograph reads "Talmud students. Trnava, Czechoslovakia, 1937."[34] Vishniac's commentary again homogenizes Jewish life in Eastern Europe:

Boys were admitted to yeshiva from about the age of four. In their dimly lit schoolroom [cheder], these youngsters read and wrote Hebrew. They became knowledgeable aboutthe Five Books of Moses — the first five books of the Old Testament — and they studied the commentaries on the Talmud, particularly the commentaries of Rashi, a famed scholar of the eleventh century. The Talmud is the compendium of Jewish law and lore that forms the basis of religious life. In the cheder, seeds of learning were planted, and "tradition" was continually renewed and reviewed. Perhaps I should call these pictures "The Faces of Learning."[35]

With a caption filled with its basic information about Jewish life and culture and an overtly metaphysical tone, Vishniac's original photograph clearly does not address Kalishers. Its target audience consists of non–Jews and its level of detail remains profoundly general and non-specific. The use of such an iconic photograph in *The Kalish Book* again contradicts this yizker book's self-appointed mission to construct memories of Kalish out of material specific to it.

What then might one make of the reversion to iconicity, and what implications might it hold for the use of yizker books in Holocaust research? On the one hand, yizker books hold great promise as sources that transcend the tendency to study the destruction of European Jewry from the perspectives and archives of those who destroyed them. Jan T. Gross's seminal study *Neighbors: The Destruction of the Jewish Community in Jedwabne, Poland* and Omer Bartov's recent *Erased: Vanishing Traces of Jewish Galicia in Present-Day Ukraine* are two exemplary works that show how yizker books may enrich our understanding about the Holocaust by challenging received narratives about perpetration and victimhood.[36] The books allow scholars to rely on sources other than those created by perpetrators, and at the same time help re-inscribe the Holocaust within the broader contours of Central European and Jewish history. But, on the other, as *The Kalish Book* shows, the volumes bring with them the danger of becoming fetishized precisely because, at least at first glance, they promise a more victim-centric way to study the Holocaust. Their ready availability in the online collections at the New York Public Library and on the JewishGen website only increases that temptation. In the final account, *The Kalish Book* is, like so many other Holocaust narratives, not just a warning *from* history. As its use of family photography and photographic forms shows, it is just as much a warning *about* history.

Notes

1. Cornelia Brink, "Secular Icons: Looking at Photographs from Nazi Concentration Camps," *History and Memory* 12:1 (Spring/Summer 2000): 135–136.

2. "The Stroop Report: 'The Warsaw Ghetto Is No More!'" http://www.holocaust-his tory.org/works/stroop-report/htm/intro000.htm.

3. David Engel, "On Studying Jewish History in Light of the Holocaust," Maurice R. and Corinne P. Greenberg Inaugural Lecture, Center for Advanced Holocaust Studies, United States Holocaust Memorial Museum, April 16, 2002. Engel suggests that modern Jewish history constitutes an indispensable part of the broad historical context out of which the Holocaust emerged.

4. I.M. Lask, trans., *The Kalish Book* (Tel Aviv: The Societies of Former Residents of Kalish and the Vicinity in Israel and U.S.A., 1967). *The Kalish Book* is henceforth abbreviated as *TKB*. For ease of reference, all citations use the image number available on http://yizker. nypl.org/index.php?id=2299. See also Jack Kugelmass and Jonathan Boyarin, eds., *From a Ruined Garden: The Memorial Books of Polish Jewry* (Washington D.C. United States Holocaust Memorial Museum; Bloomington: Indiana University Press, 1998); and Judith Taylor Baumel, "In Everlasting Memory: Individual and Communal Holocaust Commemoration in Israel," in *The Shaping of Israeli Identity: Myth, Memory, and Trauma,* eds. Robert Wistrich and David Ohana (London: Frank Cass, 1995), 146–170.

5. *TKB*, 236.

6. The different names and spelling of the Polish town Kalisz carry different implications. For the purposes of consistency, Kalisz in this article refers to the town in Western Poland; whereas Kalish, the Yiddish spelling, refers to the town from the vantage point of its Jewish residents referred to as Kalishers.

7. The United States Holocaust Memorial Museum (USHMM), "The Jewish Community of Kalisz in the Interwar Years." http://www.ushmm.org/wlc/article.php?lang=en&ModuleId =10005789. The USHMM website features a series of articles about the history of Jews in Kalisz.

8. Stary.Kalisz.pl, " ydzi w Kaliszu." http://www.stary.kalisz.pl/go_zydzi.php.

9. USHMM, "The Jewish Community of Kalisz in the Interwar Years." http://www.ush mm.org/wlc/article.php?lang=en&ModuleId=10005789

10. *TKB*, 236.

11. *TKB*, 236–247. This section of *The Kalish Book* titled "The Story and Activities of the Non-Partizan (*sic*) Relief in U.S.A." details the philanthropic work of Kalishers to benefit their hometown. Pages 236–239 concern the period up to the Holocaust; pages 239–243 describe specific, post-Holocaust memorial activities. The remaining pages discuss "The Kalish Lodge," "The Kalish Social Ferein," "The Kalisher Independent Society," and other individual Kalish *landsmanshaftn.*

12. *TKB*, 271.

13. *TKB*, 240–243.

14. *TKB*, 242–243.

15. Annette Kuhn, *Family Secrets: Acts of Memory and Imagination* (London: Verso, 2002), 160.

16. Ibid., 5.

17. Sigmund Freud, *The Standard Edition of the Complete Psychological Works of Sigmund Freud,* ed. James Strachey (London: The Hogarth Press, 1964), *Volume XXII: (1932–36) New Introductory Lectures on Psycho-Analysis and Other Works,* 21. See also Robert Clark, "Secondary Revision," *The Literary Encyclopedia.* 24 October 2005, http://www.litencyc.com/php/stopics. php?rec=true&UID=1605 (accessed June 2, 2008).

18. Kuhn, *Family Secrets,* 160–169.

19. *TKB*, 8.

20. Steven Luckert, *The Art and Politics of Arthur Szyk* (Washington, D.C.: United States Holocaust Memorial Museum, 2002), 19.

21. John Berger, *About Looking* (New York: Pantheon Books, 1980), 63.

22. See Martha Langford, *Suspended Conversations: The Afterlife of Memory in Photographic Albums* (Montreal: McGill-Queens University Press, 2001). Also, see Martha Langford, *Scissors, Paper, Stone: Expressions of Memory in Contemporary Photographic Art* (Montreal: McGill-Queens University Press, 2007), 287.

23. *TKB*, 64–124.

24. Geoffrey Batchen, *Forget Me Not: Photography and Remembrance* (New York: Princeton Architectural Press, 2004), 41.

25. Arthur A. Cohen and Paul Mendes-Flohr, eds., *Contemporary Jewish Religious Thought* (New York: Free Press, 1987), 761.

26. Katharina Hall, "Jewish Memory in Exile: The Relation of W.G. Sebald's *Die Ausgewanderten* to the Tradition of the *Yizker* Books," in *Jews in German Literature since 1945: German-Jewish Literature?*, ed. Pól O' Dochartaigh (Atlanta: Rodopi B.V. Editions, 2000), 154–155.

27. Ibid., 153.

28. Roland Barthes, *Camera Lucida: Reflections on Photography*, trans. Richard Howard (New York: Noonday Press, 1981), 96.

29. Susan Sontag, *On Photography* (New York: Anchor Doubleday, 1977), 19–20.

30. Roman Vishniac, *A Vanished World* (New York: Farrar, Straus & Giroux, 1983), iv.

31. See Jeffrey Shandler, "The Time of Vishniac: Photographs of Prewar East European Jewry in Postwar Contexts," *Polin: A Journal of Polish-Jewish Studies*, Vol. 16 (2003); cf. also Marion Wiesel, *To Give Them Light: The Legacy of Roman Vishniac* (New York: Simon & Schuster, 1993), 14.

32. Elie Wiesel, "Foreword" in Vishniac, *A Vanished World*, iii.

33. Vishniac, *A Vanished World*, v and 3.

34. Ibid., v and 8.

35. Ibid., v and 6–8.

36. See Jan T. Gross, *Neighbors: The Destruction of the Jewish Community in Jedwabne, Poland* (Princeton: Princeton University Press, 2001) and Omer Bartov, *Erased: Vanishing Traces of Jewish Galicia in Present-Day Ukraine* (Princeton: Princeton University Press, 2007).

14

The *Others* in Yizker Books

RIVKA PARCIAK

Yizker books published after the Holocaust by the former residents of devastated Jewish Eastern European towns and villages and their descendants were designed to perpetuate the memory and way of life of those places.[1] However, the scholarly reaction to the books was sometimes quite critical. Some scholars considered the information about the community unreliable because the accounts generally referred only to the positive aspects of the community concerned and either ignored or covered up its negative elements. For instance, Abraham Wien criticized the editors and writers of yizker books on the grounds that they presented a rosy picture of Jewish places that no longer existed. They failed in their efforts because in the books

> personalities and characters were removed from their natural setting and were needlessly highlighted in the various recollections of the Jewish experience there. Instead of highlighting and bringing to light the specific individual, the books dealt extensively with longings for *Shabbat* with mother, as well as for the characters such as the water-drawer, prankster, crazy person, the local entertainer, and similar figures ... and included everything they came across.[2]

Specifically, Wien criticizes the amount of space that the memorial books devote to the exceptional people in the town, such as the prankster or crazy person, whose images in the books were no more than marginal and incidental details. Wien thought that these details were included in the books without any thought or examination and made no contribution to the knowledge of the hometowns and how they should be remembered; as a matter of fact, they were worthless. Issues regarding the extent to which the information included in the yizker books was chosen selectively and controlled and the criteria used for inserting information into the books have been discussed by Jack Kugelmass and Jonathan Boyarin.[3] Kugelmass and Boyarin found that editors decided on a book's style and sought to either highlight or gloss over some facts and moods, possibly due to an emotional commitment toward the survivors and their families or unwillingness to depict certain personalities in a negative light. About that, Wein mentions that the Tomaszow Mazowiecki yizker book, which states: "The committee for the publication of the memorial volume decided at one of its meetings against writing about the bad behavior of certain Jews from Tomaszow in the book."[4]

Indeed, many yizker books tend to reduce and mitigate the deeds and behavior of whoever acted in contravention of the community's moral principles. As noted in *Sefer zikahon Trembowla, Strusow ve-Janow ve-ha-sevivah*: "No negative characters, in the vulgar sense of the word, were found in the last generation to inhabit the town of Struzov."[5] Similar statements appear in the books dedicated to Dabrowica, Lezanjsk, and Uhnow. Interestingly, in the yizker book to Stavische, all detailed references to anyone who did not behave in accordance with the moral standards that typified the ideal character of the town were erased by hand with a felt-tipped pen after the book was printed and bound.[6] The following unambiguous comment in *Sefer Dombrovitsa* makes the issue clear: "Even the thieves in our town were honest!"[7] The motivation behind all of this was to permit the life in the town to be remembered in a positive light and in a proper fashion for future generations. Usually, those interested in delving into the past tend to see it in a favorable light. As Jewish traditional sources state: "If only we could return our glory to what it once was;" "The older generations were better than the new ones;" and "Their finger nail was worth much more than the belly of later generations" (Mishna Tractate: Yomah 9), but "the generations have been in constant decline" ever since.

This chapter addresses the question: Why are *others* mentioned in yizker books at all? *Others* are defined as the deviant people in the town. They are exceptional in some way, and their character or appearance apparently deviated from the town's ideal and untarnished image. The significance of their appearance in the memorial books has neither escaped attention nor is incidental. In this chapter, I argue that those who were often described in yizker books as *others* play a role in strengthening the town's image. My examination is based on an examination of yizker books to fifty-four East European Jewish communities. I specifically look at the descriptions of *others* in those books and the ways they are remembered, as well as the portrayals of them in songs, photographs, and sketches.[8]

Categories of Others

As Erving Goffman notes: "We use specific stigma terms such as cripples, bastard, and moron in our daily discourse as a source of metaphor and imagery, typically without giving thought to the original meaning."[9] These character-istically stigmatic terms are a source for a metaphor or simile. We usually label the *other* in a manner that is not necessarily or directly related to the principal characteristic that sets the person apart as different. Thus it was quite possible that an invalid or otherwise abnormal person might be called *crazy*. The crazy person is the prototype of the *other*. Indeed, the term *crazy* or *meshugener* in Hebrew and Yiddish serves as a general category under which *others* associated with different kinds of deviations are found in memorial books. However, not all of them may be linked to mental disorders. The word *crazy* is not widely used in the written language, even though in Hebrew it does have biblical origins: "The prophet is considered a fool, the intellectual is viewed as a madman [*meshuga*]" (Hosea, IX: 7). In the spoken language, however, the term refers to a "person who is not mentally ill, but behaves in an extreme fashion or does eccentric things owing to acute sensations and does so in the extreme."[10] The word was a common expression in spoken Hebrew and was prevalent in Polish, English, German, Dutch, Yiddish, and other languages too.

In yizker books, the disabled are indentified as crazy ones, even when their problems are physical rather than mental. What is more, their economic and abnormal conditions create a parallel between them and the crazy ones. Among the outstanding examples of this phenomenon are the deaf and dumb, as well as the blind. For example, according to his profile in the Tarnow book, the wisest of men seen walking freely about the town managed to look after himself despite his tremendous physical difficulties and handicaps. Yet the writers and editors of the book place this exceptional individual in the category of *meshugener*.[11]

There are many memorial books that count the disabled among the *meshugener*. For instance, *Disna: sefer zikaron le-kehilah* counts Israel the blind man, "even though he was blind rather than crazy."[12] *Sefer Zambrow* counts a man with a distorted appearance from birth.[13] *Pinkas Zyrardow, Amshinow un Viskit* counts a blind person.[14] *Sefer yizker le-kehilat Radomsk ve-ha-sevivah* counts a water-drawer who lacked secondary sexual characteristics and "whose voice was not the voice of a male and his facial expression also seemed to be either crying or laughing but one could never be sure."[15] In *Lask; sefer zikaron*, the son of Mordechai Cajals, who is "the president of the dumb," is counted among the disabled, hunchbacks, blind, dumb, and simpletons.[16] In *Mlawa ha-yehudit*, a dumb woman figures as one of the community's "crackpots."[17] *Sefer Plonsk ve-ha-sevivah* counts a hunchback who served as the "*shul clapper*" and whose job it was to call people to prayers in the synagogue.[18]

In addition, some people are described as being possessed. *Sefer zikahon le-kehilat Iwie* recounts the story of an episode that occurred in the 1930s when a child fell sick with a strange malady. Rumors soon spread around that town that the child's body had been invaded by a *dybbuk* [evil spirit]. Rabbi Zeev Perlman, the Rabbi of Iwje, did not believe in such spirits and said: "Whoever does not believe in the *dybbuk* is an utter heretic, and anyone who does believe in him is an absolute fool."[19]

It was not only irregular behavior or appearance that might lead to a label of *other*, inferior, or insane. Sometimes an occupation led to that label. Regarding that, Shulamit Shahar outlines the division of professions and how the traditional society related to its various workers.[20] The society adopted a special attitude to professions that were connected with impurity, such as those that dealt with death, including hangmen, as well as occupations that dealt with blood, such as butchers and barbers. In addition to professions concerned with scum, there were those involving sex. These included bathhouse attendants, since bathhouses were perceived as places for sexual activity. Such occupations were spurned in the traditional society and bore negative stigma. An exception to this rule in Jewish society was made those who worked for a *chevra kadisha* [burial society]. Those workers were highly respected and constituted an elite group because of their voluntary work in granting the last rites to the deceased.

Many people who are called *others*, deviants, crazy ones, or *meshugeners* in memorial books usually worked in occupations connected with death. They might be criers at funerals, coffin bearers, gravediggers, or watchers over the dead. They might be engaged in the burial itself. However, there were also those whose work involved handling scum, such as those who carried wastewater or those who emptied the garbage. People who were disabled and came from a low socio-economic background were forced into certain vocations, such as porters, water carriers, and woodcutters. They might be *tehilim klappers*, those who would bang on people's windows in the middle of the night or in the early hours of the morning to awaken the faithful for the recitation of the psalm prayers. Sometimes, they might work as wagon drivers or cart pullers. One of these individuals, depicted in *Pinkas Zyrardow, Amshinow un Viskit*, is a man who himself was harnessed to his wagon.[21] These were people who were unable to cope with the greater or more complex demands of jobs in other fields. Their tasks needed to be simple and repetitive. Their connection with the employers was usually brief, and their only encounter with their employer was usually when an order was placed and a finished product received. *Kamenets-Podolsk u-sevivatah* describes one townsman Froike whose

> work was to serve his fellow men and women. He used to remove the buckets of slop and the baskets full of garbage from the houses ... he liked serving people, helping women carry their shopping baskets.... Froike would carry the buckets of slop from the upper floors with a sense of a purpose.[22]

The individual became identified with his particular vocation and that affixed a particular tag to him. However, the perception that these jobs were carried out for the public benefit and served the local population made the jobs legitimate pursuits. While those who engaged in such tasks might have been marginalized in society, they were certainly not banished beyond its borders. Froike is a legitimate figure because he was useful and helpful.

In *Sefer Minsk-Mazowiecki*, an author describes the water carrier who lived on the edge of society, exaggerating him in this far-reaching conclusion:

> This water-drawer did not really live among men but rather existed alongside human society on the margins of the community ... so that an entire populace lived on the edges of humanity or a whole community dwelt along the nation's periphery.[23]

Here we find a clue that links the image of the water carrier with the people of Israel who also live "on the brink of humanity" or "in the nation's periphery." This indication was probably included to enhance the image of the drawer of water and maybe to justify his inclusion in the memorial volume.

Handicapped individuals are documented at various jobs. They include the baker's assistant in Berezne, although "it was doubtful if he actually knew how to bake."[24] Additional sources document attempts by abnormal people to show that they worked or behaved as though they were employed in other jobs, such as musicians or pseudo-players; they were also people who played on sticks pretending that the sounds came from a flute or trumpet. Examples are found in the books to Mława and Kamenets Podolskiy. However, this behavior was not regarded as an occupation with the potential of making a contribution or being useful, but as merely pathological, disconnected from all reality.

Customs and tax officials are also classified as *other*. *Sefer yizker li-ḳehilot Ṭrembowla, Ṣtrusow ṿe-Janow ṿe-ha-sevivah* asserts unequivocally that no "negative characters" were found among the town's population. Although "[t]he customs and excise officials were virtually excommunicated from the community ... and what was more, they were thought of as having brought shame on the Jews. The widow of the last customs official lived to a ripe old age ... and even as a senior citizen she still suffered from her late husband's doings during his lifetime;" and moreover, *mosrim* [professional informers] are depicted in this book as people "[w]hose extortion in threatening to hand over Jews to the government because their efforts in observing their customs sometimes led to disputes with the civil law. Thus the informers had an additional source of income on the side or sometimes even earned their living in full."[25] In addition to this reference, thieves are mentioned in volumes commemorating the towns of Chorstkow, Dabrowica, Khotin, Luck, Tarnow, Uhnow, and Wojslawice.

Individuals who withdrew from the mainstream community are also categorized as *other*, as are those who converted to Christianity. Converts from Judaism are mentioned in the books to Kazimierz, Lowicz, Minsk-Mazowiecki, Pruszkow, Rudki, and Rzeszow. In those volumes, the proselytes to Judaism constitute a separate group of *others*, which is extensively recalled, but the negative nuances associated with the description with other marginal groups are omitted. Descriptions of proselytes appear in the memorial books to Ciechanowiec, Ilja, Lancut, Minsk-Mazowiecki, Przedborz, and Szczucyn.

Women as Other

Deviant women, backward, or crazy females constitute a phenomenon in their own right. Witches are a special category reserved for women. Although women may be included in all the categories of *other*, they should be discussed as a separate group. The number of women described as *meshuga'ot* [crazy females] in memorial books is proportionately fewer than their number in the community and also fewer than the number of men described in this manner. Twenty women are mentioned as *other* in eleven of the thirty-six books reviewed; whereas ninety-three men are mentioned. If we assume that in actual practice the distribution of deviant people in the population is more or less equal, with a slightly larger number of men, then we must consider the difference in the number of such descriptions of women as representing a specific social reality.[26]

Women in the small Jewish town were typically occupied in the home. It may be assumed that the women who were abnormal in any way not only constituted a potential threat to their environment but were also in danger themselves when they went outside. Therefore crazy women were usually kept at home where they could be protected. At the same time, society would be safeguarded from them in a manner that was consistent with tradition and customs. These women played no part in the community's public affairs. However, the *meshuga'ot* in memorial volumes are more unfortunate, hopeless, stricken, and abnormal than men in similar conditions. In general, the women are considered more insane than the men. The attitude in the traditional Jewish society towards *other* men differed than the attitude towards *other* women. Deviant men could totter on the margins of society, yet still remain within its borders. Abnormal men, simpletons, and the handicapped could find work that enabled them to maintain some social contacts. Their occupations were useful and accommodated their disability. Drawers of water are an example. While those men were always on the move and worked independently, they proved themselves useful by bringing water to people's homes. Their arrival was welcomed because people needed them. Some jobs were considered a means for men with limited ability to earn a living, thus keeping them within the fold of society.

Deviant people in the small town usually became a target for negative reactions. Sometimes they were subject to brutality and abuse. Women were in even greater danger in such surroundings because their environment saw sexuality as threatening and dangerous, especially if those deviant women found it difficult to exercise self-control. Here we cannot help recalling the deviant women who were considered to be witches during earlier times and were subsequently charged with having prohibited sexual relations with demons as part of their magic deeds and their relationships with demonic powers.

Mlawa ha-yehudit describes one deviant woman who was called a witch:

> She has blond hair with a few streaks of gray hair through it ... as cold flames strike out of her turbulent eyes penetrating and stabbing like spears ... all the way through to the entrails ... and she used to open her wide dry and toothless mouth and so on, and quite apart from her being a witch who skewered entrails, that same witch drove her husband to committing suicide. He killed himself—without a blessing and without a proper knife but used a simple kitchen knife.[27]

The witch's husband is also thought to be an animal. Although certain rules and tools apply to the ritual slaughter of animals, apparently, the witch made her husband ignore them and caused him to die as an animal, not as a man. Moreover, he was not even killed according to the principles of ritual Jewish animal slaughter. This cynical and grotesque description could be seen from a sexual angle insofar as the witch was depicted as a woman who used "to strip naked and then dressed like our mother Eve she would begin dancing around the *mikvah* [ritual bath]."[28] The witch from Mława gets her sexually enticing image after stripping and running naked around the *mikvah*, which is generally associated with propriety in sexual relations. Therefore this description involving the *mikvah* links the woman with wild and wanton sexual connotations, which may not be attributed to respectable women of Israel but only to a witch. Two more descriptions of women as witches are found in the book to Mława. These echo an event that seemingly had its origins in an incident dating back to the Middle Ages. According to this story, two witches "flew on chicken livers" to Szydlowiec where they poisoned the "ruler's" flocks and spread poison in the fields to blight them and consequently the witches were burnt at the stake.[29] This story has a certain similarity to the blame placed on the poisoning of wells. Although this latter charge related to damage done directly to human beings and not to fields, nevertheless those who poisoned the wells were always men. Furthermore, the activities of these men were neither involved in witchcraft nor linked to sexuality. The appellation *witch*, with all that the name conjures up, was reserved for women.

Although the story of the witches appears in the memorial volume to Mława, it is by no means clear that these women were Jewish witches because the story relates to the fertility of fields and flocks. It may be assumed that Jews, and especially Jewish women, were unconnected to agricultural fertility of all things; however this cannot be determined for certain. The question remains as to what made the book's editors include such a description in the volume, unless of course they could not resist the temptation suggested by its scintillating nature. It seems probable, however, that such legends about sorcery involving riding on a rooster were common in the area around Mława and were handed down over time. The legends also might have included the episode about the witches who rode on a chicken's liver.

Sefer Radzin depicts a dumb woman as follows: "This poor woman was insane; she wore sackcloth and went barefoot as she ran around the streets alarming the children."[30] Descriptions of crazy women are also found in the books to Dzisna and Merkine. Interestingly, although Jewish towns developed organizations and societies to look after the poor, sick, mourners, women in confinement, passersby, or other people who happened to show up, in general, the responsibility for attending to the needs of the crazy women was placed on the shoulders of the poor women alone.

In *Pinkas Zyrardow, Amshinow, un Viskit*, there is a reference to "Toivala, the fool," who was "a servant at the home of Ziskind, the butcher, and nobody knew when she came to the town or where she came from."[31] It is difficult to imagine in a small town where everyone knew everybody that a Jew could possibly enter the town, live there, and walk around without anybody knowing when she arrived or where she came from. It seems almost certain that no one wanted to take responsibility for this poor unfortunate woman, and consequently ignored her and the circumstances of her arrival. A general tendency to ignore the deviant women and write very few details about them is seen in a number of yizker volumes. For instance, *Lask; sefer zikaron* describes the *meshuga'at* from the neighboring town of Zdunska Wola whose residents paid the people of Lask "to take her in for a while.... She was covered in rags and every day she used to add an additional rag."[32] Similarly, Michel Foucault writes about the ship of fools on which the town's *meshugeners* in the Middle Ages were loaded and sent down the river to remove them from the community. However, Foucault does entertain the possibility that the story of the ship of fools was nothing more than a literary composition and not a true account of a historical event.[33] The idea of transferring a crazy woman to another town for payment is comparable to the idea that produced this legend about the ship of fools.

Descriptions of the Other

Lengthy accounts of specific individuals who are considered *other* are found in some yizker books. An example is the article in *Sefer Horodenka* about "*Moishe brecht man shubin*" [Moishe who used to break windows].[34] In contrast to these lengthy accounts, other books only contain names. For example, in the Merkiner book, Herscha and Pira-Gala are mentioned as the town *meshugeners*. In some books, *meshugeners* were depicted and given names associated with their actions, occupation, or appearance. These names originate in expressions from different geographical and cultural areas where the particular idioms were customary. They are given here as they appear in the yizker books reviewed. Along with the words *meshuga* or *meshugener*, the term simpleton or *nar* [stupid] appears in many books. There are other examples of expressions used and nicknames.

In *Mayn shtetele Berezne*, the following expressions are found: the city's strange characters, queer customers, abnormal people, confused individuals, slightly out of his mind, somewhat simple, *tsemisht* [confused], *a bisl tsedrieter* [a little rotated], and *tamewate* [naïve]. In *Brzezany, Narajow ve-ha-sevivah*, there is a description of four wretched people. They are described as *nars* [crazy, strange, abnormal people]. Leizer Pif was *shlechtfarshtiendikn lashon* [slow-witted]. Dudie Morge was *tsemisht* and a stammerer who mixed Yiddish, Polish, and German. Avremtshe Cholemke was clumsy, and Hershele Dzia Hop used to jump when he heard his nickname mentioned. In *Disna: sefer zikaron le-kehilah*, the terms lunatic and worthless people are used. In *Sefer zikaron le-kehilat Horodok*, two town lunatics are described. One of them believed he was a miracle-worker; the second believed that he had supernatural powers. *Sefer Horodenka* describes *Moishe brecht men shoibn* as a benevolent *meshugener* and a *nutslecher meshugener* [somebody who could be helpful].

In *Sefer zikahon le-kehilat Iwie*, the *others* are described as *meshugeners*, psychopaths, simpletons, people who are easily mocked, *tshudakes* [odd ones], *nit kein gabakene* [not baked enough], freak characters, exceptional in appearance and conduct in general, and *firmowe meshugeners* [deranged or officially diagnosed]. In addition, there are individuals who became demented or lost their minds due to excessive study of Torah, such as Ziedel. Besides that, there was the *kaliker* [cripple], for example Nachum-David. There was the uneducated or *bezgramatener* [an illiterate person], such as Hershel Bereziner, who was also described as a *lemishevate* [naïve, unsophisticated, and innocent as a lamb]. There was the defective person, such as Jakov-Liebe. Additional terms include the town lunatic or the merry beggar, simpleton, innocent, fool, *geshtroft durchn goral* [misfortunate], like Fishke's family; a wretched individual, a naïve person, or good-for-nothing. Cashke di zig [the goat] is described as *shvachkeit* [weak, slow, or has difficulty with understanding]. In *Kamenets-Podolsk u-sevivatah,* four people are mentioned. One is Isaac, a tragic, crippled *meshugener* beggar. The second one is Note, a flute player; the third is Simion who used to curse, and the fourth is Stroiny Czlowiek [a tall man]. In *Sefer zikaron le-kehilat Kolomey ve ha-sevivah,* there is a long description of the blind man, Chuna na Muchi, who sold fly paper in the market.

Lask; sefer zikaron mentions sick and abnormal people, *kalikes* [cripples], *nars* and the absent-minded, witless individuals, people who lost their minds, and *gots geshtrofte* [creatures afflicted by God]. This book differentiates between local *meshugeners* and those who came from elsewhere. There is also a description of quiet and unruly *meshugeners.* Some were seasonal *meshugeners;* some were insane all year like Avremale. He studied the religious and wisdom literature during the winter, but when summer came he would run around the streets talking to himself, singing obscene songs, and breaking windows. Hershl Voler was *tsedrieter* [confused]; and Jakov was *meshugene* due to excessive study of the Torah. Two crazy girls are mentioned. One was believed to be obsessed by a *dybbuk*; the other one was aggressive. In *Sefer yizker le-kehilat Radomsk ve-ha-sevivah,* there is a description of Liebele Nar, who was not blessed with intelligence or good appearance. He had no secondary gender signs and was called Leibele moid [Leibele the girl].

Additionally, *others* are described as miserable, unfortunate, spoiled, or corrupted. In *Sefer Zambrow;Zambrove,* there is a reference to Kuni Lemel, a character from Yiddish folklore. *Sefer Tarnogrod* mentions a clown and a kind of Bohemian. *Tarnow; kiyumah ve-hurbanah shel ir yehudit* refers to a naïve Jew, a simple person who knew no pranks and was *un kuntsn* [without tricks]. *Sefer zikharon le-kehilat Tomaszow Mazowiecki* mentions a nice silly little fool. In *Sefer Oshpitsin,* the description *parshoin* [persona or character] appears. *Pinkas Navaredok* contains the term *golem* [an oaf]. Overall, a rich selection of expressions and adjectives is found in the yizker books. Interestingly, most of these terms appear in Nahum Stutchkoff's Yiddish dictionary under the entry *meshuga'at.*[35]

Several expressions relate to cognitive functioning and to the fact that the people are simpletons, backward, or naive. Other expressions relate to differences, namely people who are exceptional, deviated from the norm, or weird in some way. A few expressions relate to the etiology of the deviation. These include someone who lost his mind after spending an excessive length of time engaged in studying the Torah or someone who fate or God dealt a cruel blow. Other expressions relate to arrogant people and ridicule them by using the term *parshoin,* a title originally derived from the word person and means an important personality as well as a character or exemplar, a Kuni Lemel, or dense person. Sometimes expressions bordered on awkward paternalism, such as in the case of "our nice silly fellow." Additional expressions convey compassion, such wretched individual, unfortunate one, or miserable people. Occasionally the nickname is based on a more detailed observation, such as the distinction between calm crazy people and aggressive ones or the distinction between people who only become *meshugeners* during certain seasons of the year. There are instances where the characteristics of a miracle worker are attributed to a crazy one, as though the person possessed supernatural powers. This perception of the deviant individual is not unknown in the history of mental illness. In some instances, the description is simply this: "he or she is sick." Among those labeled in such a manner are handicapped people from the lower socio-economic classes, such as the deaf, dumb, cripple, blind, or hunchback. Among the crazy ones mentioned in memorial books are those who are clearly mentally ill. However, it is doubtful if they ever underwent a medical diagnosis. These people are defined as such because they are unusual in some way. As a result of their behavior, appearance, deeds, manner of speech, or job, they were labeled *crazy*.

Additional groups of people are labeled as *other*. One group is comprised of those who are defined as insane, although they are not like the deranged individuals. This group includes Israel, the crazy man from Nowogrodek, about whom it is written: "He was not really insane; he only acted like a fool to survive, and so pretended to be crazy."[36] Those only pretending to be crazy are documented in *Mlawa ha-yehudit*. That book contains the following account. In the town of Mława lived a man who, in his youth, was conscripted in the Czar's army and pressure was brought to bear on him to convert to Christianity during his military service and also later on when he was living in the town. About him, it is written:

> He used to pretend to be mad with different manifestations of his madness on every occasion and then one day when the priest and all his attendants were all ready and prepared to welcome the wayward soul of the Jewish youth, Fischel started dancing and playing music with a stick. The irate priest and his entourage subsequently attacked him, beat him up and threw him bodily out of the church. In another incident he pretended to behave just like a regular maniac, and after stripping he began playing music with a shepherd's staff in hand, dancing like a wild man in front of the church's holy icons. Thus Fischel told his story of how his going crazy saved him from a forced conversion.[37]

The city of Pruszkow had the largest psychiatric hospital in Poland, and in *Sefer Pruszkow*, there is an entry about a man who on his attorney's advice pretended to be insane and was subsequently committed to the hospital. He took this drastic action to escape the punishment that he expected to receive for smuggling and evading the customs and excise laws.[38] This category of *meshugeners* who pretended constitute a group of people who derived some advantage from their apparent insanity and did so consciously while making instrumental use of their insanity as a solution to personal, material, or religious distress. Recall the story of King David who when he fled from Saul to Achish, King of Gath at one point acted crazy:

> He behaved in an unruly manner, leaving marks on the doors of the gate and letting his saliva run down his beard. Achish said to his servants, "Look at this madman! Why did you bring him to me? Am I short of fools that you have brought me this man and let him go insane in front of me? Should this man enter my house?"(1 Samuel XXI 14–16)

Indeed such phenomena were not unknown, even in ancient times. There is an additional group of people who actually suffered from a pathological condition. For those people, authors did not use a diagnosis or label. They simply gave a detailed description of the person's behavior, thus indicating that the person was mentally ill. In *Sefer Rypin*, there is a description of a family whose members in the wake of the death of their only son began behaving strangely. Using a rope they tied a rooster to the foot of their bed and fed it rations of grain that they weighed on scales. These classes of *others* are handled with discretion, sensitivity, and a certain degree of respect. Perhaps that was done because the authors wished to write euphemistically or because they sought to avoid any disrespect to the memory and feelings of the people concerned or their own relatives.

Means of Describing the Other

Although the *others* are usually described in a simple style or prose typical of written memoirs, some memorial books include depictions of *others* in photographs, sketches, or poems. One penciled sketch and one poem appear in *Sefer zikaron le-kehilat Horodok*. The poet describes the town with its streets and institutions, along with its personalities including the rabbi, ritual animal slaughterer, rabbinical judge, cantor, doctor, pharmacist, and local gentiles. One verse is devoted to the town's *meshugeners*. It reads as follows:

> *Meshugeners* lived in the town
> One thought he was a miracle-maker
> The second one cried, laughed and shouted out
> That he was the Messiah and could split the sea.[39]

Photographs of town *meshugeners* are found in yizker books to Berezno, Iwie, Lezajsk, Nowogrodek, Plonsk, Radomsko, Tarnow, and Zyrardow. A pencil sketch is found in the volume to Przedborz. Most of the photographs are staged, which was the practice during the period. Neither the photographer nor the individual who organized the photographs are known. Moreover, the families of the abnormal people are usually very poor, and so it seems unlikely they could have ordered such pictures. There is also no information as to whether the sketch was drawn from an actual model or drawn from memory.

Yizker books were written after the towns were abandoned by their Jewish population. They were written with a specific perspective on the past; it was a selective one that was directed towards presenting the town in a certain light. The descriptions, poems, and photographs of the town's *meshugeners*, came before the writing of the books. There is no reason to suspect that these pictures of the *others* were taken for the purpose of adorning the memorial books. The photographs give a certain fixed view from the specific point in time when they were taken, but as so often occurs with photographs, they were taken for the sake of the future. Thus, photographs focus on the future; whereas yizker books focus on the past. Questions remains as to what the photographers saw; why they documented the crazy people; why they kept the photographs; and what editors saw in the photographs to justify interspersing the pictures in the books?

Attitudes Towards the Other

The *others* are depicted in the memorial books with a feeling of repulsion, especially at their appearance. For instance, the book dedicated to Nowogrodek describes a man "who was terribly dirty and reeked of an awful moldy smell."[40] Similar descriptions are found in the books to Horodenka, Lezajsk, and Zyrardow.

In a number of books, the descriptions of the *others* are written with ridicule or mockery, as for example in the volume to Zambrow. In that work, the author depicts his abhorrence of a certain *meshuga* noting that his "face and body were like a pig walking on two feet, hopping along as he leaned on a cane."[41] A description no less depressing may be found in the book to Brzezany:

> He was extremely large and awkward with a large fleshy nose and his nose became his principal characteristic. Anyone approaching him saw his nose first and then only afterwards his face appeared.[42]

The book commemorating Lask presents the following description of a man: "He used to have spasms, causing everybody to almost die laughing."[43]

Descriptions of the abuse of deviant people are common in memorial books. However, most of the descriptions documenting a cruel and abusive attitude towards the *other* specify the behavior of the town's children towards those unfortunate people. An example appears in *Lask; sefer zikaron*:

> Nobody was more occupied with the crazy people and the disabled than we the children were ... our "treatment" of these individuals became part of life's fun, and presented us with an opportunity to enjoy "a happy hour" as we watched these people who had been afflicted by God in this world. Children, who were sadistic by nature, were delighted at such an opportunity to be caught up in the prevailing atmosphere and persecute these ill-fated human beings in the community.[44]

Sefer yizker le-kehilat Radomsk ve-ha-sevivah describes how children used to run after a man who lacked a moustache, beard, and other secondary sexual characteristics. The children teased him persistently by asking: "Do you want a bride? Then they would pull at his clothes and throw mud at him."[45] An author in the book to Iwje recounts: "We used to throw stones at him and shout ... throw wet towels at him ... and called him by derogatory names or simply shouted '*meshugener.*'"[46] While the children used to abuse the *meshugeners*, they also feared them. The book to the town of Dzisna describes Bendak, a man who used to walk around the town with a large bag and "the [children's] parents and elder siblings would warn them that if they did not behave well, they would be handed over to Bendak who would put them into his deep bag."[47]

Role of the Other *in Yizker Books*

The study questions why writers and editors included deviant characters in their volumes when the overall tendency in the books was to ignore the negative aspects of communal life. The role of the *other* in the books may be explained from the perspective of sociologists, criminologists, or anthropologists; it may also be explained from the perspective of the community members themselves.

According to Emile Durkheim, deviation is a natural and essential part of the healthy and normal activities of society.[48] Moreover, deviation may actually perform a needed service to society by drawing people together in a common posture of anger and indignation. The deviant act creates a mutual linkage between people in society because it provides a focal point for concentrating the emotions of group members. Severe events such as war, floods, or other emergencies, as well as different situations and deviations from the norm help create a greater alertness to the common interest that society's individuals share, as well as to the community's collective awareness. Normal life in the community would prove to be impossible unless it encompassed incidents involving deviant behavior. Deviants are visible reminders of the normative limits that define particular social systems. The nonconformist, or the *other*, stands in marked contrast to prescribed behavior and allows the group to develop a cohesive sense of its own membership. Polarizing and expelling individuals or groups to the periphery permits mainstream society to strength its integration as well as its self-identity, and thereby, plays an important role in the world of cultural symbols. One precondition for marginalizing an individual or group is categorization. Categorizing men and women based on their ethnic origin, common characteristics, beliefs, opinions, or manner of behavior is the primary and essential basis for defining them as belonging to the margins of society and relating to them as *other*. This very categorization is the outcome of a normative system stemming from the balance of power in society that determines the status of the individual or the group either at its core or on its fringes. The Holocaust was a severe and terrible event that created a mutual linkage between different people in society because it provides a focal point for concentrating the emotions of the group's members. These emotions find their place in yizker books. Michel Foucault, who wrote one of the major works of the twentieth century about the history of madness and about outsiders of all kinds, place sanity and insanity against each other to show that "Day and night mirror one another, reflecting each other indefinitely and giving this simple couple a sudden depth that envelopes in a single movement the whole of the life."[49] The effect of the mirror is so strong because a "lightning bolt can only stand out in gathering darkness."[50] We would be unable to understand ourselves or assess our own character if it were not for the fact that we have some way of knowing what we are **not**. Consequently, we have no way of knowing what the life of the small town was at the height of its glory unless we know what its *others* were like. The editors and writers of memorial books used a similar principle to contrast the deranged with the reasonable person; they exploited their reference to the crazy people.

The other explanation for including the descriptions of *others* in memorial books may stem from a sense of identification described in the books. This is suggested in *Sefer Kotsk*, which depicts Zlatka, "the town's mad woman." The author asks himself why out of all the possible episodes this particular memory remained so vivid in his mind? His answer is that this recollection is probably due the fact that during the war in the northern forest when people did not have proper clothing, went barefoot in the cold and freezing weather, were terrified, and were uncertain about what might happen the following day, they were all like Zlatka. He writes the following: "Like her, we just stood there in the line for a drop of soup or a piece of bread, and once we got our precious morsel we would hold on to it carefully lest it might drop;

using our tongues we would lick the last residues of the soup, for we were so much like Zlatka. As survivors who succeeded in enduring the Nazi inferno we have inscribed in our hearts those who were not lucky enough to make it."[51] Another writer recalls this: "Our mothers and fathers, sisters and brothers, all our relatives and friends, and among them we shall not forget the tragic and unfortunate souls, lest any person who lived in our community be forgotten."[52] Indeed, as Kugelmass and Boyarin note "the dead have a power over the living."[53]

Memorial books offer yet another explanation. This from *Sefer zikaron le-kehilat Kolomey ve ha-sevivah*:

> Every city had its own life style, profile and uniqueness, character and culture. It also had its own personalities, figures and characters. Some of these people ascend the social ladder thanks to their altruistic virtues or in recognition of their superior activities, while others stand out as their exceptional way of life or their deeds that ran contrary to the accepted norms capture the public's attention. These individuals do not sparkle like the pearls in a necklace, but their color is so different that it stands out prominently in the social fabric of the members of their generation.[54]

This statement dichotomously places the different and contrasting components of Jewish society in the small town. At one pole, there are the elite, the people who contributed to the community; at the opposite pole, there are the deviant individuals, the *others*. In the Lezajsk memorial book, one author establishes a dichotomy when he takes up the differences between the people in the town as the key issue to understanding the integration of the *other* in the book. He writes:

> Fate is not something absolute for it is also gauged in proportion, based on a comparison with the destiny of somebody else, either for better or for worse. Therefore everybody in the city would benefit if he or she could draw a comparison with somebody who was not as smart as he or she was, or was less successful, or accepted to a lesser extent by his or her fellow human beings, and similar comparisons. This "town fool" fulfilled this role in every city and no town among the people of Israel would have been complete without such an instrument "to grant it the honor of his disgrace" like that one.[55]

The *others* are seen in the life of the small town, as well as in yizker books in a particular manner. They serve as a general all-inclusive term covering all those in the town who fit the category; they represent insanity, backwardness, disability, rejection, and ugliness. These elements are mentioned in the books so that the reader might know that the town was *not* like what these *others* represented, but rather the place was a beautiful and untarnished town. The image of the town was purified due to the very fact that it presented the deviant characters who lived on the margins of society. The clown or the town's fool assists the group by forming the social catalyst, which unites the entire group. People who are seen as conformists are defined in contrast with those seen as deviant. The law-abiding citizen is defined by the criminal, and these law-abiding citizens need the criminal to reinforce their own self-righteousness. Social perverts benefit the group's normative structure and contribute to the well-being of its conformist members.

To quote the judge's statement as he addresses the prostitute in the play *The Balcony* by Jean Genet: "The fact that I am a judge," so he lectures the thieving prostitute, "stems from the fact that you are a thief ... if I had no longer any need to differentiate between the good and the bad, what would people need me for? The world is an apple and I slice it in two; the good and the bad. So you will agree, thank you very much, you will agree to be the bad one."[56] If we continue along the lines of the judge's way of thinking in the spirit proposed by Genet, we may complete the sentence by adding these words: in order for me to be able to be good. Or it may be concluded that the town may be depicted and preserved in the collective memory as beautiful and untarnished, because its unpleasant and deranged sides shown by the *others* have been set aside and marginalized.

Books Reviewed for This Essay

Brzezany
> *Brzezany, Narajow ve-ha-sevivah.* Ed. M. Katz. Haifa: Brzezany-Narajow Societies in Israel and the United States, 1978.

Berezno
> *Mayn shtetele Berezne.* Ed. G. Bigil. Tel Aviv: Berezner Society in Israel, 1954.

Ciechanowiec
> *Ciechanowiec; mehoz Bialystok, sefer edut ve-zikaron.* Ed. E. Leoni. Tel Aviv: Ciechanovitzer Immigrant Association in Israel and the USA, 1964.

Chorstkow
> *Sefer Chorstkow.* Ed. D. Shtokfish. Tel Aviv: Committee of Former Residents of Chorstkow in Israel, 1968.

Dabrowica
> *Sefer Dombrovitsa.* Ed. L. Losh. Tel Aviv: Association of Former Residents of Dabrowica in Israel, 1964.

Dzisna
> *Disna: sefer zikaron le-kehilah.* Eds. A. Beilin et al. Tel Aviv: Former Residents of Disna in Israel and the United States, 1969.

Holszany
> *Lebn um umkum fun Olshan.* Ed. Irgun Yotzey Olshan. Tel Aviv: Former Residents of Olhan in Israel, 1965.

Grodek
> *Sefer zikaron le-kehilat Horodok.* Ed. M. Simon. Tel Aviv: Association of Former Residents of Grodok in Israel and Argentina, 1963.

Horodenka
> *Sefer Horodenka.* Ed. S. Melzer. Tel Aviv: Former Residents of Horodenka and Vicinity in Israel and the USA, 1963.

Khotin
   Sefer ḳehilat Khọtin (Bessarabia). Ed. S. Shịtnovitser. Tel Aviv: Khotin Society, 1974.
Iwie
   Sefer zikahon le-kehilat Iwie. Ed. M. Kaganovich. Tel Aviv: Association of Former Residents of Ivie in Israel and "United Ivier Relief" in America, 1968.
Ilja
   Kehilat Ilja; pirkei hayim ve-hashmadah. Ed. A. Kopsilevitz. Tel Aviv: Association of Former Residents of Ilja in Israel, 1962.
Felshtin
   Felshtin; zamlbuch lekovod tsum ondenk fun di Felshtiner kdoyshim. Ed. Book Committee. New York: First Felshtiner Progressive Benevolent Association, 1937.
Frampol
   Sefer Frampol. Ed. D. Shtokfish. Tel Aviv: Book Committee, 1966.
Kamenets-Podolskiy
   Kamenets-Podolsk u-sevivatah. Eds. A. Rosen, Ch. Sharig, and Y. Bernstein. Tel Aviv: Association of Former Residents of Kamenets-Podolsk and its Surroundings in Israel, 1965.
Kazimierz
   Pinkas Kuzmir. Ed. D. Shtokfish. Tel Aviv: Former Residents of Kazimierz in Israel and the Diaspora, 1970.
Kock
   Sefer Kotsk. Ed. E. Porat. Tel Aviv: Former Residents of Kotsk in Israel, 1961.
Kolomya
   Sefer zikaron le-kehilat Kolomey ve ha-sevivah. Eds. D. Noy and M. Schutzman. Tel Aviv: Former Residents of Kolomey and Surroundings in Israel, 1972.
Korczyna
   Korczyna; sefer zikaron. New York: Committee of the Korczyna Memorial Book, 1967.
Lancut
   Lancut; hayeha ve-hurbanah shel kehikat yehudit. Eds. M. Waltzer and N. Kudish. Tel Aviv: Association of Former Residents of Lancut in Israel and the USA, 1963.
Leczyca
   Sefer Linshits. Ed. J. Frenkel. Tel Aviv: Former Residents of Leczyca in Israel, 1953.
Lask
   Lask; sefer zikaron. Ed. Z. Tzurnamal. Tel Aviv: Association of Former Residents of Lask in Israel, 1968.
Lezajsk
   Lizhensk; sefer zikaron le-kedoshei Lizhensk she-nispu he-shoat ha-natsim. Ed. H. Rabin. Tel Aviv: Association of Former Residents of Lezajsk in Israel, 1970.
Luck
   Sefer Lutsk. Ed. N. Sharon. Tel Aviv: Former Residents of Lutsk in Israel, 1961.
Lowicz
   Lowicz; ir be-Mazovia u-sevivah, sefer zikahon. Ed. G. Shaiak. Tel Aviv: Former Residents of Lowicz in Melbourne and Sydney, 1966.
Merkine
   Meretsk; ayarah yehudit be-Lita. Ed. U. Shefer. Tel Aviv: Society of Meretsh Immigrants in Israel, 1988.
Minsk-Mazowiecki
   Sefer Minsk-Mazowiecki. Ed. E. Shedletzky. Jerusalem: Minsk-Mazowiecki Societies in Israel and Abroad, 1977.
Mława
   Mlawa ha-yehudit. koroteha, hitpathuta, kilayona-Di yidishe Mlawe; geshikte, nyfshtand, unkum. Ed. D. Shtokfish. Tel Aviv: Mława Societies in Israel and in the Diaspora, 1984.
Nowogrodek
   Pinkas Navaredok. Eds. E. Yerushalmi et al. Tel Aviv: Alexander Harkavy Navaredker Committee in the USA and Israel, 1963.

Oswieciem
  Sefer Oshpitsin. Eds. Ch. Wolnerman, A. Burstein, and M. S. Geshuri. Jerusalem: Oshpitsin Society, 1977.
Plonsk
  Sefer Plonsk ve-ha-sevivah. Ed. Sh. Zemah. Tel Aviv: Former Residents of Plonsk in Israel, 1963.
Pruszkow
  Sefer, Pruszkow, Nadzin ve-ha-sevivah. Ed. D. Brodsky. Tel Aviv: Former Residents of Pruszkow in Israel, 1967.
Przedborz
  Przedborz-33 shanin le-hurbanah. Ed. S. Kanc. Tel Aviv: Przedborz Societies in Israel and America, 1977.
Radomsko
  Sefer yizker le-kehilat Radomsk ve-ha-sevivah. Ed. L. Losh. Tel Aviv: Former Residents of Radomsk, 1967.
Radzin
  Sefer Radzin. Ed. I. Siegelman. Tel Aviv: Council of Former Residents of Radzin (Podolsky) in Israel, 1957.
Rudki
  Rudki; sefer yizker le-yehudei Rudki ve-ha-sevivah. Ed. J. Chrust. Tel Aviv: Rudki Society, 1978.
Rypin
  Sefer Rypin. Ed. Sh. Kanc. Tel Aviv: Former Residents of Rypin in Israel and in the Diaspora, 1962.
Rzeszow
  Kehilat Raysha; sefer zikaron. Ed. M. Yari-Wold. Tel Aviv: Former Residents of Rzeszow in Israel and the USA, 1967.
Stavische
  Stavisht. Ed. A. Weissman. Tel Aviv: Stavisht Society, New York, 1961.
Szczuczyn
  Sefer zikaron le-kehilot Szczuczyn, Wasiliszki, Ostryn, Nowydwor, Rozanka. Ed. L. Losh. Tel Aviv: Former Residents of Szczuczyn, Wasiliszki, 1966.
Suwalki
  Yisker-bukh Suvalk. Ed. B. Kahan. New York: Sulvalk and Vicinity Relief Committee of New York, 1961.
Tarnow
  Tarnow; kiyumah ve-hurbanah shel ir yehudit. Ed. A. Chomet. Tel Aviv: Association of Former Residents of Tarnow, 1954.
Tarnogrod
  Sefer Tarnogrod; le-zikaron ha-kehilat ha-yehudit she-nehrevah. Ed. Sh. Kanc. Tel Aviv: Organization of Former Residents of Tarnogrod and Vicinity in Israel, United States, and England, 1966.
Tomaszow Mazowiecki
  Sefer zikharon le-kehilatt Tomaszow Mazowiecki. Ed. M. Wajsberg. Tel Aviv: Tomaszow Organization in Israel, 1969.
Trembowla
  Sefer yizker li-ḳehilot Ṭrembowla, Ṣtrusow ṿe-Janow ṿe-ha-sevivah. Ed. M. Selzer. Bene Beraḳ: Trembowla Society, 1981.
Turka
  Sefer zikaron le-kehilat Turka al nehar Stryj ve-ha-sevivah. Ed. J. Siegelman. Haifa: Former Residents of Turka (Stryj) in Israel, 1966.
Turzec
  Kehilot Turzec ve-Jermicze; sefer zikaron. Eds. M. Walzer-Fass and M. Kaplan. Tel Aviv: Turzec ve-Jermicze Societies in Israel and America, 1978.

Uhnow
  Hivniv (Uhnow); sefer zikaron le-kehilah. Ed. N. Ortner. Tel Aviv: Uhnow Society, 1981.
Wieliczka
  Kehilat Wieliczka; sefer zikaron. Ed. Sh. Meiri. Tel Aviv: Wieliczka Association in Israel, 1980.
Wlodzimerz
  Sefer Vladimerets. Ed. A. Meyerowitz. Tel Aviv: Former Residents of Vladimerets, 1962.
Wojslawice
  Sefer zikaron Voislavitse. Ed. Sh. Kanc. Tel Aviv: Former Residents of Voislavize, 1970.
Zambrow
  Sefer Zambrow; Zambrove. Ed. Y.T. Lewinsky. Tel Aviv: Zambrover Societies in USA, Argentina and Israel, 1963.
Zyrardow
  Pinkas Zyrardow, Amshinow un Viskit. Ed. M.W. Bernstein. Buenos Aires: Association of Former Residents in the USA, Israel, France and Argentina, 1961.

Notes

1. In this essay, the translation from Yiddish to Hebrew is by Rivka Parciak. The translation from Hebrew to English is by Morris Herman.

2. Abraham Wien, "Memorial Books as a Source for Jewish Historiography," *Yad Vashem Collection of Essays* Vol. 9–12 (Jerusalem: Yad Vashem, 1973) (Hebrew), 214. Also see, Nachman Blumenthal, "Memorial Books by Survivors of Communities," *Yad Vashem* (April 1958): 24–27, and Judith Tydor Baumel, "In Everlasting Memory," in *The Shaping of Israel: Identity, Myth, Memory and Trauma*, eds. Robert Westrich and David Ohana (London: Newbury House, 1995), 149–169.

3. See Jack Kugelmass and Jonathan Boyarin, "*Yizker bikher* and the Problem of Historical Veracity: An Anthropological Approach," in *The Jews of Poland Between Two World Wars*, eds. Yisrael Gutman, Ezra Mendelsohn, Jehuda Reinharz, and Chone Shmeruk (Hanover, NH: Brandeis University Press, 1992), 519–536.

4. Abraham Wien, "Memorial Books as a Source," 215.

5. M. Selzer, ed., *Sefer yizker li-kehilot Trembowla, Strusow ve-Janow ve-ha-sevivah* (Bene Berak: Trembowla Society, 1981), 51.

6. A. Weissman, ed., *Stavisht* (Tel Aviv: Stavisht Society, New York, 1961), 83.

7. L. Losh, ed., *Sefer Dombrovitsa* (Tel Aviv: Association of Former Residents of Dabrowica in Israel, 1964), 105.

8. In Yad Vashem's library, there are 1,411 memorial books. Every tenth book in the collection was chosen for this study. The result was 141 yizker books written and published by members of a community or by members of several communities. Yizker books published by the great communities of Warsaw, Lód, Kraków, Lublin, and Kiev were taken off the list. From the remaining, 136 books, 54 books or 40 percent had descriptions of *others*, that is, crazy people, *meshugeners*, cripples, disabled, or retarded men and women. The study relies on these 54 books. One of the books, a memorial volume for the community of Felshtin, was published in 1937. That early publication is an exceptional case. The other books were published at various times between 1954 and 1989, but the majority of them were published during the 1960s and 1970s. No date appeared in some books. The volumes are usually written in Hebrew or Yiddish, and the Yiddish volumes are sometimes accompanied by a Hebrew translation, which appears on the page facing the Yiddish original. Occasionally, the "Hebrew version ... is far from identical to the original Yiddish one" as argued by A. Wien (1973: 213). Some books include articles in English, French, Russian, and Polish.

9. Erving Goffman, *Stigma: Notes on the Management of Spoiled Identity* (Englewood Cliffs, NJ: Prentice Hall Inc., 1968), 15.

10. Dan Ben-Amotz and Netiva Ben-Yehuda, *Ben Yehuda's Dictionary* (Hebrew) (Jerusalem: Levin Epstein, 1975), 146.

11. A. Chomet, ed., *Tarnow; kiyumah ve-hurbanah shel ir yehudit* (Tel Aviv: Association of Former Residents of Tarnow, 1954), 796.

12. A. Beilin, ed., *Disna: sefer zikaron le-kehilah* (Tel Aviv: Former Residents of Disna in Israel and the United States, 1969), 40.

13. Y.T. Lewinsky, ed., *Sefer Zambrow; Zambrove* (Tel Aviv: Zambrover Societies in USA, Argentina and Israel, 1963), 550.

14. M. W. Bernstein, ed., *Pinkas Zyrardow, Amshinow un Viskit* (Buenos Aires: Association of Former Residents in the USA, Israel, France and Argentina, 1961), 97.

15. L. Losh, ed., *Sefer yizker le-kehilat Radomsk ve-ha-sevivah* (Tel Aviv: Former Residents of Radomsk, 1967), no page.

16. Z. Tzurnamal, ed., *Lask; sefer zikaron* (Tel Aviv: Association of Former Residents of Lask in Israel, 1968), 119.

17. D. Shtokfish, ed., *Mlawa ha-yehudit. koroteha, hitpathuta, kilayona — Di yidishe Mlawe; geshikte, nyfshtand, unkum* (Tel Aviv: Mława Societies in Israel and in the Diaspora, 1984), 40.

18. Sh. Zemah, ed., *Sefer Plonsk ve-ha-sevivah* (Tel Aviv: Former Residents of Plonsk in Israel, 1963), 285.

19. M. Kaganovich, ed., *Sefer zikhon le-kehilat Iwie* (Tel Aviv: Association of Former Residents of Ivie in Israel and "United Ivier Relief" in America, 1968), 232.

20. Shahar Shulamit, *Marginal Groups in the Middle Ages* (Tel Aviv: Ministry of Defense, 1995), 23.

21. Bernstein, *Pinkas Zyrardow*, 97.

22. A Rosen, Ch. Sharig, and Y. Bernstein, eds., *Kamenets-Podolsk u-sevivatah* (Tel Aviv: Association of Former Residents of Kamenets-Podolsk and its Surroundings in Israel, 1965), 74.

23. E. Shedletzky, ed., *Sefer Minsk-Mazowiecki* (Jerusalem: Minsk-Mazowiecki Societies in Israel and Abroad, 1977), 192.

24. M. Katz, ed., *Brzezany, Narajow ve-ha-sevivah* (Haifa: Brzezany-Narajow Societies in Israel and the United States, 1978), no page.

25. M. Selzer, ed., *Sefer yizker li-kehilot Trembowla, Strusow ve-Janow ve-ha-sevivah* (Bene Berak: Trembowla Society, 1981), 51.

26. On assessing the modern situation, the data in the report by the Ministry of Health, dated May 2, 1999, show that 9,293 men and 7,239 women were committed to mental hospitals in Israel; men constitute 56 percent of those hospitalized.

27. Shtokfish, *Mlawa ha-yehudit*, 40.

28. Ibid.

29. Compare Charles De Coster, *The Legend of Thyl Ulenspiegel and Lamme Goedzak*, trans. M. Atkinson, Vol. 2, Book 4 (London: Heinemann, 1922), 218–230.

30. I. Siegelman, ed., *Sefer Radzin* (Tel Aviv: Council of Former Residents of Radzin (Podolsky) in Israel, 1957), 146.

31. Bernstein, *Pinkas Zyrardow*, 68.

32. Tzurnamal, *Lask*, 115.

33. Michael Foucault, *History of Madness*, ed. Jean Khalfa and trans. Jonathan Murphy and Jean Khalfa (London and New York: Routledge, 1992), 14.

34. S. Melzer, ed., *Sefer Horodenka* (Tel Aviv: Former Residents of Horodenka and Vicinity in Israel and the USA, 1963), 147–149.

35. See Nahum Stutchkoff, *Der oyse fun der Yiddish shprach* (New York: YIVO, 1950).

36. E. Yerushalmi, et al. eds., *Pinkas Navaredok* (Tel Aviv: Alexander Harkavy Navaredker Committee in the USA and Israel, 1963), 48.

37. D. Shtokfish, *Mlawa ha-yehudit*, 48.

38. D. Brodsky, ed., *Sefer Pruszkow, Nadzin ve-ha-sevivah* (Tel Aviv: Former Residents of Pruszkow in Israel, 1967), 111.

39. M. Simon, ed., *Sefer zikaron le-kehilat Horodok* (Tel Aviv: Association of Former Residents of Grodok in Israel and Argentina, 1963), 7.

40. Yerushalmi, *Pinkas Navaredok*, 50.

41. Lewinsky, *Sefer Zambrow*, 359.

42. M. Katz, ed., *Brzezany, Narajow ve-ha-sevivah* (Haifa: Brzezany-Narajow Societies in Israel and the United States, 1978), no page.

43. Tzurnamal, *Lask*, 115.

44. Ibid., 119.

45. Losh, *Sefer yizker le-kehilat Radomsk ve-ha-sevivah*, no page.

46. Kaganovich, *Sefer zikahon le-kehilat Iwie*, 306.

47. A. Beilin et al., eds., *Disna: sefer zikaron le-kehilah* (Tel Aviv: Former Residents of Disna in Israel and the United States, 1969), 41.

48. Emile Durkheim, *The Rules of Sociological Method* (New York: The Free Press, 1958), 64–75.

49. Foucault, *History of Madness*, 245.

50. Ibid., 246.

51. E. Porat, ed., *Sefer Kotsk* (Tel Aviv: Former Residents of Kotsk in Israel, 1961), 166–167.

52. Ibid.

53. Jack Kugelmass and Jonathan Boyarin, eds. and trans., *From a Ruined Garden: The Memorial Books of Polish Jewry* (New York: Schocken Books, 1983), 1.

54. D. Noy and M. Schutzman, eds. *Sefer zikaron le-kehilat Kolomey ve ha-sevivah* (Tel Aviv: Former Residents of Kolomey and Surroundings in Israel, 1972), 214.

55. H. Rabin, ed., *Lizhensk; sefer zikaron le-kedoshei Lizhensk she-nispu he-shoat ha-natsim* (Tel Aviv: Former Residents of Lezajsk in Israel, 1971), 236.

56. Jean Genet, *The Balcony*, trans. Bernard Frechtman (New York: Grove Press, 1966), 17.

15

Klezmer Memories
in Yizker Books

YALE STROM

Music has been a vital aspect of Jewish culture since the biblical times, and *klezmer* music is one particular style of central and eastern European Jewish music. In general, *klezmer* refers to Jewish folk instrumentalists. Given the role of the *klezmer* in the culture, there are numerous proverbs about them.[1] Some, such as the following, express a negative view of the musicians.

> *Dray mentshn oyf der velt zingen far tsures: a khazn, a betler, un a marshalik.* [Three people in the world sing out of need: a cantor, a beggar, and a wedding bard.]
>
> *Az men tsaylt sfire, kumt di klezmer a pegire.* [When they count the omer, the *klezmer* can drop dead.]
>
> *Khasene gehat mit a klezmer iz geveyn a khusn mit knap yikhes.* [Marrying a *klezmer* is like a groom with hardly any pedigree.]
>
> *Klezmer musik, dos iz geveyn a niderike madreyge.* [Klezmer music, that's a low profession.]

Others, such as these, are positive.

> *Vos far a klezmer, aza khasene.* [The wedding's only as good as the *klezmer.*]
>
> *A levaye on geveyn iz vi a khasene on klezmer.* [A funeral without tears is like a wedding without a *klezmer.*]
>
> *Az tsvay kapstronim gayen tansn raysn zikh bay di klezmorim di strunes.* [When two paupers go dancing, the *klezmorim* play harder.]
>
> *A khasene on klezmer izerger fun a kale on a nadn.* [A wedding without a *klezmer* is worse than a bride without a dowry.]

Building on the cultural interest in *klezmer* and my own, I decided to study the accounts of *klezmers* contained in yizker books. Yizker books are special in part because they describe the complex, interesting, and diverse culture of the particular community commemorated. My previous research coupled with yizker book descriptions are the basis of this essay on the social history of *klezmorim*. I found that some stories in yizker books were written by people who were in their eighties, which means that they were describing incidents they actually witnessed as early as the 1870s. Additionally, some people recalled stories told to them in the 1880s by elderly *klezmers*; those first-person memories reach back to the first quarter of the nineteenth century! Clearly, then, yizker books are a rich source of information about these often misunderstood and quixotic figures. Thus, musicians, scholars, and others may turn to the books for details on the attitudes toward the *klezmorim*, their daily lives, their professions, and related topics.

The entries in the books are quite diverse. Some concern awkward situations, for instance, fights between *klezmorim* and their gentile employers or conflicts between religious Jews and secular Jews. Others deal with celebrations, such as the completion of a new Torah or holidays, such as May Day or Purim. Still others cover life events, such as a wedding of two orphans in a cemetery during a typhus epidemic or the wedding of a *rebe's* daughter. The harsh realities of poverty and war are also addressed. There are references to certain dances, including *brizhe*, *kutner*, *larsey*, and *tush*, for which I was unable to find any definitions, There are references to specific instruments, including double-necked ten-string guitar, bass bandura, long-tube trumpet, and bagpipes.

The Jewish wedding gives a contextual through-line to better understand the important function of the *klezmer* for his fellow Jewish and sometimes for his gentile neighbors. A wedding, the most celebrated life cycle event in Jewish culture, was never just a family celebration; it also included strangers. Sometimes the whole town was invited to participate and revel in the joy of the bride and groom. Often the preparation for a wedding kept the *klezmer* as busy as the wedding ceremony and festivities. Before the engagement, the bride's dowry was announced. Sometimes as much as a tenth of this dowry was given to the town's poor. That was thoroughly discussed and agreed upon between the prospective in-laws. Then with the help of a matchmaker, the engagement agreement was signed by all and sealed by breaking a ceramic dish in half. The groom and bride each kept a half. Sometimes gifts were exchanged between the newly engaged couple, and *klezmorim* were brought in to play for the engagement party. Details about these arrangements appear in numerous memorial volumes. From *Sefer yizker le-kehilat Radomsk ve-ha-sevivah*:

> The engagement agreements were settled, a watch was given to the groom and some gifts to the bride and the date was finally set.[2]

From *Sefer Frampol*:

> Though young people had some new ways of meeting each other, the tradi-
> tional ways of their mothers and fathers still prevailed in Frampol. The match-
> maker still played an important role in bringing together the proper mates.
> The matchmaker came from either Biłgoraj or Januv-Lubeslski. Each candi-
> date brought to the wedding canopy was described in impressive terms. The
> bride was described as coming from a family with pedigree and having money,
> being beautiful, learned, genteel and a kosher Jewish girl. The first meeting
> between the prospective couple is with the families and the matchmaker. This
> was called *ze-evdik* [seeing]. If the meeting was a success then plates were bro-
> ken and a toast was made. Then the date for the signing of the engagement
> contract was set. For the signing of the engagement a big party was made and
> everybody, friends and relatives, were invited. At the celebration there was a
> big meal and old treasured Jewish dance.[3]

Each of the four weeks preceding the wedding had a special name: iron,
copper, silver, or gold. During the first week, the wedding clothes were sewn;
special foods, such as honey cake, wine, and chicken broth made with mead,
were eaten; and the *klezmorim* played lively dances, a special *vivat* [an upbeat
dance] for the bride. During the last seven to eight days before the wedding,
neither bride nor groom was supposed to leave home. To help make the time
go by, friends would visit and the *klezmorim* would play at the homes of the
engaged couple each night, except the Sabbath. The evening before the wedding, the bride was led to the *mikve* [ritual bath house], accompanied by the
klezmorim and close women relatives and friends. The musicians "would play
in the other room while the older women drank and danced, sometimes —
and not so seldom — until their heads spun."[4]

If the groom did not live in the same town as the bride, the *klezmorim*
helped welcome him and his parents when they entered the town. Descriptions
of these greetings are found in yizker books. From *Yisker-bukh tsu Vlodava*:

> The men stopped a few kilometers outside of the *shtetl* while waiting for the
> arrival of the groom. A herald and the father of the bride harnessed up four
> horses to a coach and set forth to greet the groom with music. The groom
> and his family followed with great pride. Without any music the men would
> have not been able to walk in time. The *klezmorim* who had waited a long
> time for such a wedding played the whole time proudly and loudly. Their
> music resounded over the whole *shtetl*.[5]

For hasidic weddings, especially where the wedding couples' fathers were *rebes*
[spiritual leaders of a sect], the groom's entry into the bride's town was done
with even greater fanfare. An account of this is recorded in *Tomashover* [*Lubelski*] *yizker-bukh*:

> The day came when the oldest daughter of the Sieshnover Rebe Henela was
> to get married to the Hentshiner Rebbe's son, Rabbi Yosef Borukh. The

Sayshinover hasidim decided to celebrate the wedding in a big way to show their gratitude to their *rebe*. The wedding was the 19th of Kislev in 1934, but the preparations began in the summer. They decided that since the groom lived eight kilometers away from the town, they would meet him in his town and accompany him to the bride's town riding horses. There were three regiments of fifty hasidim, each dressed as Cossacks with swords. One regiment rode on horses that were decorated, while the other two walked carrying real guns. Those who served in the military gave the instructions on how to march and carry their weapons. The local paper had written a critical article before the wedding day, saying this was an old and wrong custom to perform. But this criticism just gave the young hasidim more courage to perform this spectacle. The day of the wedding they went to meet the groom and his family at seven in the morning. The parade was lead by Rabbi Hirsh Adler who was seventy and who served in the Kaiser's regiment in Petersburg. After him came other dignitaries, two orchestras and other officials all dressed and acting with military discipline.[6]

Like elsewhere, the finances of the couple and their families determined the lavishness or simplicity of the wedding. At the weddings of the poor, the *klezmorim* earned a small amount from the bride's family. Most of their earnings came from the guests who bought dances to honor the newlyweds by approaching the *kapelymaster* [band leader] or the *batkhn* [wedding bard] and asking to pay for either one dance or several dances in a row to be played in honor of the newlyweds. At lavish weddings, which were infrequent, the *klezmorim* could live on their earnings for a month. A description of an extravagant affair is found in *Pinkas Chmielnik*:

> Once there was a wedding so bountiful in Chmielnik that they began preparing for the wedding feast six months before the wedding day. A special train wagon had to bring the pepper for the fish, while other special wagons brought oxen, cows, and calves from nearby provinces. To kosher all of this meat ten cars had to be filled with salt. To cook all of this it took several lots of lumber from a nearby forest.[7]

On the wedding day, the *klezmorim* were extremely busy. First there was the groom's *tish* [table], the bride's *bazetsn/baveynen* [the sitting of the bride or the crying of the bride], and the *badekn* [the veiling of the bride]. All this took place before the procession to the wedding canopy. Often the music was rather solemn, reflecting the religious significance of the wedding ceremony and the seriousness of the choices the bride and groom had made about embarking on a new life together, as well as the stress and fatigue the couple experienced from the wedding fast that had begun the night before. Yizker books describe the events of the wedding day. From *Sefer Iwieniec*:

> On the day of the wedding five shiny sleighs with bells around the horses brought the bride's family to meet the groom's family. After meeting they

enjoyed some cake and whiskey. Then the groom sat in the first sleigh with two *klezmers*, Vintshe and Leybovitch who played the whole way back to town to my Uncle Moshe's house. While this happened the *badekn* ceremony took place for the bride. The cantor sang the "Al Moleh Rokhamim" for the bride's father who had died. Then the groom's attendants with the *klezmorim* walked the groom to the synagogue where the wedding canopy was standing.[8]

From *Sefer zikaron Czyzewo*:

At the groom's table there was fruit, candy and whiskey. The groom sat with his friends and family discussing the dowry and the *kest* [room and board offered by in-laws to their son-in-law] and what his duties were. Reb Yosef-Shlomo the *shoykhet* [ritual slaughterer] wrote by hand with his beautiful handwriting the wedding contract. In a room next door or in a neighbor's house sat the women around a table set with fruit and candy. Then Yudl Batkhn sang to the groom and the *klezmorim* played a *freylekhs* [common upbeat klezmer dance]. The groom was dressed in a white *kitl* [white linen robe]. Afterwards Yudl led him and the guests to the *badekn* of the bride. While they walked the *klezmorim* played a Skarbavn *nign* [hasidic melody]. When the groom arrived all the women who were waiting with the bride threw confetti on him. After the *badekn* Yudl called "With the right foot let us go in a lucky hour to the wedding canopy." The *klezmorim* played their traditional march and led everyone to the wedding canopy which was by the *besmedresh* [small orthodox house of worship]. The guest carried lit torches as it was dark out and there was no moonlight. As it was the custom on *Tishe-bov* [a Jewish day of fasting and mourning to commemorate the destruction of the first and second Temples in Jerusalem] to throw little stones, it was the custom to throw rotten fruit or pickles at the groom as he passed by. If it was winter then you threw snowballs at him. All of these customs meant to represent that this should be the most painful time ever in his life.[9]

After the crying of the parents and guests during the reciting of the seven blessings by the rabbi, the groom smashed the glass with his foot, and everyone shouted: "*Mazl tov!*" [good luck]. Immediately the *klezmorim* broke into a lively dance and led the guests either to a local inn or to the home of the bride, a wealthy relative, or a family friend. As the wedding couple left, wheat or corn kernels were sometimes thrown at them as a symbol of fruitfulness. Other times, money was thrown on the ground as charity to be picked up later by the poor in the town. And if the wedding took place in winter and there was snow, children would throw snowballs at the newlyweds for fun. A description of this merriment appears in *Ostrov Mazowiecka*:

The music was also heard in the alleys. Men danced in the snow. The youngsters made snowballs preparing for the moment when the bride and groom were led to the synagogue courtyard. In the street you could hear hasidic nigunim being played. Reb Shlomo *klezmer*'s fiddle cried, while the band, with his son Berl on bass, Abramtche on clarinet, Shepsl Klezmer on second violin, and Peysekh on violin let loose so everyone could hear.[10]

Before the newlyweds presented themselves as husband and wife, they were escorted to a chamber for *yikhed* [a private room to which the bride and groom would traditionally go immediately after the wedding ceremony to consummate their marriage]. However, in Eastern Europe the newlyweds simply had some private time together before celebrating with their family and friends. The next day, after the couple had slept together for the first time, the groom's mother came in the house to check the sheets for blood. Stains proved that the bride had been a virgin. To marry a non-virgin could bring great shame on the groom and his family, especially if his father was a rabbi. During the party, family and friends gave speeches and toasts while drinking wine and whiskey and eating delicious dishes. If a wedding was given by a rich family, the custom was to invite the poor and set a lavish table for them. A wealthy family did not want its daughter to begin her new life under a cloud of shame. If the poor were not invited or the food was not sumptuous enough, guests might disrupt the celebration and make rude comments about their hosts.

During a wedding, the *klezmorim* might perform over fifteen styles of dances, not all of which cost the same or had the same honorific value. The *sever tants* [server or waiter dance], in which the waiters danced in front of the newlyweds with a special plate of food, such as *tsimes* [a sweet casserole made from either cooked carrots or plums mixed with potatoes and beef] or the first piece of roasted goose, cost less than the *mekheteneste tants* [in-laws' dance], danced by the new mothers-in-law. In the latter dance, the bride's mother would act as if the groom were not good enough for her daughter and the groom's mother would act the same way. After displaying this mock arrogance toward each other, the music became a *freylekhs* as the two mothers-in-law danced happily hand-in-hand at the end of the dance. Because there are many dances, with some so new that guests might not be familiar with the steps, a wedding might have a special dance instructor. Details about wedding dances are found in *Dubno: Sefer zikaron*:

> All of the dances during the party were paid separately. Up until World War One the following dances were popular. The quadrille was for four couples and cost four kopeks. The dance lasted about fifteen minutes and the tempo was slow. The *sherele* [a kind of square dance] was danced by many couples. Each couple paid ten kopeks. It started slowly and ended up in a strong gallop. The *freylekhs* was usually danced with one couple at a time, a man with his wife or two people of the same sex. Sometimes four lined up one across from the other. When the music began one person would dance specific steps opposite the other. Their hands were held down by their sides and moved back

and forth. The dance lasted until one fell from fatigue. Then the other partner would grab hold of the tired partner's hands and begin to dance together with each other's hands on each of their shoulders to the *freylekhs*. Then the *klezmorim* would pick up the tempo while the in-laws all began to clap with great appreciation and ardor. Then the women would wave their handkerchiefs in the air urging on each partner to surpass the other. Such a *freylekhs* cost twenty kopeks. The *kozak* [a Cossack dance] cost the same amount. This dance was played for the in-laws and adolescents. The young danced waltzes, *krakowiaks*, [Polish folk dance] etc. There was also the Boston-waltz, a *lizginka* and the *tsherkesher* [Turkish dance] dance where one held a knife in his hand. This dance received a big noisy applause.[11]

Of all the life cycle events, the wedding was the most important family celebration. It was also the most important for the *klezmer* since weddings were the staple of his profession. Food and drink was abundant, and the salary was commensurate with the family's income. There was also plenty of revelry. What better job to have than to make people happy and help them to forget their worries for a time. However, playing music at a Jewish wedding could be dangerous. A lengthy description is in *Pinkas Chmielnik*:

One day Rabbi Abraham Yitskhok Silman, the rabbi of Chmielnik, asked Yosef-Leyb Marshalik, the leader of the town's *klezmer* band, to his home. Rabbi Silman asked Yosef-Leyb to promise that he, his children, and his grandchildren would never play at a wedding where boys and girls danced together. "I promise you this," said Yosef-Leyb.

Almost all of the *klezmorim* belonged to one large family. Yosef-Leyb played the bass, and his son Sane played the violin. His daughter Chana's children also played in the band. There was Notl, the oldest, on violin, Abraham on clarinet, and Yisroel on drum. Chane's husband Velvel also was a *klezmer* and played the trumpet, violin, and clarinet, sometimes with Yosef-Leyb. The youngest son Elye, was too young to play in the band. Eventually he studied at the conservatory in Vienna and became a well-known cellist, giving lessons in Kielc, Lodz, and Krakow. He died young in Kielc. His only son survived the Holocaust and lived in America.

In 1895, there was a big wedding in town between Hirshl Stelmakher's son Yankl Rimazh and Yakhe-Libe, Elye Penzel's daughter. The wedding took place in Yisroel Stolar's carpentry workshop. After the ceremony and customary Jewish dances, Shmuel Stelmakher, the groom's younger brother (a playboy of sorts), went up to Yosef-Leyb and asked him if he would perform more popular dances like the *kutner* and *larsey*, in which eight couples dance together. The first dance was the *kutner* dance, which cost Shmuel one ruble. The ruble was put into the tin can, which was tied to the belt of the youngest *klezmer*, the drummer. The tin can was locked, and the key was left at Yosef-Leyb's home. After the wedding all the *klezmorim* went to his home where the can was opened and the money counted. Each *klezmer* received his proper share.

The music began and so did the dancing. Eventually Sane, who played first violin, went up to the front of the crowded room to see what one of the young boys was shouting at him. Apparently the *klezmorim* had begun to play the second section of the *kutner* dance before all the couples had completed their steps. When Sane got closer to the young man, he saw he saw the boys dancing with the girls and quickly yelled something to Yosef-Leyb in *klezmer* argot. Suddenly the music stopped. It was explained to Shmuel that a promise had been made to the rabbi that mixed dancing would not take place at any wedding at which the Marshalik *klezmorim* played. Shmuel insisted that he continue to play since he paid a ruble for the two dances. Yosef-Leyb refused, and at that very moment a fight broke out. Sane's violin was broken, along with Yosef-Leyb's bass. While people were shouting, screaming, and running about Yisroel, the drummer, quickly ran out with the tin can to save what little they had earned.

The next day Libe-Elye Penzel, quite depressed, went to Yosef-Leyb's home to apologize and pay him the rest of his fee. He did not want to take it, but she insisted knowing that several instruments had to be repaired. And this was how the playboys of Chmielnik got back at the *klezmorim* for making the agreement with the rabbi.[12]

Despite the importance of the *klezmer* at Jewish weddings, his social standing was rather fluid, and sometimes his *yikhes* [lineage] was just a rung or two higher than the local *treygers* [porters]. Playing music generally paid poorly, thus making it difficult for the *klezmer* to provide for his family. *Klezmorim* were not perceived as close followers of or knowledgeable in Torah and Talmud. And to complicate matters, even though *klezmorim* traveled less at the turn of the twentieth century than in the early nineteenth century, people had the impression that they were usually away from home. That led to suspicions and rumors about them. It was believed that they fraternized with all kinds of riff-raff on the roads or in the inns and taverns, including drunks, thieves, smugglers, gamblers, vulgar gentiles, prostitutes, and Rom. Finally, to make the public even more apprehensive and wary, the *klezmorim* had their own argot, *klezmer loshn* [musician's language], which they used at Jewish and non–Jewish festivities. The *klezmorim* could use this argot to secretly speak about the people they met while traveling or about the people who hired them. The language is filled with sarcasm, disdain, humor, and sexual innuendo. As one writer explains in *Sefer Kaluszyn*:

The *klezmorim* had their own ways, customs and language so no one would understand them. For example they would say: "This *yold* [chump, sucker] doesn't understand what is permitted and does not *knasn* [recognize] the band." *Yold* here meant the male in-laws at the wedding who ordered around the band. The female in-law was known as the *yoldevke* [wife of a chump, sucker]. During the course of the wedding, *klezmorim* talked about their upcoming engagements and the beautiful manners of the Polish clerks, teachers, pharmacists and building superintendents.[13]

To many Jews in Eastern Europe, a *klezmer* was considered an avocation acceptable and necessary for a celebration, but not a vocation to which young Jewish men should aspire. Playing music as a profession gave the impression that the *klezmer* never grew up, and thus he was unable to meet the responsibilities of adulthood. There were many reasons to scorn the *klezmorim*, including their finances, travel, friends, and acquaintances. Moreover, their work was perceived as play. "*Shpil klezmer shpil.*" [play, *klezmer*, play] was yelled to the musicians at a celebration and not "*Arbayt klezmer arbayt.*" [work, *klezmer*, work]. An indication of this attitude is in *Sefer zikaron le-zekher Dobromil*:

> Yidl was an extraordinary fellow who played the violin and other instruments. He gave music lessons in the homes of rich Christians and was often invited to play at special occasions in the homes of wealthy landowners. Half the town's young women were in love with him. Yidl's girlfriend was Fadzhe, Moshele Melamend's daughter, who was gentle and was one of the most beautiful girls in town. However Moshele was a teacher and did not want a *klezmer-yung* [youth] for a son-in-law who never grew up. But after a year of persistence the wedding canopy was finally erected.[14]

The problems the *klezmorim* had with their fellow Jews was not nearly as constant and dangerous as the anti–Semitism they often experienced from the non–Jewish populace. An example from *Sefer zikaron Czyzewo*:

> My father had been a *klezmer* for forty years in Czycewo, so much so that the Christians ceased to hire *klezmorim* for their balls. This next episode is strongly engraved in my memory. Just after my grandfather's wedding when he was still young, two elegantly dressed landowner's came to him after the Sabbath. They asked him if he would come with his band to their ball that evening. It was a small village and grandfather had never heard of it. They sent a beautiful carriage with three horses that took the band on a half hour ride to the ball. The court was full of guests. The *klezmorim* were lead to a huge dance hall where they began to play for the couples. Suddenly they noticed that the dancers wore shoes made to look like chicken feet. Immediately the band felt some fear but did not know how to leave the place. They continued to play never once putting anything in their mouths for several hours as people danced. Finally after half the night went by the two landowners who had brought them said "We are so pleased with your playing. We would like to pay you. Should we pay you gold or chicken feces?" "With gold," my grandfather said with some alarm. Immediately they were assaulted. It was dark and before they realized it they found themselves in a swamp in the forest. Their violins were hanging in the trees and their cases were filled with chicken feces. It was difficult to get their violins out of the trees. Afterwards they

dragged their tired muddy selves home. That Sabbath they all went to the small synagogue and said a blessing for having survived this dangerous event.[15]

After the assassination of Alexander II in 1881, Jews found themselves in a cauldron of anti–Semitism and political agitation. Movements from anarchism to Zionism were sweeping the Pale. The proletarianization of the Jewish masses, accompanied by the *haskole* [enlightenment], was changing traditional life. Even the hasidic *rebes* could not hold back these radical changes. As a result, more and more *klezmorim* worked as artisans or day laborers full-time and played their music part-time. Moreover, if bands traveled, they usually went no more than a half-day's ride by horse and wagon. Details about the multiple occupations of *klezmorim* appear in the memorial books. From *Sefer Skierniewice*:

> There were in Skierniewice three handsome Jews, all three dear *klezmorim*. The first was named Nison the Baker, the second was Lipman the Tinsmith, and the third was Berl the Cotton Weaver.[16]

From *Kehilat Semiatycze*:

> The leader of the *klezmorim* in Semiatycze was Shepsl the Hairdresser. He was a tall, handsome, manly person with a black twisted mustache like a Polish lord. He had two professions but was entirely poor. All the *klezmorim* from his band had two professions, and they were still poor.[17]

From *Yisker-bukh tsum fareybikn fem ondenk fun der khorev-gevorener yidisher kehile Ryki*:

> In Ryki, Moshe Britzman played the bass in the *klezmer* band, but this was not his profession. He owned a coach in which he would drive people to and from the train.[18]

From *Ayaratenu Swir*:

> Elikum the Barber was known as the Paganini of the town. Elikum also had a beautiful voice and sang and played at weddings. However, his main profession was as a barber. He worked even on the Sabbath, because many of his customers were leftists and did not keep the Sabbath.[19]

At the beginning of the twentieth century, oppressive poverty and unrelenting anti–Semitism were part of the East European Jewish experience. At that time, many people were renewing their interest in Judaism. Having been enticed by acculturation and assimilation under the Russian and Austro-Hungarian empires, some in the Jewish community began to reaffirm their Jewish identity. This did not mean that those progressive Jews who were Zionists, Labor Zionists, Yiddishists, or Bundists abandoned their political ideals; rather, they incorporated them into expressions of Hebrew and Yiddish culture. For many, Yiddish became the vehicle to express one's Jewish identity.

Similar to the revival of Ashkenazic culture in America over the last thirty-five years, the Jewish artists of a hundred years ago were at the forefront of this passionate return. One outgrowth of this Yiddish creativity was the Yiddish Language Conference held in Czernowitz, Bukovina, from August 30 through September 4, 1908. At the conference, Jewish writers from Europe and the United States gathered to discuss the role of Yiddish in Jewish life. One issue was the relationship between Yiddish and modern Hebrew, which was undergoing its own renaissance in conjunction with Zionism. At the end of the conference, Yiddish was proclaimed *a* national language, which heightened its prestige considerably. The conference also made it clear to many of its participants that numerous aspects of Yiddish culture were disappearing. The *haskole* had spread into the hinterlands of Jewish Eastern Europe, proclaiming the twentieth century as the dawn of a new era. Progress meant ridding oneself of the old Jewish traditions and customs, which had developed over nearly a thousand years. A number of Yiddishists conducted ethnographic expeditions for the purpose of collecting Jewish folklore, specifically sayings, poems, songs, music, stories, photographs, clothes, and artifacts.

Additionally, numerous artists significantly contributed to the *klezmer* culture. One was Solomon Zainwil Rapaport, known as Sh. An-ski (1863–1920), who was a folklorist, ethnographer, and playwright. During his momentous ethnographic expedition from 1911 to 1914 in southern Ukraine, he collected Yiddish folksongs, *klezmer* melodies, oral histories, photographs, handicrafts, and instruments. Another was Menachem Kipnis (1878–1942), a singer, writer, and collector, who published one hundred forty Yiddish folksongs with music in two volumes in Warsaw in 1918 and 1925. Still another was Yehuda Leyb Cahan (1881–1937), a collector of Yiddish folksongs and music and one of the founders of YIVO, who published his collection of over five hundred Yiddish folksongs, many with music, in New York in 1912.

In 1888, Sholom Aleichem (1859–1916), a Yiddish writer and humorist, wrote *Stempenyu*, a novella that portrays the world of the *klezmers*, including their personalities, work, music, travel, dalliances, and argot. The work is based on the life of Stempenyu, a *klezmer* who lived from 1822 to 1879 and who came from ten generations of *klezmorim*. He eventually settled in Barditshev, where his reputation as a virtuoso and showman spread throughout southern Ukraine. About him, it has been said:

> Every place Stempenyu went, everyone waited to see him open his case. When he put the violin under his chin the rest of the violin players felt like burying themselves alive. He was envied by the men and eyed by the women.[20]

In 1892, Yitskhok Leyb Perets (1852–1915), a Hebrew and Yiddish author, wrote "The *Klezmer's* Death." This short story describes the ways in which the enlightenment movement caused pain and conflict to a *klezmer* family. In the story, the father, the old band leader, lies in bed dying, while his sons show their indifference and his hysterical wife admonishes them for their non-religious ways. She also admonishes her husband for being unfaithful. Working with paint, stained glass, and fabric, Marc Chagall (1887–1985) also portrayed *shtetl* life. His whimsical and fantastic paintings of *klezmer* violinists, wedding couples, and flying chickens became readily identifiable images and influenced other artists.

Then there was Joel Engel (1868–1927), who composed the music for An-ski's Yiddish play *The Dybbuk*. With encouragement and help from Rimsky-Korsakov, Engel established the Society for Jewish Folk Music in St. Petersburg in 1908. About that project Rimsky-Korsakov said: "Why should you Jewish students imitate European and Russian composers? The Jew possesses tremendous folk treasure ... Jewish music awaits its Glinka."[21]

While many accounts about the *klezmer* and his life appear in memorial books, there are a few entries illustrating a number of Jewish folk traditions and superstitions that disappeared with the Holocaust. Although *klezmorim* are key in each of the following accounts, their stories are unknown outside the memorial books. From *Sefer yizker le-kehilat Radomsk ve-ha-seviva*:

> In 1916, World War One was in full force. All the armies that were fighting boasted of victories. That spring a typhus epidemic came to our town. Immediately it spread throughout the town to all strata. People were dying daily. Then our "good" neighbors, the Poles, said the cause of the plague was the Jews' uncleanliness. The plague grew. There was not a home that did not have someone infected. The Polish hospitals were full and not accepting any Jews so we built our own hospitals. Those in charge of the hospital were Yitskhok Kitsov and his daughter, Dr. Mitelman, and Mr. Fishof. Soon after the hospital was built Dr. Mitelman contracted typhus. Jews were dying daily. The religious men recited psalms and their wives would go to the cemetery every Monday and Thursday to recite special prayers wearing white linen. Then the *shamas* died and the people thought this was a sign that the plague would end, but it continued. Then the second sacrifice was Rabbi Yosef Safkever. Now the cemetery was full of people who had recited psalms, so people fasted and treated the time as a *yom kipper-katan* [small Day of Atonement observed by orthodox who were not able to observe the holiday on the actual day]. Finally the Jewish community decided the last resource was to have a wedding in the cemetery. They found a bride living in the home of her mother, a widow. She was one of twelve daughters. Then there was an all out offensive to catch a groom. The groom was Shimele, a water porter who brought water from the town's pump to everyone's house. His father Moyshele was a glove maker and a follower of the Radomsker Rebe. But this was not enough for his son. Every other Sabbath Shimile prayed with another rebe, the Gerer, the Sokhotsever, etc. Then the town prankster Shlomo-Yitskhok Epshteyn

told Shimile he should not go to the wedding canopy without a dowry. With Shimile convinced about this the town immediately went to the rich folk and put together a dowry of second hand stuff: clothes, dishes, old bed linen, towels, etc. Tuesday early morning was the day of the wedding. First two religious women took the bride, who at first did not want to go, to the mikve. Then everyone else in town dressed for the wedding and at noon began walking to the cemetery. At the front of the crowd was Leybele the *Klezmer* (the old hoverer) dressed up as if he was playing for a rich man's daughter's wedding and Skurke the Batkhn (the comb maker) who made jokes at the expense of the wedding couple. At the Radomsker's Rebe's house the *badekn* took place. Then the music began and everyone led the couple, the town's amulet, to the cemetery. The ceremony was completely silent, except for the voice of Leybl-Shamas. After the glass was broken, the people in the cemetery screamed *mazl-tov* and other good wishes. At the *besmedresh*, the wedding celebration continued with food, music, and gifts. The next day, the people felt as if a heavy burden had been lifted from their shoulders.[22]

From *Apt (Opatow): Sefer zikaron le-ir va-em be-Yisrael*:

There was a tradition in Apt (Opatow) of blessing the new moon every month and of blessing the sun every twenty-eight years. In 1925, eight days before Passover, early in the morning, everyone gathered for the blessing of the sun ceremony. The rabbis had received permission to gather and greet the sunrise with music. People waited for Aryesh the *klezmer* because they knew he had composed a new melody for this special occasion. Then all of a sudden everyone heard a beautiful march. A thousand Jews gathered around the synagogue. At five a.m., the chief rabbi, Rabbi Khayim Yosef, dressed in his holiday clothes with a *shtrayml* [fur-edged hat worn by hasidic Jews on Sabbath, holidays, and special occasions] came out with the other rabbis. The *klezmorim* played the Polish national anthem, then the Hatikvah. Then the public walked to the music along a wide street to the open field near the kosher slaughterers' houses. Rabbi Khayim Yosef pointed his arms towards the east where the first rays of the sun were appearing. Everyone waited for the sign from the rabbi to bless the sun. Simultaneously the *klezmorim* took out Aryesh's music and began to play. This melody written just for the blessing of the sun was talked about and remembered for a long time.[23]

During World War Two, *klezmorim* sometimes performed popular and Jewish music in ghetto ensembles. They played for Yiddish theatres, choirs, and classes, as well as for public and private celebrations. Sometimes *klezmorim* were relegated to begging in the streets with their instruments, if they still owned one. To a degree until the ghettos were liquidated, instrumental and vocal music functioned as a source of entertainment, therapy, and hope for Jews.

Those *klezmorim* who managed to survive the ghetto and deportation often found themselves playing in a camp orchestra. In addition to their daily labor, some musicians had to perform at Nazi dinner parties and other events. If they were lucky, they might receive a little extra food for their efforts. Since musicians were not plentiful in the camps, Nazis sometimes prolonged a musician's life for a while. One result was that musicians were forced to perform while their friends and family members were being humiliated, beaten, or gassed. Psychologically this was excruciating for the musicians. Some survived these ordeals; others succumbed to them. Yizker books contain descriptions of these experiences. From *Sefer zikaron le-kehilat Kozieniec*:

> Itsik Klezmer (Nodelman) and his sons had a good reputation in town. He was the leader and first violinist in the band. Nearly everyone in his band was a family member or relative. There was Shmerl on bass, Meyer Shakhnes on flute, Yisroel the Tall with his long trumpet and Khamia on violin. The drummer was Yisroel's son Elal. They played at Jewish weddings and celebrations and at gentile landowners weddings, both in towns and villages. They were the only *klezmer* band in the Kozieneicer district. When Itsik played for the *badekns*, the wives cried and the men swayed their heads as they cried. Itsik played with great strength and was an immense artist. During the Holocaust Itsik's son Shloyme worked in the gas chambers in Treblinka. He stood by the entrance of the gas chambers and played with the orchestra as the bodies were gassed. While he stood there he saw his nine year old son being led. He grabbed his son by the hand and pulled him out of the line. A SS officer saw this laughed and kicked the little boy in the stomach. At the very moment Shloyme smashed his violin over the SS officer's head and marched with his only child into the gas chamber.[24]

The exact number of *klezmorim* murdered during the Holocaust is unknown, but of the approximately four to five thousand *klezmorim* living in Eastern Europe before the war, estimates suggest that about ninety percent perished. Fifty years after the Holocaust politicians and members of Jewish communities are beginning to accept and promote the revival of Yiddish culture in Eastern Europe and the former Soviet Union. On the surface, the resurgence mixes irony with incongruity. It took only two generations for Jewish culture, often with few or even no Jews participating, to resurface in the very countries where six million Jews were murdered.

And as for me, to be able to hear the occasional strains of *klezmer* music as I walk the streets of Eastern Europe towns where my ancestors once walked, is both hauntingly beautiful and bittersweet. I understand this sentiment from *Yisker-bukh tsu Vlodave*:

> Without the music the public didn't make a move. The *klezmer* had long looked forward to the wedding, played throughout with great pride and fanfare. His music rang throughout the shtetl.... The *klezmorim* demonstrated once again their magic by making the public sad and happy, as they had done in the past, while filling the heart and soul with bliss.[25]

Notes

1. See Yale Strom, *The Book of Klezmer* (Chicago: A Cappella Books, 2002).

2. Sara Hamer-Jaklin, "A Wedding in Przedborz," in *Sefer yizker le-kehilat Radomsk ve-ha-sevivah,* ed. L. Losh (Tel Aviv: Former Residents of Radomsk, 1967), 285.

3. Moyshe Likht Feld, "A Wedding in Town," in *Sefer Frampol,* ed. D. Shtokfish (Tel Aviv: Book Committee, 1966), 160.

4. I. Lifschitz, *"Batkhonim und letsim bay yidn,"* in *Arkhiv far der geshikhte fun yidishn teatr un drama,* ed. J. Shatzky, Vol. 1 (Vilna–New York: 1930), 33–34.

5. Abraham Barnholts, "The Wedding in Town," in *Yisker-bukh tsu Vlodave,* ed. Sh. Kanc (Tel Aviv: Wlodawa Societies in Israel and North and South America, 1974), 520.

6. Asher Reyz, "The Big Wedding," in *Tomashover (Lubelski) yizker-bukh* (New York: Tomashover Relief Committee, 1965), 441–442.

7. Leybl Fiemrikowski, "The Rich Man's Extravagant Wedding," in *Pinkas Chmielnik* (Tel Aviv: Former Residents of Chmielnik in Israel, 1960), 308.

8. Yitskhok Kuznits, "A Wedding in Iwieniec," in *Sefer Iwieniec, Kamien he-ha-seviva; sefer zikaron* (Tel Aviv: Iwieniec Societies in Israel and the Diaspora, 1973), 179–180.

9. "The Order of the Wedding Ceremony by the Groom," in *Sefer zikaron Czyzewo,* ed. Sh. Kanc (Tel Aviv: Former Residents of Czyzewo in Israel and the USA, 1961), 499–501.

10. Mikhl Grins, "A Wedding in the City," in *Ostrov Mazowiecka,* ed. Judah Loeb Levin (Jerusalem and Tel Aviv: Yad Yahadut Polin, 1966) 299–300.

11. Moshe Katshke, "Jewish Weddings and *Klezmorim*," in *Dubno: sefer zikaron,* ed. S. Eisenberg (Haifa: 1962), 666–667.

12. Moshe Leyzer Mints, "The Ruined Wedding (on Account of an Agreement Between the Rabbi of Khmelik and the Musicians)," in *Pinkas Chmielnik* (Tel Aviv: Former Residents of Chmielnik in Israel, 1960), 212–214.

13. Shmuel Ayzershtayn, *"Kaluszyner klezmorim,"* in *Sefer Kaluszyn; geheylikht der khorev gevorener kehile,* ed. A Shamri and Sh. Soroka (Tel Aviv: Former Residents of Kaluszyn in Israel, 1961), 253–254.

14. Z. Shtayn, *"Klezmer,"* in *Sefer zikaron le-zekher Dobromil,* ed. M. Gelbart (Tel Aviv: The Dobromiler Society in New York and the Dobromiler Organization in Israel, 1964), 223–224.

15. "The Order of the Wedding Ceremony," in *Sefer zikaron Czyzewo,* ed. Sh. Kanc (Tel Aviv: Former Residents of Tshizhevo in Israel and the USA, 1961), 579–580.

16. Yisroel Heler, "Three Beautiful Masters: The Baker with his Violin, the Tinsmith with his Trumpet, and the Cotton Maker with his Drum, Played a Poor Wedding," in *Sefer Skierniewice,* ed. J. Perlow (Tel Aviv: Former Residents of Skierniewice in Israel, 1955), 357–358.

17. "Shepsl the *klezmer* and Anshel the *batkhn,*" in *Kehilat Semiatycze,* ed. E. Tash (Tel Aviv: Association of the Former Residents of Semiatich in Israel and the Diaspora, 1965), 142.

18. Moyshe Taytboym, "Weddings," in *Yisker-bukh tsum fareybikn dem ondenk fun der khorev-gevorener yidisher kehile Ryki,* ed. Sh. Kanc (Tel Aviv: Ryki Societies in Israel, Canada, Los Angeles, France and Brazil, 1973), 322.

19. "Family Artists," in *Ayaratenu Swir,* ed. Ch. Swironi (Tel Aviv: Former Residents of Swir in Israel and in the United States, 1959), 190.

20. Strom, *The Book of Klezmer,* 117.

21. Ibid., 120.

22. Zev Sobotowski, "A Wedding in the Cemetery," in *Sefer yizker le-kehilat Radomsk ve-ha-seviva,* ed. L. Losh (Tel Aviv: Former Residents of Radomsk, 1967), 154–155.

23. Pinye Titl, *"Klezmorim,"* in *Apt (Opatow): Sefer zikaron le-ir va-em be-Yisrae,* ed. Z. Yasheev (Tel Aviv: The Apt Organization in Israel, USA, Canada, and Brazil, 1966), 139.

24. "Itsik Klezmer (Nodelman)," in *Sefer zikaron le-kehilat Kozieniec,* ed. B. Kaplinski (Tel Aviv: Former Residents of Kozieniec in Israel, 1969), 253.

25. Abraham Barnholts, "The Wedding in Town," in Wlodawa: *Yisker-bukh tsu Vlodave,* ed. Sh. Kanc (Tel Aviv: Wlodawa Societies in Israel and North and South America, 1974), 553.

PART V

BIBLIOGRAPHY

16

A Survey of Reference Books

ROSEMARY HOROWITZ

The references given here are divided into three types: works that discuss the memorial volumes as artifacts or as books; works that use the volumes as source documents for research; and bibliographies.

Studies of Yizker Books

Adamczyk-Garbowska, Monika. "*Żydowskie księgi pamięci i ich współczesne kontynuacje.*" In *Odcienie tożsamości — literatura żydowska jako zjawisko wielojęzyczne*, 106–121. Lublin: Wydawn. Uniwersyteta Marii Curie-Skłodowskiej, 2004.

_____, Adam Kopciowski, and Andrzej Trzciński, eds. *Tam był kiedyś mój dom ... Księgi pamięci gmin żydowskich.* Lublin: Wydawn. Uniwersyteta Marii Curie-Skłodowskiej, 2009.

Amir, Michlean. "From Memorials to Invaluable Historical Documentation: Using *Yizkor* Books as Resources for Studying a Vanished World." Association of Jewish Libraries Annual Convention, La Jolla, CA. June 24–27, 2001.

_____, and Rosemary Horowitz. "*Yizkor* Books in the 21st Century: A History and Guide to the Genre." *Judaica Librarianship* 14 (Fall 2008): 39–56.

Baker, Zachary. "Memorial Books as Sources for Family History." *Toledot, The Journal of Jewish Genealogy* 3 no. 2 (Fall-Winter 1980): 3–7.

Blumenthal, Nachman. "Memorial Books by Survivors of Communities." *Yad Vashem Bulletin* (April 1958): 24–27.

Bojczuk, Sylwia. "'Księgi Pamięci' — geneza i charakterystyka." *Scriptores–Pamięć–Miejsce–Obecność* 1 (2003): 73–76.

Friedman, Philip. "*Di landsmanshaftn literatur in di fareyniktn shtatn far di letstn ten yor.*" *Jewish Book Annual* 10 (5712/1951–1952): 81–95.

Grunberger, Michael W. "*Yizker Bikher*: The Literature of Remembrance." *AB Bookman's Weekly* 77 (1986): 1798–1803.

Halpern, Nikki. "Thunders of Silence: Yizker (Memorial) Books Between Rupture and Repetition." http://www.ufr-anglais.univ-Paris7.fr/CENTRES_RECHERCHES/CIRNA/CIRNA1/Identites/CEJA/CAHIER01/Halpern.htm. April 1, 2010.

Hoffman, Miriam. *Memory and Memorial: An Investigation into the Making of the Zwolen Memorial Book.* (Unpublished thesis). New York: Columbia University, 1983.

Horowitz, Rosemary. *Literacy and Cultural Transmission in the Reading, Writing, and Rewriting of Jewish Memorial Books.* (Published dissertation). San Francisco: Austin and Winfield, 1998.

Jones, Faith, and Gretta Siegel. "*Yizkor* Books as Holocaust Grey Literature." *Publishing Research Quarterly* (Spring 2006): 52–62.

Koss, Andrew. "*Yizker Bikher* as Primary Sources for the Study of the Ghettos in the German-Occupied Soviet Union." In *Holocaust in the Soviet Union: Symposium Presentations,* 61–68. Washington, DC: Center for Advanced Holocaust Studies, United States Holocaust Memorial Museum, 2005.

Kugelmass, Jack, and Jonathan Boyarin. "*Yizker Bikher* and the Problem of Historical Veracity: An Anthropological Approach." In *The Jews of Poland Between the Two World Wars,* edited by Yisrael, Gutman, Ezra Mendelsohn, Jehuda Reinharz, and Chone Shmeruk, 519–535. Hanover, NH: University Press of New England, 1989.

_____, and _____, eds. and trans. *From a Ruined Garden: The Memorial Books of Polish Jewry.* New York City: Schocken Books, 1983.

_____, and _____, eds. and trans. *From a Ruined Garden: The Memorial Books of Polish Jewry.* Second, expanded edition. Bloomington and Indianapolis: Indiana University Press in association with the United States Holocaust Memorial Museum, Washington DC, 1998.

Madsen, Catherine. "In the Bond of Life: Yizker Books of the Second World War." *Pakn-Treger* 46 (2004): 20–25.

Mark, Beryl. "*Yisker-bikher, vos baveynen un vekn tsum kampf.*" *Yidishe kultur* 26.6 (June-July 1964): 25–29.

Rechtman, Yigal. "What Are *Yizkor* Books and How to Use Them to Enhance Genealogical Work?" *Everton's Genealogical Helper* 52.3 (May-June 1998): 12–15.

Rosenbaum, Yankel. *The Yizkor Books of the Holocaust.* (Unpublished thesis). Melbourne: University of Melbourne, 1987.

Rotenberg, Yehoshua. "*Yizker-bikher — tsi bloyz a sheyne matseyve?*" *Di goldene keyt* 103 (1980): 155–160.

Schulman, Elias. "A Survey and Evaluation of *Yizkor* Books." *Jewish Book Annual* 25 (5728/1967–1968): 184–191.

Shapiro, Chaim. "How Not to Write a '*Yizkor* Book.'" *Jewish Observer* 14.8 (1980): 18–25.

Shapiro, Robert Moses. "'*Yizker-Bikher*' as Sources on Jewish Communities in Soviet Belorussia and Soviet Ukraine During the Holocaust," in *The Holocaust in the Soviet Union: Studies and Sources on the Destruction of the Jews in the Nazi-occupied Territories of the USSR, 1941–1945,* edited by Dobroszycki and Jeffrey S. Gurock, 223–236. Armonk, NY: M.E. Sharpe, 1993.

Shatzky, Jacob. "*A bukh vegn yidn in Plotzk.*" *YIVO Bleter* 27.1 (1946): 167–174.

_____. "*Yizker bikher.*" *YIVO Bleter* 37 (1953): 264–282.

_____. "*Yizker bikher.*" *YIVO Bleter* 39 (1955): 339–359.

Shmulevitz, I. "Our Obligation to Remember." *Yiddish* 1.3 (1974): 49–54.

Shmulevitz-Hoffman, Miriam. "*Denkmol un zikhron: An oysforshtung funem tsunoyfshtel fun Zvoliner yizker bukh.*" *YIVO Bleter* 1 (1991): 257–272.

Stark, Jared. "Broken Records: Holocaust Diaries, Memoirs, and Memorial Books." In *Teaching the Representation of the Holocaust,* edited by Marianne Hirsch and Irene Kacandes, 191–204. New York: Modern Language Association of America, 2004.

Wachtel, Nathan. "Remember and Never Forget." *History and Anthropology* 2.2 (October 1986): 307–335.

Wien, Abraham. "'Memorial Books' as a Source for Research into the History of Jewish

Communities in Europe." *Yad Vashem Studies on the Eastern European Catastrophe and Resistance* 9 (1973): 255–272.

Wieviorka, Annette, and Itzhok Noborski. *Les Livres du Souvenir: Memoriaux Juifs de Pologne*. Paris: Editions Gallimard/Juilliard, 1983.

Studies Using Yizker Books

Adamczyk-Garbowska, Monika. "Patterns of Return: Survivors' Postwar Journeys to Poland." Ina Levine Annual Lecture Occasional Paper. Washington, DC: United States Holocaust Memorial Museum, Center for Advanced Holocaust Studies, 2007.

Aleksiun, Natalia. "Gender and Nostalgia: Images of Women in Early *Yizker Bikher.*" *Jewish Culture and History* 5, no. 1 (Summer 2002): 69–90.

Glicksman, William. *Jewish Social Welfare Institutions in Poland: As Described in Memorial (Yizkor) Books*: *Studies in Jewish Communal Activities*. Philadelphia: M.E. Kalish Folkshul, 1976.

Goldberg-Mulkiewicz, Olga. *Ksiega pamieci a mit zydowskiego miasteczka. Etnografia Polsk* 35, no. 2 (1991): 187–199.

_____. *Stara i nowa ojczyzna: ślady kultury Żydów polskich*. Łódź: Polskie Towarzystwo Ludoznawcze, 2003.

Hall, Katharina. "Jewish Memory in Exile: The Relation of W.G. Sebald's *Die Ausgewanderten* to the Tradition of *Yizkor* Books." In *Jews in German Literature Since 1945: German-Jewish Literature?* edited by Pol O'Dochartaigh, 153–164. Amsterdam: Rodopi B.V., 2000.

Horowitz, Rosemary. "Reading and Writing During the Holocaust as Described in *Yisker* Books." In *The Holocaust and the Book: Destruction and Preservation*, edited by Jonathan Rose, 128–142. Amherst: University of Massachusetts Press, 2001.

_____. "The Transformation of Memory in Online *Yisker* Books." *Proteus: A Journal of Ideas* 19, no. 2 (Fall 2002): 39–42.

Kurtzer, Yehuda. "'And You Shall Recount to Your Children:' *Yizkor* Books in the Literature of Jewish Memory." (Unpublished paper). United States Holocaust Memorial Museum Center for Advanced Holocaust Studies, 2004.

Strom, Yale. *The Book of Klezmer*. Chicago: A Capella Books, 2002.

Trunk, Isaiah. *Judenrat: The Jewish Councils in Eastern Europe Under Nazi Occupation.* New York: Macmillan, 1972.

Veidlinger, Jeffrey. "...even beyond Pinsk": *Yizker Bikher* [Memorial Books] and Jewish Cultural Life in the Shtetl." In *The Jews of Eastern Europe*, edited by Leonard J. Greenspoon, Ronald A. Simkins, and Brian J. Horowitz, 175–189. Omaha: Creighton University Press, 2005.

Winker, Helen (compiler). "Jewish Music and Dance as Recorded in Yizker Books." http//www.klezmershack.com/articles/winker/Yizkerlinks.html. April 1, 2010.

Bibliographies of Yizker Books

Baker, Zachary. *Bibliography of Eastern European Memorial (Yizkor) Books: With Call Numbers for Six Judaica Libraries in New York*, edited by Steven W. Siegel. New York: Jewish Genealogical Society, Inc., 1992.

_____. "Bibliography of Eastern European Memorial (Yizker) Books," in *From a Ruined*

Garden: The Memorial Books of Polish Jewry, edited and translated by Jack Kugelmass and Jonathan Boyarin. Second, expanded edition. Washington, DC. United States Holocaust Memorial Museum; Bloomington: Indiana University Press, 1998.

Bass, David. "Bibliographical List of Memorial Books Published in the Years 1943–1972." *Yad Vashem Studies* 9 (1973): 273–321.

Fox, Cyril Albert, and Saul Issroff. *Jewish Memorial (Yizkor) Books in the United Kingdom: Destroyed European Jewish Communities*. London: Jewish Genealogical Society of Great Britain, 2006.

Kopciowski, Adam, ed. *Księgi pamięci gmin żydowskich: bibliografia = Jewish Memorial Books: A Bibliography*. Lublin: Wydawn. Universyteta Marii Curie-Skłodowskiej, 2008.

Meizlish, Penina. *Ha-Hayim ha-datiyim ba-Sho'ah 'al-pi sifre ha-zikaron la-kehilot* Ramat-Gan: Universitat Bar-Ilan, 1990.

Tahan, Ilana. *Memorial Volumes to Jewish Communities Destroyed in the Holocaust: A Bibliography of British Library Holdings*. London: The British Library, 2004.

Yizkor Books from the Library of Yad Vashem. Jerusalem: Yad Vashem, 2000.

A Survey of Collections

AMY BURNETTE *AND* ROSEMARY HOROWITZ

Introduction

With advances in electronic databases and digitizing technologies, the availability of yizker books continues to increase. As a result of a partnership with the National Yiddish Book Center, the New York Public Library, for instance, provides electronic access to 650 yizker books in its collection. Several institutions that house yizker books, such as Bar-Ilan University in Israel, even supply online access to the New York Public Library's collection. In addition to preserving the value of the original texts, online facsimiles of yizker books make their contents widely available to scholars, historians, and genealogists who use the books to analyze memoirs, testimonies, photographs, maps, necrologies, and other material.

Although these technologies grant researchers worldwide the access to view a text, they have notably affected the acquisition of new yizker books. Dr. Barry Walfish, the Judaica and Theology Specialist at the University of Toronto Library, affirms that the need to acquire additional yizker books has "considerably diminished" due to electronic availability.[1] Digitizing technologies also generate a gap between the original yizker texts published by the *landsmanshaftn* and their subsequent reprints, perhaps prompting librarians and archivists to reconsider the definition of the term "yizker" and the texts cataloged as such in their institutions. This has, in some cases, significantly impacted the manner in which yizker book collections are developed and archived. Indeed, some scholars suggest that varying definitions of the term "yizker" likely account for their fluctuating numbers in collections around the world.

Faith Jones and Gretta Siegel acknowledge this probability in their article "Yizker Books as Holocaust Grey Literature." They explain that yizker books are sometimes grouped under the broader classification of "memorial books," often referred to as "grey literature," examples of which include:

> German-language books published by non–Jews about the destroyed Jewish communities of the German-speaking countries; individual survivor memoirs; general town histories by a single author where the dominant part of the book is not about individuals; books of memories collected through oral interview by school groups in Israel; and Hasidic groups' histories of their rabbinical dynasties, which are usually associated with a particular town.[2]

Some institutions do, in fact, catalog yizker books alongside what Jones and Siegel delineate as "grey literature," perhaps explaining the uneven distribution on JewishGen.org.[3] As such, there is currently no definitive number of yizker books available to scholars and researchers.[4] It is helpful for researchers to learn the definitions used at institutions claiming to house significant numbers of yizker books.

While there have been numerous studies on the contents of yizker books and how to use them, there has yet to be an investigation of how institutions are collectively defining this term. There have, however, been bibliographies of yizker book holdings that define the term in specific regions or institutions. In 2004, Ilana Tahan, Hebraica Curator and Head of the Hebrew Section at the British Library, published a bibliography that organizes the library's yizker book holdings by language, year, and country of publication.[5] Zachary Baker, Reinhard Family Curator of Judaica and Hebraica Collections at Stanford University, also published a bibliography of yizker books in *From a Ruined Garden: The Memorial Books of Polish Jewry* in 1998. While both scholars provide definitions of the term "yizker," several collections currently rely upon Baker's definition to catalog their memorial books. The intent of this study is to build upon this scholarship by providing information on how several institutions catalog, archive, and acquire yizker books, as well as to assess the impact of digitizing technologies on this genre of literature.

Methodology

The methodological approach in this study involved the online distribution of a survey of ten questions. Each question was designed to elicit responses germane to the cataloging of yizker book collections at each institution surveyed. Surveys were sent to the head archivists and librarians of the 67 institutions named on JewishGen.org as having considerable yizker book collections. Some institutions' websites only provided e-mail addresses for general, informational questions; in these cases, the reference desk contacted the appropriate librarian in an effort to provide sufficient responses. The *Sem-*

inario Rabinico Latinoamericano in Buenos Aires, Argentina, *Bibliothèque Medem* in Paris, France, and the Institute for Strategic Studies Foundation in Krakow, Poland, were also contacted; these institutions are not included in the 67 organizations found on JewishGen.org. Each was contacted via e-mail during the months of January through June 2009; eventually 56 institutions responded to the survey.[6] Information from the holdings at the Jewish Historical Institute in Warsaw, Poland, and from the Center for Jewish Studies of Marie Curie–Sklodowksa University in Lublin, Poland was also collected. Once received, responses to the first four questions were compiled and organized to identify contact information, classify each institution, and provide the number of yizker books in each collection. (See the Survey of Collections table beginning on page 284.) Responses to the remaining questions were analyzed and measured in terms of the cataloging, circulation, definition, acquisition, and digitization of yizker books. These responses were often lengthy and provide the basis for the remainder of this essay.

Cataloging and Circulation

Yizker books were written to sustain the memory of the lives and villages destroyed during the Holocaust; the fragility and inferior quality of the paper on which many of these books were printed puts institutions at risk of losing these invaluable memorabilia due to deterioration. As such, it is critical to understand the cataloging and circulation policies of those institutions holding yizker book collections. Several of the librarians and archivists surveyed affirm that they do, indeed, keep yizker books in special rooms or collections for library use only and do not allow the books to circulate; other institutions, while allowing the circulation of texts, only permit them to do so if they are in satisfactory physical condition.

Amanda Seigel of the New York Public Library explains that yizker books are part of the Dorot Jewish Division Collection. Like the British Library, these texts may be "requested for use in the Jewish Division;" however, "the yizker books do not circulate outside of the Jewish Division's reading room," and are used for research purposes only on library premises.[7] Leah Hauser of Baltimore Hebrew University writes that her yizker book collection does not circulate, and is thus "[reflective] of their significant research value."[8] Although the books are cataloged in the general collection, Rita Saccal, Head Librarian of *Seminario Rabinico Latinoamericano* affirms that it is "not a circulating library. People can only look into the book in[side] our library."[9] Similarly, Natalia Krynicka and Sharon Bar-Kochva of *Bibliothèque Medem* catalog yizker books in the general collection, yet present them in a "distinguished part of the reading room as reference books" and do not permit their circulation.[10] Most institutions that catalog yizker books in their general collections tend not to allow their circulation.

Some institutions do allow the circulation of yizker books depending upon the physical condition of the book and/or its binding and structure. Emily Madden, Manager of the Price Library of Judaica at University of Florida, explains that its yizker books are housed in a special collection; however, many of them do circulate. Madden clarifies that their circulation is "contingent upon their physical condition. If brittle, they would not circulate"[11] Other collections depend upon the prevalence of certain yizker texts. While cataloged in the general collection, Eli Ginsparg of Hebrew Theological College affirms that the circulation of yizker books "depends on [the] number of copies and condition of the book."[12] In this case, reprints or facsimiles may grant researchers access to the text, yet preserve the condition of the original edition. According to Colin T. Clarkson, Head of the Reference Library at Cambridge University in Cambridge England, the circulation of yizker books, though "scattered" throughout the general collections, is based "partly on subject matter, but also on factors such as the physical format of the volume. A paperback or a book with folding plates, for example, would most probably be assigned to a non-borrowable class."[13] The delicate condition of a yizker book's paper would likely deter catalogers at Cambridge from allowing a book to circulate.

Other collections are organized somewhat differently. The Library of Congress, for instance, catalogs books written in the English and Roman languages in its general collection. Yizker books written in the Hebrew and Yiddish languages are in the care of the Hebraic Section, neither of which permits circulation. Similarly, the University of Pennsylvania houses yizker books in three separate locations. Ruth A. Rin, the University's Hebraica Cataloging Librarian, specifies that some of its memorial books are in the main stacks, but non-circulating copies are at the Rare Book and Manuscript Library. The yizker books at the Library of the Katz Center are cataloged separately as a "memorial collection."[14]

Interestingly, the digitization of yizker books seems directly correlated to an institution's decision to circulate the texts. To limit the wear and tear on its holdings, Madden "strongly encourage[s] users to access yizker books online via the NYPL portal"[15] Naomi M. Steinberger, Director of Library Services at Jewish Theological Seminary, writes that some of the older books and manuscripts are housed in special collections, whereas "others are contemporary and in the general collection"[16] Contemporary editions of these texts are likely the result of on-demand printing, which while protecting yizker books as historical artifacts detracts from their value as memorial texts.

How Institutions Define the Genre

Definitions of the term "yizker" vary among the institutions surveyed, with some collections relying upon the cataloging techniques of other establishments and others having no official description of the texts. With the growing interest in yizker books as source documents, an assessment of the definitions used to categorize these books is beneficial not only to librarians and archivists, but to researchers locating within these texts ancestral and genealogical connections. Furthermore, linguists, sociologists, and historians are utilizing these texts to analyze the colloquial language structures and cultural patterns specific to each village or community.

Several of the librarians surveyed catalog yizker books by using an exhaustive definition of the term; others archive the books simply as memory or memorial books. As Jones and Siegel point out, this likely explains the irregular numbers of holdings documented on JewishGen.org. Many of these books perhaps fall under the broader category of grey literature. Walfish acknowledges the "difficulty" of defining the term, adding that a narrow definition of a yizker book would be "a book published by a *landsmanshaft* to memorialize a destroyed community. Broader definitions would include personal memoirs."[17] Whether a librarian or archivist uses the term *landsmanshaftn* in the definition seems directly related to the number of yizker books an institution claims to house. Institutions that include the term generally claim to house a smaller number of yizker books than those that do not; there are, of course, exceptions. Walfish adds that University of Toronto holds just over 600 yizker books.

The Library of Congress and the St. Louis County Library define "yizker" according to the definition in *From a Ruined Garden*; similarly, the Holocaust Memorial Center defines memorial books "according to the definitions set by the New York Public Library and Zachary Baker."[18] Patricia Feeley, Reference Librarian for the Boston Public Library, also references Baker, noting that

> to give you a count, I have to define them in a sense. I have chosen to count the memorial books for Eastern European Jewish communities listed in the yizker book bibliography compiled by Zachary M. Baker in Warren Blatt's *Resources for Jewish Genealogy in the Boston Area* and annotated for the Boston Public Library's holdings plus any such books that were returned in a search for keyword "yizker" in the online catalog.[19]

Feeley adds that the Boston Public Library has between 200 and 225 yizker texts, and her definition of the term confirms the difficulties in supplying an accurate number of yizker books without first adequately defining the genre. Zachary Baker, currently the Reinhard Family Curator for Judaica and Hebraica Collections at Stanford University, defines yizker books as "collectively authored community monographs published under the auspices of organizations of former townspeople (*landsmanshaftn*)."[20] Stanford's collections holds over 500 yizker books; however, while Baker uses the term "*landsmanshaftn*" in his definition, the Library of Congress counts 1,100 yizker books and the Holocaust Memorial Center mentions 1,300, both of which are significantly higher than the New York Public Library's 700 and other researchers who have done exhaustive counts, such as Paul Hamburg.

Hamburg seems to have been the last to formally count yizker books, finding about 800 in 1998. Several of the institutions surveyed, however, have holdings well above this number. While yizker books continue to be published into the present, it seems unlikely that there would be several hundred over Hamburg's claim if there were not fluctuating definitions of the term. The Leopold Muller Library at the Oxford Centre for Hebrew and Jewish Studies, for instance, houses over 900 yizker books. The institution's deputy librarian, César Merchán-Hamann, defines a "yizker" book as "[a] memorial volume devoted to commemorating a Jewish community which suffered either partial or total destruction in the Holocaust. Of course there are grey areas, for example the matter of who composed (edited/wrote/collected) the work," which seems to include texts that are elsewhere classified as "grey literature."[21] Merchán-Hamann does recognize the ambiguity created by not specifying the text's authors.

Rather than using the term "*landsmanshaftn*," Yale University and Yeshiva University define yizker books as those works compiled by Jewish survivors of communities destroyed during the Holocaust. According to Leah Adler, Head Librarian at Yeshiva University, yizker books were written "primarily by Holocaust survivors who left their home towns before the war."[22] While Yale provides no definitive number for its yizker book collection, Adler maintains that Yeshiva houses over 500 yizker books, a realistic number given the institution's definition. James P. Rosenbloom, the Judaica Librarian for Brandeis University, maintains that the institution's 800 yizker books are cataloged as having been written by the "former residents" of the destroyed Eastern European Jewish communities.[23]

Aviva Astrinsky of the YIVO Institute for Jewish Research is aware of the inconsistency in definitions of the genre, as she provides two different definitions in her response. According to her, yizker books are "sponsored by survivors of a single town or region," which seems in line with institutions using the term "*landsmanshaftn*" as part of their definition. She continues that yizker books may be thought of as "history books devoted to a town or region, written by one or more authors, which are not necessarily sponsored by survivor societies but include details about the destruction of the town and names and other information of people who perished in that particular area."[24] The second definition is clearly a broader one encompassing memorial books by non–Jews or individual survivor memoirs that may not necessarily be considered dedicatory texts.

The collection at *Yad Vashem* contains 1,300 volumes. Dr. Robert Rozett, Director of *Yad Vashem* Libraries, defines a yizker book as a volume

> created by former residents of a given community (or sometimes larger community including nearby smaller communities). They generally provide vignettes about the history, people and institutions; tell about the period of the Holocaust; and frequently contain lists of victims in the Holocaust. We also include books produced by non–Jews along these lines (unlike most of our sister institutions).[25]

Of all those surveyed, Rozett is the only one who mentions that some memorial books honor larger communities but include smaller neighboring villages as well. Rozett's definition is critical in understanding that not all institutions catalog memorial books written by non–Jews alongside yizker books, even though they are each considered memorial texts. The fact that *Yad Vashem* catalogs these texts as yizker books surely accounts for its high total. Many of these likely fall under the category of "grey literature."

Several librarians and archivists surveyed provide insight into how their definitions and cataloging of memorial texts are being impacted by digitizing technologies. Judy Janec, archivist for the Holocaust Center of Northern California, describes yizker books as memorial texts written by survivors of destroyed communities in Europe during World War II; however, she adds that these include "later or updated editions and translated editions in our collection."[26] There are currently several texts on JewishGen.org that are partially, if not fully, translated into English for descendents who experience difficulties in reading Hebrew or Yiddish, among the many other languages in which these texts are published. Janec also asserts that the Holocaust Center of Northern California holds 505 yizker texts.

Interestingly, Vanessa Freedman, Hebrew and Jewish Studies Librarian at the University College in London, mentions that her library is "largely reliant on how [a] book has been catalogued by other libraries, as we download most of our records."[27] However, when asked if the College planned to acquire additional yizker books, Freedman responded "yes, especially in Yiddish." Thus, although the library downloads most of its records, it appears to seek physical yizker texts for its collection as well. Freedman comments that their records are usually downloaded from CURL (Consortium of University and Research Libraries) or OCLC (Online Computer Library Center).

Other institutions define a yizker book by the type of information therein, such as songs, indices of names and special places, or folklore. Spertus Institute of Jewish Studies, for instance, delineates a yizker book as a "Memorial [book] about communities destroyed during the Holocaust which includes lists of names and places, maps, stories, and recollections."[28] This definition, however, expands the parameters for authorship of a yizker text at this institution and provides markers for what constitutes a memorial text.

The libraries at Baltimore Hebrew University, now integrated into Towson University, use the same methodology as Spertus in cataloging their yizker books; however, Leah Hauser, one of the institution's librarians, provides an in-depth, historical definition:

> A collective effort was begun by [Jewish] survivors to remember those who perished and to preserve the Jewish life that was destroyed during the Nazi regime. Groups of survivors from various cities, towns, and villages compiled memorial books about the area in which they had lived. These books are known as yizker books. Several hundred yizker books, representing the cities and vicinities throughout Eastern Europe, are now in existence. They appear in a number of languages, including Hebrew, Yiddish, English, French, German, Hungarian, and Russian. Although originally published to commemorate a vanished hometown or geographic location, yizker books serve as a rich source of information for those seeking knowledge about their ancestors. A typical yizker book contains a history of the town, articles written by former residents, personal information of genealogical interest, maps, and photographs of families, groups, and individuals. There is also a memorial section, which commemorates individuals and families lost during the war.[29]

Hauser uses a definition that historically documents the tradition out of which the yizker book developed, while also referencing how others might attempt to use the information in the texts. Baltimore Hebrew University's collection is comprised of over 130 yizker texts. Hauser is careful to mention in her definition that the tradition of Jewish memorial books originated among the survivors from specific communities and villages in which they lived, and gestures that she is, indeed, referring to the *landsmanshaftn*.

The University of Pennsylvania and University of Texas at Austin document in their definitions the inclusion of Jewish community members who perished during the war. With 200 yizker books in her collection, Ruth A. Rin explains that the University of Pennsylvania primarily looks for names of residents, organizations, photographs, maps, street addresses, survivors, and the relatives of other people of a special interest in a particular destroyed community. Uri Kolodney, Interim Judaica and Hebraica Bibliographer at the University of Texas at Austin, identifies yizker books as being made up of "descriptions and histories of communities, biographical information about their population, and sometimes listings of people who perished during the war."[30] Rather than using a definition that describes the authorship of the texts, these institutions rely upon the documents and information inside the books.

Patrick J. Stevens, Selector for Judaica at Cornell University, also provides a thorough definition of the term "yizker," as well as a geographic interpretation of the term. Like several other institutions surveyed, Stevens expounds more upon the purposes of a yizker text as opposed to its authorship. Stevens explains that no formal definition is kept at Cornell; however, he fashions one for the purposes of the survey, responding:

> A yizker book (*yizker bukh* in Yiddish), when the term relates to the Shoah, is a publication whose purpose is to commemorate a Jewish community anywhere in the world, but particularly within the Nazi or Axis sphere of influence in Europe, Asia or North Africa, that suffered persecution, partial destruction or extermination as the result of direct or indirect action perpetrated as part of the Holocaust. This working definition remembers (geographically) the persecution of e.g. Arab Jews in Tunisia as it does the extermination of Ashkenazi Jews in e.g. Hungary or Poland. It also attempts to remember the disappearance of many Jews not through direct kills but through malnutrition, starvation, and illness in enclosed ghettoes such as Lodz and camps such as Buchenwald.[31]

Stevens's definition gestures at the different regions out of which yizker texts developed, which helps historians and researchers who may not know the region or country in which an ancestor lived. This is also beneficial for those researching towns and villages that have variant names and spellings. Stevens's entry is interesting in that he references the term "shoah," which is Hebrew for the Holocaust, and is how the term appears in numerous yizker texts. Stevens was one of the only librarians to use that term. This definition differs, however, in that Stevens was the only librarian who mentioned that yizker books commemorate Jewish communities anywhere in the world; other librarians and archivists specifically referenced Eastern European countries.

A few institutions respond with more technical definitions than other collections surveyed. Krynicka and Bar-Kochva remark that *Bibliothèque Medem* categorizes the texts as *livre du souvenir. Bibliothèque Medem* also arranges yizker books according to the "names of the places the book represents."[32] Similarly, Shunit Degani, Head of Classification and Qiryat Sefer Departments at the National Library of Israel and the Jewish People, explains that the institution "classif[ies] them according to the city/country they commemorate,"[33] also providing the Dewey Number for the texts, 933.5. Margo Gutstein, Technical Services Librarian for Simon Wiesenthal Center Library, affirms that her institution follows "the scope notes for the subject heading MEMORIAL BOOKS (HOLOCAUST) in LCSH."[34]

Nine of the institutions surveyed use the definition "memory" or "memorial" books; the numbers in those collections are as follows: *Seminario Rabinico Latinoamericano*, 20; Ben-Gurion University, 34; Breman Jewish Heritage and Holocaust Museum, 40; Hebrew University, no number provided; University of Haifa, 448; Florida Atlanta University, 696; Gordon Jewish Community Center, 61; Jewish Museum of Maryland, 131; Jewish Theological Seminary, 900; and Leo Baeck Institute, no number provided. Only three respondents stated that they do not have a working definition of the term "yizker." The books in those collections are as follows: Cambridge University, 6;[35] *Centre de Documentation Juive Contemporaine au Memorial de la Shoah,* 143; and Hebrew Theological College, 360.

Acquisitions and Collections Policies

Yizker book collections developed out of different acquisition methods. Many institutions were given memorial texts as gifts by surviving Jewish community members, while other institutions actively sought yizker books from dealers or private contacts. Several institutions still work to obtain new memorial books and are quite dedicated to doing so. Some librarians and archivists even seek books composed in specific languages, such as Yiddish, to expand and fulfill certain aspects of their collections. A text written in German, for instance, provides a differing cultural or community history than one composed in Hebrew. A varied collection of yizker books also provides researchers with information on how Jewish communities differed in Eastern Europe. Some institutions, however, do not actively procure new copies of yizker texts due to the increasing availability of the books through electronic databases or to the budget constraints of the library.

In addition to searching for texts in specific languages, an institution may search for yizker books from specific countries or regions. YIVO was the first library to collect firsthand accounts and interviews from Jewish survivors and has been developing its collection since 1945. Aviva Astrinsky explains that many of YIVO's books have been donated to its collection as gifts, while others have been secured from book dealers. Interestingly, she mentions that YIVO "actively acquire[s] new yizker books which are now published primarily by survivors from the Soviet Union."[36] Other librarians mention that they obtain new texts from Israel and Germany. While no formal collections policy exists at Cornell, Patrick Stevens explains that he orders titles on a selective, not comprehensive, basis, clarifying that

> purchasing at least some yizker books is ... essential, as the memory of these communities must be kept available for future generations. I select sometimes on criteria such as the relative lack of knowledge about e.g. Jewish communities in some regions of Europe that were nonetheless exterminated by the Nazis.[37]

Stevens's acquisitions guidelines for Cornell are quite beneficial for historians or genealogists seeking information on a specific region or community from which there are fewer survivors.

Katharina Hubschmann, Senior Librarian at University College London, comments that while her institution has no formal collections policy, she specifically searches for texts written in Yiddish. Most of her yizker books are currently acquired through library suppliers and antiquarian booksellers.[38] Comparably, Ilana Tahan asserts that the British Library is also working to obtain Yiddish and Hebrew material for its collection. Since the publication of her bibliography, *Memorial Volumes to Jewish Communities Destroyed in the Holocaust*, about the texts housed in the British Library, she has acquired 22 yizker books, most through book dealers in Israel. Additionally, Renate Evers, Head Librarian at Leo Baeck Institute for Jewish History, offers that her current collections policy is to obtain memorial texts "pertaining to German speaking communities."[39]

Other institutions, such as Hebrew Union College, acquire new yizker books in hopes of providing researchers with an expansive collection as possible. These books are obtained mostly through book vendors or online solicitations. Both the Jewish Theological Seminary and Yeshiva University in New York acquire new yizker books from antiquarian booksellers; both institutions have collections policies of being as "comprehensive" as possible, contrary to Cornell.[40] Margo Gutstein adds that she obtains yizker books as soon as they become available. While many of its memorial texts were donated as gifts, Gutstein is able to acquire additional texts through "used Judaica dealer[s] like Dan Wyman or Eric Haim Kline."[41] Although Simon Wiesenthal Center has no formal collections policy, Gutstein tries to "collect every yizker book [she] can obtain."[42] Similarly, Merchán-Hamann comments that Leopold Muller Library acquires yizker books through contacting "private sellers or donors [who] approach us directly," adding that the library would like to develop its collection as fully as possible.

According to Krynicka and Bar-Kochva, *Bibliothèque Medem* ambitiously seeks to possess "all existing yizker books."[43] This would, of course, be a fine resource for researchers in Eastern Europe. Comparable to the U.S. Holocaust Museum and Bar-Ilan University, Feiga Weiss, Head Librarian at the Holocaust Memorial Center, mentions that she continually seeks new volumes for her collection. Weiss remarks that she and her staff members "check book lists from publishers and read Judaica announcements," adding that the policy is to "acquire as many as [they] can and, in addition to cataloging them, we put the name of the town on the library portion on our website,"[44] which is quite advantageous to those researching the distribution of yizker books.

Instead of having a specific collections policy, some institutions group yizker books under Holocaust-related texts. Ruth Einstein, Special Projects Coordinator of the Breman Heritage and Holocaust Museum, considers the acquisition of yizker books to be "part of the collection process when speaking to potential donors of Holocaust-related materials."[45] While Ilana Tahan mentioned that she seeks yizker books in specific languages, she also acquires "material covering the entire spectrum of Jewish Studies. Yizker books are just one category of books I acquire for the collection,"[46] and thus yizker books fall under Jewish Studies material as opposed to having their own collections policy. At the University of Haifa, Yardena Lewenberg states that "there is no special collection[s] policy for yizker books. The collection is part of our 'Jewish history' collection."[47]

Some of the institutions surveyed are not actively seeking yizker books at present, mostly due to budget concerns and access to the digitized versions. Uri Kolodoney mentions that the University of Texas at Austin does not currently have a collections policy for yizker books, "mainly because other institutions already do that, and also because the majority of these unique books are available online."[48] Although Zachary Baker confirms that Stanford does, indeed add to its yizker collection as books become available, in the past, the library obtained yizker books "only when a digital version [was] not available through NYPL or when they [were] donated to the library."[49] Similar to the Breman Museum, Stanford has no official collections policy for yizker books; rather, "they are subsumed within overall collection parameters for modern Jewish history and culture."[50]

Although adding to its collection as books become available, Nanette Stahl, Judaica Curator for Yale University, demonstrates that the digitization of yizker books is impacting the acquisition of texts. Stahl maintains that it may soon be unnecessary for Yale to purchase original editions of the texts because "many are already digitized and most of them will be soon."[51] While the University of Florida does not rely upon online technologies for its acquisitions of books, Emily Madden notes that "some are acquired as reprints or facsimile editions."[52] While digitizing technologies seem to be decreasing the acquisition of new yizker books, on-demand printing and facsimiles are, undoubtedly, highly useful resources for researchers who are not within traveling distance of the original edition of a yizker text, and Madden affirms that "yizker book collection development is of elevated importance to our mission to provide materials in support of Florida programs and research regarding the study of Jewish history."[53]

Several of the institutions surveyed no longer acquire yizker texts due to monetary restrictions. *Seminario Rabinico Latinoamericano* is currently unable to purchase or obtain any books because of the poor economic situation in Argentina; all twenty texts in the institution were donated.[54] Joyce Loving admits that Allen County Public Library is currently facing a similar situation, noting that they are not seeking as actively as they have during the past because "budget cuts have caused us to carefully evaluate what material to purchase."[55] While the Holocaust Center of Northern California generally purchases yizker books as opposed to receiving them through donations, Judy Janec explains that they must do so "as budget constraints permit."[56]

Other institutions, such as Florida Atlantic University, rely solely on donations, while others choose not to acquire additional copies of yizker books because they claim to already house a sufficient number of texts.[57] Brandeis University, for instance, only acquires new yizker books through donations or advertisements. However James P. Rosenbloom, Judaica Librarian, adds that with a collection of 800 yizker books, "we have so many that we don't actually seek others." [58]The Wiener Library, Hebrew Theological College, Spertus Institute of Jewish Studies, the Museum of Jewish Heritage, and *Yad Vashem* all rely predominantly upon private donations. [59]Although *Yad Vashem* additionally notes, that "we collect any yizker book we can obtain and up to 4 copies of a given book." Interestingly, Jennifer Vess affirms that the Jewish Museum of Maryland is neither "actively collecting yizker books," nor has a "separate collecting policy for yizker books. To evaluate whether to accept one, we would use our standard archival and library collections policies."[60]

Online Catalogs

Of the institutions surveyed, only five responded that they do not include yizker books in an online catalog, and this is mostly due to institutions not having an online catalog at all. The New York Public Library has the most extensive online catalog of yizker books, with 650 of the 700 texts available online. Amanda Seigel explains that "yizker books are included in the online catalog, including links in each bibliographic record to the library's website."[61] Most online catalogs do not provide access to the full text, rather only the bibliographic record is provided. While the Breman Museum does not currently have an online catalog, titles of the yizker books at this institution are available on its website. *Seminario Rabinico Latinoamericao* hopes to launch its online catalog during the coming year, and when it does so, will include yizker books in the online catalog.

Although yizker books are included as bibliographic records in Baltimore Hebrew University's online catalog, Vess suggests that researchers interested in finding out the titles housed in its collection should visit the circulation desk. According to Vess, there is a listing of all the yizker titles in the library available at the desk, and "it is easier to scan a list than to try and figure out the spelling of a particular town to search in the online catalog."[62] Vess brings up an important point, as the names of many Eastern European villages sometimes have as many as three variant spellings. YIVO, however, has an online collection of its yizker books called "MEMOR," and a short list of all of its titles kept up to date.

A few institutions mentioned difficulties in searching through online catalogs for yizker books, and the correct number of texts does not appear when searching. When searching the online catalog at the Boston Public Library, Patricia Feeley found only 25 yizker books; she explains that "seven of them had publication dates of 1974 and later. It is possible that the other 18 are titles also found in the old card catalog so the true number of books in the collection, as opposed to records in the catalog, is between 200 and 225."[63]

The different languages in which yizker books were originally published have also causes difficulties in the launching of some online catalogs. The Holocaust Memorial Center does include yizker books in its automated catalog; however, most of the books were cataloged before the center had the capability to automate in Hebrew, and thus only the Roman language memorial books are currently available. Similarly, Hebrew Union College includes most of its yizker books in the online catalog, but many of the Hebrew alphabet items are not in the online catalog and are accessible through other catalogs provided by the institution. While digitizing technologies have demonstrated impressive research capabilities for older texts written in English, texts written in Hebrew are often difficult to locate online, especially villages and communities with more than one possible spelling. Bar-Ilan University, however, actually links parts of its online yizker book catalog to the New York Public Library. David Wilk explains: "We have also cooperated with the New York Public Library and with its permission have added links from yizker books they have scanned to our bibliographic records of those books, enabling them to be viewed online from one's home without entailing a visit to our library."[64]

In some cases, several items from card catalogs have not yet been transferred to the online catalogs. Hebrew College currently lists seventy percent of its holdings in its online catalog, but the remaining thirty percent are still in the card catalog, which, according to Harvey Sukenic, are mostly "older books."[65] New yizker acquisitions are immediately archived on the online catalog at University College London, but, similar to Hebrew College, older materials are still being converted from the card catalog and are not yet available. Half of the yizker books at the Jewish Museum of Maryland are available through its online catalog, while the other half are not yet transferred. At Cambridge University, Colin Clarkson explains that "all academic books are included in Newton, as are all non-academic books published from 1978 onwards. Older, non-academic material is gradually being added to Newton."[66] This information is especially beneficial for scholars researching the number of yizker books at specific institutions through online catalogs.

Other institutions respond by offering the subject headings by which a yizker book is identified in the online catalog. The University of Pennsylvania cross-references yizker books with memorial books; each is under the subject heading of "Holocaust." At Yeshiva University, all yizker books are classified under the online subject heading "memorial books." Cornell University catalogs memorial books "in accordance with LC MARC and LC classification conventions" on its online catalog, and at the University of Florida, yizker books are included in the online catalog by titles transliterated by ALA-LC Guidelines.

Conclusion

While this is not an exhaustive study as only not all institutions responded, this research does provide an assessment of the ways in which most of the holding institutions catalogue yizker books. With the increasing interest in the books by scholars, genealogists, and others, researchers need an understanding of how these texts are distributed and archived, which depends largely on how an institution defines the term "yizker." The definitions are perhaps the most important section of this study. Additionally, digitizing technologies are significantly impacting the genre. One result is that the definitions and acquisitions of yizker texts remain unclear, such as what percentage of an institution's holdings are reprints, facsimiles, or translations. A future study might consider researching whether or not copies located in the general collection are copies of original yizker texts, as well as analyze the differences between the memorial collection and the rare books collection. Still another study might assess the effects of digitization on the genre, and whether or not institutions plan to emulate the New York Public Library's initiative of providing electronic access to its holdings, or, as Bar-Ilan University has already done, provide access to these texts directly through NYPL. Finally, another might assess how many yizker texts included in the collections are included in the translation project, as this may contradict with the "true" definition of the term "yizker."

Bibliography

Adler, Leah. "FW: Yizker books." Message to Yeshiva University. 17 Feb. 2009.
Allen County Public Library. "Yizker collection." Message to Allen County Public Library." 21 May 2009. E-mail.

Amir, Michlean. "RE: Yizker Book collections." Message to the author. 18 Mar. 2009. E-mail.

Astrinsky, Aviva. "RE: Yizker book collection at YIVO Institute for Jewish Research." Message to the author. 21 May 2009.

Baker, Zachary. "Re: Yizker books." Message to the author. 13 Feb. 2009. E-mail.

Brumberg, Esther. "Yizker book collection at Museum of Jewish Heritage." Message to the author." 20 May 2009. E-mail.

Clarkson, Colin T. "Yizker books." Message to the author. 12 Feb. 2009. E-mail.

Degani, Shunit. "RE: Yizker book collection at Hebrew University." Message to the author. 24 May 2009. E-mail.

Dyngosz, Mateusz. "Fwd: Yizker books." Message to the Institute for Strategic Studies. 30 Mar. 2009. E-mail.

Einstein, Ruth. "RE: Yizker books." Message to the author. 5 Mar. 2009. E-mail.

Elbe, Pamela. "RE: Yizker books." Message to the author. 10 Feb. 2009. E-mail.

Emanuel, Gila. "FW: Yizker book collection at Hebrew University." Message to Naomi Alschech." 1 Jun. 2009. E-mail.

Evers, Renate. "RE: Yizker books." Message to the author. 3 Apr. 2009. E-mail.

Feeley, Patricia. "SOC 02.09.09 Yizker Books." Message to Sarah Glover. 26 Feb. 2009. E-mail.

Fleischer, Lynn. "Yizker books Nashville." Message to the library. 10 Feb. 2009.

Fleiszig, Leonie. "Re: Yizker books." Message to the author. 1 Apr. 2009. E-mail.

Freedman, Vanessa. "RE: [Fwd: Yizker books]." Message to University College London. 4 Mar. 2009. E-mail.

Ginspark, Eli. "Fw: Yizker books." Message to Rabbi Dr. Jerold Isenberg. 21 May 2009.E-mail.

Goral, Mike. "Re: Reference Question (LTK 16101759265X)." Message to UCLA Library. 24 May 2009. E-mail.

Graham, Pamela. "Re: Yizker Books." Message to the author. 10 Feb. 2009. E-mail.

Gutstein, Margo. "Re: Fw: Yizker books." Message to Adaire Klein. 11 Feb. 2009. E-mail.

Hauser, Leah. "RE: Yizker books." Message to the author. 10 Feb. 2009. E-mail.

Holtzman, Ada. "Re: Yizker book collection at Hitachdut Yotzei Polin." Message to the author. 27 May 2009. E-mail.

Hubschmann, Katharina. "FW: Special collections — Yizker books enquiry." Message to the Weiner Library." 27 May 2009. E-mail.

Janec, Judy. "Re: Yizker books." Message to the author. 9 Feb. 2009. E-mail.

Jones, Faith and Gretta Siegel. "Yizker Books as Holocaust Grey Literature." *Publishing Research Quarterly* 22.1 (2006): 52–62. Print.

Kolodney, Uri. "RE: Yizker book collection at University of Texas at Austin." Message to the author. 26 May 2009. E-mail.

Krynicka, Natalia and Sharon Bar-Kochva. "RE: Yizker books." Message to the author. 11 Mar. 2009. E-mail.

Lewenberg, Yadena. "RE: Yizker book collection at University of Haifa." Message to the author. 11 Jun. 2009. E-mail.

Loving, Joyce. "Yizker books at St. Louis County Library." Message to the author. 22 May 2009. E-mail.

Macaulay, Tatyana. "FW: Yizker book collection at Center for Holocaust Studies." Message to Betty Perkins. 27 May 2009. E-mail.

Madden, Emily. "FW: Fw: Yizker books special collections." Message to the author. 26 May 2009. E-mail.

Merchán-Hamann, César. "RE: Yizker books." Message to the author. 25 Mar. 2009. E-mail.

Mirvis, Rabbi Ephraim. "RE: Yizker book collection at Finchley Synagogue." Message to the author. 28 May 2009. E-mail.

Murphy, Sarah. "Library Question — Answer [Question #4530802]." Message to the Ohio State University Library." 8 Jun. 2009. E-mail.

Pearlstein, Peggy. "Yizker books at the Library of Congress." Message to Sue Vita. 10 Feb. 2009. E-mail.

Polani, Tsviya. "Re: Yizker book collection at Ben Gurion University." Message to the author. 25 May 2009. E-mail.

Rin, Ruth A. "Re: Yizker books." Message to the author. 11 Feb. 2009. E-mail.

Rosenbloom, James P. "Re: Yizker books." Message to the author. 10 Feb. 2009. E-mail.

Rothstein, Fred. "FW: Yizker book collection at Congregation Neveh Shalom." Message to Hilde Jacob. 21 May 2009. E-mail.

Rozett, Robert. "RE: Yizker books." Message to the a uthor. 12 Feb. 2009. E-mail.

Rudavsky, Arnona. "FW: yizker books." Message to Sarah Bernard. 20 Feb. 2009. E-mail.

Saccal, Rita. "Fw: Yizker books." Message to the author. 25 Mar. 2009. E-mail.

Seigel, Amanda (Miryem-Khaye). "Library Question — Answer [Question #4530740]." Message to New York Public Library." 31 May 2009. E-mail.

Shotwell, Camille. "Re: Yizker book collection at Institute of Jewish Studies." Message to the author. 26 May 2009.

Siegel, Leslie. "Fw: Yizker books." Message to Florida Atlanta University. 17 Feb. 2009. E-mail.

Sion, Ariel. "RE: Yizker books." Message to the author. 25 Mar. 2009. E-mail.

Slatt, Vincent. "Re: Virtual Reference Desk." Message to United States Holocaust Memorial Museum. 22 May 2009. E-mail.

Stahl, Nanette. "Re: Reference question." Message to the author. 21 May 2009. E-mail.

Steinberger, Naomi. "FW: Yizker books." Message to Dr. Mayer Rabinowitz." 10 Feb. 2009. E-mail.

Stevens, Patrick J. "FWD: Yizker books." Message to Michael Engel. 10 Feb. 2009.

Sukenic, Harvey. "RE: Yizker Books." Message to the author. 10 Feb. 2009.

Tahan, Ilana. "RE: CAS-109629-IHIK FW: Yizker books CRM:00700472." Message to the British Library." 19 Feb. 2009. E-mail.

Vess, Jennifer. "Yizker book survey." Message to the author. 4 Mar. 2009. E-mail.

Walfish, Barry. "Re: Yizker books." Message to the author. 10 Feb. 2009. E-mail.

Weisman, Yaffa. "RE: Yizker books." Message to the author. 10 Feb. 2009. E-mail.

Weiss, Feiga. "RE: Yizker Books." Message to the author. 10 Feb. 2009. E-mail.

Wilk, David. "Re: Yizker books." Message to the author. 11 Feb. 2009. E-mail.

Notes

1. Barry Walfish, e-mail message to author, February 10, 2009.

2. Faith Jones and Gretta Siegel, "Yizker Books as Holocaust Grey Literature." *Publishing Research Quarterly* 22.1 (2006): 55.

3. Jones and Siegel (ibid.) aptly note, however, that the "existence of multiple books for many of the towns, and multiple languages for many of the books add to the complexity of managing such collections," which also explains their inconsistent numbers.

4. Abraham Wein listed 400 in "'Memorial Books' as a Source for Research into the History of Jewish Communities in Europe," *Yad Vashem Studies on the Eastern European Catastrophe and Resistance* 9 (1973): 255–272; David Kranzler identified 600 in *My Jewish Roots: A Practical Guide to Tracing and Recording Your Genealogy and Family History* (New York: Sepher-Hermon,1979; and Paul Hamburg indicated 800 in "Closing Circles, Opening Pathways," *The Reference Librarian* 29, Issues 61 & 62 (April 1998): 235–243.

5. Ilana Tahan, Memorial Volumes to Jewish Communities Destroyed in the Holocaust. London: British Library, 2004.

6. Three of the 56 were not included on JewishGen.org. Thus, of the 67 institutions listed on JewishGen.org, 53 responded. Some of the institutions listed as having collections on JewishGen.org responded that they no longer house yizker books on their premises. Ada Holtzman explains that "the collection of the Yizker book of the Polish Jews Organization in Israel (Hitachdut Yotzei Polin) has been delivered to a few universities and exists no more (like the organization itself)." (Ada Holtzman, e-mail message to author, May 27, 2009). Pamela Elbe,

Collections Manager and Archivist for the National Museum of American Jewish Military History and Archives of the Jewish War Veterans of U.S.A., explains that "neither the JWV nor the NMAJMH has any Yizker books." (Pamela Elbe, e-mail message to author, February 10, 2009). Fred Rothstein explains that the yizker book collection at Congregation Neveh Shalom in Portland, Oregon were originally the property of Portland State University. Rothstein continues, "We housed them for several years, but lack of space forced us to return them to the university. We have a number of volumes listing names of Holocaust survivors, and victims, cities, and countries of 'Holocaust' section of our library."(Fred Rothstein, e-mail message to author, May 21, 2009). Tansy Barton, Special Collections Administrator, and Kate Wilcox-Jay, Reader and Technical Services Librarian, of University of London confirm that this institution does not have any yizker book holdings, e-mail message to author . In addition, Jones and Siegel's "Yizker Books as Holocaust Grey Literature" and Adam Kopciowski's *Księgi pamięci gmin żydowskich: bibliografia* = *Jewish Memorial Books: A Bibliography* also helped us identify collections.

    7. Amanda Seigel, (Miryem-Khaye), e-mail message to author, May 31, 2009.

    8. Leah Hauser, e-mail message to author, February 10, 2009.

    9. Rita Saccal, e-mail message to author, March 25, 2009.

    10. Natalia Krynicka and Sharon Bar-Kochva, e-mail message to author, March 11, 2009.

    11. Emily Madden, e-mail message to author, May 26, 2009.

    12. Eli Ginsparg, e-mail message to author, May 21, 2009.

    13. Colin T. Clarkson, e-mail message to author, February 12, 2009.

    14. Ruth A. Rin, e-mail message to author, February 11, 2009.

    15. Emily Madden, e-mail message to author, May, 26 2009.

    16. Naomi Steinberger, e-mail message to author, February 10, 2009.

    17. Walfish, e-mail message.

    18. Feiga Weiss, e-mail message to author, February 10, 2009.

    19. Patricia Feeley, e-mail message to author, February 26, 2009.

    20. Zachary Baker, e-mail message to author, February 13, 2009.

    21. Cesar Merchán-Hamann, e-mail message to author, March 25, 2009.

    22. Leah Adler, e-mail message to author, February 17, 2009.

    23. James P. Rosenbloom, e-mail message to author, February 10, 2009.

    24. Aviva Astrinsky, e-mail message.

    25. Robert Rozett, e-mail message to author, February 12, 2009.

    26. Judy Janec, e-mail message to author, February 9, 2009.

    27. Vanessa Freedman, e-mail message to author, March 4, 2009.

    28. Camille Shotwell, e-mail message to author, May, 26, 2009.

    29. Hauser, e-mail message.

    30. Uri Kolodney, e-mail message to author, May 26, 2009.

    31. Patrick J. Stevens, e-mail message to author, February 10, 2009.

    32. Krynicka and Bar-Kochva, e-mail message.

    33. Shunit Degani, e-mail message to author, May 24, 2009.

    34. Margo Gutstein, e-mail message to author, February 11, 2009.

    35. Stevens explains that Cambridge houses "a small number" of yizker books and adds that "searching for the keyword "yizker" in our Newton online catalogue (http://ul-newton.lib.cam.ac.uk/) yields only eight hits including two bibliographies." Because bibliographies are not considered yizker books, I have supplied the number "6" here.

    36. Astrinsky, e-mail message.

    37. Stevens, e-mail message.

    38. Katharina Hubschmann, e-mail message to author, May 27, 2009.

    39. Renate Evers, e-mail message to author, April 3, 2009.

    40. Adler, e-mail message; Steinberger, e-mail message.

    41. Gutstein, e-mail message.

    42. Ibid.

    43. Krynicka and Bar-Kochva, e-mail message.

    44. Feiga Weiss, e-mail message.

45. Ruth Einstein, e-mail message to author, March 5, 2009.
46. Ilana Tahan, e-mail message to author, February 19, 2009.
47. Yadena Lewenberg, e-mail message to author, June 11, 2009.
48. Kolodoney, e-mail message.
49. Baker, e-mail message.
50. Ibid.
51. Nanette Stahl, e-mail message to author, May 21, 2009.
52. Madden, e-mail message.
53. Ibid.
54. Saccal, e-mail message.
55. Joyce Loving, e-mail message to author, May 22, 2009.
56. Janec, e-mail message.
57. Leslie Siegel, e-mail message to author, February 17, 2009.
58. Rosenbloom, e-mail message.
59. Katharina Hubschmann, e-mail message to author, May 27, 2009; Eli Ginsparg, e-mail message to author, May 21, 2009; Camille Shotwell, e-mail message to author, May 26, 2009; Esther Brumberg, e-mail message to author, May 20, 2009; and Jennifer Vess, e-mail message to author, March 4, 2009.
60. Jennifer Vess, e-mail message to author, March 4, 2009.
61. Seigel, e-mail message.
62. Vess, e-mail message.
63. Feeley, e-mail message.
64. David Wilk, e-mail message to author, February 11, 2009.
65. Harvey Sukenic, e-mail message to author, February 10, 2009.
66. Clarkson, e-mail message.

The Survey of Collections[1] below is listed as follows: country, name of institution, classification of institution, postal address, website, librarian/activist contacted, and number of yizker books.

ARGENTINA

Seminario Rabinico Latinoamericano — Academic library within a religious institution; José Hernandez 1750, Buenos Aires, 1426; n/a; Rita Saccal, Head Librarian; 20

AUSTRALIA

Makor Jewish Community Library — Special library open to the public; 306 Hawthorn Rd., Caulfield South, 3162; www.makorlibrary.com; Leonie Fleiszig, Library Director[2]; 28

CANADA

Robarts Library, University of Toronto — Academic library; 130 St. George St., Toronto, ON M5S 1A5; n/a; Barry Walfish, Judaica and Theology Specialist; 600+

ENGLAND

British Library; National library — 96 Euston Rd, London, NW1 2DB; www.bl.uk; Ilana Tahan, Hebraica Curator and Head of the Hebrew Section; 322

Cambridge University — Academic library; West Rd., Cambridge, CB3 9DR; www.ul-newton. lib.cam.ac.uk; Colin T. Clarkson, Head of the Reference Department; 6

Leopold Muller Memorial Library Oxford Centre for Hebrew and Jewish Studies — Academic library; Yarnton Manor, Oxford OX5 1PY; www.ochjs.ac.uk/library/index.html; César Merchán-Hamann, Deputy Librarian; 900+

University College London — Academic library; Gower St., London, WC1E 6BT; www.wiener library.co.uk; Katharina Hubschmann, Senior Librarian; 13

FRANCE

Centre de documentation Juive Contemporaine Au Memorial de la Shoah — Library; 17 Geoffroy l'Asnier 75004 Paris; www.memorialdelashoah.org; Ariel Sion, Head Librarian; 143

La Maison de la Culture Yiddish Bibliothéque Medem — Private associative library open to the public; 29 rue du Chateau d'Eau 75010 Paris; n/a; Natalia Krynicka, Sharon Bar-Kochva; 200

ISRAEL

Bar-Ilan University — Academic library; Ramat-Gan; www.biu.ac.il/lib/; David Wilk; 500

Aranne Library, Ben-Gurion University of the Negev — Academic library; P.O. Box 653, Be'er Sheva 84105; www.bgu.ac.il/aranne/; Tsviya Polano, Reference Librarian; 34

Hebrew University, Bloomfield Library — Academic library; Mount Scopus Jerusalem 91905; www.huji.ac.il/huji/eng/library_e.htm; Gila Emanuel, Librarian of the Department of Jewish History and Contemporary Jewry; n/a

National Library of Israel and the Jewish People — Academic and public library; Givat Ram POB 39105 Jerusalem 91390; http://www.jnul.huji.ac.il; Shunit Degani, Head of Classification and Qiryat Sefer Departments; n/a

University of Haifa Library — Academic library; University of Haifa Library, Haifa 31905; http: //www.haifa.ac.il/index_eng.html; Yardena Lewenberg; 448

Yad Vashem Library — Government Institution; PO Box 3477, Jerusalem 91034; www.yadvashem. org; Dr. Robert Rozett, Director of the Yad Vashem Libraries; 1,300

POLAND

Center for Jewish Studies of Maria Curie-Sklodowksa University — Academic library; 20-031 Lublin Pl. Marii Curie-Skłodow-skiej 5 20-031 Lublin; www.umcs.lublin.pl; n/a; 32

Institute for Strategic Studies Foundation — Non-profit, non-government, inter-disciplinary institution; Mikola-sjska 4 St., I p 31027, Krakow; www.iss.krakow.pl; Mateusz Dyngosz, Projects Coordinator; 266

Jewish Historical Institute — Non-profit, non-government, inter-disciplinary institution; 00-090 Warsza-Waul Tlomackie 3/5, Warsaw; www.jewishinstitute.org.pl; n/a; 190

UNITED STATES
California
Frances-Henry Library — Hebrew Union College; Academic/special library; 3077 University Ave., Los Angeles 90007; www.huc.edu/libraries/la; Yaffa Weisman, Library Director; n/a[3]

Holocaust Center of Northern California — Private education and research center; 121 Steuart St., San Francisco 94105; http://www.hcnc.org; Judy Jane, Archivist; 505

Simon Wiesenthal Center Library — Special collections library; 1399 S. Roxbury Dr., Los Angeles 90035; www.wiesenthal.com; Margo Gutstein, Technical Services Librarian; 213

Charles E. Young Research Library Building, UCLA — Academic library; Box 951575, LA 90095; www.ucla.edu; Miki Goral, Reference Librarian; n/a[4]

Stanford University Libraries — Academic library; Green Library, Stanford University 94305; http://library. stanford.edu/depts./hasrg/jewish/jewish.html; Zachary M. Baker, Reinhard Family Curator of Judaica and Hebraica Collections; 500+

Connecticut
Yale University Library; — Academic library; Box 208240, New Haven 06520; www.library.yale. edu; Nanette Stahl, Judaica Curator; n/a

Florida
Florida Atlantic University — Academic library; 777 Glades Rd., LY 3 Room 261, Boca Raton 33431; http://www.library.fau.edu; Leslie Siegal, University Archivist; 696

University of Florida, The Isser & Rae Price Library Judaica — Academic library; PO Box 117010, Gainesville 32611; www.uf.catalog.fcla.edu; Emily Madden, Manager of Price Library of Judaica; 581

Georgia
The Breman Jewish Heritage and Holocaust Museum — Museum; 1440 Spring St., Atlanta 30309; www.thebreman.org; Ruth Einstein, Special Projects Coordinator; 40

Illinois
Hebrew Theological College — Religious institution; 7135 North Carpenter Rd., Skokie 60077; www.htc.edu; Elie Ginsparg; 360

Spertus Institute of Jewish Studies — Academic library; 610 S. Michigan Ave., Chicago 60605; www.spertus.edu; Camille Shotwell; 325

Indiana
Allen County Public Library, Genealogy Center — Public research library; PO Box 2270, 900 Library Plaza, Fort Wayne 46801; www.acpl.lib.in.us; n/a; 200

Maryland
Baltimore Hebrew University — Academic library; 5800 Park Heights Ave., Baltimore 21215; n/a; Leah Hauser; 130+

Jewish Museum of Maryland — Museum; 15 Lloyd St., Baltimore 21202; www.jewishmuseum md.org; Jennifer Vess, Curatorial Assistant, Acting Archivist; 131

Massachusetts
Boston Public Library — Public library; 700 Boylston St., Boston 02116; www.bpl.org; Patricia Feeley, Social Sciences Department; 225

Brandeis University — Academic library; 415 South St., Waltham 02453; http://lts.brandeis.edu/research/; James P. Rosenbloom, Judaica Librarian; 800

Clark University — Academic library; 950 Main St., Worcester 01610; www.clarku.edu; Tatyana Macaulay, Program Director; 50

Hebrew College — Academic Library; 160 Herrick Rd., Newton Centre 02459; www.hebrew college.edu; Harvey Sukenic, Acquisitions Coordinator; 80

Michigan

Holocaust Memorial Center — Public research library archive; 28123 Orchard Lake Rd., Farmington Hills 48334; www.holocaustcenter.org; Feiga Weiss, Head Librarian; 1,300

Missouri

St. Louis County Library — Public library; 1640 South Lindbergh, St. Louis 63131; www.slcl.org; Joyce Loving, Manager, Special Collections; 116

New York

Cornell University — Academic library; 201 Olin Library, Ithaca 14853; www.library.cornell.edu; Patrick J. Stevens, Selector for Judaica; 100

Jewish Theological Seminary — Private academic library; 3080 Broadway, New York 10027; www.jtsa.edu; Naomi M. Steinberger, Director of Library Services; 900

Leo Baeck Institute for Jewish History — Special library for Jewish-German history; 15 W 16th St., New York 10011; www.lbi.org; Renate Evers, Head Librarian; n/a

Museum of Jewish Heritage — A Living Memorial to the Holocaust; Museum; 36 Battery Place, New York 10280; www.mjhnyc.org; Esther Brumberg; n/a

New York Public Library — Public research library; 42nd St., New York 10018; www.yizkor.nypl.org; Amanda (Miryem-Khaye) Seigel; 700

Yeshiva University — Academic library; 500 West 185th St., New York 10033; www.yu.edu/libraries; Lead Adler, Head Librarian; 500

YIVO Institute for Jewish Research — Independent research library; 15 West 16th St., New York 10011; www.yivoinstitute.org/library; Aviva Astrinsky; 840

Ohio

Hebrew Union College — Religious academic institution; 3101 Clifton Ave., Cincinnati 45220; www.huc.edu; Arnona Rudavsky, Public Services Librarian; n/a

The Ohio State University Library — Academic library; 1858 Neil Ave., Columbus 43210; http://library.osu.edu; Sarah Murphy, Coordinator, Research and Reference; n/a[5]

Pennsylvania

University of Pennsylvania Libraries — Academic library; 3420 Walnut St., Philadelphia 19104; www.library.upenn.edu; Ruth A. Rin, Hebraica Cataloging Librarian; 200

Tennessee

Gordon Jewish Community Center — Special public library; 801 Percy Warner Blvd., Nashville 37205; www.nashvillejcc.org; Lynn Fleischer, Assistant Librarian; 61

Texas

University of Texas at Austin Libraries — Academic library; PO Box P, Austin 78713; www.lib.utexas.edu/subject/judaica/index.html; Uri Kolodney, Interim Judaica and Hebraica Bibliographer; 70

Washington, DC

Library of Congress — Research library; 101 Independence Ave. SE, 20540; www.loc.gov; Peggy Pearlstein, Head of Hebraic Section and African & Middle Eastern Division; 1,100

U.S. Holocaust Memorial Museum — Federal institution; 100 Raoul Wallenberg Place SW, 20024; www.ushmm.org/research.library; Vincent E. Slatt, Librarian; 667.

NOTES

[1]Adapted from the work done by JewishGen volunteers, Faith Jones, Gretta Siegel, Michlean Amir, and others.

[2]Leonie Fleiszig, Director of the Makor Jewish Community Library, notes that Makor is "the home of the database that lists all the yizker books. The other libraries are the Jewish Cultural Centre and National Library "Kadimah," Jewish Holocaust Museum and Research Centre, Jewish Museum of Australia and Kew Hebrew Congregation Library."

[3]Weismann responds "Please search under 'yizkor book.' You will find 3 possible locations CN (Cincinnati), NY (New York) & LA. We exchange books through Inter Library Loan and I am not sure how you want to count them."

[4]Goral responds, "If you go to this LibGuide for Jewish Studies, http://guides.library.ucla.edu/content.php?pid=23757&sid=273332, you can see a link to a list of the titles in our collection."

[5]Murphy responds "To ascertain how many books are in the library's yizkor collection, please search the OSU Libraries catalog. I searched the subject headings of this catalog for yizkor and was referred to 10 books.libr.

About the Contributors

Monika Adamczyk-Garbowska is a professor of American and comparative literature and the head of the Center for Jewish Studies at Maria Curie-Skłodowska University in Lublin, Poland. Her books include *Polska Isaaca Bashevisa Singera — rozstanie i powrót* (*Isaac Bashevis Singer's Poland: Exile and Return,* 1994), *Contemporary Jewish Writing in Poland: An Anthology* (2001, co-editor), *Odcienie tożsamości. Literatura żydowska jako zjawisko wielojęzyczne* (*Shades of Identity: Jewish Literature as a Multilingual Phenomenon,* 2004), *Tam był kiedyś mój dom ... Księgi pamięci gmin żydowskich* (*My Home Used to Be There ... Memorial Books of Jewish Communities,* 2009, co-editor).

Michlean Amir works as an archivist at the United States Holocaust Memorial Museum. She holds an MLS from Simmons College and is an active member of the Association for Jewish Libraries. She has written articles for numerous publications and lectured at various conferences in the United States and Israel on the subject of memorial books.

Amy Burnette earned her MA degree in English at Appalachian State University in May 2010 and entered a doctoral program at Syracuse University in August 2010.

Adina Cimet earned her licenciatura in Sociology at the Universidad Nacional Autónoma in Mexico and her Ph.D. from Columbia University in New York. She has published widely in academic journals in Spanish, English, and Hebrew and has lectured in Yiddish, English, and Spanish on historical and sociological themes. She is the author of two books: *Ashkenazi Jews in Mexico; Ideologies in the Structuring of a Community* (State University of New York Press, 1997) and *Jewish Lublin* (Marie Curie–Skłodowska University, 2009).

Philip Friedman (1901–1960) was a historian of Polish Jewry before the war. Afterwards, he dedicated himself to recording the history of the Holocaust. He helped found the first Jewish historical committee in Lublin, helped the Centre de Documentation Juive in Paris organize its collections, and worked on bibliographical projects at Yad Vashem and YIVO, among other activities.

Rosemary Horowitz is a professor of English and co-director of the Center for Judaic, Holocaust, and Peace Studies at Appalachian State University. She is the editor of *Elie Wiesel and the Art of Storytelling* (McFarland, 2006) and the author of *Literacy* *and Cultural Transmission in the Reading, Writing, and Rewriting of Yisker Books* (Austin & Winfield, 1998).

Roni Kochavi-Nehab was born, grew up and lives today in Kibbutz Hazorea, Israel. She studied literature and folklore at the University of Haifa. Her Ph.D. dissertation and the volume it inspired deal with books celebrating kibbutz jubilee. She has been a teacher, librarian, and archivist and now works as an editor of academic and literary publications.

Daniel Magilow is assistant professor of German at the University of Tennessee, Knoxville. His research centers on Holocaust Studies and 20th century German culture. He translated and edited *In Her Father's Eyes: A Childhood Extinguished by the Holocaust* (Rutgers University Press, 2008) and has published several articles about Holocaust photography.

Rivka Parciak holds a Ph.D. from the Hebrew University in Jerusalem. She has contributed essays on East European Jewish life to books and periodicals in Hebrew, English, and Polish. She is the author of *Here and There, Now and on the Other Days* (in Hebrew) (Magnes Press, 2007). That work is a study of relations between Poles and Jews on the background of Jewish cemeteries and memorial sites in Israel and Poland.

Elias Schulman (1905–1986) worked as a writer, critic, and scholar of Yiddish literature and culture. Starting in 1931 in New York, he wrote hundreds of articles, essays, and reviews. For more than fifty years, he studied Yiddish literature as a literary historian, critic, and chronicler.

Jan Schwarz is senior lecturer in the department of Germanic Studies at the University of Chicago. He is the author of *Imagining Lives: Autobiographical Fiction of Yiddish Writers* (Wisconsin University Press, 2005). Dr. Schwarz is currently completing a book about Yiddish writers after the Holocaust.

Jacob Shatzky (1893–1956) worked as a literary and drama critic, editor, bibliographer, lexicographer, lecturer, teacher, and librarian. In 1923 he moved to the United States, where he became a prominent Jewish scholar. Although his interest was the history of the Jews in Poland, he published numerous studies on all aspects of Jewish history, writing extensively on Jewish literature, literary history, folklore, and biography.

Yale Strom is one of the world's leading ethnographers of *klezmer* culture. A pioneer among American revivalists, he has conducted field research among the Jews and Roma in Central and Eastern Europe for over thirty years. His research has produced twelve books, two plays, thirteen CDs, seven documentary films, and numerous group and solo photography exhibitions. He is currently artist-in-residence in the Jewish Studies Program at San Diego State University.

Abraham Wein (1912–) was a researcher at the Jewish Historical Institute in Warsaw until 1968. Following that, he was on the staff of Yad Vashem. There he was the senior editor of the seven-volume *Pinkas Ha-kehilot, Polin*, which provide information about the history of the Jewish communities in Poland from their early days to their end. He has edited and written numerous articles on Jewish and Holocaust history.

Index